Culture, Behavior, and Personality

Culture, Behavior, and Personality

ROBERT A. LeVINE
University of Chicago

ALDINE PUBLISHING COMPANY / Chicago

ABOUT THE AUTHOR

Robert A. LeVine received his B.A. and M.A. from the University
of Chicago, and his Ph.D. in social anthropology from Harvard. He also
graduated from the Chicago Institute for Psychoanalysis and was
a Fellow of the Center for Advanced Study in the Behavioral Sciences.
He is presently Professor of Anthropology, Psychiatry and Human
Development at the University of Chicago.

First published 1973 by
Aldine Publishing Company
529 South Wabash Avenue
Chicago, Illinois 60605

ISBN 0–202–01085–6
Library of Congress Catalog Number 75–169514

Printed in the United States of America

To my parents
Aaron and Emily LeVine

Preface

This book is offered as an introduction, not to an established body of knowledge, but to the potentialities of a field of inquiry. The basic questions of culture and personality have long been recognized as worthy of scientific attention, and early theoretical statements on the subject provided a convincing sense of connection between personality, society, and culture, which stimulated a variety of research efforts in psychology, psychiatry, education and the social sciences. Although these specialized lines of investigation have been pursued at an increasing pace with a rapidly accumulating literature in recent years, the field has seemed to lose sight of its unifying perspective, and some of its central methodological problems have been neglected.

My aim in this book is to restore that unifying perspective and direct attention to the central problems that both arouse interest in the study of culture and personality and present its most difficult challenges. Rather than reviewing the literature or research findings, I present a critical overview of existing theoretical and methodological directions, followed by a statement of my own proposals for theory and method. In theory, I return for guidance to the Darwinian model of organism-environment interaction that contributed the original sense of connection inspiring work in this field. For method, I consider anew what we can learn from the Freudian clinical tradition. I hope that what has emerged will help provide an integrating anthropological perspective on culture and personality for both the student and the investigator.

At the moment, the study of culture and personality occupies an extremely uncertain place in social anthropology, sociology, and other "institutional" social sciences, for reasons that involve intellectual history more than logical argument or empirical evidence but which are nevertheless important to bear in mind. As the field of psychology developed in the nineteenth and early twentieth centuries, attempts were made to explain social, economic and political behavior in psychological terms. Men like Emile Durkheim and A. L. Kroeber, who were trying to establish sociology and anthropology as independent disciplines during that period, had to struggle against the tendency of both laymen and scholars to see institutional patterns as reducible to individual factors such as instincts and habits. They argued for the autonomy of the institutional sphere: Social facts and psychological facts were of different orders, society was a phenomenon *sui generis,* culture was "superorganic." The doctrine of institutional autonomy, strongly supported by economic theorists as well, was built into the social science fields as they became separate academic disciplines. Not everyone accepted it, however, and in the years between 1927 and World War II, some sociologists and anthropologists—most notably, W. I. Thomas, Edward Sapir, Ralph Linton, John Dollard, and A. Irving Hallowell—formulated theoretical ideas that linked institutions to individual dispositions without the psychological reductionism of earlier decades. Their formulations, together with detailed field research on individual development in other cultures by Margaret Mead, Gregory Bateson, and John W. M. Whiting, among others, laid the initial basis (before World War II) for the scientific study of culture and personality. This work was completely overshadowed in the public eye, however, by the less scholarly publications of Ruth Benedict, Geoffrey Gorer, and their colleagues, who published, during and just after the war, a series of psychologizing analyses of modern nations that were identified as culture and personality studies.[1] The wide public attention received by these studies, the support of the United States government for some of them, and the impression they gave that a diluted version of psychoanalysis could solve the major international problems of our time (in the name of social science!) called forth an indignant reaction from many social scientists, who found themselves engaged once more in arguing for institutional complexity and autonomy against attractive, oversimplified psychological explanations. There followed a sweeping rejection of culture and personality theory and research in the social sciences, even by some who had previously contributed to it, so that since the 1950's the field of study has come to be stigmatized as consisting of vulgar journalistic simplifications of the complex realities of social structure and culture.

Much of the contemporary rejection of culture and personality research among institutional social scientists is due to confusion and misconception. They confuse the fallacies of the most publicized national-character studies with the field as a whole, and more fundamentally, they confuse

1. See Benedict (1946, 1949); Gorer (1943, 1948); Gorer and Rickman (1949). Their approach was extensively defended by Mead (1953, 1954; Mead and Metraux, 1953). For a critical review see Inkeles and Levinson (1968).

the adequacy of empirical research conducted to date on a problem
with the legitimacy of that problem for scientific research. For example,
the culture and personality field has been identified by some of its
critics (e.g., Wallace 1961b) with a "uniformitarian" view in which
group differences in personality are so exaggerated as to exclude individual differences within a population. Such a view is implied in some
writings, but Ralph Linton, one of the most respected early theorists of
culture and personality, wrote in 1936:

> It is unfortunate that we have no exact, objective techniques for identify-
> ing psychological types, but general observations lead to the conclusion that
> the total range of those types is much the same in all societies. At the same
> time, different societies seem to show differences in the relative frequency of
> occurrence of the various psychological types (1936, p. 484).

This is hardly a uniformitarian view, and its concern with individual differences is also represented in many early and later writings on culture
and personality.[2] Even if culture and personality studies had been uniformly misguided on this point, however, the question of psychological
differences between human populations would remain an important one
for scientific study. No amount of deficient empirical research diminishes
its importance or the soundness of asking the question.

This is a moment at which even those who are skeptical about the
value of culture and personality study might consider stretching their
curiosity in this direction. In recent years, a number of professional political scientists and even some economists and historians have found
purely institutional analysis inadequate to account for the behavior they
are attempting to explain, and they have turned to social and personality
psychology for help. In sociology and social anthropology there is growing dissatisfaction with conventional institutional models, particularly
for the understanding of contemporary social change, which contains
all-too-frequent surprises for extant social theory. Part of the trouble is
that some of the most influential social theorists have exaggerated the
salience and stability of behavior patterns that are expressed in institutions and formal ideologies at a particular historical moment, and they
have underestimated the capacities of men to resist, transform and inno-
vate within their institutional environments. They have promulgated an
"oversocialized conception of man" (Wrong, 1961) as merely reflecting
the social pressures acting on him, a conception that is implausible to
any observer of social behavior who does not already subscribe to their

2. See Sapir's (1938) influential essay deriving the problem of culture and personality from disagreements among informants; Mead's (1939) emphasis on individual
variation in her early work on Samoa and New Guinea; Hallowell's (1938) distinction
between individual defenses and those constituted by culture; Kluckhohn and Murray's
(1948) discussion; the article by Hanks (1949).

doctrines. Furthermore, despite the atttempt to eliminate individual psychology from institutional theories, some assumptions must be made about the behavioral dispositions of participants in institutions, and these unacknowledged assumptions have often been naive, absurd, or demonstrably false. Economists since Adam Smith and sociologists at least since Durkheim, however antipsychological their views, have been trafficking in the human psyche, usually oversimplifying it no less than psychoanalysts dealing with institutions. Their failure to examine their psychological assumptions in a rational and empirical manner, or even to acknowledge them, has been a major weakness in social science theories. These weaknesses are increasingly recognized by social scientists themselves, who may be driven to take more explicit account of psychological factors to achieve a firmer basis for the prediction and explanation of social trends.

The potentially greater receptivity of social scientists to a consideration of psychological factors has its parallel in the increasing efforts by psychologists, psychiatrists and educational researchers to undertake comparative studies and work out systematic methods to deal with individual patterns at the population level. Thus the day of a new psychosocial rapprochement may be drawing near. If new attempts at interdisciplinary thinking and cooperation are to be effective, they must be unencumbered by the stale controversies and defensive postures that have inhibited the understanding of culture and personality for the past two decades. Culture and personality specialists should stimulate a return to the basic questions motivating the field and provide an intellectual framework in which issues worthy of research can be identified and rational priorities for investigation can be developed. These are my goals in this book.

Acknowledgments

I have many persons and agencies to thank for the support and intellectual influence that enabled me to write this book. I am indebted to David Riesman, my first teacher of culture and personality; to John W. M. Whiting and Beatrice B. Whiting, my intellectual parents; to Donald T. Campbell, whose influence pervades the book; to my teachers at the Chicago Institute for Psychoanalysis; to David M. Schneider, who was largely responsible for my undertaking training in psychoanalysis; and to my colleagues in the Committee on Human Development, University of Chicago, for stimulation on a broad range of topics represented herein. While working on the book I was supported by a Research Scientist Development Award (K02-MH1844) from the National Institute of Mental Health; my psychoanalytic training was made possible by a fellowship from the Foundations' Fund for Research on Psychiatry; and the manuscript was completed at the Center for Advanced Study in the Behavioral Sciences. I gratefully acknowledge the help of these agencies.

Valuable criticisms and comments on Chapters 12 through 17 were made by Frederick Crews, Raymond D. Fogelson, Marvin Zonis, and the late William Caudill, whose death is a loss for the field of culture and personality as for me personally. Alexander J. Morin's frank and trenchant criticisms prompted many improvements throughout the book. The following colleagues at the Center for Advanced Study in the Behavioral Sciences commented helpfully on the second draft; Lawrence A. Cremin, Amitai Etzioni, Max Gluckman and Monica Wilson. Bernard Weissbourd, Hildred Geertz and Robert Nozick also made helpful suggestions. Doris Portman and Doris Norgard typed the manuscript. My wife Sarah provided encouragement at times when I might otherwise have given up this task. I hereby thank them all.

An earlier version of Chapter 2 was published as "Toward a Psychology of Populations: the Cross-Cultural Study of Personality," in *Human Development*, 1966, 9, 30–46. Chapters 4, 7 and 8 are based on my article "Culture, Personality and Socialization: An Evolutionary View," in D. Goslin, ed., *Handbook of Socialization Theory and Research*, Chicago: Rand-McNally, 1969. Parts of the preface appeared in "Psychosocial Studies in Africa," *African Studies Review*, 1970, *13*, 105–111. Permissions of author and publisher are acknowledged for the quotation from Mary Catherine Bateson's "Insight in a Bicultural Context," *Philippines Studies*, 1968, and for reprinting Beatrice B. Whiting's chart from the introduction to LeVine and LeVine, *Nyansongo*, New York: Wiley, 1966.

Contents

11. *A Cost-Benefit View of Psychosocial Adaptation*   163

PART IV   THE STUDY OF INDIVIDUAL DISPOSITIONS
             IN SOCIAL SETTINGS   171

12. *Strategies in Personality Study*   173
13. *Psychoanalytic Clinical Method*   185
14. *The Couch and the Field*   203
15. *Universal Categories and the
    Translation Problem*   215
16. *Psychoanalytic Ethnography:
    Structures for Comparative Observation*   226
17. *Religious Symbols and Religious Experience*   249

PART V   CONCLUSIONS   283
18. *New Directions in Culture and
    Personality Research*   285

             APPENDIX A   291
             REFERENCES   295
             INDEX   311

Culture, Behavior, and Personality

Part I

Introduction: The
Comparative Study of
Personality and
Sociocultural Environments

Basic Questions for Culture and Personality Research

Culture and personality research is the comparative study of the connections between individuals (their behavior patterns and mental functioning) and their environments (social, cultural, economic, political). This broad field could be assigned a more compact label such as *psychosocial studies* or broken down into disciplinary components such as psychological anthropology, cross-cultural psychology and trans-cultural psychiatry. I prefer *culture and personality* because, as the original term for this interdisciplinary area, it emphasizes the continuity between the pioneering work of its founders some 40 years ago and the conception of the area presented in this book. The important questions they identified in the borderlands between psychology, psychiatry, and the social sciences remain the defining characteristics of the field and set the course for contemporary theory and research.

The terms *culture* and *personality* have acquired such diverse meanings in common speech and scientific discussion that it is necessary to indicate at the outset what I mean by them and related terms. In anthropology, *culture* is an omnibus term designating both the distinctively human forms of adaptation and the distinctive ways in which different human populations organize their lives on earth. Humans are seen as having a common set of adaptive goals, many of which they share with other animals, but as having the unique capacity to achieve them through acquired behavioral characteristics (patterns of culture) that can vary widely from one population to another. At this level of discourse, culture is often defined against the background of the physical and biological environment to which a human population must adapt in order to survive. But culture can also be seen as constituting an environment for members of a population, and it is in this sense that the term is used here. The individuals in a human population do not adapt directly and simply to

3

their physical and biological environment but to the cultural (or socio-cultural) environment that includes means for their individual survival and guides their adaptation along established channels. I use the term *culture* to mean an organized body of rules concerning the ways in which individuals in a population should communicate with one another, think about themselves and their environments, and behave toward one another and toward objects in their environments. The rules are not universally or constantly obeyed, but they are recognized by all and they ordinarily operate to limit the range of variation in patterns of communication, belief, value, and social behavior in that population. Grammatical rules, for example, are constraints on acceptable speech patterns, tending to restrict utterances to certain channels. Other forms of communication are similarly restricted by explicit and implicit rules and so are patterns of interaction between persons (in groups and other social situations), and beliefs about the worlds of outer and inner experience.

Sociocultural environments are complex and variable; their most stable features can be called *institutions*. When a pattern of behavior, belief or communication is accorded such legitimacy in a population as to assume the status of a rule recognized by all, it is *institutionalized*. This means performance in accordance with the rule is recognized as correct (given positive social sanction), while deviation from it is recognized as incorrect and may bring other negative social sanctions. The institutionalization of such a rule, or norm, thereby puts pressure on individuals in a population to standardize their social performance. Norms concerning individual response to a specific type of situation are governed by larger institutionalized programs for collective action (institutions) directed toward adaptive goals, for example, economic institutions, religious institutions, political institutions. These programs are realized through *institutional structures*, stabilized aggregates of persons interacting according to normative prescription, with each person responding to the prescriptions defining his *institutional role*. From the viewpoint of the individual, his sociocultural environment is made up of situations, roles, and institutions that represent normative pressures on him for correct performance and also offer opportunities for personal expression and satisfaction.

Personality is used here in two distinct but related senses similar to those discussed by Irvin L. Child:

> In the first meaning, personality refers to the complex psychological processes occurring in a human being as he functions in his daily life, motivated and directed by a host of internal and external forces . . . .
> The other and narrower meaning of personality refers to a more restricted subject matter within this wider range—to the internally determined consistencies underlying a person's behavior, to the enduring differences among people insofar as they are attributable to stable internal characteristics rather than to differences in their life situation. . . . Personality, in this sense, con-

sists of all those more or less stable internal factors that make one person's behavior consistent from one time to another, and different from the behavior other people would manifest in comparable situations (1968, pp. 82–83).

To put the first meaning somewhat differently, we might say that personality is the organization in the individual of those processes that intervene between environmental conditions and behavioral response. If individuals responded uniformly to all environmental conditions, as motorists do to traffic lights, we could safely ignore such processes in the prediction of social behavior. In fact, however, individuals respond so differently to so many aspects of the human condition (*e.g.*, birth, death, pleasure, pain, stress, anger, growing up, aging) and to so many of the pressures and opportunities in their cultural environments, that we are forced to take account of the intervening processes that must be involved in producing these differential responses. These processes include perception, cognition, memory, learning, and the activation of emotional reactions—as they are organized and regulated in the individual organism. The individual's mental processes, distinctively organized toward the goals of self-regulation and social adaptation, lead him to respond to environmental stimulation with distinctive patterns of responses.

A full understanding of the processes involved in personality in this broader sense will eventually include more complete knowledge of the biochemistry of the central nervous system than is presently available, not to mention the myriad connections between neurophysiology and behavior. At present, we can at least bear in mind three types of processes: (a) those intervening between an immediate situational environment and an evoked response, as in emotional arousal or cognitive problem-solving; (b) those intervening between environmental conditions experienced by the individual early in his life and his behavior at a later stage, as in memory, learning, and the developmental processes of ontogeny; (c) those intervening between the environmental conditions of the breeding population or the human species as a whole, long before the individual was born into it, and his own innate endowment for behavioral functioning, as in the phylogenetic process of natural selection. These three types can be seen, in reverse order, as a hierarchical series of constraints, each setting limits on the behavioral possibilities of the next. Thus human evolution provides the genetic constraints within which ontogeny takes place, and the latter limits the range of behavioral response to life situations. Adaptation, the shaping of the organism's response potentials toward fit with environmental conditions, goes on at all three levels, and the personality of the adult individual is the product of this complex series of adaptive processes.

This broad conception of personality, then, involves theoretical models of mental functioning and development, positing the operation of mechanisms and processes that go beyond what can be empirically demonstrated by psychological investigation to date. Personality in the second, narrower, sense, however, is based on observing behavior rather than theorizing about process. It is generated from the observation of consistencies in the behavior of the individual, consistencies across diverse situations in his life at one time as well as across diverse periods in his life. The trans-situational and enduring qualities of these behavior patterns or personality traits suggest that they are properties of the individual rather than of particular situations or developmental phases in his life.

The definition of units of behavioral consistency is quite arbitrary, since individual behavior in this directly observable sense has no inherent boundaries in time or space. Is a person to be termed "irritable," "hostile to same-sex peers," or simply "aggressive"? It depends on who is observing him, the kinds and number of situations in which he was observed, and the amount of time devoted to observation. It also depends on the terminology favored by the observer. Faced with this arbitrariness, psychologists have tended to ground personality trait descriptions in the folk terminology of Anglo-American culture, using adjectives by which ordinary persons categorize each other's idiosyncratic behavior patterns (e.g., sociable, dependent, aggressive, domineering, suspicious), though giving them more precise and explicitly operational definitions. Traits so defined are widely variable among individuals in our own population and appear to vary greatly across culturally diverse populations as well, but evidence concerning such variation is only as valid as the comparability of the situations in which the individuals were observed. Despite problems of comparison and cultural bias, however, it seems highly probable that every culture gives recognition to trans-situational, enduring behavioral consistencies of the individual in its vernacular terminology and that both behavioral consistency within an individual and variability between individuals are universal in human populations. Although there is little agreement about which dimensions of individual behavior form the most important consistencies and variations for scientific research, it is obvious that many dimensions recognized in ordinary speech and personality psychology alike are highly relevant to participation in the sociocultural environment.

In referring to "internally determined consistencies underlying a person's behavior," Child indicates another aspect of personality in the second sense: that behavioral consistencies reflect or express *dispositions* that are not themselves directly observable but are in some sense "internal" to the individual. The disposition is a *potential* for behavior that is conceived of as existing even at times when it is not being realized in observable behavior. As a stable characteristic of an individual organism, it is also conceived of as functioning *for* that individual, contributing somehow to his internal workings. These conceptions are more than theoretical postulates; they have roots in the observation of behavior. Individual behavior patterns give evidence of being dispositions by their insistent repetitiveness, intruding themselves into diverse situations even when other behavioral options appear readily available, and surviving even under a variety of unfavorable conditions. Suppose, for example, we observed a man reacting in an irritable way to his wife, castigating her for some apparently minor act that he interpreted as an attack upon himself. Later, the following observations are added: (a) He does this to his wife frequently, not only at home but in situations outside the home. (b) He behaves in this way not only to his wife but also to his secretary and, in fact, to a succession of secretaries who have worked for him. (c) He has occasionally done this in situations where it would be observed by others and regarded as socially unacceptable behavior. (d) When he was in military service, no incidents of this kind appeared for two years; on being reunited with his wife, however, the behavior pattern soon reappeared. (e) When his wife left him, he reported feeling very disturbed at being alone and soon found another woman with whom he repeated the same pattern of irritable behavior. These observations suggest a behavior pattern that is not only repetitive and consistent but also sufficiently durable to reappear after prolonged absence, sufficiently "driven" to defy potential social censure, and sufficiently important to the individual for him actively to seek to reinstate the conditions of its activation when they were withdrawn. On such grounds I, and many personality psychologists, would conclude that we had been observing the manifestations of a stable disposition that acts as a pressure on and influences the individual's behavioral adaptation, including his selection of environments, and that plays a part in the maintenance of his sense of well being. Assuming the existence of such a disposition makes the individual's behavior predictable and comprehensible, it also suggests an internal psychological organization in which that disposition is functionally embedded. In making this assumption, then, we are saying that the observed behavioral consistencies do not *constitute* personality, they are *indicators* of it, or rather of the internal dispositions that influence overt behavior.

The more elaborate and detailed one's assumptions about the internal psychological organization in which personality dispositions are embedded, the farther one moves toward personality in the first sense, as psychological process, and away from a strictly behavioral definition. There are many differing views about how much organization and structure to assume in personality, particularly about whether personality can be approached as a set of separate (or separable) dispositions or must be seen as a functioning whole and about whether dispositions should be conceptualized as needs operating in a psychic economy or system of equilibrium (see Maddi, 1968). In the present state of knowledge and methodology, I prefer to operate with a set of minimal assumptions that do not preclude a more elaborate conceptualization: that personality dispositions operate as pressures on individual behavior, as cultural norms do, but from within; that each disposition manifests itself in the individual's goal-seeking behavior, emotional reactions, cognitive activity (perceiving, associating, conceptualizing, remembering, problem-solving, learning), and communicative behavior—all of which are observable; that the imperative quality of the disposition indicates that it is functionally related to the maintenance of a psychological organization that is internally as well as environmentally adaptive and that has a history of its formation in the life of the organism; that dispositions can and should be compared across individuals and groups, with awareness of their possible varying significance in differing psychological organizations (which require comparative study in themselves). These minimal assumptions constitute the provisional concept of personality with which we can begin this book.

Some may ask: Why not remain at the level of behavior? Why deal with unseen entities of psychological organization? The answer is that just as the field experience of anthropologists provided an intuitive basis for viewing culture as an institutional organization rather than an assortment of unrelated traits, so the clinical experience of students of personality makes the assumption of psychological organization plausible. Returning to the example offered above, we could term the man's behavior pattern "hostility toward women" and leave it at that. A clinical approach, however, would take the imperative quality of this pattern as an indicator of something more and might discover that this man had excessive expectations of the women in his life, believing unrealistically that they would take care of him as he wanted to be taken care of and then reacting with anger when they did not. The desire to be taken care of by woman would come into focus as the primary disposition, accounting for his seeking to reinstate relationships that seemed to irritate him and for his unhappiness when such irritations were removed from his environment. It might also be discovered that his unrealistic expectations of women had a long history in his life, beginning with relations with his mother at a time in childhood when he was cognitively immature and lasting long afterward. In other words, it might point to a developmental history in which the conditions surrounding its formation might be identified. Furthermore, shifting focus to his unrealistic expectations of women might make it possible to understand that in his third marriage he found a woman whose behavioral style afforded him enough satisfaction of those expectations to reduce his observable hostility to women, at least in the conjugal relationship, while leaving the underlying disposition unchanged. This kind of deeper understanding of individual behavior, with

its actually greater range of coherence and its potentially greater predictive and postdictive power, is not possible without assuming that
dispositions are organized in the individual.

Another illustration can be offered from the realm of work and achievement. Two men are highly successful in their occupations due to a combination of competence, careful planning toward long-range goals, moderate risk-taking, and a great deal of hard work. They could both easily
be rated high on the psychological dimension of *n* Achievement (achievement motivation, the desire to compete with a standard of excellence).
One of them, who might be Japanese, believes that he works to please
his mother and to make him feel worthy of the sacrifices she made for
his educational success and to increase his family's social esteem. The
other believes that he works to achieve acclaim for himself from others,
regardless of who they are, that this desire for personal recognition keeps
him going in his job and makes his work an overwhelmingly important
part of his life. These self-interpretations suggest that the same behavior
pattern of achievement motivation might be embedded in different personality organizations in these two men and have differing subjective
significance for them. While it is true that both are high in achievement
behavior and the achievement motive, they probably have different work
styles, different ways of integrating work with family relations in their
lives, and different preferences in working conditions. When one tries to
predict from their contemporary success and high motivation, either
forward to their possible reactions to technological unemployment or
retirement, or backward to their formative experiences, the different
personality organizations in which their *n* Achievement is embedded are
likely to assume primary importance as a basis for prediction and
explanation.

We cannot do without the assumption that personality dispositions are
organized in the individual and have functional roles in that organization. This does not mean we have to give up the concept of personality
as behavioral consistency. Indeed, the most ambitious and comprehensive
theory of personality, psychoanalysis, is based on an attempt to relate
individual behavior as observed in clinical detail to a complex model of
personality organization. The present model, based on the assumptions
stated above, is much simpler, because I hope we can discover how
dispositions are organized rather than anticipating it theoretically. I
distinguish three levels: the observable behavioral consistencies that distinguish one individual from another and that we may think of as *personality indicators;* the *personality dispositions* that underly observable
behavioral consistencies and that are psychologically complex, having
motivational, affective, and cognitive components and multiple forms of
expression; the *personality organization* in which dispositions are embedded and to which they contribute functionally.

With these provisional definitions of culture and personality, we can return to consideration of the field in which their connections are studied. In terms of academic disciplines, it is comprised of psychological anthropology (where its roots are strongest), psychology and psychiatry in their comparative aspects, and the social sciences of sociology, political science, economics, and history insofar as they consider individual patterns of thought and action. But culture and personality as a field of study is definable not by its disciplinary affinities nor by a distinctive theory or method (which it lacks), but only by its attention to a particular set of questions about human behavior. These questions, which in one form or another have concerned men for centuries, have not yet been satisfactorily answered and remain the common focus of scientific research on culture and personality.

1. *Are there psychological differences between human populations?* We know there is wide variation in institutionalized behavior among human groups, but the question is whether there are differences in cognition, emotion, and motivation (and their organization in personality)—differences that require understanding as properties of individuals rather than of their institutional environments. This difficult scientific issue has been obscured by its confusion with popular or folk formulations of national and ethnic differences in behavior. Popular beliefs concerning foreign groups tend to be stereotyped, which is to say they are simplified, personalized, exaggerated, and highly evaluative. Group stereotypes are "psychological" in the sense that they reduce complex national societies to an image of an individual—the Englishman, the Mexican, the Arab—and attribute to such images qualities such as might characterize a person—unfriendly, lazy, cunning, belligerent, sensuous. That such attributes are absolute and unchanging is usually implied. In consequence, psychological characterizations of group differences, regardless of their scientific merit, have always been more popular among laymen than institutional analyses, and they have been used to support and justify policies of national and ethnic competition and conflict in the modern world. Such characterizations have often been dangerous and irresponsible oversimplifications of complex realities. War, for example, cannot be properly understood in terms of "warlike" and "peace-loving" peoples but only by taking into account the economic, social, political, and psychological processes that produce it. The same is true of other major aspects of the contemporary world such as variations in economic development and the rise of authoritarian governments. Psychological characterizations of a simple-minded sort have gained wide currency as explanations of these extremely complex phenomena because they are easily assimilated to group stereotypes in popular belief.

It is no wonder, then, that social scientists attempting to establish the importance of a scientific perspective on human affairs have resisted and rejected "psychologizing." But they have frequently overlooked the possibility that there is a legitimate scientific problem here that merits objective investigation by the best procedures available to psychology. Popular thought has raised an important question but has settled for quick, simplistic, and self-serving answers. The question is whether there are differences in the emotional reactions, thought processes, motives, character traits, intellectual capacities, psychopathologies, and other behavioral dispositions of individuals in different human groups. Although much of our thinking on this subject to date may have been influenced by stereotypes, biased observations, and impressionistic evidence, we cannot dismiss this question. Humans exhibit more behavioral variation from one population to another than any other species, and it seems likely that some of it is stabilized in individual dispositions that are more than immediate situational responses. A growing body of cross-cultural observation and systematic psychological evidence supports this view (see Child, 1968; DeVos and Hippler, 1969; LeVine, 1970). But problems of measurement in the psychology of personality, discussed in detail in the final section of this book, have so far prevented the generation of conclusive evidence.

Psychological variation across populations of the human species has not received the attention it requires within the field of culture and personality. In many of the older works, psychological difference between persons of different cultures was taken as a self-evident fact requiring no proof, and no sharp distinction was made between variation in cultural norms, which is tremendous and well-documented, and psychological variation, which, however personally impressive, is difficult to demonstrate. The demonstration of detailed psychological differences (and similarities) among populations has become a central focus of culture and personality research. It is now approached with a number of methods, most of them involving quantification and statistical analysis: psychometric tests of abilities, psychiatric epidemiological surveys, attitude surveys, longitudinal observation of infants and children, and a variety of personality assessment procedures. Thus investigators of diverse disciplines and training are helping to answer this fundamental question about man.

2. *What are the causes in individual development of psychological differences between populations?* To put it another way, if there is psychological diversity between human populations, what factors operating on or in individuals produce that diversity, and how do they do it? These factors may be genes, diet, early experience patterns, later learning experiences, or some combination, but they must be demonstrated to have a direct effect on developmental process in the individual rather than merely being associated with a behavioral disposition at one point in time. Categories such as "culture," "ecology" or "social structure" do

not explain the development of an individual disposition though they
may help account for its adaptive or maladaptive consequences. For
example, the language of South African Bushmen has "click" phonemes,
which means that all Bushmen children *must* learn to speak with clicks
to communicate with others, but this does not explain *how* they learn it.
To explain *how*, it is necessary to investigate the conditions under which
individual children first produce clicks, their sequence of improvement
over time, and the factors retarding or advancing their approximation
to the proper sounds as they are made by adults. So it is with psychological characteristics: They must be studied as they develop in the
individual or—if they are due to genetic or other congenital factors—as
they manifest themselves in his development, in order to provide a basis
for assessing their causal influence. It is only when this has been done
comparably in psychologically varying populations that we can draw
definite conclusions about the causes of their divergent development.

This second major question of culture and personality research, no less
than the first, leads us into fundamental issues concerning the nature of
human behavior and involves psychological knowledge, methods, and
skills. In this case, the issues concern the relative influence of hereditary
and various environmental factors on psychological development and
the means by which such factors produce individual behavioral dispositions; the psychological skills involved are those of developmental
psychology.

3. *How are psychological differences between populations related to
the sociocultural environments of those populations?* In other words, what
are the sociocultural causes and consequences of psychological variations
across groups? What effects do the personality dispositions of the individuals in a population have on the functioning of its institutions? How
do institutions affect individual development? Are there connections between the social order of a group and its mental disorders? How does
sociocultural change affect individual dispositions, and vice versa? These
questions take us into the realms of sociology and social anthropology
with their attempts to generalize about the relations between social structure and personality, normality and deviance, and social and psychological factors in culture change. Nothing is more characteristic of the
field of culture and personality than its concern with the transactions
between the microsocial domain of individual experience and the macrosocial domain of institutional functioning. It is in this area too that its
ultimate significance for social policy resides, for there are implicit here
major problems of the environmental bases of mental health, the psychological bases of social control, and the connections between social constraints and individual satisfaction. These problems will eventually have
to be studied in historical as well as comparative perspective. But effective research on these problems presupposes more progress in investigat-

ing psychological variation across human groups (Question 1) and understanding the processes of individual development (Question 2).

A serious interest in Questions 2 and 3, and in the study of culture and personality altogether, is predicated on an affirmative answer to Question 1. If there are no significant psychological variations across populations, one can hardly investigate their causes and correlates. And while there is some solid empirical evidence for psychological variation, it is not yet so overwhelming that behavioral scientists of every theoretical persuasion feel compelled to accept it. Until we have better methods for measuring personality characteristics (both within and between cultures), the answer to Question 1 must be partly a matter of assumption based on theoretical inclination. If an investigator assumes a positive answer, he will regard research on culture and personality as a worthwhile pursuit, but if he assumes a negative answer, he may well consider it a pointless endeavor. Investigators in the field of culture and personality take the view that there are cross-cultural differences in personality. They make this assumption because they believe that the great range of cross-cultural variation in institutionalized behavior, so well documented by anthropologists, requires psychological variation to support it, because their own experience with foreign peoples suggests to them profound differences at the individual level between their own and other peoples, and because a variety of anecdotal and case study materials seems to confirm it. In Chapter 2 the kinds of experience and evidence that can be brought to bear on this question are considered.

Part II is a critical overview of existing theories and methods in the field of culture and personality. In Chapter 3 I present an outline of the major theoretical positions concerning the relations of culture to personality, and continue these theoretical contrasts in Chapter 4, but with regard to the crucial problem of socialization. Chapter 5 is a preliminary consideration of approaches to the assessment of personality in cross-cultural comparison, a topic to which I return later in the book. In Chapter 6 I introduce several central problems concerning personality, social structure, deviant behavior and sociocultural change—problems on which existing views diverge but not along the lines of the theoretical positions considered previously. These four chapters represent, in capsule form, my view of where theory and method in this field stand and what is wrong with them.

In Part III I present my attempt at constructing a unifying theoretical perspective on culture and personality in the form of an evolutionary model termed "population psychology" (to emphasize its parallel with population biology). In Chapter 7 I explore the applicability of the Darwinian model of variation and selection to the domain of culture and personality. Chapter 8 contains the basic concepts of the theoretical model; Chapters 9 and 10, its formulations of psychosocial stability and change, respectively; and Chapter 11, its implications for comparative research and social policy.

In Part IV I return to the problem of personality assessment method (dealt with in Chapters 2 and 5), which I regard as the central problem of this field and the greatest obstacle to the development of the population psychology envisioned in previous chapters. In Chapter 12 I consider the failure of personality testing to produce methods of accepted validity and outline some general approaches to the scientific problem of disentangling the effects of individual dispositions and environmental pressures in the observation of adaptive behavior. Concluding that psychoanalytic clinical method embodied a solution to this problem that was rejected by academic investigators for reasons of convenience, I examine that method in detail in Chapter 13. Possibilities and difficulties in combining psychoanalytic clinical method with anthropological field work are explored in Chapter 14, and I set forth guidelines for a future psychoanalytic anthropology. In Chapters 15 and 16 I propose a series of naturalistic frameworks for comparative field research on personality, and in Chapter 17 I discuss the application of these frameworks to the psychological decoding of religious symbols.

A concluding chapter is a brief summary of the diagnosis of theory and method in culture and personality in this book, the prescriptions offered for their improvement, and my prognosis of future development.

2

Group Differences in
Individual Behavior Patterns

Are there psychological differences between human populations? In this chapter I consider the kinds of evidence that gave rise to this question and the kinds of evidence that would be required to answer it. Although it cannot be definitively answered by presently available data—particularly if the quality and quantity of the differences are to be understood—it is possible to anticipate the forms that a proper answer would take.

Our inquiry is about the distributions of individual characteristics in human populations and in that respect it resembles other population inquiries: those of population genetics on gene frequencies; anthropometrics on height, weight, and other bodily measurements; demography on the vital statistics of birth, death, and marriage; and epidemiology on the incidence of disease. Measuring the behavioral and psychological characteristics of persons, particularly to make inferences about personality dispositions, poses special and serious problems that have retarded the progress of this inquiry; these are considered in detail later in this book (Chapters 5, 12–17). Here our concern is with what the question means and how to begin thinking about it as a matter for systematic study. What kinds of experience would lead a person to suppose that populations differ in personality characteristics as defined in the previous chapter?

The Experiential Basis

All scientific inquiries can be traced back to their origins in commonsense experience or at least in the uncommon sense of men who chose to question their ordinary experience. In a field like culture and personality, which is defined not by academic discipline but by a sense of problem, it is particularly important to clarify the grounds in ordinary experience for considering the problem to be plausible. The grounds for plausibility lie primarily in the intercultural experience of travelers and immigrants, including anthropologists, and in the commonly known history of Western societies, including their immigration histories.

Anyone who has lived for a prolonged period in an alien cultural environment, trying to understand its people and their point of view and to participate in their social life, has had an experience that allowed him to distinguish between merely conforming to their standards of behavior and sharing their deeply felt preferences, tastes, interests, and aversions. No matter how successful he was in meeting their standards of speech, politeness, and social participation, in developing strong friendships and in understanding their point of view, it is unlikely that he came to replace his desires, fears, and fundamental values with theirs. He more likely became aware as never before how attached he was to so many values, concerns, and personal feelings characteristic of the people with whom he grew up. The host people too probably noticed that although he became like them in some important respects, he retained many differences in behavioral style and personal preference that were attributable to his cultural background. This is true even of many permanent or long-term immigrants and much more so of short-term visitors like anthropologists, foreign students, overseas volunteers, despite their "total immersion" in the other culture. The experienced fact is that another culture very different from one's own cannot be completely "acquired" in adulthood if in the term *culture* we include not only the most institutionalized forms of public behavior (customs) but also the more private patterns of thought and emotion that accompany these behavioral forms in their indigenous context and give them voluntary support—what has been called the "cultural patterning of personality."

The following quotation from an American anthropologist working in the Philippines exemplifies how personal contact across cultures can intensify awareness of differences in the ways in which cultural behavior is personally experienced.

The first event was a conversation between two women lasting approximately one hour. Ana was questioning Aling Binang in detail about the death of Aling Binang's youngest child, a son, at age of twenty, some six months before. Half-way through the conversation, Aling Binang began to weep, but the questioning continued almost unchanged. This is an event which gives me two kinds of data: one is the description of the conversation, as recorded by me afterwards; the other is the description of my response as a member of my own culture. The purely descriptive data would not push me to generalization and further thought were it not for urgency produced by a sense of difference. For my response as an American would be this: that Ana's behavior was unforgiveably crude and insensitive. American handling of bereavement requires that the bereaved person not be reminded of what has happened, not be asked to talk about it. Tact requires that the name of the dead person be mentioned only with extreme circumspection, that the details be glossed over, and the emotions not rearoused. As an American I felt outraged, very sorry for Aling Binang, embarrassed by the tactlessness of Ana; as an anthropologist, I knew that these feelings were probably extraneous, but useful as a cue for further investigation.

The second event was a paglalamay "vigil" in the house of people I had not yet met, near to the house where I was staying. Coming home one day, I learned that a death had occurred, and that my family would be visiting, and would I like to come? I asked a series of questions about what would be happening, got instructions on how to give an abuloy "contribution" of one peso to the young woman whose mother had died, and we went to the house; we stayed for a number of hours. Again, I have two kinds of data. One is a description of the familiar form of a paglalamay: the body laid out in the coffin with funeraria lamps, the relatives gathered, people coming and going, expressing condolences and offering money and then standing and gossiping, the young boys and girls playing word games and flirting at the door, the gambling tables and barbecues set up around the outside of the house, with general merriment continuing through the night, all these activities audible in the room where the body was laid out, overlapping and intermingling; there is no need to go into details here. The other kind of data concerns my own feelings: my strong reluctance to go to this house, an act which I as an American conceptualized as a terrible intrusion by a stranger; my extreme, almost paralyzing embarrassment over the act of giving the abuloy; the difficulty of entering into the word games, laughing, and imitating animal noises. American handling of death requires silence and stiff decorum, requires that the privacy of the bereaved be respected (they are supposed to want to be alone), and includes a suspension of all reference to the material facts of every day, represented to me in this situation by the money and the food (Americans may even be obscurely ashamed to discover that they are hungry on returning from a funeral).

The third event was the death, only a few hours after his premature birth, of my first child, in a Manila hospital. On the afternoon of that day I was able to describe, so that my husband and I would be prepared, the way in which Filipinos would express sympathy. They show concern, in this as in many other contexts, by asking specific factual questions and the primary assumption about those who have suffered a loss is that they should not be left alone. Rather than a euphemistic handling of the event and a denial of the ordinary course of life, one should expect the opposite. Whereas an American will shake hands and nod his head sadly, perhaps murmuring, "We were so sorry to hear," and beat a swift retreat, a Filipino will say "We were so sorry to hear that your baby died. How much did it weigh? How long was labor? Etc. Etc."

Had I not been in a position to make these generalizations and predictions, the most loving behavior on the part of Filipinos, genuinely trying to express concern and affection, would have seemed like a terrible violation and intrusion. In order to handle the affront and to control myself against breaking down in the face of sudden reminders of grief, I would have had to impose a rigid self-control which would have reinforced in the Filipinos the belief that many hold, that Americans don't really grieve. In a situation of this sort, the foreigner is somewhat protected by the knowledge of Filipinos that their behavior may not be appropriate, which produces a general reticence and a hesitation to approach. However, those who overcome this reticence are likely to be those who most genuinely wish to be helpful. It is important to understand that the most alien customs can be comforting once their rationale is understood, as an agnostic may be touched to receive a Mass Card when he recognizes in the strange form, gentleness, concern, the wish to help. Some societies organize their recognitions of bereavement around an effort to help the bereaved control himself and forget, while other societies are geared to help him express and live out his grief (Bateson, 1968, pp. 609–612).

In this frank account, the anthropologist describes her behavior and experience in three situations: first as an observer of a conversation about a young man's death, then as a mourner making a condolence call, and finally as a bereaved mother accepting the condolences of others. Situations involving death of a close relative or other loved one are psychologically significant because they arouse intense emotions concerning interpersonal loss and the suffering of others. A person's inner and outer responses to bereavement in himself and others are likely to reflect, however imperfectly, the quality and intensity of his enduring relationships, their meanings to him, his freedom or inhibition about expressing emotions in front of others or in sympathy with them, and other characteristics that I would not hesitate to call personality dispositions.

The relative ease with which the anthropologist learned to behave in accordance with the condolence customs of her hosts and even to understand them intellectually, is contrasted with the relative inflexibility of her emotional responses. In making a condolence call according to instructions, she suffers an "almost paralyzing embarrassment" that she relates to having been raised as an American. In other words, her emotional reactions—which are psychophysiological processes—have been so thoroughly programmed by her earlier normative environment that when she attempts to behave according to a different set of norms, even while knowing that what she is doing is appropriate and that an anthropologist is supposed to conform to local custom, she experiences internal resistance and discomfort. Later, in the role of the bereaved, she prepares herself with knowledge of local custom to interpret her neighbors' condolences in positive terms and to derive comfort from them. But it is comfort from recognition of the benevolent intent lying behind the condolence behavior rather than from the explicit questioning itself. The anthropologist manages to behave appropriately but leaves no doubt that she does not experience what a Filipino must experience in the same situation. The distinction between their norms, which she has mastered behaviorally and intellectually, and her own "American" emotional patterns and preferences, remains largely intact. Acquiring the situationally appropriate overt behavior of another culture does not eliminate the emotional response patterns acquired early in life from one's own culture.

This does not imply that all Americans would behave identically in the situations recounted above; on the contrary, some might experience less internal resistance than Dr. Bateson in adjusting to Filipino norms, and many would undoubtedly experience so much more that they would be unable to go through with the performances she managed. No American, I believe, could fail to experience some discomfort in playing the "intrusive" or "intruded upon" role (from an American perspective) in Filipino mourning customs, but the amount of discomfort, its most salient qualities and personal meanings, and the means of handling it would vary considerably from one American to another. Similarly, Jean Briggs (1970) has given a candid and detailed account of her field work with an Eskimo family and the difficulties she experienced in suppressing her "emotional volatility" to conform to Eskimo standards of unemotional response. It seems to me obvious that most white Americans would find it difficult to conform to the Eskimo norm of never being visibly irritated or upset in face-to-face situations. Some might find it less of a strain than Dr. Briggs, while others would experience it as unbearable and abandon the field work. By contrast, however, most Eskimos seem to find conformity to this norm compatible with their deeply felt personal preferences and to experience no discomfort in handling their emotional reactions this way. There are unquestionably variations in this among the Eskimos too, for personality dispositions are variably distributed rather than homeogeneous in a population, but a large difference between the central tendencies of the Eskimo and white American distributions seems plausible to assume for this dimension of variation.

What the outsider experiences, then, is that not all the differences in individual response between his home and host groups are conscious, controllable, acquirable, and reversible. He can usually learn to behave in accordance with the host group's explicit customary rules and even empathize with their hopes and fears, but without acquiring the spontaneous feelings and beliefs that give these rules and motives deeper meanings and a culturally distinctive style of organization and integration. After he has learned all they can tell him and show him about how and why they behave as they do, there still seems to be much more left that differentiates his home group from them and that appears to be essential to how they think about themselves and organize their behavior but that they cannot easily express in words. He finds this is equally true of himself: There are aspects that he may not be able to conceptualize but is not free to give up or replace, and these aspects—however idiosyncratic their form—bear the stamp of his home group's culture.

In the following propositions I attempt to extract from intercultural experience some plausible assumptions about cultural variation in individual dispositions.

1. Some culturally distinctive patterns of thought and feeling are not readily accessible to verbal formulation or voluntary control but seem to influence the individual's decisions about regulating himself and adapting to his environment.

2. These patterns are not easily reversed even when the individual is outside the cultural environment that normally reinforces them.

3. The individual can adapt behaviorally to the demands of novel cultural environments without eliminating these patterns of thought and feeling, although their behavioral manifestations may be temporarily inhibited or situationally restricted.

4. The relatively unconscious, involuntary and persistent qualities of these patterns and the difficulty of their being acquired by an exotic adult through conscious imitation indicate that they are normally acquired early in the life of the individual.

5. The persistence of these patterns in novel cultural environments and the probability of their childhood acquisition suggest that they should be thought of as representing dispositions of the person (personality dispositions, as defined in the previous chapter) rather than simply of the environmental situations that foster them.

6. Their conceptualization as reflecting personality dispositions is also supported by their apparent salience in the individual's structure of subjective thoughts and emotions about himself as a separate and continuous entity and by the apparent relevance of that structure to his decisions about self-regulation and adaptation. In other words, they play a part in the organization of his personality, as discussed in Chapter 1.

These propositions are roughly consistent with intercultural experience at many times and places, and they represent an argument for the dispositional and culturally variable view of personality. According to this argument, personality dispositions are not uniformly distributed across human populations, and culturally distinctive ones are resistant to extinction in novel cultural environments. Intercultural experience provides the intuitive grounds for accepting as plausible, without systematically collected evidence, the assumption that there are psychological differences of some importance between human populations; it gives face validity to the search for those differences.

The same kind of intuitive evidence based on experience, however, tells us that even what we choose to call personality dispositions are not completely unmodifiable in the lifespan of the individual. The degree to which change is possible when a person moves from his home group to a host group seems to be dependent on many factors; the quantity and quality of cultural difference between the two groups, the amount of pressure on him to change, his personal flexibility in adapting to new environments, differences in relative prestige and other incentives between the two groups, the types of opportunities available to him in the new group, his rejection of the home group or its values before leaving, his age and psychological development at the time, and so forth. When these conditions are favorable, persons do change and become drastically acculturated or resocialized to a new set of environmental values, either abruptly, as in religious conversion or "thought reform," or more gradually through increasing participation in the new and decreasing attachment to the old. It is not entirely clear how many of these observable changes are permanent or fundamental, but they suggest the modifiability of recurrent behavior patterns under special conditions. They do not contradict the assumption that those patterns we call personality dispositions are resistant to extinction but rather suggest that the resistance has limits, some of which are environmentally determined. On the whole then, at least some culturally distinctive dispositions are experienced by most persons as salient parts of themselves to which they are emotionally attached, and they are not easily given up; thus continuity in these dispositions through adulthood is more prominent than change for most persons.

We know from historical evidence that, however stable culturally distinctive dispositions appear in the individual lifespan, they can and do change in response to environmental conditions over longer periods of time. The massive acculturation of rural migrants from underdeveloped areas in Europe and Asia to industrial occupations and urban life styles in the United States, Australia, England, and other Western countries, and the transformation of some of them from traditional peasantry to middle class in two or three generations constitute the best known example of this phenomenon in the recent past. Although immigrant groups are not simply homogenized culturally, there can be no doubt that in most cases their behavior and values eventually shift toward those prevalent in the new environment. Some of the founders of culture and personality as a field of study undoubtedly based their axiomatic belief in the power of "culture" to mold a person's behavior and values in childhood on their personal observation of the children of immigrants whose Americanization in public school and community appeared so strikingly thorough. Longer-term history, without immigration, is even more convincing. Who can doubt that before the advent of Victorian sexual puritanism and romanticism, Englishmen in the late 18th century were different in fundamental values and personal tastes, particularly concerning self-discipline, from their class counterparts a century later? And who can doubt that the differences had something to do with the major changes in British institutions (scientific development, industrialization, urbanization, imperialism) during that period? Many other periods and places in the known history of the West would illustrate this same point. Given a long enough time and enough obvious institutional change, the culturally distinctive behavior patterns of a population—including the private thoughts, emotions, and personal preferences of its individual members—change, and the direction of that change bears some relation to alterations in the institutional environment.

The basic assumptions of research on culture and personality, grounded in unsystematic experience and historical considerations, thus concern the relative durability of personality, once formed, during the individual lifespan, and its relative modifiability over the generations in response to environmental change. These assumptions imply the existence of psychological differences between human populations as great as the environmental variations in their past and present conditions. What kinds of evidence can be obtained regarding population differences in personality characteristics?

Types of Group Differences

Variability in behavior among human individuals exists at many levels. Kluckhohn and Murray gave succinct recognition to this in their dictum:

Every man is in certain respects
a. like all other men,
b. like some other men,
c. like no other man (1948, p. 35).

Culture and personality studies are primarily concerned with those respects in which a man is like some other men, particularly his fellow group members, in contrast to members of other groups. The respects in which he is like all other men are the biosocial and psychological universals that form the background categories within which significant between-group variations are found. The respects in which he is like no other man are the objects of inquiry in the psychology of individual differences, which are a function of the variability within any population, no matter how clearly defined. Investigators of culture and personality can ill afford to ignore biosocial universals, psychological universals (such as those in semantic structure), and individual differences, but their special attention is reserved for variations between groups.

This does not mean that culture and personality study assumes a spurious uniformity of behavior within populations and overlooks variations between individuals; on the contrary, it is the genuine group differences that go beyond the individual variations of any one population that are the central subject matter of the field. If it were to be discovered that a vast variety of sensitive and sound instruments of psychological measurement could uncover no significant differences among ethnic groups and national populations, there would be little need for a subdiscipline of culture and personality, since its main goal is the explanation of such differences. Conversely, the demonstration that such differences do indeed exist is a first order of business, and this chapter is concerned with illustrating and classifying those types for which we have some evidence. Since culture and personality is only one kind of group psychology, this discussion is not concerned with all psychological differences between all kinds of groups. It is deliberately limited to personality characteristics and relatively stable populations.

Personality characteristics include three levels of abstraction: (a) personality indicators, observable consistencies in behavior that are not attributable to a temporary external or internal condition of the individual and that distinguish him from some other individuals; (b) personality dispositions, which operate as internal pressures on the individual's response to a variety of conditions, creating consistencies that unify diverse psychological processes (*e.g.*, cognition, emotional activation) in the pursuit of a particular set of goals relating to his self-regulation and social adaptation; (c) personality organization, the ordering of personality dispositions for a given individual, including hierarchical and interdependent relations among them, permitting orderly response to stimulation and the fulfillment of self-regulatory and adaptive functions.

Only consistencies in behavior are observable; they are the indicators from which we infer the existence and operation of personality dispositions and their organization in an individual. Some specific consistencies indicate dispositions that, though varying across human populations, may fall outside our definition of personality. For example, there is good evidence (Segall, Campbell, and Herskovits, 1965) that populations vary in their susceptibility to standard optical illusions, and it has been suggested that this has something to do with the occurrence of right angles in their childhood visual environments. No suggestion has been made that the variable disposition involves any psychological function but visual perception or that it is salient in the self-regulation or social adaptation of the individual. Until it is shown to be more psychologically complex or central to goals of individual functioning (as has been argued for another perceptual characteristic, field dependence-independence; see Witkin *et al.*, 1962), illusion-susceptibility may be regarded as a psychological characteristic but not a personality characteristic.

A population, in this discussion, is an aggregate of persons who share a culture (organized body of rules) that they transmit from generation to generation. This type of aggregate is often referred to as a culture or subculture, but the term *population* is preferred here because it does not imply internal uniformity. The use of a population unit excludes temporary groups bringing together heterogeneous persons for limited functions; thus the riders of a subway car would not constitute a population (except insofar as they are drawn from the same larger population), nor would the employees of a large insurance company. The Italian-

Americans of New Haven, the Japanese-Americans of Chicago, or the lower-middle-class residents of Cincinnati are populations in the sense used here because they have defining attributes that indicate similarities in the rules by which they live, including those concerning interpersonal relations within and outside the family, and an endogamous ideal that helps maintain those similarities over the generations. The boundaries of a population as here defined are dependent on the scope of the comparison. For some purposes, one would want to compare working-class residents of Philadelphia with middle-class residents of the same city and would, therefore, consider them separate populations. If one were to compare them with villagers in Japan and India, however, it might well be appropriate to consider both classes of Philadelphians as parts of one population. In one case, the focus would be on a narrow range of variation; in the latter case, the Asian-American differences could be so gross as to make variations between working-class and middle-class Philadelphians pale into insignificance.

In a discussion of the scientific study of group differences aimed at clarifying the realities underlying group stereotypes, Gordon Allport (1954, pp. 95–103) provided a typology that is applicable to variations in observable behavior patterns (personality indicators) among populations. These cross-culturally variable behavior patterns are the crude ore from which investigators of culture and personality attempt to extract plausible inferences about variations in personality dispositions and their organization. In considering each of the four types described below, we must consider to what extent the observed behavior can be plausibly interpreted as indicating the operation of a personality disposition.

J-CURVE OF CONFORMITY BEHAVIOR

This refers to a kind of behavior expected of every member of one population and actually performed by most of them, but not occurring at all in the populations with whom they are being compared. One can see this most clearly in the case of religious prescriptions and proscriptions. For example, Hindus—in contrast to most other peoples—are prohibited from eating beef, and the vast majority of them have never done so, but a smaller number have eaten it at some time in their lives, and a few eat it regularly. A hypothetical distribution of conforming individuals may be plotted as in Figure 2.1. The frequency curve drawn to the histograms resembles the letter J.

The J-curve is thus a graphic representation of the large proportion of members in a population who conform to a cultural norm that is nonexistent in another population. The decay in such a curve over time, so that it stops resembling the letter J, is, as Allport pointed out, a graphic representation of change in normative behavior. Many descriptions by social anthropologists of the peoples with whom they worked imply the

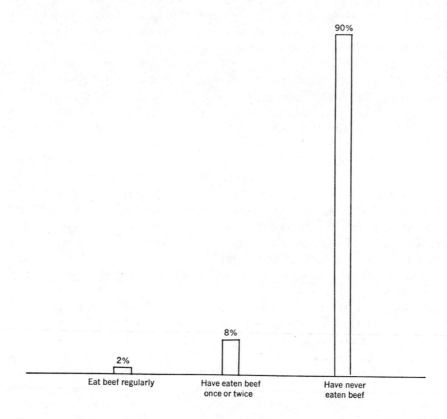

FIGURE 2.1. *Hypothetical percentage of Hindus who refrain from eating beef —a conformity attribute.*

existence of J-curves. For example, a statement like "The Zulu practice mother-in-law avoidance" implies that most Zulu conform to such a rule and that anyone who did not would at least be recognized as deviant and probably punished; the implicit comparison is with populations in which mother-in-law avoidance is unknown. Insofar as a social anthropologist describes the most distinctive features of institutionalized behavior he observes, he is generating J-curve data.

Since conformity behavior is very problematic as a personality indicator, J-curve data by themselves provide weak evidence concerning the distribution of personality distributions in a population. While it might be asserted that large-scale conformity to the Hindu beef taboo reflects personal conflicts over cannibalistic impulses directed at the father, but displaced onto the sacred cow, or that most Zulu avoid their mothers-in-law because of repressed hostility or sexual feelings toward their own mothers, it seems more plausible that a majority in both populations conform because there are rewards for normative behavior and punishment for deviance. The burden of proof for explanations involving personality dispositions lies on those who propose such explanations. Admittedly, the simple conformity explanation does not help us understand how the beef taboo or mother-in-law avoidance got started or how it is maintained when other rules are dropped, but those are separate questions. For the Hindu or Zulu individual, the pressure of social sanctions may be enough to enforce his conformity without invoking any deeper psychological factors.

The J-curve as a simple statement of recurrent conformity behavior is an inadequate personality indicator, but its psychological significance can be increased through careful analysis and additional data. We must consider what kinds of evidence would convince us that the behavior served a deeper psychological function than enhancing respectability. If we knew a Hindu, for example, who was thrown into a panic at the thought of eating beef even when living among non-Hindus, who expressed detailed ideas about the horrors of slaughtering and eating cattle, who dreamed about such horrors, and for whom these thoughts, ideas, and dreams were related to ideas about himself and significant others that aroused similar emotional responses—we might become convinced that his food abstinence reflected not only conformism but other personality dispositions as well. And if further investigation indicated that a large proportion of beef-abstainers had similar ideas and emotional reactions related to similar interpersonal content and to sacred cows, this would be evidence concerning the psychological function of that taboo in that population. Thus we must ask about a particular pattern of conformity behavior: What relations does it have to environmental reinforcement and to the emotional reactions, thought processes, and interpersonal relations of the person who performs it?

My field work in Nigeria affords a more realistic example of the ways in which one can find evidence concerning whether J-curve behavior should be regarded as a personality indicator. I worked in a Yoruba town in southwestern Nigeria and several years later in a Hausa town in the northwestern part of the country. Both were densely settled urban communities with walled residential compounds and prominent marketplaces, but there were many differences in the social behavior of the people. A most obvious difference had to do with sociability: The Yoruba engaged in a great deal of jovial public conversation with many different persons, often accompanied by laughter and other indications of friendliness. The Hausa, though also sociable, were much more restrained in their expressions of friendly interest. Their norms of interpersonal behavior differ, and so did the behavior I observed; each population held to its own J-curve, at a different level on a sociability axis. The Yoruba sociologist, Fadipe, wrote:

The Yoruba is gregarious and sociable. . . . [The] Yoruba is more of an extrovert than an introvert. The self-contained, self-reliant person who can keep his mental and physical suffering to himself so that others may not express their sympathy for him is regarded as churlish and one to be feared. The Yoruba looks upon expressions of sympathy offered to a man who is experiencing temporary or permanent injury as helping to lighten the pain. A person who is ill but keeps his illness from the knowledge of his mates for fear of being obliged to them or even out of consideration for their peace of mind is roundly scolded (1970, pp. 301–303).

In contrast, the Hausa value highly the personal quality called *fara'a* ("consistent geniality, cheeriness, pleasant manners, being unruffled"; Bargery, 1934, p. 302), which has the connotation of a calm, stoical pleasantness no matter what the stress or provocation, and they admire the quality termed *fillanci* and *filako*, which connote reticence, the denial of one's own needs in public, and the ability to endure severe pain without complaint.

These differences in the normative ideals of sociability and sharing one's suffering with others seemed to be widely realized in the actual behavior I observed. In the Hausa town there was a small Yoruba population whose public interpersonal behavior stood out against the background of Hausa reticence as flamboyant and boisterous, even intrusive. Physicians and nurses in the local hospital reported that Yoruba women cried out and moaned freely during childbirth, while Hausa women hardly ever made any sound even during difficult deliveries. Here is evidence that conformity with their respective cultural ideals is achieved even during the pain and stress of this universal biological event. This suggests that the observed pattern is not merely conformist behavior but is programmed into personality functioning, determining emotional response to pain. If more comparable evidence of this type were available, it would be possible to evaluate the hypothesis that the observed differences in sociability between Yoruba and Hausa were related to average differences in personality dispositions in the two populations.

This example, incomplete as it is, indicates the lines along which we would want to pursue this inquiry further, the questions that must be answered to make a psychological interpretation of any conformist behavior which has a J-curve distribution in a population:

How general is the behavior across situations? The more general it is in the situations that make up the individual's life space, the more it requires of him, and the more likely it is to be programmed into his functioning personality.

To what extent is the behavior performed in private situations, where "no one is watching," as opposed to public situations, which are clear occasions for social evaluation? The more the behavior persists in the private realm, the more independence it shows of direct public scrutiny, the more justified we are in considering it a property of the person and assuming it is relevant to a disposition in his personality.

To what extent does the behavior persist despite stress, pain or other personal sacrifices that might have to be made for conformity? If persons are under severe pressure not to perform the behavior and they nevertheless do so, it is likely to be more than a perfunctory act of conformity. The Hausa women, for example, who undergo prolonged and difficult deliveries in a hospital without anasthesia and with hardly a whimper, are conforming to a Hausa normative ideal, but under such pressure to deviate that the very strength of their conformity must be thought of as a personality indicator.

To what extent does the conversation of individuals show them to be consciously preoccupied with the behavior and aware of it as salient in their personal ethical code, their emotional stability or other aspects of their representations of self? The more individuals are preoccupied with the behavior and see it as part of themselves and functioning for them in ways other than simply obtaining social approval and avoiding disapproval, the more we are able to interpret the conformist behavior as relevant to a personality disposition.

To what extent does the behavior persist among migrants who have left their home area to reside among people of a different culture who do not have the same normative ideals? In other words, does the practice persist among individuals when its normal social supports are removed? Of course, segregation among immigrants can maintain these social supports, but it is usually possible to find immigrants from the same cultural background varying in the degree to which they maintain these supports (see Cronin, 1970), and the more the practice continues without support, the more reasonable it is to see it as a personality indicator.

Even with the information to answer all these questions positively, so as to confirm a psychological interpretation for at least *some* of those who conform to the behavioral norm, we would still need to ask for what proportion of those who conform the psychological interpretation is valid. It is not only possible but probable that in the same population will be found individuals who perform a practice merely because it is a social imperative and those for whom the practice is more deeply embedded in their psychological processes. A satisfactory interpretation of J-curve behavior from the viewpoint of culture and personality research would require information on the proportion of individuals falling into each of these categories.

Thus an ethnographic description that tells us most persons in a population behave in accordance with a norm raises more psychological questions than it answers. J-curve distributions can be taken as personality indicators only after these questions have been answered. When normative change occurs, however, and J-curves begin to flatten out, the possibilities for interpreting social behavior in personality terms are greatly increased. Wolf (1966, 1968, 1970) describes the situation among the Chinese in Taiwan, whose custom of parentally-arranged marriages decayed in this century. When all marriages were arranged by parents, it was not possible to interpret the universal conformity of bride and groom as signifying how they felt about each other. Later, when choice by the prospective spouses was legitimized as an option, the nature of the choice could be psychologically significant. Wolf argues that those young people who had been betrothed as infants and raised together but who refused to marry each other as adults when such choice became legitimate, were indeed inhibited by psychological processes. When choice is itself legitimized, selection of one option over another can be a personality indicator in a more obviously valid way than choosing to do what almost everyone else is doing and feels must be done. But J-curve behaviors are, nevertheless, of great psychosocial interest because they distinguish one population from another rather than merely individuals from one another within a population, and they are not immune to psychological interpretation.

RARE-ZERO DIFFERENTIALS

Some traits thought of as characteristic of a given population are actually rare within it but are totally absent in the populations with which it is being compared. This kind of comparison is graphically represented in Figure 2.2. Very few people in India lie on beds of nails or walk on burning coals, but no one in most other countries performs such feats, so we think of them as distinctive of India.

The most obvious personality indicators that have this rare-zero distribution across populations are unusual mental diseases such as *piblokto*, the "hysterical flight" syndrome of the Polar Eskimos; *windigo* psychosis, characterized by cannibalistic fantasies, among the Ojibwa Indians; *latah* or "arctic hysteria," involving purposeless imitation of others and violation of controversial modesty, among Central Asian and Siberian groups; and *amok*, the temporary homicidal violence found in Malaya and Indonesia. All of these conditions are rare in the populations mentioned but are believed to be absent elsewhere; insofar as they are truly absent in other populations, they represent genuine rare-zero differentials.

This type of contrast is not limited to mental diseases, however. Any individual pattern of social responses that is recurrent in a population, limited to a minority of individuals within it, and absent in compared populations, falls into the category of rare-zero differential. This includes any unusual or esoteric pattern of religious, esthetic, or political behavior that might be taken as an indicator of personality. Celibacy in Catholic populations is restricted to the relatively small number of persons who are priests, monks, and nuns, but compared with non-Catholic groups in which celibacy does not exist, it may be said to be a characteristic of the Catholic groups. The literature on esoteric religious practices and deviant sects is full of such examples. Some attempts to use specialized art productions as indicators of personality contrasts across groups involve rare-zero comparisons. Certain types of poetry, novels, dramas, styles of painting and sculpture may be highly distinctive, even unique, productions of a particular population, with no counterpart elsewhere, yet their

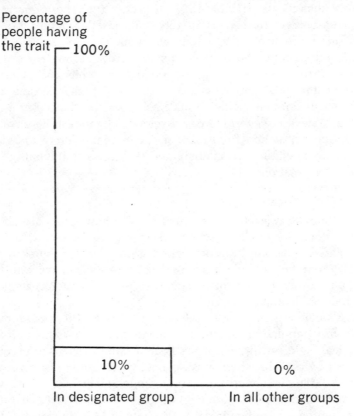

FIGURE 2.2.   *A rare-zero differential.*

production and even their appreciation may be limited to a small segment of the population. The leaders of a group may recurrently exhibit tendencies peculiar to that group but not widely shared within it.

One of the drawbacks of the rare-zero differential as a category for personality comparisons is the difficulty of establishing the absence of certain characteristics. Wallace (1961a) has suggested that the symptoms of *piblokto* among the Polar Eskimo are by no means peculiar to them if the syndrome is analyzed into its component parts, and he claims that related phenomena can be observed in our own society. This may be true of other unusual mental disorders as well (see Yap, 1969). The danger is that a rare-zero difference may be mistakenly assumed to exist when one population exhibits the characteristic in a highly institutionalized, conspicuous form, and another population has the same characteristic but does not give it the same degree of public recognition. For example, in comparing some West African groups with Americans of European ancestry, we might notice that possession by gods and spirits plays an important role in West African religious practices, particularly on the part of the specialist practitioners, and that it plays no comparable role in American religions. This might lead to the conclusion that possession as a psychosocial pattern linking trance or "hysterical dissociation" with supernatural beliefs is a distinctive characteristic of the West African groups. The study of unorthodox religious sects in America and in the European countries from which many Americans derive, however, indicates that very similar behavior is a recurrent and persistent pattern in the religious history of Christianity and Judaism (see Lewis, 1971). Thus what might seem in the first examination of the most institutionalized patterns to be a rare-zero differential is merely a difference in emphasis or relative frequency, which is not at all the same. The rare-zero differential implies a sharp discontinuity in behavior between two populations, and it is important to know whether their behavior really is discontinuous in respect to the particular characteristic.

In spite of this difficulty, there is no doubt that there are true rare-zero differentials in behavioral characteristics across populations, and they raise special problems of explanation. Since, by definition, the characteristic is exhibited by only a small proportion of the population to which it is attributed, in what sense is it representative of the whole group? What relation do these unusual individuals have to the majority who lack the characteristic? There are four kinds of explanation used to justify regarding such rare behavioral phenomena as distinctive of the whole population in contrast to other populations:

The rare behavior may be, as Allport suggests, a decayed or decaying J-curve, a cultural survival from a period in which it was required behavior for all group members. Kosher food practices among eastern European Jewish immigrants to the United States were originally J-curve norms. As the immigrants and their descendants became acculturated to prevailing American food habits, the number of deviants rose until now, for the American Jewish population as a whole in contrast with other Americans, the custom of "keeping kosher" is a rare-zero differential. Riesman (1950) argues that the "inner-directed" character type was the norm in late-nineteenth-century America, but that it survives primarily in rural areas and small towns. It is in process of becoming, according to him, a rare characteristic, though still distinctive of America as compared to non-Western countries.

A majority of the population may provide a social environment favorable to the invention and survival of the rare behavior. This would tend to be true particularly if the characteristic were associated with an elite social group or with leadership roles. The majority may not impose strict abstinence on themselves or give lengthy, emotional speeches, but they may appreciate their religious or political leaders' doing so, in contrast with populations in which such leadership behaviors are totally absent. In this sense, then, the behavior pattern exhibited by the leaders is interpreted as indicative of values present in the larger population, although the motives involved in accepting the leadership behavior pattern may be far from clear. When art productions are involved, the population may be consumers of or an audience for the creative efforts of a small group of specialists; in this case too, the survival of a particular form or style indicates its acceptance, at least among those members of the group who are not apathetic to it. Nevertheless, individuals who accept and support a given mode of behavior may be extremely different psychologically from the specialists who produce it (the audience for and performers of jazz in America illustrate this), and this presents a major difficulty for the psychological interpretation of rare-zero differentials in esthetic forms.

The rare behavior may be an exaggerated form of a behavioral tendency that is widespread in the population. Parker (1960) has argued that the *windigo* psychosis of the Ojibwa Indians represents a conflict shared by all Ojibwa men but precipitated in this extreme form by stressful economic conditions. Where this is so, the rare pattern may be seen as epitomizing a unique or unusual tendency of the population compared with other populations. This is analogous to a malnutritional disease syndrome affecting only a small number of individuals in a population which suffers generally from malnutrition; the state of the larger group makes it likely that some individuals in it will experience the more serious effects of malnutrition. This kind of reasoning, not always adequately demonstrated in comparative personality study, is also behind assertions that the content of Hollywood movies exemplifies in extreme form the values of Americans generally and similar generalizations about specialized symbolic productions. The hypothesis that leadership qualities represent the embodiment of ideals toward which most individuals are striving is also based on this conception.

Finally, rare behavior patterns may be seen as inverted forms of widespread behavioral tendencies in the population, reactions against J-curve behavior. Wallace (1959) distinguishes two types of such reactions: "cathartic" and "control." Cathartic reactions involve a release from the pressures and restrictions of social conformity. Koestler (1961) suggests that the norms of behavior in Zen Buddhist monasteries, especially the apparent verbal and physical hostility involved in instruction, represent an attempt to escape the polite formalities and pleasantries of conventional Japanese social life. The Plains Indians custom of *berdache,* an institutionalized form of transvestism in which certain men took on the dress and duties of women, has been widely interpreted as an escape from the rigid requirements of courage and military vigor involved in the ordinary male role in those societies. This is not "cathartic" in the usual sense, but it is a waiver of some of the duties required of others in the same population; this waiver allows the expression of personal tendencies that are ordinarily forbidden. Control reactions involve the deviant imposition of restrictions on tendencies that are currently finding widespread expression in the population. Puritanical reform movements that begin with a small group observing self-imposed restrictions are examples of this phenomenon. Both cathartic and control reactions are often interpreted by social analysts in terms of a behavioral dialectic in which the deviant pattern is taken as a sign of the cultural norm that it inverts.

These four widely varying conceptions of the ways in which a trait that is rare in one population but absent in others may be considered distinctive of the whole population indicate that the interpretation of a rare-zero differential may depend on theoretical premises concerning the relation of psychotics, artists, leaders, or religious fanatics to personality distributions in their respective populations. Since some of the theoretical premises are questionable and lack empirical confirmation, rare-zero differentials between populations must be interpreted with great caution.

OVERLAPPING NORMAL CURVES OF DISTRIBUTION

The two types of group differences discussed so far are finite and can be summarized in terms of presence and absence. However, human characteristics that can be measured on a quantitative scale allow each individual to be assigned a numerical value that he may share with no others in the same population; thus we compare the distributions of these values in different populations. The most frequent pattern for these distributions in graphic form is a bell-shaped curve (see Figure 2.3). As Allport states:

> We speak of the curves as "normal" for the reason that a great many human characteristics are found to occur in this symmetrical pattern of distribution. Few people stand extremely low and few extremely high; most are moderate in the trait in question. This "bell-shaped distribution" is particularly common for biological qualities (height, weight, strength) and for most measures of ability (intellectual capacity, learning ability, musical ability, and the like). It holds also for most personality traits (1954, p. 100).

If we give one of the usual kinds of personality tests to a sample of individuals from a given population and record their numerical scores on a particular trait, we can expect the distribution of scores to approxi-

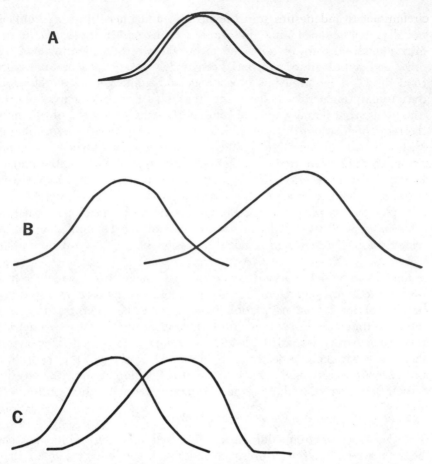

FIGURE 2.3. *Varying degrees of overlap in curves of normal distribution.*

mate a bell-shaped curve. This is also true of responses to tests of cultural
values (see Kluckhohn and Strodtbeck, 1962); many persons cluster
around a population mean, while extreme responses are considerably
fewer. It is somewhat less obvious, though equally true, that certain kinds
of child-rearing variables are normally distributed within populations,
although the dispersion is often concealed behind an ethnographic description of J-curve behavior: "Mothers (in a particular society) wean
their children from the breast when they are 18 months old." In fact, a
survey conducted in the society for which such a statement was made
would be virtually certain to find that a majority of mothers wean their
children when they are between 16 and 20 months and that some are
weaned earlier than 16 months and a few later than 20 months. The ages
at which many developmental events take place are likely to be normally
distributed, often around a socially approved average that individual

circumstances and desires impel some parents to accelerate and others to delay. Unless an ethnographic account specifically states that a developmental event invariably takes place on a particular birthday of the child, it can be assumed that the ages of its occurrence are normally distributed.

An important fact about normal curves is that when they are plotted for two human populations on a single characteristic, they frequently overlap. This means that there are some individuals in each population whose numerical values fall within the range of the other. Strangely enough, this is even true of characteristics that appear to differentiate populations very clearly. For example, the nasal widths of West African Negroes and Scandinavians seem, on the basis of impressionistic observation, to be extremely disparate. Measurement of a Nigerian population with the greatest nasal width and a Swedish one with the smallest shows that the bell-shaped curves nevertheless overlap considerably, as in Figure 2.3, c. Thus some of the Nigerians have narrower noses than some of the Swedes, even though on the average the Swedish nasal width is less. So it is with normally distributed personality characteristics; the average tendencies of two populations may be disparate, but this does not mean that every individual from one group will be higher on a scale than every individual from the other. Awareness of this alerts us to the dangers of leaping to conclusions about personality differences between populations.

Understanding that the curves overlap, the student of culture and personality is nevertheless interested in comparing the two populations is terms of central tendency, by using the means, medians, modes, or modal classes (a specified range of scores about the mode) to represent the groups. If he finds the distributions overlap greatly, as in Figure 2.3, A, he may conclude that the difference is a slight one that cannot be relied upon to discriminate the two populations in regard to personality. If he finds little overlap, as in Figure 2.3, B, he may decide that he has discovered a dimension on which the two groups differ significantly. If the overlap is intermediate, as in Figure 2.3, C, he will probably need a statistical test of significance to determine the likelihood that the difference is due to chance. In the last case, which is very common, the range of differences within each group is wider than the differences between the means of the two groups, so that intragroup differences account for a large proportion of the total variation present.

The value of statistical tests of significance in interpreting normally distributed psychological test responses can be illustrated by Wallace's (1952) Rorschach test study of the Tuscarora Indians. Wallace (1970) used the results of that study to support his theoretical argument that populations are heterogeneous with respect to personality characteristics: "Wallace was able to state that the modal type of personality, defined on twenty-one dimensions of observation in a certain Indian population, was shared by only 37 percent of the sample tested" (1970, p. 153).

Reference to the original study (Wallace, 1952, pp. 104–110), however, shows that fewer than 5 percent of a comparison sample of Ojibwa Indians shared the Tuscarora modal personality type according to the same criteria. The difference is statistically highly significant, indicating that the Rorschach responses are not randomly distributed across these two Northeastern Indian groups. Thus, though 37 percent may fall short of the subjective expectation of intrapopulation homogeneity that Wallace originally brought to the study, the figure indicates (in comparison with the Ojibwa) a group difference of greater interest than the question of whether the Tuscarora are homogeneous or heterogeneous in personality. We have no reason to expect personality characteristics to be more homogeneous than biological ones, which vary within and between populations, and we have at least as much reason to assume that cross-population differences in personality, if not based on chance, have adaptive significance.

Culture and personality study is not focused on, nor does it attempt to explain, the entire range of variation of psychological dimensions; between-group/ differences are its special objects of inquiry, and these differences pose important problems for scientific investigation even though they represent a relatively small segment of the total range. Thus the comparative psychology of populations seeks to find differences in the mean scores of different groups on psychological tests and to take these average differences as starting points for cultural inquiry.

CATEGORICAL DIFFERENTIAL

When a particular category is present in all populations being compared and the category is of such a nature that each individual can be classified as either falling into it or not falling into it, population differences in terms of a categorical differential can then be expressed. Human biology provides a familiar illustration. Every person has gene loci for the alleles that make him classifiable as having blood type A, B, AB, or O. If one blood type such as B is taken as the category for comparison, we find that in one population 10 percent of the individuals have B blood while in another population 27 percent fall into this class. Demographic variations are also frequently expressed in this way: birth rates, death rates, rates of infant mortality, and so forth. Categories universal to all populations are used to show striking and dramatic cross-population differences in frequency.

Whenever common categories of behavior can be established, they can be used as units for comparing the frequencies of different groups. Rates of homicide, suicide, and other crimes; rates of divorce and social mobility; the incidence of common mental diseases; frequencies of patterns of sexual behavior (such as virginity at marriage)—all of these are widely variable across populations. The availability of institutionally collected statistical information on some of these variables makes the categorical differential one of the most documented types of behavioral differences between groups. Comparisons of suicide rates among countries of the world, alcoholism among American ethnic groups, psychoses and neuroses among American social classes, and sexual patterns of American religious groups, have revealed gross differences in frequency. Public opinion surveys often uncover categorical differentials, not only among regional, occupational, and educational groups, but also between national populations in terms of percentage responding "yes" or "no" to questions on public issues. Many of the group differences revealed by official statistics, opinion polls, and social surveys are only tangentially related to personality; others, such as rates of alcoholism or schizophrenia, are fairly direct indicators of behavioral tendencies that might be considered personality dispositions. Too few students of culture and personality have tried to use available information on categorical differentials between populations as a means of entry into deeper and broader personality differences between groups. J. H. Straus and M. A. Straus (1953) attempted this in relating the extremely high homicide rate in Ceylon to the social characteristics of various ethnic groups in that country.

A categorical differential may be simply another means of expressing differences between overlapping normal curves of distribution; thus if we compare the proportion of individuals who score higher than 75 on a personality scale, we might come out with 13 percent for one population, 37 percent for another, 86 percent for a third. Other categories are not based on continuous distributions; for example, a person either commits suicide or does not, is a diagnosed alcoholic or is not. These are dichotomous categories in which no intermediate degrees are recognized. Rates of deviance (crimes, mental diseases, etc.), usually expressed in dichotomous categories, share with the rare-zero differential the quality of measuring the behavior of a small fraction of the population. Although Ceylon may have a much higher homicide rate than Eire, even in Ceylon the vast majority of persons never commit homicide. All of the problems involved in interpreting deviant behavior as distinctive of a whole population, discussed above for rare-zero differentials, apply also to categorical differentials. There is usually better evidence for the existence and stability over time of some of the latter, however, so that their interpretation may be carried out with a greater degree of confidence.

Although the most familiar examples of categorical differentials are variations in rare behavior such as deviance rates, comparative personality study benefits greatly from the development of comparable behavior categories that apply more generally to the individuals in each population compared. For example, the method for thematic analysis of dreams devised by David M. Schneider (see Dorothy Eggan, 1961) uses categories such as sexuality and aggression (directed against the dreamer or used by him against others) that appear to occur in some dreams in all cultures, for comparing the frequencies with which dreams of a particular category occur across populations. The same kind of analysis may be made of projective tests, open-ended interviews, and values questionnaires in which the alternative categories of response are relatively limited; one can contrast the frequencies of the several alternatives in different populations.

Summary and Conclusions

Culture and personality is by necessity a comparative science, for the personality characteristics shared by individuals in a population cannot be understood except by comparison with other human populations that are somewhat different. Personality differences between nations, ethnic groups, and other populations are popularly recognized in stereotyped images and literary clichés that exaggerate the homogeneity of groups and attribute rare or average behavior to every member of a group. All of us are influenced by such stereotypes, and they affect our perception of cross-cultural differences in behavior. It is essential that culture and personality research rise above these popular distortions and concern itself with actual behavioral differences between populations. The types of actual differences that occur must be specified and distinguished in comparative study. Insofar as this is not done, culture and personality work will be liable to the popular errors of exaggerating internal uniformity, emphasizing the bizarre and unusual, and failing to discriminate between the rare, the modal, and the universal within a population.

Four types of group differences in individual behavior patterns are recognized: the J-curve of conformity behavior, in which a rule that is absent in contrasting populations is adhered to by most individuals in the group under study; the rare-zero differential, in which a behavior pattern not found in contrasting populations is recurrently characteristic of a small number of individuals in the group under study; overlapping normal curves of distribution, in which a sample of the behavior of each individual in several populations is placed along a single numerical scale and the central tendencies of the populations are compared; and the categorical differential, in which a category of behavior present in all populations under comparison is used to detect variation in frequencies of the behavior populations.

These types are not entirely disparate; in fact, some of the types are different ways of expressing the same thing, and some may be seen as altered forms of the others. It is extremely important, however, to know which of these types one is referring to when formulating a cross-cultural variation in personality. Confusion of rare behavior patterns with those characteristic of an entire population and confusion of a behavioral norm imposing the same requirement on everyone (J-curve) with an average tendency emerging from individuals widely dispersed along a behavioral continuum (normal curve) are particularly serious conceptual traps for students of culture and personality. The typology presented has the advantage of requiring that anyone who decides to take a rare behavior as characteristic of a population or a behavioral rule as synonymous with a normally distributed behavior pattern must lay bare his assumptions about the relation of deviance to normality or of cultural values to individual conformity.

Each of the various behavioral sciences concerned with culture and personality has tended to concentrate on a particular type of group difference. Anthropologists, because of their concern with normative behavior and their goal of extending the known range of human behavioral variation, have often used J-curve behavior and rare-zero differentials, the two types that involve the discovery of unique behavior patterns and the least degree of quantification. Psychologists, wedded to individual testing procedures and quantitative scoring, have most frequently examined overlapping normal curves for group differences, and they have been followed in this by anthropologists interested in projective techniques. Sociologists, with their tradition of analyzing social statistics for rates of various kinds and their development of opinion survey methods, have tended to concentrate on categorical differentials between populations. There is no reason, however, why all of these types should not be used in attacking specific problems in the comparative study of personality, and there are signs that investigators in one discipline are discovering the advantages of using formulations of group differences that have been the specialty of another. This methodological cross-fertilization is highly beneficial to culture and personality study and has only begun to have its effect on the field.

No matter what formulations are employed, cross-cultural differences in personality are the true starting points for culture and personality study. This is one reason why a general knowledge of world ethnography or specific knowledge of some diverse cultures is so useful for students of this field; it enables them to know what aspects of institutionalized behavior are variable cross-culturally, and it sharpens their perspective in the search for psychological variations across groups.

Part II

An Overview of Existing Theories and Methods

3

Theoretical Conceptions of
Culture-Personality Relations

Lacking a systematic theory of its own, culture and personality has provided a fertile field for the extension of theories from a variety of disciplines, including cultural anthropology, psychoanalysis, and sociology. A number of differing viewpoints on the relation between culture and personality have thus developed and influenced investigators in this field. Since it is virtually impossible to understand the contributions of these investigators without being acquainted with the range of their conceptions of culture-personality relations, this chapter is designed to review the fundamental theoretical orientations extant in the field.

The several existing positions on the relation of culture to personality appear to fall into five main classes: anti-culture-personality positions; reductionist positions; the personality-is-culture view; the personality mediation view; the "two systems" view. Each position includes not only a general model of culture-personality relations in a stable society but also assumptions concerning the socialization of individuals (see Chapter 4) and how personality should be assessed (Chapter 5).

Anti-Culture-Personality Positions

Despite the psychological inclinations of such major contemporary theorists as Harold Lasswell (1930, 1948, 1968) and Talcott Parsons (1964), the dominant theoretical positions in the "institutional" social sciences of anthropology, economics, history, political science, and sociology do not favor acceptance of the basic assumptions on which the study of culture and personality is based. Their general line of reasoning, insofar as it can be collectively summarized, follows.

Men everywhere strive to live rather than die, to maximize pleasure and minimize pain in their lives. When the survival of the individual or

43

his group is jeopardized, it becomes the paramount consideration in his life and gives rise to adaptive responses based on a rational (or quasi-rational) calculus of environmental probabilities for survival. For most men at most times and places, survival has been uncertain enough that such considerations have given their adaptive behavior its primary shape. Even when survival is relatively certain, however, human behavior is shaped by the coercive pressures of "social survival"—the maintenance and enhancement of career, reputation, status, and the esteem of others. Just as individuals must organize their behavior in accordance with the environment to avoid starvation and death, they must do so to avoid being socially stigmatized and to obtain the rewards available in their community; in both cases individual behavior reflects environmental contingencies calculated through application of the individual's capacities for perceiving and logically processing information about environmental demands. If there are vast differences in institutionalized patterns of behavior between prehistoric and modern man, Western and non-Western societies, and groups of differing cultural traditions, we must look to their environments for the explanation—to the differences in the ecological, institutional, and ideological conditions to which they had to adjust. Such differences reflect the processes of sociocultural evolution (including technological and institutional development and differentiation, urbanization, bureaucratization) that have directional properties of their own that coerce the adaptation of individuals in all times and places. Understanding these processes and their outcomes does not require delving into the psychology of the individual apart from recognizing that he, like all other normal humans, has the capacity for appraising and adapting to his environment so as to maximize his rewards and minimize his risks.

This statement represents a view that is at least tacitly and often militantly accepted by a large proportion of institutional social scientists, regardless of their positions on other issues. Those sociologists and social anthropologists who follow Emile Durkheim in his concern with the moral order or Max Weber in his interest in ideology might take exception to the rationalistic emphasis of the statement, but on the whole they, too, have most often formulated the relationship between the individual and the normative order in such a way that the latter is seen as an environmental system to which the individual must adapt but which he cannot alter. For them, too, the socially relevant aspects of individual behavior are predictable from knowledge of the environmental context in which the individual functions without reference to other characteristics of his own behavioral organization.

Within this common framework, institutional theorists antagonistic to the culture and personality position have a variety of views on personality as it is studied by psychologists. Some anthropologists (*e.g.*, Hart,

1954) go so far as to assert that there are no significant between-group differences in personality; personality types or traits have a single normal distribution replicated in each human society. The "discovery" of individual differences in personality within populations is regarded as *prima facie* evidence for the falsity of other culture and personality approaches, which are accused of positing that all individuals in a given culture are identical. Since this accusation is incorrect and used primarily as a polemical device, this position would seem to be patently invalid. It nevertheless serves to raise the important methodological question of whether there are measurable personality differences between human populations. The gibes of critics who answer "no" to this question on the basis of insufficient evidence should act as a stimulant to more precise and wide-ranging attempts at cross-cultural personality assessment.

A more serious attack on the field of culture and personality comes from those social scientists who claim that how populations differ psychologically is of little social significance. In its most extreme form, this position is associated with single-cause theories of culture, *viz.* ecological, economic, structural, or organizational determinism. In these theories, an environmental system external to the individual (*superorganic* is the term used by some anthropologists) is conceptualized as containing the cause of cultural variations in behavior. The motives and habits of individuals are seen as conforming automatically to the requirements of these powerful external determinants, so it is unnecessary to measure individual characteristics independently. For example, economic determinists may assume that a market system or a capitalist economy has certain consequences wherever it exists regardless of the psychological attributes of the participating individuals. Culturologists (for example, White, 1949) emphasize the power of a cultural tradition antedating the present generation of individuals to determine the direction of cultural behavior and the powerlessness of each generation to change the tradition without the intervention of external supraindividual forces. Ecological determinists do not expect that the reactions of populations to arid conditions, a hunting and gathering subsistence base, or irrigation will vary with the personality characteristics of their members. The assumption throughout is that personality differences are irrelevant to the operation of these strong determinants of behavior and can neither impede nor facilitate them.

A less extreme form of this position involves the concession that differences in personality and values can impede or facilitate the operation of supraindividual behavior determinants in the short run but that they are irrelevant to long-term trends. From the macrohistorical perspective of cultural evolutionists, the psychologically determined resistance of a population to a basic advance in subsistence technology and its consequent increments in societal complexity, will, if social and environmental conditions are right, delay but not prevent the expected set of changes. Similarly, most conceptions of stages in economic growth and mathematical theories of economic development are based on the assumption that the psychological characteristics of populations make minor differences that are eventually overwhelmed by economic forces and may therefore be ignored in the long-range view that they take. Thus, industrial development may be seen as involving changes in social structure that are unaffected in form or sequence by psychological variables, although the latter may alter the immediate capacity of a population to begin changing.

Such points of view are not necessarily incompatible with comparative personality study, although their proponents consistently minimize the significance of personality factors. In effect they are saying: "Personality factors account for such a small and ephemeral portion of the variance we are trying to explain that we cannot waste our time with them." This is not a doctrinaire position but one that puts the burden of the proof on culture-personality investigators, to demonstrate through empirical research that personality factors do account for substantial portions of the variance in socially significant behaviors. The confrontation of structural with personality-oriented positions in attempts to explain juvenile delinquency, for example, is likely to be beneficial for research development in that area (see Inkeles, 1963). Furthermore, it is usually acknowledged by proponents of the long-range view that their scientific objectives differ somewhat from those of culture-personality investigators; the short-run differences that they acknowledge may not be relevant to their predictions but may be of great import to the subjective satisfactions and emotional condition of great masses of people.

At the present time the most fundamental theoretical challenge to the basic assumptions of the culture and personality field comes not from social scientists concerned with large-scale institutional systems and processes but from sociological social psychologists of the "symbolic interactionist" school (e.g., Becker, 1970; Brim and Wheeler, 1966; Cottrell, 1969; Goffman, 1959a, 1961a, 1961b, 1963, 1967; Shibutani, 1961; Turner, 1956; Young, 1965). Although they share the environmentalist and rationalist position summarized above, they concentrate on the individual's view of his immediate social situation (the phenomenological perspective), emphasizing the normative pressures in that situation that induce him to behave as he is observed to behave. As followers of the philosopher George Herbert Mead, the members of the symbolic interactionist school operate with the notion that the individual's concept of self is generated from social interaction in the situations that make up his life. The self comprises the only characteristics of the individual's psychological organization that one must know about to understand his social adaptation, but it is itself derived from his social environment and changes with that environment through his lifespan. Understanding the individual's social behavior, therefore, is achieved through intensive examination of the situational environments to which he is responding, to discover the composition of his social self and the options available to him for maintaining self-esteem and the esteem of others. The basic assumption is that variations between groups in observable behavior can be explained in terms of situational pressures experienced by the individual, without evidence about deeper psychological factors.

Thus symbolic interactionism brings the argument between sociological and psychological interpretations of social behavior down to the immediate environment of the individual, the situation in which his adaptation occurs. Where the culture and personality theorist would see the behavioral expression of a personality disposition, the symbolic interactionist sees a self-esteem-maintaining response to a situational constraint. The symbolic interactionist position represents, at the level of the situation, all those social theories that deny the autonomous influence of enduring personality dispositions on social behavior.

The general strategy of symbolic interactionists is to demonstrate by situational analysis that a pattern of social behavior that might be accounted for in terms of personality dispositions is more properly understood as reflecting situational pressures to which the individual is responding. Thus Goffman (1963) argues that the behavior of patients in mental hospitals should be seen not as the expression of their psychotic personalities but as the outcome of the way they are treated in that institutional setting, and he provides detailed ethnographic evidence to support his interpretation. Thus Young (1965) argues that male initiation ceremonies in non-Western cultures function, not as a means of resolving the identity conflicts of boys (as proposed by Whiting, Kluckhohn and Anthony, 1958, and Burton and Whiting, 1961), but as a solution to the problem of organizational continuity for the men of the community. In a similar vein, though without explicitly invoking the symbolic interactionist position, MacAndrew and Edgerton (1969) propose a social explanation of drunkenness in human populations:

> [We] have attempted to document the inadequacy of the conventional understanding of the effects of alcohol on human conduct and to present a radically social-psychological formulation in its stead. Rather than viewing drunken comportment as a function of toxically disinhibited brains operating in impulse-driven bodies, we have recommended that what is fundamentally at issue are the learned relations that exist among men living together in a society. More specifically, we have contended that the way people comport themselves when they are drunk is determined not by alcohol's toxic assault upon the seat of moral judgment, conscience or the like, but by what their society makes of and imparts to them concerning the state of drunkenness (p. 165).

The lesson that symbolic interactionists intend to teach is that explanations involving unobservable psychological processes are made unnecessary by careful observation and analysis of the situation in which the individual is functioning. Like behaviorists of the social-learning school (Bandura, 1969), they are particularly critical of psychoanalytic explanations for locating the causes of behavior in hypothetical complexities of personality structure rather than in the visible contingencies of the situation faced by the individual.

Although much symbolic interactionist writing has a doctrinaire and polemical quality, particularly in its anti-Freudian attack, it poses a problem of the most profound significance for culture and personality studies. The problem is that the institutionalized behavior of humans, like many adaptive animal behavior patterns, represents a fit between the action of the individual and his environment that is inherently ambiguous in its origins: Is correspondence between what the individual does and what the environment rewards him for doing achieved by the individual's possessing the appropriate adaptive equipment before his contact with the environment or by learning through experience with that environment? The symbolic interactionists focus on experiential effects and minimize the influence of the individual's adaptive equipment, thus reversing an emphasis found in much writing on culture and personality. Controversies over sociological versus psychological interpretations of social behavior patterns have not solved the problem. We need a reexamination of the kinds of evidence that would demonstrate the contributions of organism and environmental pressure to observed adaptive behavior. My own effort in this direction begins with Chapter 12.

Reductionist Positions

Psychological reductionism or psychological determinism is the point of view from which individual psychological factors are seen as independent causes of cultural and social behavior. This point of view is by no means limited to the theorists discussed here, but they give it such an exclusive place in their theoretical systems that other views of cultural and social behavior are overlooked or minimized.

Psychological reductionism has a long history in nineteenth- and early twentieth-century social thought, most of which is of only marginal interest today. (See Allport, 1968, for a review of the relevant literature.) The major contemporary reductionism has been Freudian, and the pioneer in applying psychoanalysis to anthropological materials—after Freud himself—was the psychoanalyst-anthropologist Géza Roheim (1950; see Wilbur and Muensterberger, 1951, for a bibliography). For Roheim, the developmental patterns described in the works of Freud (*i.e.*, the stages of psychosexual development, including the Oedipus complex) were human universals which determined interpersonal behavior and group fantasy in all cultures. In the manner of Freud's analysis of primitive belief and ritual, by assuming that unconscious meanings discovered in clinical work with Western patients were applicable in all cultural contexts, Roheim analyzed the myths, folk tales, and beliefs of peoples ranging from the peasants of his native Hungary to the Australian aborigines with whom he did field work. In so doing, he—and others working along similar lines—claimed to have discovered recurrent symbolic formulations in which, for example, snakes and other reptiles represent the penis, children devour or are devoured by their mothers, and sons kill their fathers. The belief systems of folk cultures were seen as the direct outgrowth of the invariant developmental patterns and as serving psychological functions for the individuals whose anxieties, hostilities and other unconscious motives were represented in religion and folklore. While his field work in Australia and Melanesia made an innovative contribution to method in culture and personality (see Chapter 14), Roheim's theoretical formulations were focused on speculative issues like the origin of culture, issues that lend themselves to lofty generalizations tending to be either self-evident but vacuous (*e.g.*, "Human culture as a whole is the consequence of our prolonged infancy," Roheim, 1969, p. 50) or outrageously over-simplified (*e.g.*, "Civilization originated in delayed infancy and its function as security. It is a huge network of more or less successful attitudes to protect mankind against object-loss, the colossal efforts made by a baby who is afraid of being left alone in the dark," 1943, p. 100). Roheim asserted the primacy of intrapsychic motives and their fantasy derivatives over man's rational and adaptive capacities, as in the following statements:

> [The] bulk of human culture, even in its adaptational or ego-aspects, arises out of play or ritual activities. The reason for these activities lies in the infantile situation, and they acquire survival value secondarily by assimilating a part of the environment to man's needs. . . . Our tools are the projections of our body and we owe the art of making fire to a displaced play repetition of the genital act or of masturbation (1969, pp. 46–47).

Roheim never presented the logical argument that might have connected such statements with common sense and endowed them with plausibility. He seemed to delight in making uncompromisingly flat assertions that would convince only those who already agreed with him, and he apparently felt that operating within the Freudian theoretical tradition he had no need to construct a systematic theoretical formulation of his own. In consequence, his reductionist position has never been taken very seriously by anthropologists.

Roheim's naive psychological reductionism is also blind to history and institutional process; considerations of time sequence in the culture pat-

terns being analyzed, where they came from, how they were introduced
and institutionalized, whether surrounding groups have them—all questions of great concern to the anthropologist who wants to know whether
and how he can legitimately link a culturally shared imaginative production with the underlying motives of the population—are simply ignored.

The most distinctive and fundamental weakness of Roheim's approach
to culture, however, is that it does not seriously attempt to explain cultural differences. Culture patterns are, for the most part, seen as expressions of motives, emotional constellations, and preoccupations that are
panhuman; the emphasis is more on universal themes and symbols than
on variation along psychosocial dimensions. Roheim believed that cultures varied in their infantile traumata and thus in their expressive
behavior, but this was not the major focus of his work. Although it has
contributed some understanding to the cultural forms taken by panhuman
situations, such as the mother-child relationship and the anatomical differences between the sexes, analysis of this sort is largely irrelevant to
the central concern of culture and personality work: the assessment and
explanation of group differences in personality. Ironically, the major
contribution of psychoanalysis to culture and personality so far has been
made not by those who took literally the more speculative theorizing of
Freud concerning the invariant properties of development and cultural
fantasy, but by those who saw Freud's wide-ranging attempts to uncover
unconscious motives and residues of childhood experience as a possible
basis for explaining the cultural differences documented by ethnographers. Psychoanalysts such as Kardiner, Fromm, and Erikson, who concerned themselves with cultural variation, did not adhere to a strict
psychological reductionism; they admitted geographic, economic, and
structural factors as causal variables in their theoretical formulations.

A more sophisticated and scientific reductionist approach to culture
and personality is that of David C. McClelland, a personality psychologist. He looks back upon previous reductionist efforts and isolates the
reasons for their failure:

> Psychology as the basic science of human behavior ought to be able to
> contribute to other disciplines interested in man like history and economics,
> but to date its contributions have not been impressive. It has made attempts
> to be helpful, but they have nearly always involved such extensive extrapo-
> lations beyond observed facts that social scientists have by and large remained
> unimpressed. For example, Dodge discovered years ago that human beings
> showed a built-in variability of response, that the same response—e.g., the
> knee jerk reflex—could not be elicited twice in succession without a short
> pause. He tied this in on the one hand with the refractory phase of the
> nerve impulse and on the other with the observed tendency of societies to
> avoid doing the same thing twice in a row. He suggested, for instance, that
> the fact that the United States holds a national election only once every

four years might reflect the basic human tendency to avoid immediate repetition of an act, a tendency which should incidentally contribute to the survival of the species by leading to discontinuance of unsuccessful responses. No political scientist that I know of has ever made anything of Dodge's suggestion. . . . The reason is not hard to find: Dodge made no suggestions as to how the variables in his hypothesis might be measured nor did he suggest any concrete series of intervening behavioral events by which refractory phase in reflex behavior gets transformed into refractory phase in social institutions. So his extrapolation from simple human behavior remains untested and perhaps even untestable (1958, p. 518).

McClelland notes that the more recent, psychoanalytically influenced, psychological reductionism, although dealing with what would seem more socially relevant variables, has also failed to gain social science acceptance. He considers the analysis by Gorer and Rickman (1949) of Great Russian attitudes toward political authority as related to the swaddling experience which Great Russians undergo as infants, and comes to the following conclusion:

> The fact is . . . that the hypothesis is neither more nor less testable than Dodge's. It is simply not easily testable. Neither Gorer nor Rickman nor anyone else has gone about systematically testing what the reactions to swaddling are in Russia or elsewhere and attempting to build a concrete series of empirically established links between such reactions and social institutions. Until we can measure both psychological reactions to swaddling and degree of "firmness of political control," the hypothesis cannot be tested and social scientists have a right to remain skeptical about it (1958, p. 519).

The position taken by McClelland, explicitly and implicitly, is that psychological reductionist propositions deserve to be taken seriously when (1) independent operational measures are proposed for both the psychological antecedents and the social or cultural consequences, (2) the intervening connections between the psychological antecedents and the social consequences are spelled out in considerable detail, (3) the hypothesized connections are submitted to replicable and repeated empirical tests using methods of statistical inference prevalent in behavioral science research. For research linking motives to social action, he emphasizes the first of these requirements, obtaining "estimates of the average motivational level of social groups which are independent of the behavior of those groups." Given these stringent conditions, it appears that the more remote the psychosocial connection proposed in a hypothesis, the less likely it is to survive empirical testing if it lacks validity.

In his own research, McClelland (1961) proposes a connection between the average level of achievement motivation in a population (as measured in the content of its imaginative productions) and its level of economic and cultural achievement (as measured primarily by economic

indices and secondarily through the consensus of historians). He argues
not only that populations with a high level of achievement motivation
have more productive economic activity than those with a low level of
need for achievement, but also that in the history of a single society a
rise in achievement motivation precedes economic growth and a fall in
need for achievement precedes economic decline. The motives of individuals are seen as causes of cross-cultural variations and large-scale
socioeconomic changes.

It is true that McClelland sees the shared motives of individuals in a
population as having cultural origins, because they are produced by child-
training practices that are caused by the prevailing religious or ideological conditions. In this respect he is close to the views of Kardiner, Whiting, and Child. In spite of this and despite his plea for a balanced interpretation of history rather than a one-sided psychological one, there are
several reasons for regarding McClelland's theoretical position as basically reductionist. He posits an influence of personality on culture that
is not limited to clearly affective and "expressive" aspects of culture such
as religion, art, and interpersonal relations but applies as well to "instru-
mental" and seemingly impersonal kinds of social behavior such as economic development and fluctuations in the business cycle. Second, his
approach to role systems is explicitly reductionistic: He analyzes them
into the individual capacities and performance patterns required for
their successful operation, links the acquisition of these capacities and
performance patterns to unconscious motives of the individual, and con-
cludes that the operating level of the role system is caused by the population-wide strength of the unconscious motives. Finally, McClelland
argues the general case for motives as independent driving forces in
history, criticizing those "who have tended to think of man as *reacting*
to the demands and pressures of the environment rather than as actively
molding and reshaping it to suit his needs." The strength of McClelland's
reductionism, as contrasted with that of previous psychological determinists, lies in its being harnessed to an empirical method of verification
and in its ingenious and relentless search for objective indexes of human
motives.

The Personality-Is-Culture View

The theoretical position of Ruth Benedict, Margaret Mead and some of
their co-workers (notably Geoffrey Gorer), sometimes called the configurational approach to culture and personality, represents the application of cultural relativist doctrine to the phenomena of personality psychology. Cultural relativists hold that human populations vary widely in
their cultural values, in their conceptions of what is good, true, and beau-
tiful, and that the understanding of a culture different from one's own

requires seeing it from the indigenous point of view. Anthropologists taking a strict relativist line seek to document variations in cultural values and to demonstrate that the differences are so great and so pervasive that there are hardly any universal aspects on which to base cross-cultural comparison; they see attempts to classify or rank cultures as necessarily involving ethnocentric neglect of the indigenous context from which customs derive their distinctive and noncomparable meanings. Benedict and Mead extended this view to the subject of personality, demonstrating that psychologists had ethnocentrically presumed the universality of patterns of child rearing, personality development, sex-role behavior, and mental disorder that were in fact variable from one culture to another (Mead, 1928, 1930, 1932, 1935; Benedict, 1934a, 1934b, 1938, 1949). This demonstration had a profound and irreversible effect on psychology and psychiatry, but Benedict and Mead were trying to prove that personality patterns not only varied across human populations but were integral parts of pervasive, culturally distinctive configurations that gave them meaning and apart from which they could not be adequately understood. Personality was, in other words, an aspect of culture, the aspect in which the emotional responses and cognitive capacities of the individual were programmed in accordance with the overall design or configuration of his culture (the "cultural patterning of personality"); social relations, religion, politics, art, and recreation were programmed in accordance with the same design.

This is the theoretical perspective in which Benedict and Mead rejected the conceptual distinction between culture and personality. For them, separating the two would be equivalent to saying that personality could exist without being culturally patterned. Both "culture" and "personality" refer to configurations of behavior that are manifested and carried by individuals but are characteristic of a group. They would agree with the psychological reductionists that culture can be studied and psychologically interpreted in the behavior of individuals and in collective products such as myth, ritual, and art; but they reject deterministic formulations of psychological causes for cultural effects as doing violence to the basic equivalence of culture and personality.

In place of a causal conception of culture and personality, the proponents of this school of thought assume and attempt to describe the configurations that are reflected or expressed in almost every sphere of activity, communication, and interpersonal relations, so that whether one observes interaction in a given society or analyzes its films and magazines, he will find the same underlying patterns. The configurations are described not as "causing" their diverse cultural manifestations but as characterizing the unified, consistent quality inherent in the behavior of people of a particular cultural group. The question of how these configurations developed historically is often ignored or briefly presented.

In this view, the relation between culture and individuals is the problem of the transmission of configurations from generation to generation. How do human infants of basically similar behavioral potentialities come as adults to exhibit the distinctive patterns of the cultures into which they were born? This formulation of the problem leads to the emphasis on child-rearing practices for which this school of thought is well known. In some of Geoffrey Gorer's analyses of child rearing in particular societies (1943, Gorer and Rickman, 1949), the argument takes on a deterministic flavor; he seems to be saying that the toilet training of Japanese infants or the swaddling of Great Russian infants makes them what they are as adults. Margaret Mead (1954) disputes this interpretation of Gorer's work, however, and has laid down what may be considered the official position of this school on the subject of child rearing. According to her (and Benedict, 1949), child-rearing practices are primarily significant as indicators or clues to the cultural values and emotional attitudes of a particular cultural group. As a universal situation that can be variously structured, parent-child interaction reflects culturally dominant preferences concerning role relationships and the handling of impulses, preferences that guide parents in the rearing of their offspring. Child rearing is a sample of parental behavior and indicates as much about adult values as about the personality development of children. Nevertheless, it has some special significance as the first contact of the child with the configurations of his culture.

The transmission of culture from generation to generation is, in Mead's view, a process of communication in which many aspects of the growing individual's cultural environment relay the same messages to him, messages reflecting the dominant configurations of his culture. He acquires his "cultural character" by internalizing the substance of these consistent messages. The first set of messages is transmitted to him by his parents in infancy and early childhood. They enter into communication with him by making certain (culturally approved) reactions to his cries, his performance of bodily functions, his attempts to move and grasp; much of this communication is nonverbal and implicit. It lays a basis for the later transmission of the same underlying messages in a thousand other ways, some of them more explicit, as the child increasingly participates in the various aspects of adult culture. Child rearing is fundamental in the acquisition of cultural character, but it is only the first of many formative experiences, each reinforcing the other in communicating cultural configurations to the individual. Mead and her co-workers (Mead and Wolfenstein, 1955) have particularly emphasized the role of esthetic aspects of culture, such as drama, dance, and children's literature, in this communication process.

Three major criticisms have been made of this position on the relation of culture to personality. (1) It exaggerates the internal consistency of culture by an exclusive focus on patterns that pervade all aspects of cultural behavior and by using subjective methods of analyzing cultural materials that prevent disproof of alleged configurations. Many social scientists argue that the correspondence of different aspects of culture with one another is a question for empirical inquiry, not to be incorporated as a basic assumption in a theory. (2) When culture and personality are assumed to be equivalent, there is no way of assessing the degree of adjustment between the individual and his cultural norms; we are forced to assume a good "fit" that may not exist. This conceptual fusion of culture and personality can lead to the interpretation of all cultural products, from myths to magazines, as directly expressive of the motives, habits, and values of a population of individuals. The possibility of more complex relations of such products to the expressive behaviors of individuals in the population is ignored. (3) A circular concept of personality development that avoids the problem of what causes particular patterns of behavior to develop in individuals is assumed. Child-rearing practices and art, for example, are both regarded as being simultaneously formative and expressive of cultural character. This formulation is presented as being more in tune with a complex reality than child-rearing determinism is, but it is also more vague and less susceptible to empirical test. Several aspects of culture may reinforce each other in the education of the child, but this does not relieve us of the task of isolating their separate effects. A parent may be expressing cultural values in the ways he rears his child, but this does not tell us whether the child actually acquires those cultural values in that situation or whether he learns them later on in a different context. While Mead's view of the development of cultural character avoids the obvious fallacy of a unicausal child-rearing determinism, it obscures the picture of development by raising culture to the status of a general determinant operating simultaneously in so many ways that there is no use attempting to isolate specific causes. We are asked to forfeit the aim of explaining cross-cultural differences in personality in favor of simply appreciating them.

In essence, the personality-is-culture view takes culture as its central organizing concept while reducing personality to a mere individual reflection of culture, and personality development to the intergenerational transmission of culture. Those associated with this view, however, have often taken a modified psychoanalytic approach involving child-rearing determinism in studies of personality formation in various cultures.

The Personality Mediation View

Abram Kardiner (1939, 1945), a psychoanalyst, in collaboration with the anthropologist Ralph Linton (1936, 1945), first formulated the personality mediation view. In 1953 the anthropologist-psychologist team of

John W. M. Whiting and Irvin L. Child published their own theory along very similar lines. In essence, the position involves splitting culture into two parts, one of which is seen as made up of determinants of personality while the other consists of expressions of personality. Personality, then, is a connective or mediator between two aspects of culture.

In Kardiner's first formulation, the two aspects of culture are the *primary institutions*, consisting of the socioeconomic structure and child-rearing practices that comprise the environmental constraints and influences on the development of personality, and the *secondary institutions*, consisting of the religion, art, folklore, and other expressive media that are influenced by and satisfying to those aspects of personality shared by members of a society. In the Whiting and Child version, the environmental determinants of group personality are divided into two parts: the *maintenance system*, which is the institutionalized ecology, economy, and sociopolitical structure, and functions for the survival of the group in relation to its external environment; and *child training* or *socialization*, which operates within the constraints set by the maintenance system, shaping personality in accordance with the adaptive needs of the group but often against the needs of individuals. The expressive aspects of culture are referred to as the *projective system;* they are shaped by the common-denominator personality needs that have been socialized in child training but not eliminated as pressing personal motives. In both theories, child-rearing practices are seen as operating within the constraints of the socioeconomic structure to form personalities in a society with common needs and motives reflected in the religion, art, and folklore of the group.

A recent revision of the Whiting theory is shown in Figure 3.1 (from LeVine and LeVine,*Nyansongo,*1966). For Whiting and Child (1953) as opposed to Kardiner, the cultural causes (or antecedents) of personality and its cultural effects (or consequents) are seen as analogous to the independent and dependent variables in a learning experiment in which half the animals are given special rewards or punishments for behaving in the trial situation that the other half are not; the effects of reinforcement on performance are then sought in subsequent behavior in the same trial situation. Cross-cultural variations in child training constitute the experiment, and concomitant variations in projective systems represent its permanent behavioral effects. The personalities of members of the societies are the intervening variables, connecting early experience with religion, folk belief, and esthetic forms. Both Kardiner and Whiting and Child, however, attempted in their theoretical formulations to reconcile sociological and cultural approaches with that of psychological reductionism by giving the latter its place in respect to the projective systems—secondary institutions—while assigning causal priority to socioeconomic structure and the socially structured environment of childhood.

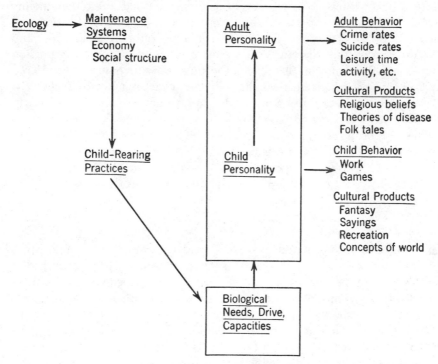

FIGURE 3.1. *The relation of personality to culture.* (Source: LeVine/LeVine, *Nyansongo,* © 1966 by John Wiley & Sons, Inc.)

In both formulations, personality—"basic personality structure" (Kardiner) or "typical personality" (Whiting and Child)—is seen not only as mediating causal influence between two aspects of culture but also as actively integrating them with one another. Implicitly or explicitly, culture is held to be a system of interdependent parts (including economy, social structure, and religion) in which personality plays an integrating role as the common denominator of individual factors that makes these disparate institutions consistent with one another in social action. Having made their own compromise between socioeconomic demands and their own needs as developing organisms, the individual members of a society shape a normative structure in the expressive institutions that tends to maintain that compromise for future generations.

Whiting's views on the functions of cultural beliefs and values have changed over the years. Although in earlier formulations (Whiting and Child, 1953; Whiting, 1961), he regarded magico-religious beliefs as reflecting the drives frustrated in the socialization process and the interpersonal residues of childhood experience, his recent work on values (Whiting *et al.*, 1966) is somewhat different. Cultural values, including the central religious beliefs of a people, are held to reconcile childhood-derived unconscious goals with adult assessments of social and economic realities; insofar as the two are discrepant, values reduce the sense of incompatibility (cognitive dissonance) between them. Thus the Zuni Indians resolve the dissonance between the prohibitions on aggression they internalized in childhood and the aggressive behavior engendered by their crowded housing through values emphasizing belief in the harmony of the universe. Religious and other values are thus designed to give cognitive comfort to members of a society in the face of their unfulfilled needs. Their function is no less defensive than that in Whiting's earlier statements, but the emphasis now is on the attainment of cognitive consistency when psychological needs and socioeconomic reality conflict. This view of religion is discussed further in Chapter 6.

The "Two Systems" View

This conception, formulated by Inkeles and Levinson (1954) and Spiro (1961a) and based in part on ideas from Parsons (1964) and Hallowell (1955), represents (modal) personality and sociocultural institutions as two systems interacting with each other. Each system is comprised of interdependent parts and has requirements for its maintenance. Both sets of requirements make demands of individual behavior, the personality system for satisfaction of psychological needs, the sociocultural system for socially valued performance in the roles that are institutionalized in the social structure. Stability in the interaction of the two systems is attained only when their respective requirements are functionally integrated by standards of role performance that permit the individual to satisfy his psychological needs and meet sociocultural demands at the same time. Psychologically satisfying conformity, as Spiro (1961a) conceives of it, makes possible what Inkeles and Levinson (1954) call *functional congruence* between the personality and sociocultural systems. Since this congruence is, in the long run, essential for societal survival, every society must provide for it through socialization of the child and adult; and in every existing society congruence should exist as either a strong tendency or an accomplished fact. Thus, for example, societies with highly authoritarian social structures should be found in comparative study to have a larger proportion of members with authoritarian personality characteristics than societies with less authoritarian social structures.

Inkeles and Levinson (1954) do not assume that the stable state of functional congruence is universal; noncongruence may be induced by changes coming from either system, what they call *institutionally induced noncongruence* and *personality-induced noncongruence*. The change in one system necessitates a change in the other for congruence to be regained and stability restored. The emphasis in this and other work by

Inkeles (1955, 1966a, 1966b), however, is strongly on institutionally induced noncongruence, as in a society undergoing industrialization or
socialist revolution. Parents are seen as the mediators of change, transforming novel institutional demands into personal characteristics as they
socialize their children. Spiro (1961b, 1965, 1966, 1967), however, is primarily interested in the ways in which personality affects the operations
of the sociocultural system, in stability as well as change, and he has
argued (1961b) that this should be the primary task of psychological
anthropology. His own work emphasizes the influence of personality on
religion, and in this he shares the psychological mediationists' view that
religion is a projective system for personality needs, providing institutionalized solutions for the unconscious conflicts of individuals (see
Chapter 6). Spiro and Inkeles thus differ in the theoretical emphasis of
their empirical work and in some of their underlying assumptions concerning psychological vs. sociological determinism, but their overall
models of culture-personality relations are basically similar.

Summary

These five conceptions of culture-personality relations—the anti-culture-
personality positions, psychological reductionism, personality-is-culture,
personality mediation and two systems—presented briefly above can be
summarized in even more abbreviated fashion as follows:

Anti-culture-personality	$C \to P$
Psychological reductionism	$P \to C$
Personality-is-culture	$P = C$
Personality mediation	$C_1 \to P \to C_2$
Two systems	$P \leftrightarrow C$

Only the personality mediation and two systems views are maintained
by active investigators in the field. Anti-culture-personality positions
characterize outsiders to the field. Psychological reductionism has been
persuasively revived by McClelland, but even he uses it as an element
in a more complex conception closer to the personality mediation view.
Personality-is-culture remains as an influence on contemporary research
but is no longer seen as a tenable position on which to base empirical
study. But all five positions represent directions of thought that have
given rise to the concepts of socialization, methods of assessing personality and other conceptions that will be considered in the next three
chapters.

4

Concepts of Socialization

The socialization of the human individual, his transformation from an infant organism to an adult participant in society, has emerged as the foremost topic of interdisciplinary concern in the behavioral sciences. Within the problem area defined by the term *socialization,* research is being actively conducted by primatologists, developmental psychologists, psychoanalysts, psychiatrists, psycholinguists, sociologists, anthropologists, political scientists, and legal scholars. Even more remarkable than the disparity of researchers is that the overlap and mutual relevance of diverse investigations in this field has received widespread professional recognition—in an extensive collection of reviews by members of a Social Science Research Council committee (Clausen, 1968), in the 1100-page *Handbook of Socialization Theory and Research* (Goslin, 1969), in the volume on socialization produced by the Association of Social Anthropologists in Britain (Mayer, 1969), in the third edition of *Carmichael's Manual of Child Psychology* (Mussen, 1970), which has a large section devoted to socialization, in an issue of the *Journal of Social Issues* devoted to legal socialization (Tapp, 1971), and in a large and growing literature on political socialization (see Langton, 1969; Dawson and Prewitt, 1969; Greenberg, 1970). Throughout these recent discussions of theory and data there is explicit awareness of the fact that no single discipline can solve the intellectual problems in the study of socialization by itself.

In this chapter, rather than attempting to recapitulate the systematic reviews of the literature already available, I will summarize those theoretical trends most evident in the culture and personality field and most closely related to the theoretical positions outlined in the previous chapter. Three different views of the process of socialization, corresponding roughly to the disciplinary orientations of cultural anthropology, personality psychology, and sociology, have dominated behavioral science theory and research. Socialization has been seen as enculturation or the intergenerational transmission of culture, as the acquisition of impulse control, and as role-training or training for social participation. Each view has taken a simple form in which a single set of factors has been emphasized to the exclusion of others, often with a naive assumption that its operation was self-evident, and one or more complex forms in which account was taken of interacting and limiting factors with a greater attempt to spell out the mechanisms involved.

Socialization as Enculturation

From the viewpoint of anthropologists who regard themselves as cultural relativists and cultural determinists (particularly of the configurational or personality-is-culture school), a basic problem of human life is the preservation and continuity of distinctive patterns of culture, their transmission from generation to generation. Some have preferred the term *enculturation* to *socialization* because it explicitly brings to mind the notion of acquiring, incorporating, or internalizing culture. Indeed, in the simpler form of this view, enculturation is seen as an automatic process of absorption in which the child as tabula rasa acquires culture simply by exposure to it. Because his entire environment is culturally determined, and because the innate equipment of children everywhere is the same and is favorable to the acquisition of culture patterns, children absorb culture in every aspect of their experience. This pervasive absorptive process may be studied in many areas of cultural life, but it is conceived of holistically and can be presumed to take place, at least in an intact and stable culture. In addition to the use of the term, *enculturation,* which has not gained a universal currency, the process has been termed *education, cultural transmission,* and *cultural conditioning,* although the last, as Hallowell (1954) has pointed out, was not used in the technical sense of behavioristic learning theory. In its earlier conceptualization by anthropologists of the Boas school, including Benedict (1938), no particular learning mechanisms were regarded as specific to the process of cultural acquisition, since the child was seen as internalizing culture through instruction, observation and imitation, reward and punishment, only as parts of his exposure to the total culture and its patterns.

The more complex forms of this viewpoint involve some attempt to conceptualize the mechanisms involved. Mead (*e.g.,* 1964) and her coworkers have looked at enculturation in the terms of communication and information theory. Child rearing is seen as a process of communicating culture to the child, encoded as implicit and explicit messages in behavior. In this translation of the configurational view into the language of a more precise theoretical system, essential aspects of the earlier formulation have been retained: its conception of the child as a passive receiver of culture; its holism, that is, the assumption that a stable culture provides mutually consistent content in the apparently diverse environment of messages to which children are normally exposed; and the insistence that specific cause-effect relations cannot be meaningfully isolated from the overall mutually reinforcing patterns of communicative events.

A considerably more complex view of the enculturative process can be found in works by psychological students of cognitive development such as Greenfield and Bruner (1969) and Kohlberg (1969). In this view, it is acknowledged that children acquire cultural beliefs and categories of thought but within the limits set by sequences of cognitive development common to all humans. The study of enculturation becomes the study of the interaction of cultural beliefs transmitted to the child through teaching and social experience with universal stages of cognitive development.

Socialization as the Acquisition of Impulse Control

Psychologists and psychoanalysts of the drive-theory persuasion conceive of humans as born with drives that are potentially disruptive to social life, and they see the problem of socialization in terms of taming disruptive impulses and channeling them into socially useful forms. The broadest and perhaps earliest concept of socialization is that in which the socialized individual, whose impulse life is harnessed, regulated, and controlled in accordance with the fundamental requirements for social order, is contrasted with the unsocialized child, whose selfish pursuit of drive satisfaction could bring harm to others and to the fabric of society unless checked and channeled by those who raise him. Feral children allegedly raised apart from human contact are offered as examples of the unsocialized individual in physical maturity, nonsocial humans.

The simple form of this concept of socialization is presented by Freud in *Civilization and Its Discontents* (1930). The conflict between the biological drives of individuals and the requisites of social organization[1] is stated in its most emphatic form. According to Freud, social organization requires that the sexual drive be sublimated into aim-inhibited forms allowing group formation and fellow feeling without possessiveness and that the aggressive drive, being such a threat to social order, be turned inward in the form of an aggressively self-policing superego. These aims of socialization are achieved through identification with the father as the resolution of the Oedipus complex (Freud, 1923). The costs of harness-

---

1. Although the German term *kultur* has been translated as *civilization,* it is clear throughout his work that by this term Freud is referring to what contemporary social scientists call *social organization.* Hence I use the latter term.

ing the sexual drive are the neurotic symptoms arising from the repression of incestuous wishes, and the cost of repressing aggression is the neurotic sense of guilt. Social organization exists, benefits, and advances through attenuating one drive and reversing the other, causing immense suffering to many individuals. Freud sees few genuine compatibilities between society and the individual and hardly any ways in which social and cultural life serve the individual's needs rather than the reverse. The one-sided character of his view makes it simpler than later concepts derived from the drive-theory position.

Among the more complex views of socialization as the acquisition of impulse control is the ego-psychology position developed within the mainstream of psychoanalytic thought by Hartmann (1958) and others. In this position, there is room for neutralized drive energy, which can be discharged in forms not disruptive to the social organization, and a conflict-free sphere and secondary autonomy in the ego, in which the forces of biology and society are not pitted against one another. The socialization of the child is seen as including the development of adaptive capacities that will serve himself as well as the social organization.

The psychoanalytic behaviorism of Miller and Dollard (1941) and Whiting and Child (1953) is the complex version of this basic orientation that has had the greatest influence on socialization research. In this view, the child's primary (innate) drives form the basis for his later social adjustment by acting as reinforcers for socially valued habits and for secondary (acquired) drives that reinforce the acquisition of a wide variety of positive social behavior patterns, including the internalization of models for appropriate behavior in social roles. The emphasis is on the effects of drive reduction as social reinforcement and on a simultaneous gain for the individual and the organization of social life. While harnessing the potentially disruptive impulses of the child is seen as a primary goal of the socialization process, it is not regarded as its only goal; and while Freudian concepts such as displacement and the sense of guilt are retained, they are interpreted in terms of their positive functions for social order. Whiting and Child's discussion (1953, pp. 218–262) of the origins of guilt, stressing the part it plays in social control rather than the suffering it causes the individual, is a particularly good illustration of this departure from the Freud of *Civilization and Its Discontents*. Even so, the acquisition of socially functional impulse control is viewed as leaving the individual with anxious preoccupations that find cultural expression in magic, religion, and other forms of collective fantasy and ritual. In the personality mediation theory of culture-personality relations, child-training customs like the severe socialization of aggression cause personality patterns like strong anxiety about aggression, which are expressed in projective customs like belief in sorcery.

Socialization as Role Training

The third major concept of socialization is that of training the child for participation in society, a participation that is seen as occurring on terms set "by society" (by institutional goals) rather than on the individual's own terms. The emphasis is on the social purpose of socialization, a process conceived as designed to achieve the conformity of individuals to social norms and rules. Although there is some resemblance to the Freudian formulation, this sociological view differs in stressing positive social prescriptions, rather than proscriptions or prohibitions, and in seeing no necessary conflict between conformity and individual satisfaction.

In the simpler, sociologistic, form of this conceptualization, it is taken for granted that the purpose of child training is social conformity, that the content of the training is dictated by social norms, and that conformity is so routinely and automatically achieved for the majority of individuals that the individual side of the process producing it is hardly worth studying. If one knows the norms and sanctions of the social structure, he can predict the aggregate social behavior of individuals without attention to the details of learning and other modes of acquisition. Adequate socialization is a given of the normal operation of a social system; only where it does not occur (in deviant behavior), is it necessary to raise questions of how and why.

In role theory terms, social structure consists of institutionalized roles antedating any particular generation of individuals. If the structure is to survive, persons must be found to fill these roles. Socialization of the child is a necessary but by no means sufficient method of attaining this goal. Most mature persons have been adequately socialized to be responsive to societal demands and incentives, but the problem remains of placing them in positions where they will contribute most effectively to the maintenance of the social system.

The processes of recruitment and selection are the means society has of solving this problem. In recruitment, the social structure finds institutionalized procedures for attracting and channelling persons to valued roles, and selection (differential recruitment) operates to match individual skills with role requirements, to put square pegs in square holes. Individuals are thought of as they would be in the personnel office of a firm, as manpower with preexisting capacities for filling preexisting positions. It is the firm that sets the criteria for job performance, establishes incentives for optimal performance, selects applicants on the basis of capacities appropriate to different jobs, and provides on-the-job training where needed. In this simple personnel office view, which has considerable currency among sociologists, the successful or unsuccessful operation of the social system is traced to strengths and weaknesses in the institutional system of social placement, social sanctions, and role structures rather than to characteristics of the individuals filling the roles.

In the more complex forms of this conceptualization, primarily related to the two-system view of culture and personality, the compatibility of early socialization with later role demands is seen as problematic rather than assumed. Conformity is not taken for granted but regarded as an adaptive accomplishment to be explained in terms of complex mechanisms integrating individual behavior dispositions with the needs of the social structure. In the formulations of Parsons (1949), Parsons and Shils (1951), Inkeles and Levinson (1954) and Spiro (1961a), as discussed in the preceding chapter, personality and social structure are conceived as separate systems with their respective requirements for system maintenance, consisting of drive reduction in one form or another on the personality side, and role demands on the side of the social system. These requirements do not necessarily take similar behavioral forms but must be brought into some minimum degree of compatibility to insure the survival and stability of society. In other words, whatever its role demands, the social system must allow individuals sufficient satisfaction of their intrapsychic needs; and whatever their press for satisfaction, individuals must perform appropriately in their social roles; when these conditions are not met, change toward a more stable situation must occur.

In contrast to the simpler view, these complex theoretical positions assign a central place to socialization processes. Parsons (1949) distinguishes between primary socialization, which occurs early in life and lays down the basic structure of the personality system, and secondary socialization, a more specialized role training oriented to institutional requirements of the social system. In addition, however, Parsons (1964), Brim (1966), and others have shown that even primary socialization is socially structure experience and that the psychoanalytic theory of object relations and identification can be translated into the language of role and social structure through the medium of G. H. Mead's interactionist view of the self.

The model of socialization emerging from these theoretical discussions is that of the social system operating in two major indirect ways to influence the early experience of individuals: (a) through family structure, which determines the nature of the child's earliest interpersonal experience (leaving a normative residue) but which in turn is affected by the wider social system with which it is integrated; and (b) through parental mediation (Inkeles 1955, 1966a) in which parents deliberately train their children for successful adaptation to a changing social order. This model offers an explanation of some of the mechanisms by which the personality system of the individual laid down early in life is made amenable to the demands of the social system. Admitting reciprocal influence between personality and social system, the Inkeles version of this model nevertheless strongly emphasizes the influence of the latter on the former and underplays the costs of social conformity in individual frustration and conflict. (Spiro, 1961a; and Whiting *et al.*, 1966, explicitly include factors of "psychological cost" in similar functional models of personality-social structure relations.)

Although theories of this sociological-functionalist persuasion have made their strongest efforts to reconcile role theory with psychoanalytic views of personality, behavioristic psychology is more obviously compatible with their position, particularly the parental mediation hypothesis. As Parsons (1949) recognized some time ago, the conceptualizations of sanctions (+ and −) in the social system, and values (+ and −) in the cultural system, are analogous to positive and negative reinforcement in stimulus-response theories of learning. In parental mediation, as pointed out by LeVine, Klein, and Owen (1967), the sanctions and values of the sociocultural order are translated by parents into rewards and punishments, or encouragement and discouragement, for childhood behavior that has relevance to adult role performance. The social-learning position of Bandura (1969), stressing response-reinforcement as opposed to acquired drives, is quite congenial to this sociological position. The shaping of children's behavior in the direction of cultural values and norms has been recognized by anthropologists for many years, although without explicit knowledge of the law of effect (see LeVine, 1963b), and the Hullian anthropologists of the 1930's and 1940's (*e.g.*, Murdock, Gillin, Whiting) combined reinforcement notions from psychology with functionalist concepts from anthropology and sociology. If the image of parents reinforcing responses that are eufunctional in a social or cultural system constitutes such a plausible convergence of ideas from different disciplines, it may be because both "reinforcement" and "social function" are intellectually descended from the Darwinian model of selective survival and adaptive fit that has so strongly influenced the way we think about man and his environment.

These three directions of thought about socialization have been presented as divergent views on the subject, but it is clear that they are not necessarily incompatible with each other. At the most commonsense level, children do absorb their culture through diverse exposures and communication; they do have their impulse life harnessed and channelled; and they do receive training for social participation. The authors of the more complex forms of the positions reviewed above have attempted in more sophisticated language to do justice theoretically to this variety of tasks and consequences of socialization within their respective theoretical frameworks. They all see early experience as leaving permanent residues in the individual; they all view socialization as socially purposive to some degree; and most envision some version of adaptation as integrating individual development and societal goals. These common elements suggest the possibility of developing a comprehensive view of the socialization process by the more explicit application of the Darwinian model that has proved so fruitful in other fields.

5

Methods of Assessing Personality

The theoretical diversity of culture and personality is more than matched by its myriad of research methods, and while competing theories invigorate research, methodological dispute can debilitate it. No one can doubt that the field of culture and personality, so promising in its theoretical statements, has foundered on the question of what kinds of evidence are necessary and sufficient to solve the important intellectual problems it represents. To a large extent this uncertainty reflects the divisions and doubts of personality psychology which, having never resolved its methodological disagreements, is now beset by questioning and rejection of virtually all its methods and techniques (see Chapter 12). To these difficulties, however, culture and personality adds a few that are distinctively its own, which have plagued the field for years and discouraged several generations of students interested in its problems from undertaking research on them.

The crux of the matter is that the organization of behavior in the individual is so complex and variable that it has not proved amenable to valid measurement and prediction by formal procedures devised for other purposes; when studied in its full complexity and variation, it is difficult to reduce to intersubjectively replicable judgments. Cross-cultural study of personality is further complicated by linguistic and cultural obstacles to understanding a person in another culture and by the question of whether culture patterns can be taken as personality indicators. In the face of these ambiguities, most investigators have adopted or devised methods congenial to their own theoretical positions, thereby diminishing the area of their agreement.

This chapter is an overview of the methods used in the study of culture and personality and a consideration of some fundamental issues represented by the extant research literature. The question of how better methods might be devised is taken up in the final section of the book (Chapters 12–17). Here we begin with consideration of whether ethnographic material can be psychologically assessed, move to a review of personality assessment procedures, and conclude with a discussion of the validity problem in cross-cultural personality assessment.

Psychological Analysis of Cultural Material

When Freud, in the first chapter of *Totem and Taboo* (1913), noted the resemblances between neurotic symptoms of patients he had observed clinically and the ritual practices of peoples he had read about in the anthropological literature of that period, he initiated one of the most controversial lines of research into culture and personality. The psychological interpretation of other cultures' beliefs and practices seems to invite speculative, often ethnocentric, psychologizing, in which external resemblances are taken as positive proof of underlying similarities in personality functioning, allowing extensive analysis on the basis of fragmentary evidence. There is a considerable literature of this kind of interpretation, much of it naive psychological reductionism based on Freudian and Jungian premises without any attention to the canons of the ethnographic method or, for that matter, to those of the psychoanalytic method as outlined in Chapter 13. I shall not discuss this literature here except to indicate that it has evoked a strong backlash among professional anthropologists and aroused a great deal more controversy than it is worth. But a similar controversy over methods accused of psychological reductionism has surrounded research representing the personality-is-culture and personality mediation views, which require serious attention.

The configurational or personality-is-culture view posits a virtual equivalence of personality and culture in which all individual behavior can be seen as cultural material ("culturally patterned personality") if its cultural context is fully understood; conversely, cultural material necessarily reflects the preoccupations of the individuals who produce, consume, and maintain it and who are themselves cultural products. Psychological and cultural interpretations of ethnographic data are from this point of view, only different and equally valid ways of looking at the same material; it is unnecessary to collect different kinds of data for assessing culture and personality. This means that a wide variety of cultural products—folktales, drama, literary fiction, films, school curriculum content, published child-rearing advice—can be used to assess personality in the cultural group from which it was collected. This approach, advocated by Mead (1953, 1954) and illustrated in Mead and Metraux (1953) and Mead and Wolfenstein (1955), does not involve formal content analysis; the personality assessment is woven into a descriptive interpretation of the particular culture under study. Comparability is not sought, since each cultural context is unique, but when it is achieved through the study of a universal biosocial context like child rearing, comparison is used for the purpose of showing not only how great variation is but also how intimately linked to the unique configurations, the dominant ideational patterns of the cultures compared.

This approach has been strongly and effectively criticized elsewhere (Inkeles and Levinson, 1954; Duijker and Frijda, 1960; Singer, 1961), and it is no longer being used in research on culture and personality. Its greatest weakness was that if one were to take seriously its basic methodological principle, that of understanding the ideational context in which behavior occurs, each cultural group would seem to comprise not one such context but a myriad of them defined by subcultural and even individual differentiation. This was even clearer in the modern nations to which the approach was applied in the works cited than in the small homogeneous societies in which it had its origins. Psychological interpretations of ritual and folklore offered as part of the ethnographic description of a small "traditional" community might be superficially plausible, but using the same method on a complex mass society exposes its oversimplification and virtually demands the addition of data on individual personality. Without questioning the theoretical premise that the content of folklore, literature, and the mass media somehow reflects the culturally patterned personalities of those who produce it and those who appreciate it, one can reject a method that fails to spell out the processes by which such content is produced, consumed, and maintained by the individuals involved. Many who accept Margaret Mead's premises about the cultural patterning of personality and the psychological patterning of cultural behavior have in fact rejected this method as a naive and misleading short cut to the study of an extremely complex phenomenon. If the individual can be dispensed with in psychocultural study, this is not the way to do it.

In the Whiting and Child (1953) version of the personality mediation view, personality is a set of intervening variables between two sets of customs described by ethnographers: child-rearing practices and magico-religious beliefs and practices. Their view is based on an analog with laboratory experiments on learning involving the stimulus-response paradigm. Since most of these experiments are done with animals, it is usually impossible to measure the ideational or other processes intervening between stimuli (or reinforcing conditions) and response (or performance), which are often referred to as the "black box." Applying this paradigm to published ethnographic data on individual development and cultural institutions, Whiting and Child operationally regarded child-rearing customs as the stimuli, adult beliefs as the ultimate responses, and personality as the intervening black box, not directly assessed. In their cross-cultural surveys of a worldwide sample of as many as 75

societies (predominantly non-Western and nonliterate), they sought correlations between hypothetical cultural causes of personality and its
hypothetical cultural consequences without measuring personality itself.
They discovered a number of interesting statistical relationships bearing
on the psychoanalytic hypotheses that they had recast in stimulus-
response terms, and their method has been frequently used in the ensuing years (for reviews see Whiting 1961, 1969; LeVine, 1970a; Naroll,
1970).

Although it was a model of operational explicitness, control of inter-
pretative bias and scrupulous consideration of alternative explanations,
the Whiting and Child study has been criticized on methodological
grounds that apply as well to other studies in the same research tradition.
The central problem concerns the intervening links that appear in their
theory (see Chapter 3) but are relegated to the unmeasured black box
in their research: the links between child rearing and child behavior,
child behavior and adult personality, and adult personality and cultural
beliefs. Since child behavior and adult personality are not assessed, one
is forced to assume hypothetically that child rearing has its expected
effects on child behavior and that cultural beliefs reflect adult personality. The latter is questionable on several grounds. First, even if one
believes that personality characteristics in a population influence its
cultural beliefs, there may be a time lag such that the beliefs at one
point in time as described by ethnographers may represent the personalities of previous generations and that the present generation is conforming to a tradition that is no longer completely congruent with their
personalities but which they have not yet replaced. Second, the ethnographic facts of magical theories of disease, which Whiting and Child
use to measure personality-influenced culture, may be too complex to
reduce to the few ratings they use. Their ratings, according to this argument, reflect an oversimplification of the facts by the ethnographer (particularly in the old and rather sparse accounts on which they leaned
heavily) or the data analyst, in either case yielding spurious scores. In the
more complete ethnographic descriptions of disease published since the
Whiting–Child ratings were done, multiple alternatives for disease interpretation abound; in other words, the better the data, the harder to fit
them into their analytic categories. Third, ethnographic description even
at its best is only a crude estimate of what, for purposes of personality
study, should be studied at the individual level and aggregated. The
proper way of using disease beliefs and practices as personality indicators in populations is to design an individual interview on such beliefs
and practices, administer it to a sample of individuals from each cultural
group, and compare the distributions of responses.

The answer that Whiting and Child (1953) and Campbell (1961) give
to such criticisms is that the very indirectness of their assessment pro-

cedures and the possibilities for slippage between personality and cultural belief would only tend to reduce their correlations and therefore make it all the more remarkable that positive results were obtained; their findings are likely to be conservative estimates of the actual relationships. Furthermore, Whiting and Child considered and at least attempted to test alternative explanations of their findings so that whatever hypotheses they are still able to endorse have survived a harsh series of tests. In essence, they argue pragmatically, "If our measures weren't right, how could we find what we did? And if our data supported our hypotheses as strongly as they did, they thereby supported our judgments about personality measurement as well." This is the argument of construct validity, to be discussed later in this chapter.

From a viewpoint made possible by the passage of two decades since publication of the Whiting and Child study, the construct validity defense seems weaker than it once did. The studies done since then have shown many customs to be correlated with many other customs, sometimes in support of contradictory theoretical formulations. It no longer seems so remarkable that Whiting and Child obtained some predicted positive findings, and it seems more likely now that an investigator could invent and find support for plausible alternative explanations that exploited the large unmeasured gaps in their causal chain. Since the validity of their view of cultural beliefs as personality indicators rests primarily on the empirical support for their hypotheses linking child training and beliefs, any alternative explanation that could account for the empirical relationships without involving personality as an intervening variable would also erode support for using cultural beliefs as personality indicators. These difficulties are recognized by Whiting and Child; a year after publication of their 1953 volume they embarked on the Six Culture Study of Socialization (Whiting, Child *et al.*, 1966), which included systematic observation of child behavior as well as other individual measures. Whiting also worked with individual interview data from three culturally different groups in the United States Southwest (Whiting *et al.*, 1966), and has been working for some years on an individual personality test to measure sex identity cross culturally.

In retrospect it can be seen that the methods reviewed above for analyzing personality through cultural material were methods of convenience rather than choice. The "study of culture at a distance" by Benedict, Mead, and their co-workers originated as investigations of countries that could not be visited during and after World War II. Similarly, the Whiting and Child study was an attempt to salvage information from available publication at a time when large-scale psychological comparisons were not yet practical. Many, including Whiting, would argue that the cross-cultural survey remains our only way of testing hypotheses on a truly worldwide basis, but they (*e.g.*, Naroll, 1970) concede that the indirectness of personality assessment and the difficulty of extracting causal inferences from correlational data make cross-cultural surveys of child training and cultural beliefs particularly problematic. The recent expansion of cross-cultural research by psychologists working in different parts of the world has made armchair assessment of personality less tolerable than ever, and increasingly high standards of ethnographic description demand that psychological characterizations of culture be validated by independent psychological evidence.

The Assessment of Individual Personality

The measurement of personality in individuals separate from the analysis of culture is required by the modern psychological reductionism of Mc-Clelland (1958, 1961), who insists on demonstrating rather than merely asserting or assuming the relationships between personality and cultural variables. It is also demanded by the two systems view that, positing a personality system and a sociocultural system, makes their possible correspondence, congruence, or conformity its primary question for research. Thus Spiro (e.g., 1965) and Inkeles and Levinson (1954) require individual psychological assessment of samples of individuals drawn from the populations whose sociocultural systems are being compared through independent ethnographic or sociological assessment. The cross-cultural covariations of individual and sociocultural data are necessary to test the hypotheses derived from their theoretical formulations. In this, Spiro is pursuing a line of research in psychological anthropology begun by Hallowell (1955) and carried on by Spindler (1961), Spindler and Spindler (1955), Wallace (1952) and numerous others (see Lindzey, 1961; DeVos and Hippler, 1969; and Edgerton, 1970, for recent reviews). Inkeles (1959, 1963) sees himself carrying on a methodological tradition in sociology initiated by Durkheim's (1895) study of suicide but rarely linked with the concept of personality. Spiro and others of the same research tradition tend to use projective tests that seek to assess the deeper levels of personality functioning referred to in psychoanalytic discourse, whereas Inkeles (Smith and Inkeles, 1966)—like many other sociologists—is concerned primarily with the measurement of conscious attitudes and values that are closer to the social surface of normal personality functioning.

The preference of some investigators for depth and others for surface in personality assessment, according to their theoretical and disciplinary inclinations, raises the question of which aspects of personality should correspond to social or cultural patterns. This has been a matter of dispute. Kaplan (1961) argued that one should not expect a one-to-one correspondence between specific personality traits and sociocultural institutions but rather that *modes of conformity* are the personality characteristics that are most plausible in correspondence with institutions. Yet, Inkeles (1961) expects congruences between specific individual values and political systems (along an authoritarian-democratic dimension) and LeVine (1966a) tries to show covariation between a specific motive (the achievement motive) and the type of status-mobility system. For Spiro (1965) and some others who use Rorschach test categories[1] having little self-evident linkage with sociocultural variables, the search is not necessarily for highly specific correspondence in symbolic content between a personality characteristic and a culture pattern, though this is not theoretically precluded (see Spiro, 1961a). For others who use projective tests, however, of whom DeVos (1961, 1968) is most prominent in cross-cultural studies, personality characteristics linked to specific cultural content are sought, even through the Rorschach test. In general, those investigators preferring the Rorschach test tend to use categories that are relevant to issues of psychopathology, whereas those who prefer the Thematic Apperception Test and other tests with explicit interpersonal content are looking for personality dispositions of direct relevance to a specific area of culturally patterned interpersonal relations or institutional participation. These differences are not necessarily in contradiction and are in any case matters to be clarified through empirical research rather than logical argument. Since empirical research has not yet produced sufficient clarifying evidence, they remain arbitrary decisions made by the investigator.

The recent review by Edgerton (1970) of method in psychological anthropology shows the bewildering variety of psychological assessment procedures, most of them designed to tap some aspect of personality, that have been or are being used by anthropologists. They are largely personality tests borrowed from psychology, sometimes with extensive modification for use in non-Western contexts. Like the psychologists quoted in Chapter 12, Edgerton expresses dissatisfaction with the state of personality testing as represented in the literature to date. In this unsettled situation, it hardly makes sense to present here an instruction manual for the various personality assessment procedures; instead, I shall present a perspective in which they can be viewed and evaluated comparatively.

Every personality assessment procedure is an attempt to obtain a small sample of an individual's recurrent observable behavior in order to make inferences about the enduring dispositions that account for the

---

1. There are many ways of analyzing Rorschach test results, but the most commonly used categories are perceptual-cognitive (*e.g.*, form *vs.* color) that are scored for their frequency and interpreted in terms of intrapsychic dynamics such as the capacity to express emotion, usually oriented toward signs of psychopathology. Cross-cultural comparison is focused on these purportedly pan-cultural categories rather than on cultural content. DeVos' (1961) symbolic analysis of the Rorschach is focused on culture-specific content.

structure and functions of his behavior. Since personality is inferred from individual behavioral consistencies that cannot be reduced to contemporaneous environmental constancies and therefore require the postulation of individual dispositions, in attempting to assess personality through the observation of behavior we seek or construct environmental situations offering the individual options from which to choose. It is from his decisions in choosing among environmental options that we make inferences about the dispositions that can be plausibly attributed to him as an individual rather to the situations in which he lives. Our assumption is that if we knew his decisions among environmental options in all situations we could uncover their patterns and make valid inferences about the underlying dispositional rules which govern them. In sampling his decision-making behavior, we hope to gain insight into those rules by observing him in a situation whose options are regarded as particularly critical or diagnostic. Since it is often difficult to identify such situations for each individual and then to give the observer access to them, psychologists have preferred to construct common-denominator diagnostic decision-making situations into which they induce those individuals they are seeking to study.

The situations constructed by psychologists to observe decisions diagnostic of personality vary significantly in the narrowness of the limits imposed by the investigator on the options available to the person under study. Some of these situations are multiple-choice paper-and-pencil tests like the Edwards Personal Preference Test, the California Personality Inventory, the Minnesota Multiphasic Personality Inventory, in which the individual is offered a few explicit alternatives ("Do you prefer a bath or a shower?") over a wide range of life situations and personal experiences that are regarded as diagnostic of personality characteristics. At the other extreme are completely open-ended clinical interviews about dreams, life history, description of self ("Tell me about yourself/your life/your childhood"), in which the investigator puts hardly any explicit limits on the options available to the person questioned and is not even aware of the alternatives from which the response is chosen until he compares it with the responses of others. In between these two extremes are the projective and semi-projective tests—the Rorschach, Thematic Apperception Test, Sentence Completion Test, in which the individual is offered a series of pictorial or verbal stimuli designed to limit the options available to him, implicitly rather than explicitly, allowing him a wide and unrestricted range of verbal expression in his response.

There are a great many pros and cons about these procedures, but the point of greatest importance here is that the farther one goes toward the forced-choice extreme, the more the investigator assumes he knows in advance the critical diagnostic options available to the person studied, and the more he must know about the environment of the person and what options are realistically available to him. While asking an American male whether he prefers a bath or a shower might conceivably be diagnostic of masculine or feminine trends in his personality, it is obviously meaningless in those parts of the world where the plumbing, or lack of it, allows no such choice. It is less obviously but even more critically inapplicable in those cultures where, although the choice is or has been available, the prevalent choice of men is opposite to that of their American counterparts. Considerations of this kind, though less gross, require the drawing of special TAT pictures for each cultural setting so that scenery, housing, clothing, and interpersonal situations are realistically portrayed in terms of the local environment. No matter how wide or narrow are the limits on options available to the person taking the test, however, the investigator is always trying to replicate in the stimuli an environmental situation in that person's life.

Some assessment procedures like the Rorschach test, open-ended clinical interviews, and dream collection have been favored for cross-cultural use by some investigators for the very reason that they do not involve replication of environmental detail and therefore have two advantages: They can be used in identical form in all cultures, and they free the investigator from having to find out what options are available in each cultural environment. This comparability, however, is more apparent than real. It is based on the assumption that culturally differing populations do not vary with respect to the options they experience and respond to in a testing or interviewing situation. This assumption can only be based on ignorance of the extreme variability in cultural norms regarding interpersonal privacy and self-revelation, conversing with foreigners or those of different status, responding verbally to novel problems posed by others. Such norms structure the situation for the person observed so that he responds to options other than those deliberately imposed by the investigator. This is fairly obvious when he is hesitant to respond or gives brief responses, as is frequent in personality studies of non-Western persons.

The same phenomenon can occur without being obvious, however, as in my own collection of dream reports from Nigerian secondary-school boys (LeVine, 1966a), which was replicated in a suburban American high school (Strangman, 1967). Although frequency of achievement motivation in dream reports in the Nigerian samples was relatively high (34 percent overall) and significantly distributed by ethnicity and other variables, it was surprisingly low (21 percent) in the American sample and unrelated to social and cultural variables. In retrospect it seems probable that the appearance of an American professor in the Nigerian schools inflated the frequency of achievement imagery for the whole sample, whereas the appearance of an American graduate student (who was a community resident) in the American school had no such effect. This is supported by the incidence of dreams of leaving Nigeria to study abroad and indirectly by the fact that Nigerian students waiting for the results of their school certificate examinations reported significantly more achievement dreams than the sample as a whole, indicating the influence of another uncontrolled factor on dream reporting. The Nigerian students may have been responding to aspects of the measurement situation that were not deliberately imposed and that were not retained in the American "replication."

Personality researchers have long been aware that small aspects of the measurement situation can have a great effect on the motivation manifested in test responses. For example, McClelland *et al.* (1953) showed that the wording of the instructions in administration of a TAT could raise the frequency of achievement imagery, and Beardslee and Fogelson (1958) showed that playing music while subjects were taking a TAT raised the frequency of sexual imagery for women but not men. These are examples of ingenious exploitation of the responsiveness of test-taking behavior to the test-taking environment. The more recent work summarized by Berg (1967), Rosenthal (1966), and Rosenthal and Rosnow (1969) indicates that the environmental conditions under which behavior is observed by psychologists often have massive effects on the responses measured whether or not the investigator consciously intended them. The conclusion emerging is that in responding to the situations constructed by psychologists for the diagnostic observation of behavior, persons respond to what is often a more limited set of subjective options than the investigator intends or knows about due to social pressures they experience in the situation. If this is true in the investigator's own culture, how much more likely it is in one with which he is unacquainted!

This perspective on personality assessment, which is growing among psychologists, allows us to see psychological testing and experimentation as a species of social interaction in which one person, the investigator, is attempting to define the situation in a formal and explicit way so as to structure the other's options, without recognizing that he (as experienced by the other) is influencing the other's choice of options in numerous informal and implicit ways. The indeterminacy involved is particularly damaging to a formal operationist approach in which a psychological characteristic is defined in terms of the instrument used to measure it rather than as a plausible disposition for the assessment of which the instrument is one fallible approach (see Campbell, 1969). It erodes the distinction between the formal test-experiment-interview approach and other forms of observation, and in fact favors the development of nonreactive measures in which the observer is removed in time or space from the behavior observed (Webb *et al.*, 1966) and of naturalistic measures in which the investigator observes a wider range of potential causes and effects than he could possibly anticipate.

Nonreactive measures that could be used for comparative personality assessment include a variety of official statistics (*e.g.*, rates of crime, suicide, litigation, voting), epidemiological figures (especially of psychosomatic disorders), and historical records (quantitative, biographical, and anecdotal). Naturalistic observation is part and parcel of ethnography but requires special procedures to make inferences about the personality system rather than cultural or social institutions (see Chapters 14–17).

The methods of observing individual behavior in situations not formally structured by the observer, and in which nonverbal behavior is taken into account, also vary greatly in the observable limits set on the range of options available to the individual, in which Barker and Wright (1955) have called the "coerciveness of the behavior setting." At one extreme there is the action taken by a voter in deciding whether to vote for the Republican or Democratic candidates for president of the United States. Although this is a purely dichotomous choice, it is possible for social scientists (Campbell, Converse, and Miller, 1960) who interview a large sample after the election to obtain, from the socioeconomic and attitudinal correlates of those decisions, a great deal of information relevant to the social-psychological processes that led up to them. In this case, of course, the decision is of intrinsic interest in itself rather than being used as a diagnostic sign of a personality disposition, but it could be used as a very limited indicator if there were many other indicators available from the same person. The point is that even behavior in a forced-choice situation, which is highly "coercive," is evidence about the person.

Many other coercive settings appear to be forced-choice situations because of normative prescription and other social pressures, but they can yield a good deal of information about the person if their formal prescriptive definition is not taken too seriously by the observer. A common illustration of this can be found in the incumbents of high government and ecclesiastic offices who, although accorded great authority, usually seem at any point in time—or even in an analysis of the options available to them—to be so encumbered by prescriptive tradition and constraints outside their control that they can only fulfill the role set for them. Yet if one thinks of Presidents Eisenhower, Kennedy, Johnson, and Nixon or Popes Pius XII, John XXIII, and Paul VI, it is apparent that each man fulfilled the role in a highly distinctive way, expressing many aspects of his personality in public behavior despite the limits of office he shared with other incumbents. This is recognized by political scientists (Barber, 1968) and journalists who refer to the "style" of performance in an office, and it is true, though less obvious, of many other apparently coercive settings: The style of responding to demands and choosing among limited options is indicative of personality dispositions, and distinguishes one person from another in the same environment.

The same reasoning and method is applicable cross culturally, with settings as coercive as those of bureaucracies in which stylistic elements of behavior reflect cultural and idiosyncratic features against a relatively uniform structural backdrop. The identification of such universal backgrounds for observation of behavior in settings that appear to be extremely uncoercive is discussed in Chapter 16. The less coercive the setting, the more ethnographic and case-study observation is required to discover the range of available options in the environment as experienced by the individual.

The Problem of Construct Validation

The most active investigators of culture and personality during the last two decades have rejected the informal and impressionistic methods of earlier work in favor of scientific method, largely as defined in academic psychology. They sought to transform empirical research in the field so that instead of merely adding psychologizing commentary to the ethnographic description of a culture they could attack significant theoretical problems concerning group differences in personality and their causes and consequencies. An integral part of this transformation was the development of personality assessment procedures designed to measure the crucial variables in hypotheses to be tested cross culturally; these procedures had to be replicable in both their data collection and analysis phases. That replicable procedures have been devised and used is unquestionably shown by a perusal of major research reports (e.g., Whiting and Child, 1953; McClelland, 1961; for reviews see DeVos and Hippler, 1969; Edgerton, 1970; LeVine, 1970a). There is still little agreement, however, about which methods of personality assessment are valid or even preferable. This lack of consensus in the relevant scientific community about the basic evidence is a major obstacle to the accumulation of scientific information. It is the treadmill of culture and personality research, which generates new methods in abundance without producing acceptable data.

Why has so much systematically conducted research resulted in so little unchallenged evidence? It is not, in my opinion, merely because of divergent theoretical positions, but rather that some of the best investigators in the field have relied too heavily on a strategy of construct validation rather than seeking to establish the validity of their methods independently of their theoretical orientations and hypotheses. Construct validation in psychology means offering evidence favoring a construct (theoretical concept) about a behavioral disposition as support for the validity of the indicator or measure of that disposition (see Fiske, 1971, pp. 167–171 for an introductory exposition). Thus if I hypothesize on theoretical grounds that boys from broken homes are more likely to be emotionally disturbed than boys from intact homes, and I find that boys from broken homes receive higher scores on my test of emotional disturbance, I may offer that finding as evidence that my test is a valid measure of emotional disturbance. Construct validation of an indicator or measuring instrument is most heavily relied on when one cannot validate it by demonstrating its correspondence with independent indicators of the same disposition (as in convergent or criterion-related validation), when the disposition must be measured in a single operation. This is frequent in personality psychology. It is also, unfortunately, the situation in which construct validation is most vulnerable, for as Fiske points out, results that partly confirm and partly disconfirm the expectations generated by the construct are ambiguous about whether "the experimenter must modify or redesign his test, must modify or rewrite his definition of the construct or his propositions involving it, or both" (p. 169).

The mixed findings of the Whiting and Child (1953) study could be interpreted as requiring modification in theory, as its authors did, but were interpreted by some of their critics as invalidating their method of assessing personality. This might have been avoided if Whiting and Child had demonstrated that their measures of personality in folk theories of disease and cure (in which, for example, a belief that death and disease were due to eating and drinking was taken as an indicator of negative oral fixation in the population) were validated by correlations with independent measures of the same personality dispositions (*e.g.*, manifestations of oral anxiety in other aspects of the culture); then their method and hypotheses would not have to stand or fall together. As it is, however, views of the Whiting and Child findings depend on the subjective plausibility one finds in their constructs or their measures.

The construct-validity defense of the Whiting and Child personality indicators depends on the lack of plausible alternative hypotheses that might account for the findings without their personality constructs; as soon as someone formulates such an alternative, the methods are called into question along with the propositions to which they are tied. The more indirect are the procedures used to assess the constructs (personality dispositions), the larger the number of possible explanations that can compete with the investigator's basis for prediction and the stronger the feeling in the scientific community that someone could come up with an even more plausible explanation if he took the trouble to try.

This problem is by no means limited to the cultural indicators of personality used in cross-cultural surveys. It is probably most acute in the most extensive series of comparative psychosocial studies done to date, that of McClelland (1961) on personality in relation to economic and cultural behavior. McClelland's central personality construct is the achievement motive, which he sees as accounting for major group differences in economic and cultural achievement across cultures, nations, and historical periods. Achievement motivation is viewed as the result of child training, reflecting parental values that have been influenced by religious ideology. In his book, *The Achieving Society* (1961), McClelland tests the propositions involved in this hypothetical causal chain, using evidence from cross-cultural surveys of the Whiting and Child type, cross-national surveys (of contemporary nations) along similar lines, comparisons of samples of individuals across nations, and comparison of historical periods within a nation. The achievement motive and achievement values are measured in a variety of ways in these studies: by the original TAT measure; by a doodle test that is correlated with the TAT measure in American samples but used without concurrent validation in Brazil, Japan, and Germany; by the analysis of religious beliefs in cross-cultural surveys, school primers in cross-national ones, and popular literature in a historical study.

The methodological ingenuity is impressive, but the findings derive their plausibility in support of McClelland's theoretical framework primarily from his interpretation of them and of the measures on which they are based. In his research strategy, the procedure for measuring achievement motivation in any single study derives its validity as a procedure from the support its findings give to the framework and their consistency with other studies using other procedures. Although it is unquestionably true that his hypotheses have survived a diverse series of tests, he does not succeed in dispelling reasonable doubts that plausible alternative explanations of his results could be devised. A major element in this doubt is the knowledge that even in our own culture, different methods of measuring achievement motivation in individuals (*e.g.*, TAT and forced-choice questionnaires) produce results that do not correlate with each other; they lack concurrent validity. McClelland makes a consistent picture of his results, but given the diversity of measures and their unknown relationships with each other in other cultures, could not someone else make an equally consistent but utterly different picture of them? It is unfair to reject his theory unless a better explanation of the data has actually been offered, but it is important to understand the thinking that retards acceptance of his explanation. In his cross-cultural work, McClelland has made acceptance of his central personality data depend too heavily on construct validity, without enough attention to considerations of face validity and concurrent validity, which played important roles in his earlier studies (McClelland *et al.*, 1953).

McClelland's more recent cross-cultural research on achievement motivation (McClelland and Winter, 1969) has been focused not on improving the face and concurrent validities of his methods in other cultures but on striving for predictive validity through experimental study. Whatever these experiments demonstrate about increasing the achievement motivation and performance of adult businessmen through formal training, they have little to say about the relations of such motivation to the naturally occurring cross-cultural variations in child rearing, religious ideology, and economic growth that were the focus of McClelland's original (1961) formulation. Methodological doubts about the achievement motivation construct as a pan-cultural variable related to patterns of institutional behavior have not been dispelled.

We need methods of personality assessment in culture and personality studies that have face validity—primitive plausibility that they are measuring what they claim to—or concurrent validity—a demonstrated relationship in the same sample with a procedure that has face validity. Given our current methodological situation, we must revalidate each procedure in each new cultural setting and use multiple procedures to measure each disposition. Behavioral measures in situations of visible environmental options, such as the frequency of individual drunkenness in a Mexican village (Fromm and Maccoby, 1970), yield data that speak for themselves when they involve significant social behaviors; they are immediately plausible as indicators of personal dispositions, even though it might not be clear what the underlying disposition is. As measures of verbal behavior and fantasy approach this kind of behavioral plausibility, they increase in face validity while indicating the subjective significance of the behavior, and both kinds of evidence (behavioral and ideational) are required to establish assessment procedures that can be accepted by the scientific community. Until such methods are developed, the field is vulnerable to unresolved controversy over the psychological and sociological (situational) interpretations of the individual behavior sampled by assessment procedures. Our present position resembles what would be true of medicine if there were a strong but unconfirmed suspicion among physicians that the results of blood tests were attributable in large measure to the time of day the blood was taken and the way in which the syringe was inserted rather than to the effects of disease on the human body. In the concluding section (Chapters 12–16), I return to this large problem and make suggestions about how it might be handled.

6

Institutions, Deviance and Change

The field of culture and personality includes within its scope some of the major problems of social science: the relations of the individual to social and cultural institutions, of personality to sociocultural change, and of deviant behavior to norms and normality. From the comparative perspective of anthropology, these problems can be summarized by the question posed in Chapter 1, "What are the relations of psychological differences between populations to sociocultural environments?" In this chapter I present the major viewpoints that have developed in attempts to answer this question, which do not fit neatly into the positions outlined in Chapter 3, and criticize some of the extant formulations. The topics involved are so broad and the relevant empirical literature so vast that the chapter is limited to a selective consideration of the most general theoretical issues and positions without reviewing the more specific problems on which research is conducted.

Institutions and Social Behavior

The major contribution of the early theorists of culture and personality, from W. I. Thomas to A. I. Hallowell, was to indicate the points of contact between sociocultural institutions, as conceived in the developing functionalist sociology and anthropology of their day, and the personalities of individual members of society. This theoretical emphasis has flowered into the central area of research and thinking in culture and personality, uniting all its leading theorists and investigators regardless of disciplinary affiliation or viewpoint. My purpose in this discussion is less to present their shared premises than to highlight a critical issue that they have overlooked.

The issue arises in an implicit disagreement between the personality mediation view of Kardiner and Whiting and the modern psychological reductionism of McClelland (see Chapter 3). Kardiner and Whiting divide institutions into two classes, those that form personality and those that are formed by it. A group's ecology, economy, settlement pattern, social stratification system, and other "hard" institutions that seem to act as constraints on individual behavior fall into the first class; and its religion, magical beliefs, disease therapies, art, folklore, and other "soft" institutions that seem to permit expression of individual needs fall into the second class. The "hard" institutions represent reality, which must be adapted to; the "soft" institutions represent fantasy, the cultural expression of individual motives. Thus do these theorists formulate in cultural theory the Freudian opposition between drives and reality and simultaneously reconcile the imperatives of Durkheim's social constraints with those of Freud's unconscious motives. Whiting et al. (1966) have recently brought Weber's ideology into the picture by recognizing a third class of institutions, values, which serve as defensive beliefs to reduce the cognitive inconsistency between motivational goals and reality demands.

This dichotomy (or trichotomy) of institutions viewed from a psychosocial perspective is ingenious and plausible, but it is recognized even by its proponents as something of an oversimplification. The family, for example, does not fit easily on either side of the line; it is part of social structure and formative of personality but also an important arena for emotional expression. It has become conventional to grant the family a special place in both classes of institutions (e.g., Bell and Vogel, 1968). The family may not be unique, however; Kardiner felt it necessary to distinguish between subsistence economy, reflecting realistic survival imperatives, and prestige economy, representing personality expressions, rather than to put economic institutions as a whole in the first class.

The cross-cultural research of McClelland (1961) helped place the problem in a different perspective by treating the economy as a "projective system" rather than as a "maintenance system" to which individual behavior must adapt. McClelland argues that simple or minimal maintenance can be achieved with or without economic expansion and growth and that the rate of growth is dependent on the amount of energy and initiative that members of the population invest in economic activity. Economic growth reflects entrepreneurial activity that in turn reflects the frequency in the population of individuals high in achievement motivation. The importance of economic growth (as opposed to mere subsistence) in the modern world, and the unanswered questions about what accounts for it, make McClelland's carefully argued case less easily dismissed than earlier attempts at reductionism. His accomplishment consists of having examined economic roles closely enough to discover that they are not merely demands and constraints on individual activity but opportunities for the pursuit of individual goals. Through these socially structured opportunities, the motives of aggregates of individuals in a population can affect the operations of a national economy and thereby accelerate or retard its growth.

Lasswell (1930) and a number of other political scientists have presented similar arguments for roles in political institutions; Levinson (1959) has done the same for bureaucratic roles. Political and bureaucratic roles do not simply prescribe behavior but also provide a public vehicle for the satisfaction of private motives. Spiro (1961a) proposed a general theoretical model for role behavior that would include behavior in economic and political roles as a response to inner needs as well as societal demands. He has also described (1957, 1958) a utopian community in Israel, the founders of which designed its socioeconomic and political structure on the basis of an ideology to which they were emotionally attached. Thus the "hard" institutions of economy, polity, and social structure can plausibly be seen as expressive or projective institutions as well as constraints on individual behavior.

It is equally plausible to think of the "soft" institutions as comprised of constraints on the individual rather than expressions of his needs. When religious institutions become specialized and bureaucratized they can represent traditional norms that demand conformity of the individual as much as they offer him concomitant satisfaction. Certainly aspects of religious functioning are expressive, but they are often combined with coercive aspects in a single institutional structure, as Spiro's (1966) formulation suggests. Once a collective activity is institutionalized, it cannot be responsive to or reflective of individual motives in any simple way; the institutional behavior of individuals is always an amalgam of their response to the pressure of established norms and their exploitation of the available opportunities for satisfaction of personal motives.

The division of institutions into two classes (primary and secondary, maintenance system and projective system), one of which constrains individual behavior while the other expresses it, is excessively simple and empirically misleading. It is better to think of all institutions as environments that limit the range of options available to the individual but do not dictate the choices he will make among those options. The patterns of choice will be dictated by his personality; insofar as his patterns are shared with others in the same institutional environment, they may act as a pressure for normative change. The relationship between personality and normative constraint in any institutional setting should be treated as an empirical question. The investigator should examine the role as an ecological niche in terms of the demands it puts on the individual and the opportunities it offers him in order to distinguish the components of situational pressure and personal disposition in observable role behavior. The "projective system" of a culture is not a certain class of its institutions but a certain component of its population's social behavior in all institutional settings. This component will probably vary in the amount of its contribution to social behavior from one institutional setting to another, but this is a matter for research rather than a priori assumption.

Some will object to this view on the grounds that the projective system as Whiting and Child (1953) and others of the personality-mediation position conceptualize it consists not merely of the contemporaneous social behavior of individuals but also of the elaborate cultural systems of belief passed on to them from previous generations. I do not deny this but insist that the projective or personality-expressive component in cultural belief can be validly identified only through the observation of social behavior, of the ways in which individual participants in socio-cultural institutions use their cultural heritage to gain personal satisfaction, pleasure, comfort, relief. We need to conceptualize these ways and the somewhat unstable social conventions that regulate them rather than focusing exclusively on the stable but remote institutional context in which they operate.

The problem lies with the concept of institution that has dominated the thinking of social scientists until recently (see Buckley, 1967) and tends to impose an unrealistic dichotomy on social behavior. According to the prevalent paradigm of conformity and deviance, social structure consists of institutionalized roles, and an institutionalized role entails normative prescriptions and proscriptions enforced by positive and negative sanctions. An individual's role behavior is either in conformity with the normative rules or deviant from them, and he receives social rewards and punishments accordingly. This paradigm is not false but it accounts for only a small proportion of social behavior, even in coercive settings. Most social behavior is not clearly classifiable as conforming or deviant because norms are not so explicitly defined or uniformly enforced, and thinking of it in this way is misleading. It is misleading in the same way that the United States Constitution is not an accurate description of contemporary government in the United States or that the playwright's script does not describe the dramatic performance. Much intervenes between script and performance and between constitution and government action, and it is that intervening area between institutionalized role and the social behavior of the individual that constitutes the proximal environment, the ecological niche, in which he functions. Institutions are the most visible forms of social behavior to an observer from outside. But they are, like the tips of icebergs, indicators of something bigger and deeper.

One way of illustrating this point is to divide the conformity-deviance dimension into as many degrees as we seem normally to recognize in everyday thought. For example, behavior may be:

1. Proscribed and punished but not effectively eliminated, as with many criminal activities.

2. Proscribed but not consistently punished or even consistently regarded as punishable, as with many illegal or socially prohibited acts that are, in effect, permitted so long as they are clandestine or restricted in location or magnitude.

3. Permitted but not expected; these are areas of open choice in an institutional environment.

4. Expected (socially) without conscious recognition, as in ethnocentric expectations that are brought to awareness only when a child or a foreigner violates them but are normally universal (within the group) and regarded as part of human nature.

5. Consciously expected but not prescribed, as with frequently chosen options that are nevertheless optional.

6. Prescribed by norms, but with informal enforcement procedures, for example, group pressures, rather than legal sanctions.

7. Prescribed by norms with formal enforcement procedures such as dismissal from position or legal sanctions.

A longer and more rigorously formulated list could certainly be made, but this one serves to illustrate how much of the social behavior that is personally significant to us does not easily fall into the classes of "normal" or "deviant" behavior (categories 6 and 7, and 1 and 2, respectively). Much more is covered by categories 3, 4, and 5, the area outside explicit institutional prescription or proscription, and many gradations could be spelled out for category 2, especially in complex and changing societies. But no set of discrete categories would do justice to the complex realities of normative pressures as they relate to the individuals who experience them. The fault lies with the institutional approach to social behavior, which tends to be legalistic, often taking (or mistaking) the most explicitly formulated and heavily enforced rules as representing the operative societal consensus. It seems more consistent with ordinary experience and more relevant to the environment of the individual to assume that the greatest societal consensus is represented by those unchallenged shared values that need not take explicit ideological form or be enforced by formal procedures and may not even be conscious (category 4), whereas institutionalization represents the tension between social norm and individual motive caused by attempts to impose normative change or to resist it. If this assumption is made, the normative environment of the individual needs to be studied in a different conceptual framework, less susceptible to the legalism and formalism of the institutional approach.

A more satisfactory approach to social behavior, closer to the proximal normative environment in which individuals actually function, is represented by the works of Goffman (1959, 1961a, 1961b, 1963, 1967). By a kind of ethnographic reportage, he explicates the rules of face-to-face interaction in numerous social settings in our own society, revealing the subjective calculus involved in communicative acts that have implications for the evaluation of self and others. His conceptual framework, which is not systematically formulated and will not be expounded here, includes concepts like *role distance*, the display of personal disaffection from the role behavior being performed. His accounts show individuals actively manipulating institutional settings for their own advantage and to protect their relationships with others, always anticipating the emotional implications of their acts and behaving according to rules worked out within the large loopholes of institutional prescription and enforcement. These rules appear to have psychological reality in the sense that they represent the options individuals experience in environmental situations rather than those formally defined for them by the institution. It is only through knowledge of these communicative rules that behavior in institutional settings can be validly analyzed into its person-specific and situation-specific components.

Thus the relations between the institutional structure of society and the personalities of its members can only be properly studied comparatively when we reformulate the problem in terms of the individual and his sociocultural environment, which has *distal* and *proximal* parts (Brunswik, 1956). The distal environment of the individual consists of the institutions in which he participates and their prescriptions and proscriptions for role performance, as described by institutional ethnography. His proximal environments consist of the norms and expectations of face-to-face situations within those larger institutional contexts, and it is to these proximal situations that his behavior should be seen as primarily adapted. At the level of proximal environment, it is plausible to expect a rather close fit between personality and norms, partly because the latter lack formal definition. The fit between personality and institutional norms, as indicated by covariations across cultures and historical periods, should be somewhat looser because of the remoteness of institutional norms and their tacit permission of situational variants at the level of small groups. This can be seen in the case of the family, which constitutes the proximal environment intervening between more distal institutional environments and the early socialization of the child. The relations between those distal environments (*e.g.*, the values and demands of the occupational structure) and the ways in which children are reared are necessarily loose because they are indirect, with the family as the crucial mediator of normative pressures (Inkeles, 1955; Kohn, 1967; see discussion in Chapter 7). This suggests among other things a delay in the transmission of new values and demands from extrafamilial institutions to the processes of child rearing and means that comparative studies at any one point in time should find a significant but modest degree of correspondence. Since adult lives too are lived in face-to-face situations and are only indirectly constrained by formal institutional demands, a similar delay should be expected to account for the imperfect correspondence between personality and institution.

Deviance

Deviance is no more a unitary phenomenon than conformity to institutional norms, and the line between deviance and conformity is less sharp than it often seems. Social scientists, including students of culture and personality, have paid more of their attention to the more extreme forms of deviance—psychosis, recorded crime, suicide, alcoholism—than to those more problematic in their distinction from normal behavior. As with covariations of personality and institutional norms, so covariations of the latter and deviance rates will probably turn out to be modest because there are so many intervening links between them. It is the nature of these intervening links that has been the major focus of theoretical speculation and research in the study of culture and personality. There are three basic models of deviant behavior in the literature, each with its own concept of the links between institutional environment and personal behavior.

Deviance as exaggeration of norms. This refers to the view, illustrated in Chapter 2, that a cultural environment may predispose individuals to a form of deviance (particularly mental disorder) that represents an exaggeration of normal and culturally distinctive behavior. The high suicide rate in Japan and the values in Japanese culture favoring self-sacrifice are an example: The large number of persons who commit suicide there could be seen as carrying a cultural value to its logical but statistically deviant extreme. To understand why some Japanese commit suicide while most do not would require examination of the operative proximal norms of self-sacrifice in small-scale environmental situations, even before personality variables could be considered. The implication might be (typical of this type of analysis) that the Japanese cultural environment predisposes individuals to suicide not only by making issues of self-sacrifice salient in their personal lives (presumably through socialization of the child) but also by offering them suicide as a culturally formulated resolution of their personal conflicts. This view of deviant behavior as culturally constituted defense resembles Spiro's (1965) conception of religion, and indeed Spiro argues that Burman culture offers young men who might otherwise become seriously impaired in their psychosocial functioning a normative alternative in the role of Buddhist monk.

A similar line of reasoning, with other points of contact between deviance and religion, can be found in the comparative analysis of schizophrenic symptomatology. Tooth (1950), for example, found that in modernized southern Ghana, schizophrenic delusions contained television and other communication technologies; in monarchical central Ghana, they contained fantasies of royal birth and royal affiliation; and in animistic northern Ghana they contained images of spirits and ancestors. The assumption is that the psychopathology is the same but draws its ideational content from the dominant imagery of the culture. Many students of this subject would agree that psychotics and other deviants use cultural themes in the deviant resolution of their personal conflicts, but they differ in the extent to which they see the underlying conflicts as themselves culturally patterned and explicable in terms of personality development (Wallace, 1961a).

Deviance as opposition to norms. This is a dialectic viewpoint in which normative pressures are seen as operating to suppress or repress individual motives; insofar as they fail, deviant behavior occurs. In one version of this view, that of Freud (1930), it is the over-conformity of the individual that results in neurotic pathology. Social institutions make exacting demands for self-discipline that conflict with basic human drives, causing widespread neurotic suffering and symptoms. Many investigators in the culture and personality field have been influenced by this model, attempting to identify culturally distinctive normative constraints that have become sources of neurotogenic stress (*e.g.*, Lee, 1968). The emphasis is on the suffering inflicted on the individual by his pathology rather than on his being treated as a social deviant.

The other version of this view, while agreeing that normative pressures generate deviance, also emphasizes the role of norms in defining the boundaries between normality and deviance. For example, Schooler and Caudill (1964), comparing the symptomatology of schizophrenics in matched hospitals in Japan and the United States, find more violence among the Japanese and more hallucinations among the Americans. They relate this to Japanese norms emphasizing nonaggressive behavior and American norms emphasizing reality-testing, implying not only that these norms might generate culturally distinctive psychotic rebellions but also that the normative preoccupations of each culture would make people more likely to classify a violator as psychotic and put him in a mental hospital. This model of deviance is more familiar outside of psychopathology, for example in the relationships between puritanical norms and pornographic deviance, religious orthodoxy and religious heresy, bourgeois culture and its underground counter-culture. In all of these cases, the norms have been seen as creating deviance by the suppression of individual needs in those who become deviant, and in all of them, the norms entail the cultural category of deviance into which those individuals are placed. In this version of the psychosocial dialectic, the enforcement of repressive norms requires deviant rebels, to be punished for the deterrent effect on others and to be observed for the vicarious enjoyment of their wrongdoing.

Deviance as breakdown of norms. In this view, originated by Durkheim (1895) and very influential in sociology, deviance results not from the pressures of social constraints but from their loosening or breakdown under conditions of social disintegration. Durkheim called the situation of the individual *anomie,* or normlessness, and he meant the condition of the individual whose "liberation" from traditional norms has left him without collective moral guidance in his social adaptation. Many investigators (*e.g.,* Leighton *et al.,* 1963) have sought and found higher rates of psychiatric symptoms, crime, psychomatic disorders, divorce, distrust, and subjective anxiety associated with rural-urban migration and particularly with social dislocation in various parts of the world. Controversies still rage, however, about the importance of social disintegration in accounting for particular types of deviant behavior.

These three models of deviance share the assumption that mental disorder, crime, suicide, *etc.,* are to be understood in terms of their relations to cultural norms and normative pressures. Although they differ in the type of relation posited, they are less contradictory than variants of the same basic position, each with its distinctive area of applicability to be identified in empirical research.

Change

The relation of personality to sociocultural change is another major problem in the study of culture and personality, though there is some question as to whether it is properly regarded as a separate problem or a dimension of every aspect of the field. In any event, I have found it convenient to think of in terms of the following four models of change in culture and personality:

Persistence. Anthropologists, following Hallowell (1955), have often sought to demonstrate that the sociocultural institutions of a people can change without a drastic alteration of their personalities or of the proximal environment of values that facilitates the transmission of personality. Material and institutional change is likely to be more rapid than changes in the personality dispositions by which adaptation is achieved. Most of the work along this line (*e.g.,* Spindler, 1955, 1968; Bruner, 1956a) has been done among non-Western peoples (particularly American Indians) whose macrosocial environments have been radically altered under colonial control and influence but who have found ways of retaining their values.

Breakdown. This is the viewpoint, presented in the preceding section, that links social disintegration with psychological disorder. In the present context, its proponents emphasize that sociocultural change induces stress and anxiety in individuals and can lead to psychopathology. Change is seen primarily as the disintegration or breakdown of old social constraints that guided individual behavior and gave life meaning. Its impact on the individual is normlessness, the burden of having to make novel decisions, the bewilderment of complex and fluctuating situations, fear of the new situation and its real and imagined dangers, separation from traditional objects of attachment. The persons most affected are those who are most uprooted and socially dislocated and who have not yet acquired the competence required for adaptation in the new environment.

Progress. The concepts of acculturation, modernization, and achievement motivation entail a model of persons as acquiring new forms of competence appropriate to innovations in their sociocultural environments. In acculturation, this is conceptualized as a process of exposure and imitation (Bruner, 1956b); in modernization, it is seen primarily as occurring through participation in modern occupational and other institutional structures (Inkeles, 1966a). In the work on achievement motivation (see De Vos, 1969, for a review), however, the new acquisition is seen as determined by preexisting psychological characteristics found more frequently in one population than another. All of these concepts share a view of the individual as being more or less prepared for participation in a new environment, and individuals are compared in terms of how much progress they have made along that line.

Revitalization. In the concept of revitalization processes, Wallace (1956, 1970) has formulated a model of the psychology of culture change that is considerably more complex than the previous three and in fact incorporates them in what might be thought of as an ideological theory of change. When the equilibrium of a sociocultural system is disrupted by forces internal or external to it, it becomes unable to meet the needs of its participants, including their needs for orderliness and predictability in their social life. They become disillusioned and discontented, which leads to an increase in deviant individual behavior, including crime and mental disorder, followed by the institutionalized flouting of conventions by groups of people seeking comfort or advantage in alcohol, violence, illicit sexual and economic practices, as social trust and security deteriorate further. Then a prophet who has undergone an altered state of consciousness in which he has been able to devise a new synthesis of ideas drawn from the traditional ideological resources of the culture, proposes this as a new and more satisfying code of values. The code (a religious or political ideology) may emphasize cathartic (release) or control (discipline) elements but in any case is sharply contrasted with the existing but unsatisfying value system. Individuals are converted to the new code and experience psychotherapeutic effects that reduce their symptoms and their need to engaged in disruptive behavior. Insofar as it wins large numbers of adherents, the new code becomes institutionalized and restores confidence in the sociocultural order. Although the new order is based on the old, it represents an innovative resynthesis of old ideas in a form that meets the needs of individuals better than the preceding established ideology. Wallace (1956) argues that such revitalization movements, failures and successes alike, have been extremely numerous in the history of Western and non-Western societies and represent a major form of sociocultural change.

The revitalization model suggests that these four models of change are not necessarily incompatible and that an adequate theory of psychosocial change must take all of them into account. They are predominantly focused on institutionally induced change to which individuals react. The problem is discussed in more detail with an equal emphasis on personality-induced change in Chapter 9.

Summary and Conclusions

In Part II I have taken a critical look at the main trends in culture and personality theory and method. Five theoretical positions concerning relations between personality and sociocultural environment were outlined, with their respective (though not always mutually exclusive) concepts of socialization and methods of assessing personality. These differing positions, except for the anti-culture-and-personality views, should be seen as tendencies in a fairly homogeneous though unintegrated field of thought. In approaching the major problems of the present chapter and discussing briefly the various models of deviance and change in the field, it was not possible to connect them directly to the more general theoretical positions of Chapter 3, since the proponents of these positions have not built comprehensive systems covering this full range of problems within consistently distinctive theoretical frameworks. In this section I review criticisms made earlier and emphasize what I regard as the major problems facing the field of culture and personality at the present time.

The following paragraphs summarize my conclusions about the various positions:

Anti-culture-and-personality (C → P). The diverse theoretical attempts to account for cross-cultural variations in social (economic, political) behavior and culture patterns without granting an explicit role to psychological factors share a number of defects: implausible reification of institutional entities while ignoring the indispensable element of individual motivation, unacknowledged and simplistic assumptions of a psychological nature, lack of interest in the subjective reactions of individuals to their institutional environments, tendencies to exaggerate either the stability of institutionalized behavior patterns or the inexorability of social trends (according to the ideological predispositions of the theorist).

Some of the positions involved here nevertheless provide perspectives that are indispensable in culture and personality work, perspectives emphasizing the historical and institutional contexts in which individuals live, to which they must adapt, and in which they are observed. The most vital contribution of those social scientists who tend to dismiss the concept of personality, particularly the sociological symbolic interactionists, is their social psychology of the situation, in which individuals are seen as responding to normative pressures, in situations of face-to-face interaction and social participation, rather than to internal motivational pressures. This view continues to represent the most important and valid challenge to the culture and personality approach and one that must be constantly faced in research in this field.

Psychological reductionism (P → C). This is also a diverse category, including the older fairly simplistic approaches, which often were irrelevant to the problem of cross-cultural variation and nonempirical in their methods, as well as the modern reductionism of McClelland, whose empirical method represents a major advance. McClelland's examination of economic roles in terms of their opportunities for personal gratification emphasized what Lasswell and other political scientists suggested earlier: that the behavior of individuals in their social roles reflects their personalities as well as role requirements and that this is as true in economic and political institutions as in religion and art.

Personality-is-culture (P = C). The configurational view of Ruth Benedict, Margaret Mead, and their co-workers was very prominent in the early literature of culture and personality. It is virtually nonexistent in contemporary research because of its conceptual ambiguities and its subjective methods, which permit undisciplined psychological interpretations of cultural materials. The general recognition by investigators that the personality system is distinct from the sociocultural environment and that the two must be assessed and described independently has made its descriptive approach obsolete. The contribution of this point of view, however, in illustrating the effects of cultural patterning in many diverse arenas of social life, was an important one, analogous in many ways to Freud's demonstrations of the influence of unconscious motives in diverse arenas of individual functioning.

Personality mediation (C_1 → P → C_2). This formulation, advanced by Kardiner and Whiting, incorporated psychological reductionism into the larger theoretical frameworks of structural-functional sociology and cultural ecology by positing a causal chain in which personality was an intervening variable formed by one set of institutions (the maintenance system and child rearing practices) and shaping another set (the projective system of religion, magic, folklore, art). Whiting's version stimulated a good deal of field research on child-rearing practices as well as cross-cultural surveys using published ethnographic reports, in which aspects of child rearing and cultural belief, ritual, or expression were shown to be correlated with each other and with aspects of socioeconomic structure. This point of view has been criticized, here and elsewhere, on both theoretical and methodological grounds. Theoretically, the distinction between the two sets of institutions seems conceptually weak, since—from the individual's viewpoint—all institutions represent sets of constraints entailing options among which he can choose. McClelland's treatment of the economy as a projective institution, the ambiguous position of the family in such a scheme, and the convincing suggestions by political scientists of psychological influences on political behavior all indicate that the distinction is not empirically tenable. The central methodological deficiency is that in most empirical studies personality was assessed not directly but only through cultural indicators, making the validity of those indicators dependent on confirmation of the hypotheses. The weakness of the construct validity approach, which applies as well to much of McClelland's cross-cultural work, is that it presupposes more face validity than many social scientists are willing to grant to psychological interpretations of cultural data, ignoring the many alternative explanations of findings based on measurement artifacts. Given these alternatives, positive findings do not constitute unambiguous evidence for the hypotheses derived from this theoretical position.

Two systems (P ↔ C). This position, as advanced by Inkeles, Levinson, and Spiro, is another attempt to deal with personality within the structural-functional framework, by viewing personality as a system with its own internal properties, interacting with the sociocultural system in a relation of limited interdependence. The most important implication of conceiving personality as a separable system is that it must be assessed independently of the patterns in the sociocultural system with which it is hypothetically integrated, since relations between the two systems are the major foci of empirical inquiry. The general formulation permits of variants leaning toward sociological determinism, as in the work of Inkeles, or psychological determinism, as in the work of Spiro, but there is no a priori assumption that certain institutions are formative and others reflective of personality; institutions are regarded as complex compromises that must be empirically studied to discover the psychological and sociological elements in their integration. The weakness in this reasonable position is in its emphasis on institutions. Since individuals adapt to constraints and opportunities in their environments other than those institutionalized as role requirements, the system-integration paradigm can be unrealistically dichotomous. It favors gross characterizations of system attributes based on the most conspicuous features of the environment, those that are institutionalized, rather than fostering a search for those proximal environmental features to which the individual is responding.

This critical overview of theory and method in the culture and personality field leads me to two conclusions:

1. Although different positions have generated divergent concepts and methods, there are no serious theoretical disputes among contemporary culture and personality theorists. Most assume that there is some kind of adaptive fit between the personality characteristics of a population and the sociocultural environment of that population. Most also assume that individual personality, no less than the sociocultural system, is a functioning system with dispositions that manifest themselves in social behavior. The terms of the adaptive fit and the conditions of its manifestation are matters of divergent emphasis; but there is general agreement that empirical research must resolve these questions. Developing a theoretical formulation that will be of greater use should involve not casting out earlier theory but rather recasting the theoretical consensus in terms of the evolutionary paradigm implicit in it. The following section (Chapters 7–11) is a preliminary attempt to do this, not merely to produce a theoretical synthesis but to construct a framework that, in its analogous and direct connections with the evolutionary formulations of other fields, can act as a plausible and compelling guide to research.

2. The major difficulties and controversies in culture and personality are methodological. They concern the problem of what kinds of evidence can be used as a basis for making inferences about the personalities of individual members of society. The most active researchers of recent years, Whiting and McClelland and their associates, have relied heavily on a strategy of construct validation of personality assessment methods. This strategy has produced a situation in which existing assessment instruments produce evidence that serves only to convince those who already believe the hypothesis to be tested or at least the theory from which it was derived. This contributes to the intellectual isolation of culture and personality research from the other social sciences. We need ways of studying personality that will produce evidence that can be more generally accepted as manifestations of personality. The last section of the book (Chapters 12–17) is devoted to the construction of such methods.

Part III

Population Psychology:
An Evolutionary Model of
Culture and Personality

7

The Applicability of a Darwinian View

In the behavioral sciences as in biology, the Darwinian model remains our most plausible means of conceptualizing the interaction between organisms and environments. Much of the theorizing relevant to culture and personality has been based on the assumption that individual behavior is adaptive to the social and physical environments of the individual and that socialization of the child is preadaptation of growing individuals to their future environments by incorporating into their early learning the fruits of experience of earlier generations of adapting adults. In one form or another, this view is taken as axiomatic by psychologically-minded anthropologists and sociologists and socially-minded psychologists and psychoanalysts. It was as characteristic of theoretical statements of 40 years ago as it is today. For example, W. I. Thomas, one of the originators of the culture and personality field, asserted, "The human personality is both a continually producing factor and a continually produced result of social evolution," and he went on to state:

> The whole process of development of the personality . . . includes the following parallel and interdependent process:
> (1) Determination of the character on the ground of temperament;
> (2) Constitution of a life-organization which permits a more or less complete objective expression of the various attitudes included in the character;
> (3) Adaptation of the character to social demands put upon the personality;
> (4) Adaptation of individual life-organization to social organization (Thomas and Znaniecki, 1927, Vol. II: 1863).

From the viewpoint of research priorities and strategy, the assumption of personality-culture adaptation implies that there is great value in studying comparatively the environmental characteristics of social and

101

cultural systems in relation to distributions of individual behavioral dispositions within populations, as in what Inkeles (1959) calls correlations between a state (*i.e.,* a global or integrative characteristic of an environmental system) and a rate (*i.e.,* an index of behavior aggregating individual responses for a population). As Inkeles (1963) points out, although Durkheim's 1895 classic study of suicide was such an investigation, the field of culture and personality is still far from having a comprehensive body of generalizations validated by research and systematically related by theory.

The future of culture and personality study as a science of Darwinian ancestry may be foreseen by examining some of its more prodigious cousins in the comparative fields of human biology, for example, population genetics, human ecology and demography, and epidemiology.[1] In those fields, sufficient consensus has been achieved concerning the measurement of individual characteristics, the means by which they are transmitted, and the definition of population units, that investigators have been able to generate substantial bodies of accepted generalizations, as well as mathematical formulations of the complex interaction of variables and the dynamics of stability and change. In culture and personality, we have to solve a myriad of methodological problems before making this kind of progress, but it will be useful at this stage to attempt a more detailed application of the Darwinian model to our own subject matter. Campbell (1966) has outlined the general conditions for such applications:

> The most exciting current contribution of Darwin is in his model for the achievement of purposive or ends-guided processes through a mechanism involving blind, stupid, unforesightful elements. In recent years, the cyberneticist Ashby (1952), Pringle (1951), and others have pointed out anew the formal parallel between natural selection in organic evolution and trial-and-error learning. The common analogy has also been recognized in many other loci, as in embryonic growth, wound healing, crystal formation, development of science, radar, echo-location, vision, creative thinking, etc. . . . The three essentials are these:
>
> 1. The occurrence of variations: heterogeneous, haphazard, "blind," "chance," "random," but in any event variable. (The mutation process in organic evolution, and exploratory responses in learning.)
>
> 2. Consistent selection criteria: selective elimination, selective propagation, selective retention, of certain types of variations. (Differential survival of certain mutants in organic evolution, differential reinforcement of certain responses in learning.)
>
> 3. A mechanism for the preservation, duplication, or propagation of the positively selected variants (the rigid duplication process of the chromosome-gene system in plants and animals, memory in learning) (pp. 26–27).

1. See Alland (1967) for an application of the Darwinian model of culture as studied by anthropologists.

Given these conditions, an evolution in the direction of better fit to the selective system becomes inevitable.

The primary purpose of this chapter is to attempt a preliminary application of this cybernetic model to the interaction of culture and personality.

Applicability of The Variation-Selection Model
To Culture and Personality

To explore the applicability of the variation-selection model outlined by Campbell, we must lay bare three assumptions concerning personality, the sociocultural system, and adaptation.

1. Distributions of personality dispositions, like the distributions of genetic and other biological traits, are statistical characteristics of populations, aggregated from measurements taken on individuals and exhibiting considerable variation, which can be expressed for comparative purposes by measures of central tendency (*e.g.*, mean, median) and by population frequencies (*i.e.*, percent of population exhibiting the trait). There is no contradiction in assuming both intrapopulation variability and cross-population differences in central tendency; many normally distributed biological traits (*e.g.*, adult stature) show significant variation across human populations. While many of the personality traits of greatest interest in comparative studies are likely to be normally distributed within populations, others may be discrete traits of very frequent or very rare occurrence (see Chapter 2). It is expected that some personality traits will vary significantly across intrapopulation groups defined by sex, age, occupation, status, and other aspects of differential social participation and differential exposure to cultural influences.

2. A sociocultural system, as a selective environment interacting with individual behavior, is a structure of institutional demands and opportunities. The demands are for conformity to norms and entail punishment for failure to conform as well as social rewards for conformity; the opportunities are socially acceptable pathways for individuals to gain satisfaction of subjectively experienced needs. Each institution makes demands of and offers opportunities to individuals, although some institutions may appear to be structured around demands, others around opportunities (as in Kardiner's distinction between primary and secondary institutions and Whiting's concept of maintenance and projective systems). Certain personality traits are more compatible than others with successful conformity to certain norms and with certain pathways for satisfaction. Individuals differing in such traits will perform differently in their social roles and in taking advantage of opportunities and will experience correspondingly differing degrees of reinforcement from their sociocultural environment.

3. The individuals in a given population are not necessarily aware of the evolved adaptations between personality and institution in which they

participate. This needs to be emphasized because the purposive, profit-and-loss language of a theory of selection and adaptation seems to imply the operation of conscious rational choice by individuals of the means required for the best environmental "payoff." It should be remembered, however, that this evolutionary model is borrowed from fields in which consciousness and purposive foresight are out of the question. As Campbell says,

> It is through such a process of selective cumulation of the unlikely that the extremely improbable and marvelous combinations found in plants and animals become, in fact, highly probable. As understood by present-day biologists, the elegantly engineered and complexly coordinated animals have been developed through this uncoordinated, unforesightful, unplanned, elementaristic process (1966, p. 27).

In the context of human culture, it is unlikely that members of a society are aware of the broader adaptive functions of customs assuring their survival, for example, the part played by dispersion of settlement and intergroup warfare in maintaining the man/land ratio within a particular subsistence level.[2] This seems true as well of cultural adaptations to high infant mortality rates. For example, Whiting (1965) suggests that a prolonged taboo on post-partum sexual activity of women operates to insure the survival of infants in populations with low-protein diets, by allowing the infants a longer period of breast feeding. If one asks a woman in such a population why she is refraining from sexual activity, she will offer reasons of morality or the belief that breast milk is poisoned by the husband's seminal ejaculation during coitus. Whatever reason she offers, she is unaware of the nutritional inadequacy of her customary diet, although this may have acted as the selective pressure favoring a longer post-partum sexual taboo. Adaptations of this sort seem to develop so gradually that their survival advantages over previous customs are not noticeable to any given generation of individuals, even though each may be responding subliminally to selective pressures. Furthermore, as soon as the practice becomes institutionalized, it is surrounded with a protective covering of normative pressures and associated nonempirical beliefs, which increase its incentive value and thereby insure its performance more securely than would any rational calculation of survival chances. Each individual then sees the custom as having immediate value for his social adaptation (conformity to norms) and for other immediate personal concerns (often ideologized or rationalized in moral or religious terms), but he may remain unaware of the custom's relevance to individual and group survival. Thus a bifurcation develops between the manifest and latent functions of the custom.

2. See Alland (1967, pp. 221–223) for discussion of this point.

Humans are, nonetheless, the only animals that *can* become aware of and consciously direct their adaptive behavior. It is thus safe to assume that humans need not be aware of more than a fraction of the adaptive values of individual behavioral dispositions but that they can become conscious of a wide range of such values, with important consequences for socialization of the child (discussed below).

Having stated these assumptions, we can proceed to apply the Darwinian model to culture-personality relations. First we must ask whether our subject matter meets the three conditions stated by Campbell to be essential for such an application: the occurrence of unplanned variations, consistent selection criteria, and a mechanism for the preservation and duplication of positively selected variants. The first is to be found in personality characteristics, as conceptualized in the psychology of individual differences. Personality characteristics in this sense are certainly variable, not only within a population as a whole but even among the children of a single set of parents. This variation is generally thought of as produced by the interaction of genetic constitution and early experience in complex ways that are not yet adequately understood but in which uncontrolled or "accidental" factors such as innate reaction levels, sibling position, parents' personality, and infantile traumata are critical. Thus there is unplanned variation in abundance.

Consistent selection criteria are provided by the sociocultural environment in its normative aspect, which includes positive and negative standards of behavior (*e.g.*, ideal personality types and rules of personal conduct as well as criteria for successful role performance), and a system of comparative social evaluation in which personal rewards and punishments are differentially distributed.

The cognitive activity of socializing agents preserves positively selected variants, and deliberate socialization acts toward duplicating them in the next generation. Every adult individual perceives the environment around him and notices to some degree the evaluative and distributive operations of the sociocultural system. From observation of individual instances of conformity and nonconformity, positive and negative evaluation, success and failure, social reward and punishment—in a process equivalent to the vicarious trial-and-error or observational learning of reinforcement theorists—he draws conclusions about which behavioral dispositions are favored and which disfavored. These inductive conclusions become part of his cognitive structure, joining the attitudes, beliefs, and values already there, and becoming consistent with them to some degree. From this cognitive structure as repeatedly modified by social perception and his own normative experience comes his definition of the situation in which he sees his children growing up and his prescriptions and proscriptions for their adaptive performance. This is his ground plan for the deliberate socialization of his children, guiding their training toward certain goals and away from others. The socializing agent's beliefs and values concerning various personality characteristics and their outcomes are shaped by his perceptual experience as a participant observer in a normative environment and serve in turn to dictate the direction in which he shapes his children's behavior. The adult in his role as parent or socializing agent performs the function of feedback from selective experience that is performed by reproduction in population genetics and by memory in trial-and-error learning.[3]

This evolutionary model of culture-personality relations is of course grossly oversimplified. Indeed, even in population genetics and trial-and-error learning, matters are not so simple as the bare statement of the variation-selection system seems to imply. The simplification of primary interest here concerns the duplication of positively selected variants. The truth is that there is much slippage between the preserved information about selective pressures and what subsequently becomes manifest in observable form. In genetics, what is encoded in the genes (the genotype) is not fully expressed in the phenotype of anatomical structure unless environmental factors (*e.g.*, nutrition) are facilitating; in trial-and-error learning, complex processes of remembering, including forms of inhibition, intervene between memory and performance and prevent much that is stored in the memory from being expressed in behavior. The counterpart in socialization is that the explicit goals of socializing agents are frequently not realized in the behavior of those they train. First, the socializers are at best imperfect psychological engineers (they do not command the necessary but as yet ill-known laws of behavior acquisition); second, they must operate within the limits set by their trainees' preexisting behavioral dispositions, acquired genetically and through "accidental" events of early experience over which the socializing agents have little conscious control. Recognition of this slippage between environmental information and subsequent performance brings to our attention two major sets of variables related to socialization: the conscious aims, concepts, and knowledge of the socializers and the relation between unplanned and deliberate influences in the child's behavioral development.

The cognitive structures of the socializers mediate between selective pressures in the environment and the socialization process to which the child is subjected. The intelligence and cognitive complexity of the parent, his conceptual and verbal apparatus (including ideological formulations), the information about the environment that is available to him—all of these are thus determinants of how environmental experience in the adult

3. In the more differentiated societies the storage and selective propagation of information about the environment is institutionally specialized and performed by schools, libraries, religious, and political organizations, rather than by ordinary parents. Here, as elsewhere in the discussion, parents are used as illustrative of the category of socializing agents rather than exhaustive of it.

world is transformed into training experience for children. This can be illustrated by three hypothetical societies.

In the first society, a nonliterate agricultural group, the emphasis during the first two or three years of life is on feeding and caring for the child so that he will live despite a high infant mortality rate. Parents do not think of shaping his behavior during this time; their concept of socialization is of a training that is postponed until the child is old enough to understand and be useful. When that time comes, their primary goals are concrete and straightforward: to teach the child to submit to legitimate authority (probably requiring physical punishment because the child is introduced to external controls fairly late in development) and to teach him to participate responsibly in the economy (beginning early and with simple task performance). These goals are sometimes summarized by the parents as "obedience" or "respect." The goals have proved valuable for social adaptation for many generations; there is no serious thought of changing them; and their correctness and necessity are perceived as absolute by adults in the society, who have never contemplated any alternatives. Socialization is rarely discussed in abstract language but usually in terms of concrete social and economic situations.

The second group is a Protestant sect in Western Europe or America, in the 17th to 19th centuries. For adult members of the group the world is defined by the scriptures as interpreted by their founder and other leaders in written works and oral instruction. These teachings, internally consistent and forming a deductive system of thought, present a single ultimate goal of conduct—salvation—and detail the ways in which salvation is to be achieved. Alternate forms of behavior are explicitly considered and frequently condemned as idolatry, sin, satanism, and popishness, leading to damnation, the opposite of salvation. Members of the group are taught to see every act as having moral and religious significance, leading toward or away from salvation. This applies with great force to the raising of their children. Child rearing practically from birth onwards is prescribed by religious leaders and designed to foster qualities such as self-control and self-reliance, which help provide the individual with the means for his own salvation. Even the feeding, sleeping arrangements, and tending of infants are infused with moral considerations, and parents apply abstract terms derived from religious teachings to their concrete behavior as socializers and to their children's behavior. They have explicit nonempirical religiously based beliefs concerning the relation between parental acts and their behavioral consequences in the child. In a word, socialization of the child has become ideologized, made part of an abstract set of ideas concerning what happens and ought to happen in real behavior.

The parents of this hypothetical Protestant sect differ cognitively from those of the hypothetical nonliterate society in a number of important ways. Most basically perhaps, the Protestant parents view the conduct of infants, children, and parents in abstract terms, seeing each behavioral event as an instance of a general dispositional quality, which has as much reality for them as the concrete social and economic situation has for the nonliterate parent. The latter is less accustomed to applying abstract labels to his parental behavior, and he is, therefore, considerably less aware of what he does as a socializer. Self-awareness is another feature distinguishing the thought of the Protestant parent from that of the nonliterate. The latter, having relatively little experience in generalizing about or applying general labels to his parental behavior, is also inexperienced in considering alternative patterns of behavior and defining his own contrastively against them. In his phenomenal absolutism (see Segall, Campbell, and Herskovits, 1966), he tends to see his own behavior as automatic and stemming necessarily from the universal situation of child and parent; the categories in his thought for other ways are neither salient nor elaborated. The Protestant parent has a salient and elaborated conceptual category—the sinful ways of the nonbeliever—and he has been trained to define his own behavior contrastively, in terms of polar opposites. His self-awareness as a socializer, although limited to poles of good and evil, is greater than the less differentiated view of the nonliterate parent. A third difference lies in the coherence or unity of the two cognitive structures: The Protestant parent operates within an explicit ideology that has the appearance of a deductive system in which diverse prescriptions are unified by their derivation from a single set of axiomatic premises. The nonliterate parent's concept of his child-training program gains some unity from its simplicity, but his actual child-training practices, being less verbalized and less self-consciously performed, are likely to be less forced toward mutual consistency. Such a parent notices inconsistencies less and is less bothered by them than a parent guided by an explicit ideology. The parents in the two groups differ in the abstractness, contrastive self-awareness, and coherence of the cognitive structures by which they mediate between their environment and their children.

The third group is a cluster of university-educated families in contemporary America. The ways in which the parents think about their child training resemble in some ways both of the other groups. Like the nonliterate parents, they are concerned about the health and economic future of their children, and they have "inherited" from the Protestant cultural ancestry of America much of the ideology of self-control and self-reliance (though shorn of some of its religious axioms) that characterized the Protestant sect. There are two important ways, however, in which they differ drastically from the other two groups. First, the contemporary parents assume that the sociocultural criteria for evaluating behavior change from generation to generation and that their children will be judged by somewhat different standards as adults than those by which the parents were judged. Hence they search for information from the environment concerning the new selective pressures to which their children will have to adapt in the future; in so doing, the parents enter into a more deliberate interaction with the social and cultural system, self-consciously acting as mediators of environmental feedback to their children. (As Riesman [1950] has pointed out, sometimes the children in such subcultures are in closer touch with new trends and may transmit environmental information to their parents who, recognizing the power of change, alter their socialization accordingly.) Second, the parents in this group believe that science, rather than religion or tradition, can tell them how to produce desirable behavioral dispositions in their children. They seek advice from and are responsive to pediatricians, educators, child psychologists, and other "experts" on child rearing concerning the best ways to produce intelligence, emotional stability, and other adaptive qualities in their children. Since "expert" advice is not based on a substantial body of validated generalizations, the opinions of scientists, practitioners, and quasi-scientific journalists and writers fluctuate, and parental beliefs and practices follow these fluctuations.

From this perspective, the concepts of child rearing and training held by these contemporary parents represent an attempt to rationalize the process of socialization by consciously gearing both its ends and means to information feedback from a changing environment. In this attempt, the goals of socialization can be altered according to shifts in selective pressures favoring certain personal qualities and discouraging others, and the means are alterable as new information is received concerning the methods that experts believe to be optimal for the fostering of adaptive personal qualities. This type of cognitive structure has much more flexibility and self-awareness and a great deal less coherence than that of the Protestant sect members because of its openness to diverse and changing sources of prescriptions for behavior.

Although parental socialization concepts in all three societies are adapted to selective pressures operative in their respective sociocultural systems, the major differences lie in the parents' awareness of their adaptation and of what they have adapted to, the abstractness and generality of their thinking about it, their sense of conscious choice among alternative practices, and their responsiveness to environmental change. Since the cognitive structure of the parent determines in great measure how and to what extent he translates his selective environment into training experiences for the child, it can be seen that the nature of socialization as a process mediating between adult experience and child training is dependent on whether the parent's concepts of socialization are abstract or concrete, differentiated or undifferentiated, verbalized or unreflective, ideologized or rationalized, absolute or relativistic, deductive or pragmatic, rigid or flexible, coherent or disunified. Cultures vary widely in these dimensions of parental cognition. Consequently, it is untenable to think of socialization as a uniform mechanism for the propagation of positively selected variants, operating identically in all populations as genetic reproduction does. We need a more complex view that takes account of cultural variation.

These considerations of cross-cultural variability in parental cognition bring us back to the relation between unplanned and deliberate aspects of socialization. Campbell's presentation of the variation-selection model places great weight on the unplanned, haphazard, or unforesightful quality of the variation that is acted upon by selective criteria in such a way as to effect differential propagation of variants. But in human affairs the dividing line between the unplanned and the deliberate is not constant; it varies with the cognitive differentiation, purposiveness, and environmental information of individuals.

This is even true for the genetics of populations. Humans, being the only species with consciousness of the means by which innate characteristics are transmitted, are in a unique position to create a more efficient, tightly controlled system of selective propagation than could occur through natural selection. Selective breeding in animal husbandry is an example that antedates Mendelian genetics. Eugenicists have argued that human breeding should not be left to the haphazard vagaries of personal choice, that existing scientific knowledge be used to extend purposive control over human reproduction by formulating general policies of selection that harness mating practices more tightly to societal goals. Although the mutation process that generates haphazard variation could not be controlled with present knowledge, the adoption of eugenic proposals would certainly reduce heterogeneity and push back the line between the deliberate and the unplanned in mating behavior.

So it is with socialization; the counterparts to eugenic proposals have been adopted by numerous groups, most conspicuously nonconformist religious sects, utopian communities, and totalitarian societies. In those groups an effort is made to remove child training from the sphere of individual choice and make it part of a grand design conceived by the leaders and centrally administered for the entire community. As in eugenics, the aim is to reduce haphazard and possible deleterious variation in the interest of achieving societal goals. One way of doing this is to make the grand design or ideology part of each parent's cognitive map and to instruct him in the ways he can contribute to achievement of the common goals by shaping his child's behavior. This parental collaboration is necessary but not sufficient; in fact, such groups tend to remove much of the child-training function from parents and the family altogether and assign a larger part of it to bureaucratically organized educational institutions whose policies can be more easily and efficiently controlled by the central administration. The desirability of such an arrangement was foreseen by Plato in *The Republic* and realized in its most extreme form in the Israeli Kibbutz described by Spiro (1957, 1958), where even infant care is bureaucratically organized, with children in group residences supervised by specialized nonfamilial caretakers from the first year of life, and where a myriad of environmental details are dictated and standardized by ideological considerations. Such arrangements do not alter the individual variation generated by differences in genetic constitution and traumatic accidents, but they do make the conditions of early life more uniform and could conceivably diminish the effects of sibling position on personality. It is doubtful that such centrally planned socialization could be as successful as intended, because humans have less complete knowledge of behavior acquisition processes than they do of genetic transmission. Nevertheless, it must be admitted that these planned societies have reduced sources of intrapopulation heterogeneity and pushed back the line between the deliberate and the unplanned in socialization so as to minimize the latter realm.

By their extreme contrast with the more usual situation in which families are left to train their own children as they see fit, cases of maximally planned child training illustrate the variability in location of the boundary between deliberate and unplanned aspects of socialization, but this variability is by no means limited to such cases. Families influenced by different religious and political value systems differ significantly in how they train their children (see Whiting *et al.*, 1966), and some of these value systems involve tighter and more conscious control over the details of socialization than others. In their comparison of Zuni Indians, Texans, and Mormons in New Mexico, Whiting *et al.* (1966) show that the value systems of the three communities emphasize different types of behavior as particularly important to socialize (aggression among the Zuni, dependence among the Texans, sexuality among the Mormons), with a correspondingly greater degree of conscious attention and explicit normative regulation in their respective focal areas of behavior. What is relatively unregulated and unplanned in one group is the object of intensely deliberate socialization in another. This study of groups occupying the same physical environment stresses the area of proscriptive control, but Barry, Child, and Bacon's (1959) cross-cultural study of subsistence economy and child rearing (showing an emphasis on obedience and responsibility in agricultural and pastoral societies and self-reliance and achievement in hunting and gathering societies) suggests that a certain prescriptive area of socialization may be isolated for greater conscious elaboration as well. Where religious ideology plays a part, as in Zborowski's (1949) example of the emphasis on book learning in the socialization of Eastern European Jewish boys, the amount of deliberate planning of prescribed child-training routines is likely to be even greater. Thus the boundary between unplanned and deliberate aspects of socialization varies widely across cultural groups and across different areas of child behavior within a culture.

A further complication concerning the factor of conscious planning in socialization is the tendency of parents to justify, rationalize, and explain their practices on ideological or pragmatic grounds of a purposive nature that are unrelated to the historical causes for their adoption. Outside artificially created systems like those of utopian communities where the discontinuity with past socialization can be historically documented, the observer is tempted to take the post facto explanations of parents as representing the ideological origins of their practices. This is extremely unreliable unless independent evidence shows that the belief preceded the practice for, as Whiting and Whiting (1959) have argued, beliefs are frequently constructed to reduce the cognitive dissonance between a child-training practice (caused by ecological or structural pressures) and incompatible ideals in the culture. We are likely to find, for example, that where many persons live in one household, children will be carefully trained not to fight, presumably to prevent disruption of the household solidarity needed to maintain cooperation in economic and other tasks. The ubiquity of this relation between household size and severity of aggression training cross culturally (see Whiting *et al.*, 1966; Minturn and Lambert, 1964) confirms this functional explanation and suggests as a plausible possibility that large households came first and required suppression of overt hostility for their maintenance. But explicit recognition of this adaptation by parents would require verbalizing the very hostility the household members are trying to suppress. Thus there is cognitive dissonance between the parent's awareness of the adaptation and his cultural ideals of interpersonal behavior; the dissonance is reduced by adopting the cultural explanation that anger will make a child ill or that fighting will offend the gods or disrupt the harmony of the universe. Apart from their role in reducing dissonance, such beliefs relate an adaptive practice to an existing cognitive structure in the parent—the religious, ethical, or cosmological system in which he already believes—and hence he can more readily assimilate them and less easily forget or neglect them. From the outside observer's point of view, this state of affairs means parents will present their child-training practices as the deliberate application of general ideological principles when they were in fact developed under the pressure of unmentioned ecological and social-structural factors. One generation's practical necessities become the next generation's exalted ideals.

This confounding of the deliberate and the unplanned (but adaptive), which we encountered earlier in this chapter in the case of the taboo on post-partum sexual intercourse, brings us back to the familiar phenomenon of the multi-functional nature of customs well embedded in the culture and the fact that some functions are manifest and others latent. An evolutionary viewpoint easily encompasses the idea that those customs having multiple functions are more likely to survive and that certain functions will be more visible and obvious than others of no less importance. Although the phenomenon is comprehensible in the broader theoretical framework, nevertheless, it often presents a serious problem for understanding which environmental stimuli the parent is responding to. Does he give his infant toys to play with because of a conscious or preconscious goal of intellectual enrichment geared to ultimate educational and economic success or because he simply enjoys seeing the child enjoy himself, with this vicarious enjoyment pattern having been unconsciously selected in generations of worldly success through cognitive enrichment? The answers to such questions, or their reformulation in answerable form, cannot be simple, and no adequate answer can fail to take account of the cognitive complexity and variability of human cultures.

Summary

In discussing the applicability of the variation-selection model to culture-personality relations we have found that Campbell's highly generalized statement, in a form as applicable to radar, embryonic growth, and creative thinking as it is to organic evolution and trial-and-error learning, is oversimplified for our subject matter. The slippage between available selective information and subsequent propagation, inherent in other applications of the variation-selection paradigm, is of critical importance in the study of culture and personality because it is not constant across human populations but varies widely, making it difficult to construct a single working model of environmental feedback and duplication for all societies. The major sources of variation are the cognitive structures (their complexity, purposiveness, and responsiveness to environmental change) of the socializing agents who stand between the adult environment and the reinforcement schedules of the children. Variations in the purposive ideologization and rationalization of child-training concepts across populations make it impossible to draw a universal boundary between deliberate and unplanned elements in the socialization process, and the blurring is compounded by post facto cultural explanations that make unplanned adaptive practices appear to have developed from preordained policies. Even in the most planned societies, genetic constitution and accidents of early experience generate a core of haphazard heterogeneity in personality characteristics; but heterogeneity appears to be greater in less planned societies, with adaptation probably occurring through a closer analogue to natural selection in the latter case. Strict application of the generalized variation-selection model will not do, and we must seek a more complex and variable evolutionary framework for culture-personality adaptation.

8

Basic Concepts in an Evolutionary Model

The attempt to construct an evolutionary model of personality-culture relations analogous to those that have proved fruitful in the comparative aspects of population biology was originally based on the assumption that, as in that more advanced field, our subject matter concerns statistical distributions of individual characteristics and the selective operation of environments. Intergenerational transmission of characteristics, selective pressures on individuals and populations, processes of adaptive equilibrium and adaptive change, are additional foci of common concern. The first part of an evolutionary model designed especially for relations between personality and the sociocultural system is presented in this chapter. Initially the focus is on the processes of personality development and socialization, and the basic concepts are personality genotype,[1] personality phenotype, and deliberate socialization.

The Personality Genotype

This refers to a set of enduring individual behavioral dispositions that may or may not find socially acceptable expression in the customary (or

---

1. The terms *phenotype* and *genotype* were introduced into personality psychology by Kurt Lewin (1935) to distinguish the "immediate perceptible appearance" from "the properties that determine the object's dynamic relations" (p. 11). It is in this sense rather than in the biological sense related to genes that the terms are used here. *Genotype* refers to the individual's personality dispositions and their organization, as discussed in Chapter 1; *phenotype* refers to the consistencies in individual behavior that are accessible to observation by the community and by the investigator making inferences about the underlying dispositions. It should also be noted that I use the word *genetic* to refer to the action and transmission of the genes in the biological sense, rather than using it as psychoanalysts do to mean "developmental" or "pertaining to ontogeny." (They use *genic* in referring to the biological genes and their action.)

institutionalized) behavior of a population. Its major characteristics are early acquisition (through the interaction of constitution and early experience); resistance to elimination in subsequent experience; and capacity for inhibition, generalization, and other transformations under the impact of experiential pressures. It acts as a set of constraints on later learning and on the adaptive flexibility of the individual.

The personality genotype has its origins in certain distinctive features of human ontogeny: an extended period of psychological as well as physical immaturity, in which the environment is mediated by caretakers, and a capacity for acquiring ideational representations of experience from the earliest years of life. The higher-order capacities for logically processing environmental information do not mature, according to Piaget, until the years from seven to eleven. Long before that time the child has acquired a stable psychological organization for regulating tension and adapting to his caretakers. This intellectually primitive organization is subordinated by the higher-order processes that govern adult adaptation but continues as an active substratum of motivation and a reservoir of affective imagery for expressive and creative activities.

Three broad classes of dispositions comprise the personality genotype:

(1) Basic, probably genetically determined, parameters of individual functioning, such as general activity level and thresholds for perceiving, discriminating, and reacting to stimuli (e.g., arousal and irritability thresholds). These dispositions set gross limits on the quantities of behavioral output and stimulus input characteristic of one individual compared with another.

(2) The motivational residues of early experience. The child's representations of his wishes and fears concerning other persons in his early life provide unconscious prototypes for his emotional response to others in subsequent environments. These early social motives, developed by the cognitively immature organism in coping with his interpersonal environment and inner needs, become stabilized long before they are integrated into a mature adaptive organization, and they continue as influences on adult behavior. In their original emotional intensity, these wishes and fears must be defended against to maintain the child's sense of well-being, and these primitive defensive resolutions are experienced in adulthood as deeply felt preferences and aversions.

(3) Adaptive organizations that monitor and regulate responses to stimuli coming from the external environment and from internal needs. These include a basic perceptual organization (e.g., self-other differentiation, reality-testing), a drive organization (e.g., capacities for stable affective responses to human objects including the self), and the functions of information processing (perceptual discrimination, memory, thinking, learning), control (e.g., delay of gratification, moral restraints), and synthesis (ability to mediate between drives, controls, and environmental demands).

The personality genotype is complexly formed but has at least the following sources: genetic constitution; patterns of stimulation, gratification, frustration, and attachment to caretakers in infancy; patterns of childhood separation (temporary and permanent) and perceptions of threatened separation from love objects causing fear and hatred of others in the immediate environment and giving rise to intrapsychic conflicts, their representation in unconscious fantasies, defenses against the conflicts, and identifications with objects perceived as lost; traumatic experiences—the influx of greater stimulation than the child can master, causing developmental arrest or regression and the subsequent formation of a repressed motivational complex.

These influences act to form the personality genotype as an organization of motives, cognitions, and adaptive habits during the first five or six years of life, but many of their separate effects are manifested in infancy and early childhood as individual differences in activity or passivity, irritability, dependence, hostility, sociability, inhibitions, imitativeness, masculinity-femininity, and other observable (phenotypic) behaviors. Determinants acting earlier form constraints on subsequent development. For example, genetic differences in perceptual thresholds may determine whether a given amount of stimulation will be traumatic. In like manner, if we assume that self-other differentiation and capacity for delay of gratification, in their most developed forms, are contingent on optimal frustration during a critical period of infancy, then it follows that infants who do not experience optimal frustration at that time will develop defects in cognitive and control functions that will affect the way they perceive and experience separation and potential traumata during childhood. A proper understanding of the development of the personality genotype would include a telescoping series of developmental constraints as one form (among many) of interaction between innate and environmental, and earlier and later, determinants. In its final form the personality genotype is itself an organized set of constraints on the later development of the individual.

These sources of the personality genotype are, with the exception of genetic constitution, social stimuli impinging on the infant and child and are parts of larger patterns of social interaction that are in turn aspects of social structure. The events in infant care and child life that lead to attachments, aversions, separations, traumata, and their complex psychological residues can be seen as outgrowths of social structure and therefore as varying concomitantly with structural variations among populations. For example, the number of nuclear families sharing a courtyard and cooperating in domestic tasks may determine the likelihood of multiple mothering of infants. The presence, absence, or frequency of polygyny and its associated rules of husband-wife relations may determine the time interval between births and therefore the average age at which children experience the birth of the next sibling. The clustering or

dispersal of residences in local communities, and the density of settlement, may determine the availability of children from outside the family
as playmates. The degree of mother's participation in occupational roles
such as cultivator and trader may determine the amount of time she has
available to attend to her children and the likelihood of her using supplementary caretakers. The marriage pattern, particularly the frequency
of stable unions, may determine the number of households in which
fathers are available as objects for love, hate, and identification; and the
rate of divorce or conjugal separation may determine the number of
children who become separated from one or both parents. In these (and
many other) cases, abrupt or recurrent events having an impact on the
child's experience, and consequently on his personality development, are
unplanned and usually unconscious byproducts of variations in the structure of family, community, and occupation.

The relations between social structure and typical patterns of childhood
experience pose two important problems: Are such relations accidental,
evolved through an adaptive variation-selection process, or the product
of purposive social policy? Do they reduce variation among the personality genotypes of a population?

In dealing with the first of these problems we return briefly to the
question of consciousness and purpose discussed in the preceding chapter.
At the most superficial level, an answer is easy. Adults respond to the
coercive pressures of their social and economic environment—for example, the need to grow food or find a job in the face of potential scarcity,
the need to cluster and cooperate for mutual defense against invaders—
and they create living arrangements designed first and foremost to solve
these practical problems of survival. Child rearing must be adjusted
accordingly, fitted into a pattern of family and community life already
fashioned for other purposes. From this point of view the resultant patterns of childhood experience are accidental consequences of socioeconomic adaptation. But there are limits inherent in the raising of
children: Each generation must survive the high mortality period of
infancy and early childhood characteristic of most human populations
until recently (and of many today), and they must be capable of carrying
on basic subsistence tasks as their elders decline in vigor. If these conditions are not met the population will not survive, no matter how successful their mode of production or defense.

It seems altogether plausible that some populations have at times
reacted to ecological shifts with new structural arrangements that failed
to meet these conditions—for example, an organization of work in which
infants and children were neglected physically and emotionally, with a
consequent rise in infant mortality and decline in the educability of
children for their occupational roles. There would then have to be a
modification in the new structure to allow better child care, or the popu-

lation would be threatened with demographic and economic collapse and eventually disappear or become absorbed into neighboring populations that had better adapted child-care practices. In other words, selection would operate, across both historical and interpopulation variation, to eliminate structural variants incompatible with the basic conditions for child care and to propagate structural variants that do meet those conditions. If this has indeed happened in human history, we would be justified in stating that customary patterns of childhood experience are not entirely accidental byproducts of social structure but have adaptively evolved through haphazard variation and selective retention. To put it more accurately, limits on the impact of social structure on childhood experience have probably been evolved through variation-selection. Within these broad limits, so long as structural arrangements do not endanger the survival or occupational trainability of children, social structures are free to vary in accordance with ecological demands and to alter the shape of childhood experience in a nonpurposive way.

A further qualification on the proposition that childhood experience is an accidental byproduct of social structure is required for those populations in which the basic conditions of infant and child care are self-consciously planned to achieve developmental goals dictated by a general ideology. The analogy with eugenics is apposite here, for eugenicists desire central and selective control over what is normally a rather haphazard process. Societies that have consciously organized the social experience of the infant and child in accordance with ideological goals are not so hard to find as those that have adopted eugenic policies, but they are the exceptions that prove the rule. The rule, the normal state of affairs in most human societies, is that infant and child care is conducted in multi-functional social units (such as the family) by persons having other tasks and responsibilities, so that child rearing takes place in a social context largely established for other purposes. Although for ideological reasons, mothers in some societies more than their counterparts elsewhere may seek to stimulate, gratify or frustrate their infants and children, no more than a fraction of the significant social-emotional experience in early life can be attributed to purposive manipulation. Present evidence does not allow us to say with any certainty how influential this fraction may be in personality development. What we can say, however, is that the effects of early influences on the complex structure of motives, cognitive patterns, and capacities, here called the personality genotype, are still so imperfectly known, even by scientific investigators of child development, that manipulative intent on the part of parents is no guarantee of success.

It is inherently difficult to discover what the preverbal child perceives and experiences and what parts of his environment are particularly significant to him, and this lack of feedback reduces the advantage that deliberate manipulation of early environment has over unconsciously evolved practices in achieving long-range developmental goals. (In this regard, the emphasis put on the early development of speech in the child by modern parents, with their consciously manipulative intent, should be especially noted.) Thus, though populations vary widely in the extent to which they aspire to manipulate the preverbal environment of the child, and though sociocultural evolution seems to have set limits on the range of child-rearing possibilities, the social-structural sources of influence on development of the personality genotype are predominantly unplanned consequences of small group interaction patterns. Parents, in their social roles (as husband, wife, kinsman, producer, consumer, etc.) and social behavior, are unwittingly generating an environment that profoundly affects the emotional development of their children.

The other question posed by relations between social structure and childhood experience is whether the structural determination of childhood environments tends to homogenize the early experiences that form personality genotypes in a population. In general, social structure operates to make social behavior more uniform. When an aspect of behavior comes under normative regulation, it may no longer be varied freely without being stigmatized as deviant and punished by social sanctions. In the absence of normative regulation of family life, characteristics such as legitimized marriage, divorce, polygyny, birth spacing, father absence, might be randomly distributed. The fact is they are not randomly distributed; there are sharp discontinuities among human populations in norms of marriage and family life, and the frequency distribution curves for relevant behavioral characteristics are distinctly different in different populations. Most frequently, such curves are either J-curves in which a large majority conform to a norm (e.g., legitimized marriage among middle-class Americans) or bell-shaped curves in which variation is normally distributed around a population mean that represents a normative ideal (e.g., family size among middle-class Americans). There may be no variation among population members in their recognition of a normative ideal, but there is always variation in the incidence of actual social behavior patterns. Thus, in a population universally regarding polygynous marriage as ideal, there will be some men who remain monogamists because of poverty, causing variation in the social experience of their children. Conformity to social norms does not in practice mean uniformity of childhood social environment.

The timing of structurally patterned events in a family also creates variations in childhood experience. For example, the oldest children in a polygynous family may spend their first few years of life in a monogamous unit, whereas those born after their father has several wives are exposed to a very different environment. The developmental cycle through which domestic groups pass in many societies (see Goody, 1958, and Gray and Gulliver, 1964) diversifies the experience of children in the "same" family.

A population may have a high divorce rate, but any particular divorce, occurring at a different point in the life of each of the several children of the union, is likely to affect them differently. Potentially traumatic events and separations, though caused by widespread patterns of family structure, are likely to have different effects even on children in the same family. Environmental differences among siblings is even greater where norms select first or last children (or sons) for special treatment, as in primogeniture or the practice of keeping the last child home. When we consider the preexisting genetic variations among siblings with which these environmental variables interact, we can see that the number of combinations and permutations among factors influencing the personality genotype is very great indeed. Structural determinants narrow the range of variation but they do not eliminate it. Thus, we might expect a given trauma or separation experience to be more "characteristic" of (more frequent in) one population than another but not uniform within it.

In sum, the personality genotype is an enduring organization of drives, cognitions, and adaptive capacities; is formed early in life; varies widely among individuals and (in frequency and central tendency) between populations; and acts as a series of constraints on later development and learning. Many of the formative influences on the personality genotype can be seen as indirect outcomes or byproducts of social structure, to which certain survival-oriented limits have probably evolved, and which necessarily narrow the range of genotypic dispositions in a population sharing a social-structural environment. Nevertheless, these formative influences are in most societies sufficiently variable in their impact on individual experience and sufficiently free of manipulative intent to be considered unplanned and nonnormative sources of personality variation.

The dispositions comprising the personality genotype are by definition latent and do not always find socially acceptable expression. It is as generalizable constraints on later learning and performance that their influence is manifested. The constraints stemming from the drive residues of infancy and childhood (as shaped by patterns of stimulation, attachment, and separation) act as internal motivational pressures for gratification, provide a symbolic interpretation of later social experience, and give direction and content to free choice behavior (as in interpersonal relations and fantasy). The constraints resulting from early ego development act as limits on the complexity and intensity of stimuli (external and internal) to which the individual can respond effectively and, therefore, constitute thresholds of perceptual discrimination and stress tolerance.

The Personality Phenotype

This refers to the observable regularities of behavior characterizing an adult functioning in the variety of settings comprising his environment. The personality phenotype of an individual includes his patterns of performance in social roles, in formal and informal settings, in interaction and alone, in coercive and free-choice situations, under stressful and relaxed conditions, in verbalization and actual behavior. It includes his conscious attitudes and values, his skills, competence and knowledge, and his preferences and tastes in recreational and hedonistic activities. If the individual is functioning normally, his phenotypic personality is a stable organization of characteristics that affords him satisfaction of his perceived needs, enables him to meet social demands and take advantage of sociocultural opportunities, and protects him from excessive anxiety.

The phenotype is not independent of the genotype; in a sense, it *is* the personality genotype modified by prolonged normative experience, through the deliberate socialization by parents and through direct participation in the wider social system. The phenotypic personality develops within the constraints of the genotype and, when formed, allows the unconscious motivational components of the latter normatively regulated expression in overt behavior. The most noticeable expressions in phenotypic behavior are idiosyncratic mannerisms, inhibitions, and other facets of distinctive behavioral style. These character traits, as they are called by psychoanalysts, are fixed stabilized expressions of defenses against unconscious impulses, and they frequently incorporate into their content some of the original impulse that is being defended against.

We are aware of the unconscious motivation of character traits when they are idiosyncratic and approach the limits of social acceptability, but we are generally incapable of seeing them in members of our own population when the behavior patterns involved are very common and completely acceptable. It takes a foreigner to point out to us the arbitrary, irrational, and perhaps compulsive quality of the behavior and make us realize that what we had seen as "natural," "normal," "rational," or "adaptive," because of its familiarity and normative acceptability, might be as unconscious in origin and defensive in function as an idiosyncratic mannerism. (For a general discussion of the "phenomenal absolutism" underlying culture-bound perception, see Segall *et al.*, 1966; for the use of outsiders' judgments in group personality assessment, see LeVine, 1966b.) It is not only idiosyncratic character traits that are defensive expressions of genotypic conflicts but also character traits widespread in the population; this is what Fromm (1941) and others have referred to as "social character." In the present perspective, social character refers to all character traits positively valued and relatively frequent in a population, and includes nondefensive (conflict-free) dispositions of the personality genotype that become enduring features of social behavior.

One of the most important integrating characteristics of the personality phenotype is a self-concept, an internal mental representation of the self that includes boundaries between, and identities with, the self and other individuals, groups, and ideologies. In his functioning as a member of society, the individual uses this enduring self-concept to monitor his own behavior and to determine the extent to which each of his behavior patterns is ego-syntonic, that is, consistent with his image of himself. This self-concept, having been produced in part through normative social experience, represents social norms as it selects among possible behaviors (in a manner analogous to other forms of variation and selection) those that are consistent with the socially acceptable image the individual wants to present to the world. In the category of unacceptable are behaviors seen as immoral, impolite, childish, stupid, crazy (or their nearest equivalents in other cultures); these are viewed as ego-dystonic, except under especially permissive conditions, and are eliminated in favor of more acceptable behaviors. When the individual loses the capacity to suppress certain behavior that he himself regards as unacceptable in one of those senses, when he is unable to keep his behavior ego-syntonic, he develops a neurotic symptom. When he alters his self-concept to include the defensive contents of a neurotic symptom (e.g., develops a rationalized inhibition out of a phobia), he has developed a neurotic character trait.

The distinction between genotypic and phenotypic personality contains elements of familiar behavioral science polarities—unconscious versus conscious, latent versus manifest, subjective versus objective, general versus specialized—but two other elements require further emphasis. First, the phenotypic personality is responsive to contemporaneous environmental pressures—in the form of real, threatened, or promised social rewards, punishments, incentives—whereas the genotype is the relatively unchanging "internal environment" of the personality, responsive only to its own past, and can be used for or against adaptation without altering its direction and content. In their phenotypic expression, genotypic dispositions may be suppressed and disguised for purposes of social adaptation and conformity but are not thereby eliminated.

Second, the personality genotype is inherently more variable and heterogeneous in a population than the phenotype; the former reflects individual constitution and experience, whereas the latter reflects the normative consensus of society. Insofar as populations have intact functioning social structures, there must be such a consensus represented in the phenotypic personalities of its members, no matter how diverse their underlying genotypic dispositions. In measuring these dispositions, the closer the investigator comes to what is explicitly prescribed by norms, the more agreement and homogeneity he finds in a population, whereas the closer he comes to normatively permissive areas of behavior—in which "free," (genotypically expressive) choice is possible—the more heterogeneity of response within the population. This has been less clear than it might be because terms such as *values* have been used to cover dispositions varying widely in their degree of normative prescriptiveness; hence some (usually

sociological) investigators, measuring individuals' perceptions or expectations of norms, find populations homogenous on values, while other
(usually psychological) investigators, measuring personal interests and
tastes, find a heterogeneity of values. It is in the nature of genotype-
phenotype relations, as conceptualized here, that the former will be
more variable than the latter unless a radical breakdown in social consensus has occurred.

Deliberate Socialization

This refers to the intentions and actions of the parents (or substitutes) in
training the child. In this process there are several factors: the child and
his presocialized behavior, the goals of the parents, the means they use
to achieve their goals, and the consequences of applying these means.

The argument can be anticipated briefly as follows: Parents use reward,
punishment, and instruction to shape the child's behavior, already genotypically influenced, in the direction of social norms; the typical result is
a phenotypic personality involving both preparedness for adaptation to
the adult environment and unsatisfied needs stemming from conflicts
between personality genotype and normative demands. The model of
training is that of behavioristic response-reinforcement theory, with the
added assumptions that the major formative influences on the child's
personality are ordinarily outside parental control and have acted before
deliberate parental training, and that parental reinforcement schedules,
whether effective or not, have unintended motivational consequences of
great importance for personality-culture interaction.

The child. No matter how early parents begin deliberate training, they
find neither a *tabula rasa* nor a passive receiving instrument in their child.
Even the infant is an active organism, striving and exploring within the
constraints of his constitutional dispositions and developmental immaturity. Parental training must deal with the child's unprovoked behavioral
output, and it must be geared to his perceptual thresholds and his
tolerance limits for particular types of stimulation. Some active infants
seem intractable to their parents; others are resistant to manipulation in
more passive ways, and parents may find the difficulties so great that they
postpone training to a later age. With the exception of the most consciously manipulative and ideologized parents, most parents in most
societies postpone the first onset of serious behavioral manipulation until
the child can talk, and they begin more intensive training in useful skills
when the child has "sense," usually at about five or six years of age. (In
some societies there are clear-cut phases of this type, while in others the
intensity of training is gradually increased.)

The child's behavioral development goes on regardless of whether
anyone is attempting to manipulate it and to produce desirable habits.

Maturational processes make new forms of behavior possible; and the child is continuously interacting with his environment, experiencing gratification and frustration, suffering trauma and separation, acquiring attachments and avoidances, observing the behavior of others, spontaneously imitating what he sees, developing pleasant and frightening fantasies and increasingly differentiated patterns of thought and action. Anyone who has observed two- and three-year-old children in a society where socialization in any serious purposive sense begins later than that, has seen behavior patterns of personal and cultural distinctiveness, obvious precursors of adult behavioral styles. These are early phenotypic expressions of the personality genotype, preceding the onset of manipulative training. Whenever the parent begins deliberate training of his child, be it at two or six years of age, he confronts not a completely unformed mass of clay ready to be shaped, but a set of genotypic dispositions that already give the child's behavior shape and purpose of its own not necessarily consistent with the parents' purposes. The parent, unlike the animal experimenter, cannot dispose of his subject and obtain a more tractable one; he must render the child tractable and amenable to training by persistent effort, by increasing reward and punishment as seems necessary, and by finding within the child dispositional allies that can be harnessed to the parent's goals. The personality genotype of the child sets the stage for impending conflict in the socialization process. And since each child in a family has a different personality genotype, each poses for its parents a different set of training problems.

Parental goals. The parent (assisted by other socializing agents and agencies) has the task of directing the behavioral (phenotypic) development of the child toward normative socially valued goals. Insofar as he performs this task, the parent is acting as a feedback mechanism, the mediator of environmental information to his child, implicitly communicating messages about discrepancies between the child's current behavior and environmental norms of behavior as he attempts to eliminate those discrepancies through training. More immediately, however, the parent's training program is determined by his phenomenal field, a field in which environmental information is only one of several forces and may be muted in its effect on parental behavior.

The phenomenal field of the parent is his view of the child-training situation as influenced by factors internal and external to that situation. In such a field of forces, a number of determinants contribute (positively and negatively) to a few resultant outcomes. The outcomes in this case are decisions concerning child training; the determinants are all the sources of pressure, constraint, belief, and value that influence his training decisions. Some of these sources are in the parent's personality; some are in the social system in which he participates; and some are in the behavior of the child with whom he interacts. Research into parental phenomenal fields has been fragmentary and incomplete so that we do not have a clear picture of how the diverse forces combine, or what their valences are, or how they are assigned valences that account for their relative contributions to the resultant decisions. We do have some idea of the range of forces involved. Brim (1959) has referred to this complexity:

> With respect to the six causes of parent behavior considered here, one recognizes that the individual operates or behaves in his parent role as part of a social system. The parent engages in behavior vis-a-vis the child in interaction situations which are regulated by social norms or rules as to what is appropriate and inappropriate. As an individual, the parent is also restricted by repressed and unconscious motives which work to determine his behavior in parent role performance in ways unknown to him. Moreover, the pressures of time and the demands of the conflicting social situations involved in a large family as well as restrictions placed upon behavior by the absence of certain economic goods, whether these be living space, the absence of toys, or more generally, the simple absence of money, all work to limit the rational and self-controlled performance of the role (p. 55).

Some of the influences on child-training decisions are enduring parameters of the parent's personality: his intelligence, his internalized moral and social values (reflecting in part normative information from the environment in which he grew up); his preferences, sensitivities, and aversions derived from unconscious genotypic dispositions. Other influences originate in relatively permanent aspects of his life situation: concepts of competence based on his occupational experience, concepts of his social and economic environment based on the breadth of his experience (including travel), the structure of housing and settlement in which he is raising his child, and traditional folk beliefs concerning child training. Still other influences are long-term but recurrent pressures generated by the life situation: work fatigue, marital adjustment, other family relationships. Then there are influences that change with the development of the family, including the number of other children and their ages, the parent's experience as a trainer of children, and the generalizations he has drawn from observing the effects of previous child training. Finally, there are the immediate, but not necessarily recurrent or developmental, pressures such as short-run economic necessity, which may give one parent less time to spend with the child or make the child's early occupational maturity seem more important, current child-care fashions, and other potentially relevant persuasive communications to which the parent is exposed (e.g., through the mass media). All of these interact with the child as perceived by the parent, who may attempt to tailor his training program to what he sees as this particular child's individual characteristics. The complexity of this interaction can be illustrated by the case of the parent whose first male child, being particularly demanding, reactivates in the parent jealousy from his own early experience with a younger brother, and who therefore is particularly punitive in training this child, affecting the entire training process with this inappropriate emotion.

These influences on the parent's definition of the child-training situation operate, as Brim suggests, to limit his role as a simple mediator of environmental norms; they act as a filter through which environmental information must pass if it is to affect the training of the child. The parent lacking in the ability to think abstractly may see no connection between environmental events and his child's behavior; the ignorant or provincial parent may be simply unaware of the broader environmental context of his life; the parent engaged in marital conflict may not pay attention to external events and norms; the parent dominated by unconscious wishes and fears may misperceive environmental cues or inaccurately transform them into child-training practices. If a parent is under intense pressure to adjust to difficult domestic or economic conditions, these may come to dominate his thinking to such an extent that he thinks only of his child's adaptation to similar conditions, neglecting other goals. The parent, then, is often not a smoothly operating child-preparation machine.

Given so many possibilities for faulty transmission between adult performance criteria and child-training goals, one might wonder how parents are able to perform this function at all. They are able to do so in relatively stable societies because the more enduring influences on their phenomenal fields are not independent of contemporaneous environmental information concerning future adaptation of their child; the parents' internalized values and life experience and their current life pressures approximate the child's future environment well enough to act as adaptive guides to training even in the absence of accurate and conscious parental transmission of environmental information, and child training is thus overdetermined. In rapidly changing societies or immigration situations, however, discontinuities between past, present, and future environments force parents to attune themselves to the environment and seek from it novel information about adult performance criteria or see their children suffer the effects of serious maladaptation as adults (see Inkeles, 1955; Miller and Swanson, 1958). It should be no surprise, then, that rapidly changing societies provide our best examples of parents attempting to rationalize their child training in terms of feedback from the environment, as well as our most familiar instances of maladaptation, for example among rural immigrants to the city who fail to change their child-training goals rapidly enough to provide their children the competence they need for economic viability and mobility in urban industrial society (see Inkeles, 1966a).

Despite the complex determination of parental phenomenal fields and the equally complex variations in the filtration they provide for environmental information, the theoretical model of parental mediation is a simple one. Parents want their children to be able to meet societal demands and to take advantage of the opportunities for personal success or fulfillment (social, economic, political) that the sociocultural environment offers. These are their most general training objectives. To attain them, the parents must anticipate what demands and opportunities the child will face in adulthood, through generalization of their own direct and vicarious experience as participant observers in a sociocultural system approximating that of the future adult, or through a conscious search for new information about social norms and payoffs, or both. This information about the normative environment as the parent sees it gives him a view of what he is preparing the child for, and can be translated into criteria for evaluating behavior patterns manifested by the child. Although there can be a good deal of slippage between the objective sociocultural environment and evaluative decisions made by the parent, parental mediation is at least theoretically self-correcting in that, in situations where the parent's own past experience is not an adequate guide for the child, the social payoffs for adaptation and penalties for maladaptation increase in value and hence in salience for parents, increasing the pressure on them to notice discrepancies between their children's behvaior and societal norms.

One set of conclusions the parent draws from participant observation in his normative environment concerns the kinds of personality traits and types that lead to respectable, righteous, and pragmatically successful adult behavior. He sees persons varying in personality characteristics receive varying amounts of endorsement or resistance from the sociocultural system, and he aggregates these instances and arrives at inductive generalizations concerning personality ideals that, if compatible with other parts of his cognitive structure, will act as a guide to the qualities he will attempt to reinforce and eliminate in his child.

Parental means. To give normative shape to the child's behavior, the parent has a number of means at his disposal. First is his power to reward and punish the child, based not only on control of resources seen by the child as necessary or desirable to his welfare but also on the child's emotional attachment to and dependence on the parent. No less important is his knowledge of adaptive skills in which to instruct the willing child. Since the parent, especially in the more differentiated societies, does not himself command all the skills he wants his child to learn, he delegates part of the training task to specialists—as tutors, and in schools and institutionalized apprenticeships. Although he certainly uses reinforcement procedures himself, the parent is not simply an administrator of rewards and punishments but an executive of sorts, making decisions about what kind of training is needed, who should give it to the child, and what level of performance the child should reach.

The role of verbal and behavioral feedback is critical in distinguishing the processes of deliberate socialization from the unplanned acquisition of behavioral dispositions through early experience. In deliberate socialization, the parent is specific enough in his goals and the child developed enough in his responses that it is possible for the trainer to gauge his immediate success or failure in attaining a training goal and then modify the quantity or quality of his reinforcement accordingly. The feedback permits establishment of a self-correcting system of training, with parental training being varied in response to the child's performance until the desired performance is achieved, a highly efficient way of shaping behavior. As mentioned before, parents who seek to extend purposive manipulation into the early life of the child are particularly concerned that their children acquire language skills as early as possible so that they can obtain verbal feedback as to the effectiveness of their training procedures. But feedback from nonverbal behavior also enables the parent to adjust his training to the child's performance and improves his ability to obtain desired results. Feedback is also essential in parental decisions concerning nonparental training: a parent who sees his child doing badly in school may decide that special tutoring is required to insure the child's admission to a higher school later on. The ultimate in self-regulation is achieved if the child acts on the basis of his own feedback to correct his mistakes and improve his performance, which children do when they have internalized adult standards of performance.

Through these conditioning processes the child acquires a range of adaptive skills that, along with earlier patterns of social behavior, become habitualized in a normative direction. It must be emphasized, however, that deliberate socialization operates predominantly on overt behavior, on the behavioral phenotype, and modifies only the overt expressions of the personality genotype—suppressing some genotypic tendencies, permitting restricted expression of others, disguising some for socially sanctioned behavior, and using others for adaptive purposes. The resultant character structure is thus based on but not reducible to the personality genotype that, in the process of deliberate socialization, has its first but far from last encounter with the normative pressures of the sociocultural environment.

Consequences. Socialization has intended and unintended products. Its intended products are skills and inhibitions, skills for adaptive performance, inhibitions of genotypic tendencies incompatible with normative demands. Unintended products include the various motivational side-effects of suppressing or attenuating genotypic tendencies.

The cross-cultural evidence taken as a whole indicates how extremely effective deliberate socialization is in producing adaptive skills in growing individuals. At the level of skills related to subsistence activity and dominant cultural values, the old idea that "culture" can turn the child into anything "it" wants seems to receive strong support: In groups to whom waterways are importantly involved in subsistence, children learn to swim early and well (Mead, 1930); in some agricultural groups, six-year-old children can cultivate fields (LeVine & LeVine, 1966); children of political elites learn respect behavior when they are tiny (Read, 1959). The evidence concerning the acquisition of skills in children so strongly suggests their great malleability that it is virtually taken for granted that if pressures are exerted in a given aspect of training, the majority of children in a population will comply even if the tasks are complex.

The matter of inhibitions is more complex. At one level, this type of socialization is highly effective, too, in producing compliance with social constraints. There is little question that if enough negative pressure is brought to bear in the socialization process, highly motivated behaviors such as sexuality and aggression can be suppressed so thoroughly in most of the population that they seem almost nonexistent to the casual observer. But suppression is not elimination, and while phenotypic expressions can be brought into line even with strict cultural prohibitions, the underlying genotypic dispositions, both motivational and cognitive, cannot be "extinguished." Indeed, Whiting and Child (1953) have argued that the inhibition of a motive through socialization actually increases its strength, although altering its direction in favor of objects dissimilar to those that were culturally prohibited (displacement).

The impossibility of eliminating common genotypic motives through socialization of the child is frequently encountered in studies of particular cultures. For example, in my own work (LeVine, 1959) I found that the Gusii, although known among the peoples of Western Kenya for their sexual prudishness, and although maintaining strict sexual prohibitions in many areas of life, had a very high frequency of rape by local and cross-cultural standards. Gusii socialization of sex, being strict and repressive concerning public manifestations of sexuality but relatively permissive concerning sexual feelings and clandestine sexual acts, was predicated on the existence of enforcement procedures (inter-clan feuding) that had broken down during British colonial administration. At the time of my field work, the strict sex-training practices, although still effective in maintaining conformity to intra-clan prohibitions, did nothing to prevent inter-clan sex offenses and could even be seen as promoting rape by raising the average level of male sexual frustration and making females resistant to heterosexual advances. Hence the paradox of an ethnic group notorious for both its prudery and its sex crimes. Whiting *et al.* (1966) present another example in the case of the Zuni Indians, whose well known emphasis on harmony and peaceful solidarity is belied by their intense and frequent malicious intrigues over witchcraft. The authors argue that the strict socialization of aggression in Zuni children is necessitated by the crowded housing conditions in which they are raised but that their aggressive motivations find an outlet in witchcraft beliefs and clandestine intrigues.

In both these instances, socialization of the child brings about overt conformity to prohibitive standards in one arena of social life but leads to unintended consequences based on the suppressed genotypic dispositions in other arenas. The social system "pays" for social control in visible primary group relations with a certain amount of disruption and strain behind the scenes or beyond the confines of the primary group. This social "cost" factor appears to be present wherever social norms require suppression of motives in the socialization of the child. Parents are then put in the position of unwittingly fostering deviant behavior as they consciously attempt to build into their children the inhibitions that will enable them to conform to institutional demands, although quite possibly institutional functioning gains more from the conformity than it loses in the deviant behavior; an evolutionary model would require this for a stable system. Where socialization of the child's impulse life is so thorough that he becomes a self-policing individual, it may be, as Freud proposed, that the cost is paid not by the social system but by the individual, who turns his socially unacceptable impulses against himself and suffers self-punishment, painful neurotic symptoms, and crippling inhibitions. This situation may be optimal for institutional functioning, unless the incidence of psychopathology and discontent become so great as to exact their own toll from the social system.

Thus adaptation of the individual to his sociocultural environment begins in the process of child socialization but is not successfully completed there, partly because the parent is an imperfect mediator of environmental pressures and often cannot anticipate them accurately, and partly because deliberate socialization can have unintended consequences that are maladaptive. This means that adaptation must be a continuing process in adult life, although many of the basic patterns of adaptive behavior are established in the training of the child. But there are, as we have seen, limits to the modification of individual behavior in the interests of adaptation to institutional environment, limits stemming from the personality genotype as a highly resistant organization of motives and cognitive dispositions. The genotypic tendencies can be suppressed, disguised, and diverted, but they are hardly ever eliminated in socialization through the life cycle. They seek expression in overt behavior, and no social system is so prescriptive and coercive as to prevent such expressions; there are always loopholes in normative prescriptions for role performance, areas for choice, and alternative possibilities. Therefore, the sociocultural environment must bend at points before these inflexibilities of the personality system, and adaptation is achieved through compromise. Institutionalized forms of adaptation between personality and sociocultural systems can be seen as compromise formations in which constraints and demands of both the personality genotype and the normative environment are represented. They have evolved from the interaction of environmental and genotypic pressures operating over time. Although movement is toward a steady state in which the more pressing demands of both sides are adequately satisfied, many particular institutionalized adaptations are "bad" compromises, in which one side or another is over-represented. The forms of institutionalized adaptation and the processes of stability and change constitute the second part of this evolutionary model and are presented in the next two chapters.

Conclusions

On the basis of this first part of an evolutionary model of culture-personality relations, it is possible to locate those points at which processes analogous to the Darwinian mechanisms of variation and selection seem to be operating and to identify relevant problems for empirical research.

1. *The adaptation of early child-care customs to ecological pressures.* Since infants must survive a period of high mortality and acquire basic adaptive skills for a population to survive, it is reasonable to assume that the infant-care customs of stable or growing populations are a product of an evolutionary process in which poorly adapted populations failed to survive, were absorbed into better adapted populations, or radically changed their customs of infant care. This process requires evolving limits on the extent to which the structure of primary groups in which children are raised can be altered in accordance with the requirements of the wider social structure. It may be, however, that this process makes more positive contributions to personality-environment adaptation. For example, Nimkoff and Middleton (1960) have shown that families in hunting and gathering societies are smaller than in agricultural societies, and we know from studies within our own culture (see Clausen, 1966) that smaller families produce children different in certain behavioral dimensions (*e.g.*, higher on achievement even with social class held constant). This accords with the finding of Barry, Child, and Bacon (1959) that parents in hunting and gathering societies emphasize self-reliance and achievement in child training, but it does not necessarily support their assumption that it is the deliberate socialization of the parents that produces requisite amounts of these dispositions in their children to maintain the subsistence economy.

Could it be that children raised in small families have early experiences that equip them with genotypic dispositions making them easier to train in self-reliance and achievement? That this greater potential for self-reliance and achievement helped give small families a selective advantage in hunting and gathering groups? Or perhaps more reasonably, could it be that the greater potential for obedience and responsibility of children raised in large families contributed to the selective advantage of large domestic groups once the food-producing revolution had occurred? These are difficult problems to study, but they raise the possibility that the structure of the primary groups in which children are raised may be more tightly adapted to ecological pressures than is readily apparent, with the personality outcome of early primary group experience being a factor in the evolution of more adaptive forms. Although the mechanisms involved are far from clear, this type of evolutionary conceptualization, closer to the original Darwinian model, is a challenging source of rival hypotheses for theorists who tend to assign to conscious parental mediation and deliberate socialization the central roles in child rearing.

2. *The initial adaptation of genotypically varying personalities to normative pressures through deliberate socialization.* In this process, the distribution of personality genotypes provides the unplanned variation, and the parent's values and decisions concerning child training constitute the selective criteria. The variation-selection model fits at the level of the population, in which normatively agreeing parents act selectively on the randomly varying personality genotypes of their children, and at the level of the parent-child dyad, in which the child's behavioral output, at first haphazardly compatible and incompatible with parental goals, is shaped toward greater compatibility by the differential reinforcement of the parent. To a degree not adequately documented and undoubtedly variable cross culturally, the parent acts as an agent of society and in response to its changing norms, so that child training helps prepare the child for future normative environments. This preparation cannot be completed in childhood because child training cannot anticipate in all their specificity the micro- and macroenvironments to which the future adult will adapt. So this is initial adaptation, in which the child develops some skills and inhibitory controls that will facilitate his subsequent adaptive behavior.

3. *The secondary adaptations of individual personality to normative environments through selective social behavior.* This has to do with differing genotype-phenotype relations within the personality of the individual as he occupies differing normative environments (including social roles) successively or simultaneously. The personality genotype is a continual source of impulses, wishes, and ideas that constitute unplanned variation from the viewpoint of performance in social roles. The individual has in the normatively shaped self-image that is central to his phenotypic social character a set of criteria for selecting among these genotypic impulses. Furthermore, each role or other ecological niche he occupies provides its own criteria for evaluating and administering rewards and punishments for behavior of varying degrees of compatibility with his genotypic dispositions. Operating within the limits set by his

own (perhaps temporarily) stabilized self-image, he responds to the demand characteristics of the microenvironment, experiencing or antici- pating reward and punishment for genotypically derived behaviors until some of the underlying dispositions are selected for expression in overt behavior, others for suppression, displacement, or disguise, in a stabilized adaptation to the niche. On a similarly experimental basis he selectively regulates the amount and kind of genotypic expression in the various environmental niches that comprise his life situation, until a total life adaptation is reached. If he moves from one role or status position to another or otherwise alters his life situation, the selective process will be repeated.

4. *The adaptation of aggregate personality characteristics of populations to normative environments through the selective pressure of social sanctions.* This refers to the means by which the frequency distributions of phenotypic character traits in a population come to fit the society-wide normative ideals of role performance, or at least to be skewed in that direction, compared to societies with other normative ideals. The details of this are presented in Chapters 9 and 10 and can be dealt with only briefly here. Phenotypic character traits, although normatively influenced and shaped, are still highly variable in a population because they are embedded in different personality structures, with varying genotypic capacities for approximating ideal role performance. Some persons have genotypic personality traits that are favored by the normative environ- ment in which they function; in consequence they manifest greater talent, skill, and fluency in role performance, are able to take greater advantage of opportunities, and achieve greater success and other social rewards. Other persons, though able to acquire normatively sanctioned character traits through socialization and subsequent secondary adapta- tion, have a harder time conforming and performing in roles because their genotypic dispositions are less compatible with environmental de- mands and opportunities; in consequence they do not manifest excellence in role performance, are less able to gain success and social rewards, and are more likely to engage in deviant behavior and incur negative sanctions. This variation in social competence (see Inkeles, 1966a) is con- stantly being acted upon by social sanctions, with the effect of differen- tially distributing social rewards and punishments (*e.g.*, success and failure, upward and downward mobility, honor and stigma, prestige and disgrace) in accordance with demonstrated level of competence on a more or less permanent basis.

In addition, the operation of this selective procedure is highly visible to actors in the social system, particularly in societies in which status mobility is possible, so that knowledge of which character traits are associated with competence becomes widespread and affects the deliber- ate socialization of children. There is thus a feedback from the selective pressure of social sanctions on adults to parental training of children, inducing parents to train their children to meet operative standards of competence. Over time, this feedback, if consistent, results in the production through socialization of a higher frequency of persons with character traits labeled as competent, until some stable state is reached. In societies where relatively little mobility is possible, stability may have been reached such a long time before that the feedback is no longer necessary, since parents' internalized norms are an adequate guide to socially approved competence without redundant observation of environmental selection. This conception of personality-environment adaptation is applied by LeVine (1966a) to relations between status-mobility systems and frequency of achievement motivation in research on three Nigerian ethnic groups.

The Darwinian variation-selection model provides a plausible conceptualization of culture-personality relations in adaptive terms, so long as one identifies those junctures in social and psychological functioning at which unplanned variation and cumulative selection can reasonably be thought to operate. Rather than a single adaptive process bringing personality and sociocultural environment into some kind of fit, there are variation and selection mechanisms operating at numerous levels toward stable integration of individual dispositions and social norms. The fact that human adaptation of this kind is not attained through a single fixed mechanism probably permits greater flexibility and efficiency of adaptation and more rapid adjustment to environmental change.

In terms of research implications, this model permits great variability among populations in responsiveness to environmental feedback and in tightness of conscious control over selection, and assigns a central role to the purposive behavior of parents and other socializing agents. It is parents who decide how to organize relations between environments and children, and we need to know much more about the cognitive and other bases for their decisions before we can understand how these relations are organized in culturally differing populations.

From this theoretical perspective, then, the most urgent objective for empirical research on socialization is to understand the relation between the planned and unplanned aspects of social learning, how this relation varies among societies, and the kinds of adaptations that are made possible with varying degrees of conscious linkage between environmental feedback and deliberate socialization. In their central position as socializing agents, parents are able to act on their perceptions of the child's personality and the environment's demands and opportunities to create the basis for adaptive fit between personality and culture; it is essential that we investigate more intensively what these perceptions are and how parents organize their perceptions to arrive at training decisions.

9

Adaptive Processes I: Stability

This chapter concerns the varieties of psychosocial adaptations that become stabilized in socially acceptable patterns of behavior. Its basic premise is that the operative social expectations for phenotypic (observable) behavior in a given role represent a stabilized compromise between private motives of high frequency in the personality genotypes of role incumbents and normative pressures stemming from public definitions of the role. The concept of a compromise formation originates in the work of Freud, who in 1896 proposed that neurotic symptoms could be seen in these terms and later extended their applicability to dreams (1900) and many other imaginative and "accidental" acts of the individual. In 1923 he summarized the concept and its usage succinctly:

> [Analytic] work has shown that the dynamics of the formation of dreams are the same as those of the formation of symptoms. In both cases we find a struggle between two trends, of which one is unconscious and ordinarily repressed and strives toward satisfaction—that is, wish-fulfillment—while the other, belonging probably to the conscious ego, is disapproving and repressive. The outcome of this conflict is a *compromise-formation* (the dream or the symptom) in which both trends have found an incomplete expression (1923b, p. 242).

The compromise formed in the dream or symptom is a creative synthesis of the two trends, involving imaginative disguises for the repressed wish, according to the principles (of condensation, displacement, etc.) which Freud presented in *The Interpretation of Dreams* (1900). Here we are concerned with cultural forms that are compromises of this type, integrating norm and motive, or what Spiro (1961a) has referred to as "duty and desire." The problem was formulated in approximately these terms by Fromm (1941) and has been discussed in functionalist terms by Parsons (1949, 1964), Inkeles and Levinson (1954) and Spiro (1961a).

These discussions, and particularly that of Spiro, which is most relevant here, are focused primarily on the "optimal" case in which normative demands and personal motives coincide (are "functionally congruent," in the terminology of Inkeles and Levinson), so that a single set of role behavior patterns satisfies both; they attempt to account for this adaptation in terms of the processes of socialization and social control that maintain it. In the present treatment, this type of compromise, which satisfies both parties, is seen as a special case among psychosocial adaptations; "bad" compromises are given more attention because they appear to be no less frequent and because their greater potential for instability makes them essential to the understanding of psychosocial change. My evolutionary model differs from the functionalist framework in putting less emphasis on the need to maintain equilibrium and more on the variety of stable and unstable adaptations that exist at one point in time.

Three major types of psychosocial adaptations, or motivational bases for conformity to cultural norms, are outlined below: willing conformity, coerced conformity with motivational displacements, and normative pluralism.

Willing Conformity

This is the adaptive pattern presented in theoretical detail by Spiro (1961a); in it, role behavior serves vital functions simultaneously for the social system in which the role is located and for the personality system of the role incumbent. This optimal compromise is based on a congruence in the behavioral imperatives of institutional norms governing role performance and of genotypic personality dispositions of high frequency. Optimal adaptive fit, at this level of organism-environment relations as at others, can be achieved in several ways. The fit can have evolved through a process of selective institutionalization so that the institutional norms transmitted from the previous generation are designed, so to speak, to give personal satisfaction to the present generation. This is the model of fit that Spiro and other functionalist theorists have in mind. But it is not the only possible one.

Another model of optimal adaptive fit between the distribution of genotypic personality dispositions and institutional norms is one in which the norms permit enough latitude for each individual to develop his own adaptive solution through trial-and-error and selective propagation. This model is the explicit ideal of American graduate education, at least at the dissertation level, for it is believed that original scholarship cannot be institutionally formulated in detail but must be worked out by each student in terms of his own interests and capacities, within the broad constraints of scholarly standards. Such a model of optimal adaptive fit is widely applicable, even in bureaucratic and other formal organizations (see Levinson, 1959). The criteria of success in economic and political competition (where competition is itself institutionalized) are broad enough to allow a variety of adaptive solutions developed by individuals to meet their own needs and the demands of their ecological niche. The situation in which the normative mandate or prescription is loose enough to allow individual variants based on individual preference and choice is very common in human societies. Although the nonindustrial societies in which many anthropologists work often seem inclined toward traditional adaptive solutions, the bias of relatively short-term ethnographic observation may exaggerate this tendency, obscuring the normative latitude that has permitted role incumbents to refashion traditional prescriptions while maintaining the appearance of rigid conformity to them. We are justifiably impressed by how often persons want to do what they must do, but we need to pay a great deal of attention to the extent to which cultural norms allow them to redefine what they must do and to do it on terms dictated by their inner needs rather than those received from the institutional program. This requires a finer-grained ethnography than we have had to date.

Willing conformity as the optimal adaptive fit between personality genotypes in a population and normative pressures in its sociocultural environment, worked out through both selective institutionalization and individually selective variation, contributes to sociocultural stability and represents the goal toward which processes of psychosocial change are continually moving. But it is not the only stabilized form of psychosocial adaptation, and thinking of it as such can be misleading, as the following discussion of other forms will illustrate.

Coerced Conformity

The opposite form of psychosocial adaptation is coerced conformity, in which the individual submits to the normative pressures in a role that effectively forbid expression of private motives aroused in that role. This situation is widespread among persons in subordinate castes, servant roles, and subject populations under repressive dictatorships, and it can also occur in a variety of less obvious circumstances where personality genotype and normative pressure make incompatible behavioral demands. Spiro (1961a) argues, quite correctly, that coerced conformity is motivated behavior and can operate only with motivational predispositions of the individual. It is, nevertheless, true that norms of role performance vary in the prescriptive and proscriptive constraints they impose on the individual and on the enforcement of those constraints through fear of punishment or concern for survival. When the spontaneity of role incumbents in performing according to norms is expected to be low, formal constraints may be imposed on their behavior and negative sanctions employed to enforce them; the more formal and explicit the constraints and the harsher the sanctions, the closer phenotypic role behavior is to coerced rather than willing conformity. Coercion is most frequently found when the role performance situation itself arouses the motive (activates a disposition in the personality genotype) but forbids it expression. Another way of putting this is that the institutional regulation of individual behavior through coercion is usually focused on the possible selection of personally attractive behavioral options in the role situation that would interfere with institutional norms. This holds for incest taboos, relationships between persons of unequal status, and interaction between rich and poor; the most strict proscriptions are associated with the most immediate temptations. I do not mean that conformity in these situations is normally attained by a rational calculus of pains and pleasures but rather that mass conformity can only be assured by adding an element of coercion to the role situation.

Since the genotypic dispositions of individuals are not eliminated by normative regulation, their prohibition in one institutional domain usually means individuals will seek to express and satisfy them in another, and a cultural belief or ideology may be required to give cognitive consistency to the differential behavior. The legitimized displacement of the motivated behavior and the cognitive framework for it can be seen as a culturally constituted defense mechanism or defensive structure, in the conceptualization of Hallowell (1955) and Spiro (1965). Cultural norms deny private satisfaction in one domain, permit it in another, and provide a way of thinking about it that helps maintain this institutional segregation of individual behavior. As the examples that follow indicate, such a model of coerced conformity with motivational displacement has many parallels with the psychoanalytic theory of neurotic symptom formation.

Four distinct, but not necessarily incompatible, types of culturally constituted defenses can accompany coerced conformity: psychophysiological palliatives, ideological palliatives, institutionalized deviance, and compartmentalized rebelliousness.

Psychophysiological palliatives are forms of recreational behavior involving the use of alcohol, narcotics, sexual discharge, or strenuous exercise that serve to release the *tension* of coerced conformity without a cultural prescription for the *ideational content* of the expressive behavior. The culture provides legitimacy for devoting part of one's daily or weekly cycle of activities to experiencing the release occasioned by these psychophysiological interventions, and it also provides the conventionalized understanding that motivational expression in that state can be disowned by the person as not being part of the public image by which he is to be socially evaluated. The cultural category of play or recreation (or its nearest equivalent) serves to deny the reality and importance of the motives that find expression while tension is being released; it is part of a cognitive framework in which phenotypic coerced conformity is accepted at face value, while recreational behavior, within prescribed limits, is denied the status of genuine public information about persons. Under conditions of coerced conformity, recreational institutions will be actively exploited by those who experience the coercion and will become important avenues for the partial expression of personal antisocial impulses. The term *palliative* is used to indicate the relationship between the coerced role performance and the motivational displacement; the latter—institutionally confined to the recreational portion of the person's life and accompanied by the release of psychophysiological tension—makes the former tolerable and thereby helps to maintain it. The recreational patterns of subordinate castes and classes—involving periodic bouts of drunkenness, brawling, sexual activity—provide many obvious examples.

Ideological palliatives are cultural beliefs that offer relief from suffering or heavily disguised expression of forbidden motives. Like psychophysiological palliatives, they represent displacements from the domain of coercive regulation to another institutional domain, but ideological palliatives provide cognitive *binding* of the tension rather than its immediate release in acting out (although the two may be combined in spirit possession and ecstatic religious experience). In this case, the culture prescribes the ideational context that the individual uses to satisfy his needs, and in its institutionalized form it is usually accorded a higher place in the public life of a community than recreational behavior. A most familiar example is to be found in religious doctrines of a paradisiacal life after death or progressively improving reincarnations, when they help make tolerable oppressive conditions of life. Sundkler (1948) provides striking evidence of how the Zulu, deprived of their political autonomy, displaced their political (and many other) aspirations into the religious activity permitted them by the South African government. The most wish fulfilling religious sects, however, clearly make coercive conformity tolerable rather than threatening to change it. Spiro has argued (1966) and illustrated (1967) that religion serves to alleviate individual suffering, and certainly there would be suffering even if there were no normative coercion. But I believe that where coercive conformity exists as a form of psychosocial adaptation, religion will be used as a means of alleviating and partly rationalizing the resultant suffering on a regular basis, and can thereby become an indirect psychological support for coercive regulation. Both kinds of palliatives involve motivational displacement within the temporal structure of the individual life; other kinds of displacement are described below.

Institutionalized deviance permits permanent release from coercive conformity for a small proportion of the population providing they bear the visible stigma of their deviation. This serves the double function of providing a regular place in the social structure for those who might otherwise rebel against it while reminding others that the price of deviation is to be stigmatized as not entirely acceptable in all social contexts. The Plains Indian *berdache* (male transvestite exempted from military duty) is a familiar example, but many types of professional entertainers and religious specialists in many societies also fall into this category.

Finally, there is compartmentalized rebelliousness, which in a sense involves the least displacement from the locus of coercive regulation but perhaps the greatest attenuation of the regulated motive. I refer to a rebellious style or manner of role behavior which, while interfering with the explicit institutional functions of the role to only a minimal degree, nevertheless communicates the resentments that would seriously interfere if they were given greater expression. This is not uncommon in servants and those employed in serving occupations who are extrinsically motivated and find the role incompatible with their self-concepts. In their style and manner (termed "role distance" by Goffman, 1961b) they release tension, assure both themselves and others that their self-concept does not fit the role, and yet manage to retain their means of support.

These four kinds of culturally constituted defensive structures are hardly exhaustive or rigorously defined, but they illustrate the cultural means available for maintaining coercive conformity as a psychosocial adaptation in certain institutional domains by providing both alternative pathways of tension release and a consistent cognitive framework for synthesizing normative constraint with the genotypic motive it displaces.

Normative Pluralism

The above discussions of willing and coerced conformity include the assumption of a single society-wide set of cultural norms for role performance, but in socially differentiated societies there are many norms, reflecting the division of society into culturally distinct social strata, geographical regions, rural and urban communities, ethnic groups, religious sects, sodalities, occupational groups, and so forth. Where membership in these groups is not hereditary but at least partly a matter of voluntary association, it is possible for a person to choose those whose norms are compatible with the motives in his personality genotype. In complex mobile societies like our own, persons do indeed choose occupation, church, recreational club, political party, civic association partly on the basis of what they call their "interests," a term by which they represent their motives to themselves. In complex but more traditional societies like those of India or the Yoruba of Western Nigeria, within a single religious system there are many cults of different gods and goddesses serving distinct functions and appealing to persons with particular kinds of afflictions, problems, and interests. Whenever alternative normative environments are available to the individual, there will be a process of selective recruitment by which individuals will find groups that best match their personality genotypes. Thus specialized psychosocial adaptations will occur in a variety of ecological niches.

It might be argued that the result is simply willing conformity, differentiated within a society. That is true in a descriptive sense, but it is important to note the different processes by which willing conformity is achieved under conditions of normative uniformity and normative pluralism. Where there is a single set of society-wide institutional norms differentiated only by age, sex, and status roles, as in many agricultural and hunting-and-gathering societies, the problem is posed of developing a psychosocial compromise between the relatively constant normative demands and an entire population's range of variation in personality genotypes. This tends to be solved partly through deliberate socialization, which is largely completed before puberty and is designed to endow the child with a permanent prescription for adaptive and satisfying behavior. Insofar as a single prescriptive solution does not work for all individuals because of genotypic variations and differentiated normative demands, two other mechanisms are used. One is permissible variation in certain areas of role performance, without stigmatizing that variation as deviant or even granting it social recognition. It is possible for some norms to be maintained by maintaining the pretense that they are rigidly enforced on a uniform basis, while permitting a great deal of individually expressive variation that escapes social notice. This is evident, for example, in societies with a structure of formal leadership based exclusively on kinship and age: when incompetent persons attain office, norms concerning the relationships of leaders and their advisers are often violated without public recognition. Thus there are institutional domains of loose normative regulation.

The other mechanism, in domains where tighter normative regulation is dictated by institutional demands, is the use of ritual, in which emotions are collectively evoked by cultural symbols to give a more homogeneous direction to the social behavior of individuals, while allowing disguised expression of some antinormative motives. This is exemplified by those African "rituals of rebellion" (Gluckman, 1963) in which traditional political loyalties and sex-status norms are publicly reinforced as followers and women ritually express their resentments. It is early and relatively rigid deliberate socialization supplemented by a combination of ritual regulation and permissive unrecognized variation that constitutes the formula for compromise between uniform norms and genotypic variation in a population. Insofar as this compromise formula for willing conformity does not work, sanctions to coerce conformity provide an institutionalized supplement.

The processes contributing to psychosocial adaptation are quite different in socially differentiated societies with normative pluralism. This type of compromise is first of all based on a cultural value of ethical relativity; it is understood and accepted in the population that its members do not conform to a single set of norms but may select a normative niche on the basis of personal preference. This value affects deliberate socialization, encouraging parents to permit the child's development of preferences that might determine his future adaptation rather than attempt to give him a permanent prescriptive solution. Social maturity is postponed until the individual is regarded as capable of making normative choices for himself, and the processes of choice (occupational, religious, recreational, and so forth) by the individual and selective recruitment by the normatively differentiated institutional structures of society are socially recognized and institutionalized in formal recruitment and admissions procedures. This is not the willing conformity of the normatively uniform society, but one that is consciously based on a self-motivated selection among socially accepted alternatives and that includes a consciousness of the alternatives that were rejected as incompatible with the individual's perception of his genotypic dispositions. For a proper understanding of the stability and flexibility of psychosocial adaptation, and the personality dispositions involved, it is essential to understand the social-psychological processes by which it is achieved, in addition to understanding its product in an observable compromise between individual motive and cultural norm. This emphasis on psychosocial adaptations as diachronic processes rather than synchronic products is a major point of distinction between the present model and functionalist formulations on personality and sociocultural systems.

Institutionalization and Psychological Process

The varieties of adaptive compromise have been discussed in this chapter as outcomes of processes operating within the individual's life space and lifespan, but they should also be seen in historical context—something frequently out of focus in functional analyses. Sociocultural environments as described by functional anthropologists often seem to be coherent and rational systems with logically connected parts, geared to fulfillment of both individual and collective purposes. Such descriptions usually provide an understanding of adaptive relationships without explicating the processes by which they came about or their differing values for the individual. In my view, institutional environments are not rational systems but are continually being rationalized in the ideologies that are presented to ethnographers by their informants. The process of making norms or beliefs fit together cognitively accompanies the institutionalization of that norm or belief and contributes to its psychosocial transformation over time. It is analogous to the secondary revision of dreams as described by Freud (1900), which he himself attempted to apply to folk explanations for taboos in nonliterate societies (Freud, 1913, pp. 94–99):

> I have said that animism is a system of thought, the first complete theory of the universe, and I shall now go on to draw certain conclusions from the psychoanalytic view of such systems. Every day of our lives our experience is in a position to show us the principal characteristics of a "system." We have dreams during the night and we have learnt how to interpret them during the day. Dreams may. . .appear confused and disconnected. . . . [It] must be added that whatever the original material of the dream-thoughts has been turned into by the dream-work is then subjected to a further influence. This is what is known as "secondary revision," and its purpose is evidently to get rid of the disconnectedness and unintelligibility produced by the dream-work and replace it by a new "meaning." But this new meaning, arrived at by secondary revision, is no longer the meaning of the dream-thoughts.
>
> The secondary revision of the product of the dream-work is an admirable example of the nature and pretensions of a system. There is an intellectual function in us which demands unity, connection and intelligibility from any material, whether of perception or thought, that comes within its grasp; and if, as a result of special circumstances, it is unable to establish a true connection, it does not hesitate to fabricate a false one. . . . Thus a system is best characterized by the fact that at least two reasons can be discovered for each of its products: a reason based upon the premises of the system (a reason, then, which may be delusional) and a concealed reason, which we must judge to be the truly operative and the real one (pp. 94–96).

Freud then applied this analytic principle to examples of ritual prohibitions that are rationalized in folk explanation but can be seen to have their roots in hidden motives. In doing so, however, he did not take into account the possibility that the cognitive distortions produced by secondary revision might acquire from the sociocultural environment secondary functions beyond their functions of concealing unacceptable impulses and making intellectual sense of unconsciously derived fantasy. Elsewhere, he took such a possibility explicitly into account in the distinction between primary and secondary gain from neurotic symptoms.

> When a physical organization like an illness has lasted for some time, it manifests something like a self-preservative instinct; it establishes a kind of *modus vivendi* between itself and other parts of the mind, even those which are at bottom hostile to it; and there can scarcely fail to be occasions when

it proves once again useful and expedient and acquires as it were, a *secondary function* which strengthens its stability afresh (Freud, 1916–17, p. 384, italics in original).

Thus the neurotic sufferer finds some side-effects of his symptom that are beneficial to him, as in the special attention or extra care he gets as someone who is socially treated as sick. Even though these benefits did not motivate the formation of the symptom, they contribute to its preservation.

However difficult it may be to maintain the distinction between primary and secondary gain in contemporary views of neurosis (see Katz, 1963), it is highly relevant to the concept of institutionalization presented here. When an innovation in behavior or belief is institutionalized, it is communicated, first from its innovators to the larger community that legitimizes it and provides for its preservation, and thence to subsequent generations of institutional participants. For its innovators, be they charismatic prophets, saints, or more humble souls, the new pattern of behavior or belief has an immediate relation to their own psychological resources. Drawing upon their genotypic personality dispositions, they created a set of symbols (*e.g.,* a religious or political ideology) that they found deeply satisfying in a personal sense. As their message is transmitted to others, however, it is altered in ways resembling the secondary revision of dreams, but which are social rather than merely intrapsychic. The cognitive processes involved were described by Bartlett (1932) for his experiments on the serial reproduction of stories and drawings and by Allport and Postman (1947) in their work on rumor communication. Bartlett writes of simplification and rationalization as the story or picture is transmitted from one person to another, and, in a chapter on the process of conventionalization, he applies these concepts to the problem of what happens "when cultural material is introduced into a group from the outside" (1932, p. 268). His conclusion is:

> [When] any cultural features come from outside, they may be transformed, not only by assimilation, by simplification and elaboration, and by the retention of apparently unimportant elements, but positively *in the direction along which the group happens to be developing* at the time at which these features are introduced. . . . The most general effect of this positive influence is probably to weld together elements of culture coming from diverse sources and having historically, perhaps, very diverse significance (1932, p. 275, italics in original).

Allport and Postman (1947) identify as major processes in rumor communication *leveling* (abbreviation) and sharpening ("the selective perception, retention and reporting of a limited number of details from a larger context" [p. 86]). They emphasize that "leveling and sharpening. . . do not occur haphazardly but take place in essential conformity with the past experience and present attitudes of the rumor spreaders" (p. 136). Thus is the original innovative message selectively reworked as it gains acceptance and legitimacy. It does not seem far-fetched to assume that by the time it is institutionalized, it has been cognitively transformed to be more consistent with the conscious ideological system of the group. A crucial aspect in this cognitive transformation is that it is increasingly seen by its converts, followers, or consumers as having personal and social uses other than those imagined by its creator. Once it is fully institutionalized, of course, the innovation is surrounded by normative pressures and concomitant rewards and punishments that act as secondary gains for believing and participating in it. It then becomes predictable that at least some who believe and participate in the newly institutionalized adaptation (*e.g.,* a new religion) do so not because its message matches the symbolic content in their genotypic personalities but out of conformist or pecuniary motives that have nothing to do with that symbolic content.

This transformation of a symbolic message in transmission from its innovators, who derived primary (psychological) gain from it, to the larger community that institutionalizes it and broadens the psychological basis of its appeal, was explicitly recognized by Max Weber (1947) in his concept of the *routinization of charisma.* According to Weber (pp. 363–386), the disciples and followers of a charismatic religion or political leader are motivated to make their ideological community consistent with the requirements of everyday social life by their concern for the continuation of the community and for their personal security and material interests. If they do so, the movement is obviously transformed, but if they do not, it will not survive. Wallace (1970, pp. 188–199) describes this process in detail for religious and political revitalization movements.

What this view of institutionalization means for the study of psychosocial adaptations in a given society is that it is necessary to make certain distinctions on a historical basis: between the meanings of a given belief or practice for its originators and its place in their psychological functioning; the "official" meanings of that belief or practice as handed down to the current generation in stitutionalized ideology; and the meanings assigned to the belief or practice in the current generation of institutional participants and its place in their psychological functioning. We may expect a shift from the emotional enthusiasm, ecstasy, or charisma (indicators of primary psychological gain parallel to that experienced in dreams, hallucinations, and neurotic symptoms) of the originators toward a more pragmatic conformity (suggesting secondary gain) in the current generation. We must also expect, however, a shift from a relative homogeneity of subjective meanings and psychological functions among the originators to a diversity in subsequent generations. This diversity is a product of institutionalization, as outlined above, that makes the belief or practice consistent in cognition and action with existing institutions and social trends, thus broadening its motivational basis beyond those whose personality genotypes were in harmony with its original emotional appeal.

As one observes the present generation adapting to beliefs and practices received from their forebears, it should be possible to identify those who are finding in them psychological satisfactions resembling those of their predecessors, those who are also obtaining expression of their genotypic personality dispositions through the attribution of new meanings made possible by the broadening of institutionalization, and those who are participating in the institution not to obtain such personal expression at all but to gain respectability, power, or material reward (secondary gain). Since individuals experience their institutions at multiple levels and work out their own adaptive compromises, many persons will not fit simply into one of these categories; they may be optimal cases of willing conformity who are pushed in the same direction by deep-seated genotypic motives and more or less rational responses to environmental contingencies. But it is essential to recognize that willing conformity is itself a psychologically heterogeneous category, including those for whom secondary gains are more important than primary ones, as well as those whose primary psychological gains diverge along lines related to the historical (cognitive) transformation of the belief or practice from its origin to the present. The institutional symbols and organization, in all their complexity, "organize" this psychological diversity (to use Wallace's (1970) concept of "the organization of diversity") through normative limits on the range of permissible psychosocial adaptations.

Psychological Diversity and Institutional Compromise

The Roman Catholic Church provides examples of both psychological diversity in relation to institutional symbols and ritual and the historical transformation of their meanings and psychological functions. A central ritual practice, such as the Eucharist, wtih the ingested wine and wafer explicitly symbolizing the blood and body of Christ in which the communicant is mystically participating, can have a variety of subjective meanings for those who practice it now, regardless of what conscious and unconscious meanings it had for the earliest Christians. In addition to those who find its explicit content emotionally satisfying, there is the theologically educated intellectual who sees the experience in self-consciously symbolic terms as part of a larger ideological system whose basic premises attract him, the conformist who is concerned to do whatever is necessary to appear appropriately devout, and so forth. For these persons the secondary gains from receiving communion outweigh the primary psychological gain of emotional response to the symbolism of the

Eucharist itself. It is, then, an empirical question as to how each person experiences the ritual and to what degree its symbolic content is related to and expressive of genotypic dispositions in his personality.

This kind of variation in the experiencing of symbols institutionalized by the Church is not merely a matter of individual diversity; it occurs culturally across the widely divergent communities participating in Catholicism. Anne Parsons (1969) illustrates this in her psychosocial account of the "Madonna complex" in Naples:

> The importance of the Madonna complex throughout the Latin world is evident to even the most casual observation; in the South Italian villages she stands in every church and along with the saints may be carried through the streets in procession, and in even the poorest quarters of the City of Naples she is likely to occupy some niche or other, decorated with the flowers or even gold chains brought by her children grateful for her favors. Moreover, every home has a private shrine in which pictures or statues of the Madonna appear along with photographs of deceased relatives illuminated by a candle or lamp.
>
> As a figure in Roman Catholic theology, the Madonna, of course, is only one element in a much wider religious complex. However, popular religion in Southern Italy does not always conform to theological doctrine, for example, in that it has a considerable admixture of magical beliefs and in that the Madonna and the saints are conceived of more as persons whom one can ask a favor (Italian *grazia*, or a grace) than as ideal figures in a moralistic sense. The Madonna may also be seen in characteristic folk manner as a quite familiar figure who is very much part of daily life. . . .
>
> The most important characteristic of the Madonna is that her love and tenderness are always available; no matter how unhappy or sinful the supplicant, she will respond if she is addressed in time of need. Acts of penitence may be carried out for her, for example, pilgrimages or even licking the steps of the church one by one and proceeding to the altar (today only in the most traditional rural areas). Even such acts of penitence, however, are apt to be conceived of as means of showing one's devotion in order to secure a favor, such as the recovery of a sick child. In this sense, the Madonna complex is based on an ethic of suffering rather than sin; the devotee seeks comfort for the wrongs imposed by fate rather than a guide for changing it.
>
> The Madonna is quite obviously the ideal mother figure, and the relation-shop of the supplicant to her is conceived of as that of a child. The other family figures in the Christian pantheon are, of course, not lacking, that is, the father and the son. However, God the Father is usually conceived of as being so distant that he is unapproachable except through the intermediary of the Madonna or a saint. . . . Christ, on the other hand, is perceived. . . either as the good son who is truly and continually penitent or else in the context of suffering; as dramatized in Lenten rituals, the Madonna weeps when he dies martyrized by a hostile world. Of the three figures, it is the Madonna who has by far the greatest concreteness in the popular eye.

Moreover, of all her characteristics one of the clearest is her asexuality; she conceived without sin and so became mother without being a wife (pp. 16–18).

Parsons goes on to show how closely the Madonna complex as a religious pattern is related to the emotional attitudes of Neapolitan family life, and how emotionally significant the symbols of the Madonna complex are for Neapolitans as individual participants in the Catholic Church. It is not that they openly reject other elements in orthodox Catholicism, but they have selectively reworked it to bring it closer to their own personality dispositions and thereby made it more personally satisfying for themselves. The Madonna complex and the saints represent the central images, symbols, and feelings they bring to bear in their religious participation—their primary gain; whereas other aspects of official and institutionalized Catholicism are accepted at a more pragmatic level, presumably for the secondary gains of respectability and access to the institutional assistance of the Church. In a long series of developments that could be historically reconstructed, the Church has in effect struck a bargain with the Neapolitans and other South Italians in which they are allowed to pursue their own local form of religious expression so long as they operate within the confines of the official structure and pay lip service to its universal forms.

This kind of accommodation or compromise between an official religion and its local more emotionally expressive folk or popular variants, has been described by anthropologists and other students of comparative religion for the Catholicism of Latin America, the Caribbean, and the Congo, as well as for Hindu India, Buddhist Southeast Asia, and many parts of the Islamic world. The official religion protects itself from rejection and revolutionary change by legitimizing or overlooking the expressive popular religions of its provinces. The distinctive character of such accommodations, from the present perspective, is that they combine willing and coerced conformity within a single institutional framework, with several significant consequences.

The consequence for the individual is that the expression of his genotypic dispositions is not displaced outside the arena of institutional coercion (as in the recreational displacements described above) but is permitted within the same institution—coercion and personal expression coexisting in the institutionalized religion. The consequence for the institution is that it is able to retain a complex structure of traditional and contemporary elements by building both primary and secondary (psychological) gains into its motivational support instead of either discarding elements as they lose their primary gain for individuals or attempting to coerce a meaningless conformity on the basis of secondary gains alone. The institutional compromise in turn permits individuals a greater variety of possible psychosocial adaptations than either of these extremes would. The consequence for the investigator is that he is faced with psychosocial complexity: Persons participate in ritual and belief with varying degrees of emotional involvement, and it is only by examining their patterns of participation that it is possible to assign meanings to those rituals and beliefs in terms of the primary and secondary gains for participants. Exaggerating the primary gain is the psychological reductionist fallacy, prominent in the literature of applied psychoanalysis; exaggerating secondary gains is the sociologistic fallacy, based on the "oversocialized conception of man" as a simple and rational reflection of his environment. A valid approach must be more empirical than either.

It could be argued that this kind of creative compromise within a single religious institution is not a feature of human societies generally but is a special characteristic of socially differentiated literate societies in their interaction with largely nonliterate homogeneous small communities, which acknowledge the dominance of the literate tradition but prefer to retain their local forms. I believe, however, that the combination of primary and secondary gains is universal among institutionalized religions, and indeed, all sociocultural institutions. I would argue, for example, that the religious situation in autonomous nonliterate populations, though lacking a clear institutional differentiation between official and variant forms, is comprised of motivational elements resembling those mentioned above. At any point in time numerous persons have vested interests in (get secondary gain from) the preservation of certain rituals and beliefs that might well be discarded if the personality dispositions of the present generation were the only factors on which their survival depended. In initiation rites, for example, there is the tendency of the young to want to undergo them because they are gateways to a higher age status, while those who conduct them enjoy the public esteem and the exercise of specialized competence involved in managing the rituals. In some groups, like the Gusii of Kenya (LeVine and LeVine, 1966), the initiation rites are conducted at harvest time when food and beer are abundant enough to warrant a festival of some sort. In other groups such rites have become connected with the demands of military activity, economic exchanges between kinsmen, the marriage system, and other institutional patterns. All of these involve secondary gains that may be of little relevance to the original meanings of the rites themselves but that help preserve them by building them into the rationalized structure of sociocultural institutions. This means one has to look closely at the patterns of participation to sort out which elements in the rites afford primary gain in terms of the expression of genotypic motives, which are experienced as traditional mumbo-jumbo one endures in order to obtain secondary gains, and which are direct "encroachments" of other institutional patterns (involving clear secondary gains) resulting from institutionalization and routinization of the ritual as originally inspired. This kind of approach, which is proposed in methodological detail in Chapters 12–17, can be applied to subsistence activity or any other institutional domain.

Although I believe the understanding of primary and secondary gains from social participation to be of great potential value in the study of psychosocial adaptation, I must add a qualification parallel to that of Katz (1963) in his discussion of primary and secondary gains from neurosis. Some social behavior that appears to be motivated by secondary gains such as the desire for material gain, social prestige, and power, in fact reflects deeper genotypic motives in which these common human desires are magnified in the context of idiosyncratic unconscious meanings. It would be a mistake to assume that every time a rational objective based on a hedonistic calculus is encountered in the investigation of social behavior, it should be interpreted as independent of genotypic motives that obtain satisfaction in social behavior merely through symbolic expression. An unconscious wish for limitless personal aggrandizement may find its behavioral expression in a pattern of striving for money, esteem or power, in which rational means are used to achieve adaptive goals but where the expressive content is as important as the manifest goal itself. It is then a matter of discovering the extent to which the behavior is symbolically linked to this deeper motive, through examination of behavioral intensity, rigidity, repetition in the absence of adaptive value, and above all, comparison with other persons in the same situation. Recognition of the possible influence of genotypic dispositions on apparently adaptive components in behavior does not diminish the importance of distinguishing primary from secondary gains in social behavior; it merely calls attention to the possibility that the secondary gains too have developed within the same personality and reflect a development to which genotypic dispositions have contributed and in which their effects may still be observed.

10

Adaptive Processes II: Change

Changes in patterns of psychosocial adaptation can originate with either side of the compromise they represent, personality genotypes or normative pressures. Inkeles and Levinson (1954), positing functional congruence between personality and sociocultural system as the stable condition, mention institutionally induced and personality-induced noncongruence as the conditions of change. In this chapter I discuss the processes of change implied by these general categories, giving equal or greater weight to the most neglected area, that of personality-induced change.

It is widely recognized that when the institutional environment changes, individuals must adapt to survive or at least to get satisfaction of their personal needs. Most social science investigations of the relation of institutional change to the individual have dealt with the effects of sociocultural change on individual behavior and personality. I begin with categories of institutional change in their effects on individuals and then move to the processes by which personality change affects institutions.

Institutionally Induced Change in Psychosocial Adaptation

In terms of impact on the individual, there are three distinguishable types of changes in his institutional environment that can affect his psychosocial adaptation:

1. *Changes in the content of normative demands for role performance or in the enforcement of such demands.* This refers to roles in the proximal environment of the individual whose requirements he must meet to avoid being stigmatized as deviant. If an individual moves to a new place with norms differing from those to which he is accustomed, he faces having to change his social behavior or be stigmatized as deviant and punished. If he happens to be located in a rapidly changing society, the same thing may happen to him. Legislation may outlaw his adaptation and

153

set new standards to conform to, enforced by law. Processes such as industrialization, urbanization, modernization, may make his previous adaptation obsolete, requiring him to give it up or lose income, status, prestige. Adapting means changing not only behavior, but the attitudes and experience that accompany the behavior. It also means raising one's children to be able to conform to the new norms. This is the standard model of acculturation, widely applicable to situations of the diffusion of cultural norms in populations at all levels of development. Barkow (1970) shows, for example, how the local version of "Islamization," occurring among the Hausa of Northern Nigeria after the Fulani conquest of 1804–1810, confronted the ordinary Hausa villager with the choice of becoming a Muslim and changing his norms of social conduct and self-evaluation to a considerable degree or suffering the increasingly severe penalties of political subordination and social exclusion associated with retaining traditional norms.

2. *Changes in the opportunity structure.* Changes can occur in the individual's environment that do not force him to change or suffer penalties but offer him new opportunities for personal satisfaction. The idea is familiar with respect to economic opportunities: New lands, new jobs, new markets or new technologies open up possibilities for pecuniary activity that the individual can, but need not, take advantage of. The same idea is equally applicable to education, science, religion, the arts, recreation, and popular entertainments, particularly in differentiated societies with plural norms. If there is normative pluralism, a situation can occur in which institutional innovations are genuinely optional, coexisting with older forms rather than replacing them and attracting rather than coercing conformity.

The line between attraction and coercion with respect to institutional innovation can be difficult to draw in a rapidly changing society. For example, for a young American headed for a career as a business executive in 1920, university education was an opportunity he might refuse without damaging his career; in 1970 he could not be employed as an executive without a university degree. What was optional, and therefore dependent on personal preference, has become prerequisite regardless of personal preference. If one adopts the long-term historical view, one sees every advantageous innovation as an incipient coercion or at least a coercive pressure to conform to a future norm. But the view of the individual involved is often quite different; he responds not to a coercive pressure for survival but to a novel opportunity for personal expression that his environment had not previously offered. A Marxist might say that only the long-term historical view is correct and that the individual is simply short-sighted, but this argument denies the psychological reality in which individuals actually function. Phenomenologically, persons can and do respond to environmental innovations that have incentive value because they offer a form of personal satisfaction not previously offered and function as incentives without material want or conformist pressure. Some of these innovations become institutionalized and lose their optional quality; others do not because their opportunities were more apparent than real or because their incentives did not function as such for a large enough proportion of the population. The capacity of persons to respond to opportunities for satisfaction beyond the dictates of material need and normative demand must not be overlooked in considering how socio-cultural environments can affect psychosocial adaptation. Innovations sometimes appear to offer more than they produce in satisfaction, inducing persons to give up previous adaptations without finding a stable alternative.

3. *Changes in the scope and complexity of selective environments.* When the boundaries of population units sharing a set of normative and other selective pressures expand or contract, individuals will experience different demands and opportunities. This type of environmental change entails the two foregoing types but takes into account the distinction between proximal and distal environments, both experienced by the individual. For example, the political and economic integration of diverse ethnic-linguistic groups into nation-states in Africa and other places has brought to many in these areas a new set of normative standards by which to evaluate themselves as well as new opportunities for advancement and enjoyment. These innovations are often superimposed, in a novel pluralism, rather than replacing local norms and opportunities, though replacement might finally result. In the meantime, persons function in a more complex environment than before, one full of potentially contradictory values but operating at different levels and in different situations.

These three categories of changes in the institutional environment of the individual represent three major directions of change that individuals experience: alterations in normative demands, opportunity structures, and the scope and complexity of selective environments. A great deal could be and has been written on this subject, but its very familiarity requires compensatory attention to the other side of the coin: personality-induced changes in psychosocial adaptation.

Personality-Induced Change in Psychosocial Adaptation

In the evolutionary model presented here, personality-induced changes in psychosocial adaptation result from changes in the effective distribution of genotypic personality dispositions in a population, weakening support for existing psychosocial compromises and creating the basis for new ones. The question of how such distributions effectively change must be addressed before considering their ultimate psychosocial outcomes.

The frequency of genotypic personality dispositions in a population will change when those environmental factors contributing to formation of the personality genotype change for that population. Thus major changes in the birth rate or in infant mortality, insofar as they are translated into alterations in the child's early interpersonal experience (*e.g.*, larger or smaller families, greater or less space between children), will affect personality frequencies. Other aspects of demographic change, for example a larger proportion of adults surviving into old age or a decrease in frequency of deaths of parents and siblings during childhood, could also have this effect. Changes in customs surrounding marriage (decrease in the age at which women marry and first give birth or increase in divorce, separation, and foster care) are also likely to have an impact. Finally, shifts in housing, residence, and settlement pattern, dictated by a variety of considerations concerning access to resources related to family economy and comfort, can have consequences for the frequency of genotypic dispositions. We do not have the evidence to prove these assertions or even specify them adequately, but what we know so far is consistent with the idea that the early interpersonal experience of the child, as shaped by the domestic group in which he lives, contributes to the formation of his personality genotype and that the influential constituents of the domestic group are subject to change under the impact of demographic and institutional trends.

Even when the actual frequency of genotypic personality dispositions does not change, shifts in deliberate socialization, acting upon the genotype, can have unintended influence on the phenotypic social behavior that affect the stability of psychosocial adaptations. Deliberate socialization in childhood sets the pattern for the kinds of adaptive compromises between internal environment (personality genotype) and external environment (normative pressure) the individual will be capable of making later in life; a population-wide change in this pattern resulting from changes in parental values is likely to make existing adult compromise formations less satisfactory and to build pressure for change. If there were a religiously induced shift toward puritanism among parents, for example, with self-control becoming a more important goal of deliberate socialization, the generation of individuals raised in the new manner might differ considerably from their predecessors. They would have novel capacities for self-regulation that they might want to exalt, utilize, and justify in various ways, while the pressures of self-regulation would create certain tensions in them requiring release in forms disguised so as not to threaten the new morality. In short, both their capacities and their needs for tension release would tend to make existing psychosocial adaptations obsolete and to favor innovation. These changes are unintended consequences of deliberate socialization acting with new force upon an unaltered distribution of genotypic dispositions, so as to create a new set of regulatory standards by which those dispositions are expressed in phenotypic behavior; the novel internalized regulations generate novel psychological tensions that must be socially accommodated.

Another source of change in the effective distribution of personality genotypes in the population has to do not with their frequency in the entire population but with a shift in their social location. Thus when ethnic or socioeconomic groups within a population are significantly different in frequency of personality genotypes, and when migration or social mobility alters the location of group members in space and status, the psychosocial adaptations in old locations with new incumbents are likely to change. When economic and social conditions permit the rise of large numbers of working class persons into the middle class or force the movement of large numbers of rural people to the cities or attract particular ethnic groups into particular occupational categories, the adaptive compromises in the receiving locations (middle class, city, occupational category) will be influenced by the influx. This can be mitigated by selective recruitment, so that the only persons recruited into the group or category are those whose personalities match past incumbents or whose phenotypic behavior gives that impression, but such a procedure is possible only when very few persons are involved. When there is mass social relocation of persons across the boundaries of groups that differ in frequency of personality dispositions, there will be change in accepted compromise formations.

These are some of the ways in which genotypic personality dispositions can change in their frequencies or in their access to phenotypic expression within the sociocultural environment of a given population. The point to be emphasized about these sources of psychosocial change is that they are almost always unplanned and unintended byproducts of macrosocial processes like demographic transition, ideological conversion, urbanization, and social mobility.

Turning to the means by which effective change in genotypic distribution alters psychosocial adaptive compromise, the following are the major processes involved:

1. *Cultural drift.* When the distribution of personality dispositions among individuals in a given role changes, when the distribution of the new generation differs in central tendency from that of its predecessor, this aggregate shift will find gradual but cumulative expression in phenotypic behavior to a point where the norms of acceptable phenotypic behavior will be changed. The change begins with exploitation of the "loopholes" in normative prescriptions. As I pointed out in Chapter 9, role behavior is never completely prescribed; the normative environment of a role allows the individual numerous options, explicit and implicit (Levinson, 1959). Individuals who resemble each other in personality will select the same or similar options in exploiting the environment for

personal satisfaction. Insofar as there is close institutional regulation of the role domain, the change in phenotypic behavior will be slow enough to escape notice but consistent in direction and therefore cumulative. The style of role performance might be the first indication of change, reflecting "compartmentalized rebellion." Areas in the role domain where institutional regulation is least coercive and where personal choice is explicitly permitted will also be affected early.

Through processes of interpersonal influence such as imitation, observational learning, and persuasion, the innovative choice patterns of individuals—similarly motivated to begin with—will gain momentum and coherence as they aggregate to alter the texture of average expectations in the environment. The cumulative alterations may remain so gradual that no sense of deviation from institutional norms is consciously experienced, though individuals may recognize retrospectively that change has taken place. This process of cultural drift, reflecting cumulative change in a consistent direction, is similar to linguistic drift but seems capable of normative change in a shorter period of time. Drift in language and culture, as in population genetics, represents the effect of microscopic selective change, aggregated from individuals and cumulated over time in a gradual adaptive process. Its socially subliminal nature, highly adaptive in coercive institutional environments, makes it difficult to study as an ongoing process and easy to overlook as a cultural phenomenon. But cultural drift is one of the major means by which norms are brought into accord with personality dispositions in evolving adaptive compromises.

2. *Organizational competition and selection.* In socially differentiated societies, each institutional domain in which normative pluralism occurs usually has a plurality of organizations competing for the membership, support, and commitment of individuals. Religious cults and sects, political parties and factions, and other kinds of voluntary associations present the individual with an array of options from which he can choose on the basis of personal preference. Each group forms a public image of itself, including an ideology, that represents an adaptive compromise (between normative and motivational pressures) in which its founders and members find personal satisfaction and which they are proposing as an adaptive solution to others. Its ideology, its program, its symbols and the ritual in which they are embedded, and its concepts of membership and participation offer the individual a distinctive and complex compromise formula not only for synthesizing norm and motive in phenotypic behavior but also for disguising certain aspects of reality and the expression of certain motives. The organization offers a formula for resolving the motivational conflicts of individuals; it is, in the words of Hallowell (1955) and Spiro (1965), a culturally constituted defense mechanism or defensive system. But it is not the only such culturally constituted formulation

available to the individual; normative pluralism means that diverse solutions compete, each with organized group of adherents and proponents.

From the process of organizational competition, some groups emerge as dominant by virtue of attracting more members, participants, and supporters. Thus personal decisions in the aggregate select certain adaptive compromises and give them a stronger public status than their competitors, surrounding them with the aura of legitimacy that comes from knowledge of widespread popular support, and sometimes institutionalizing them so that adherence becomes to some degree mandatory rather than optional. Insofar as the effective frequency of genotypic personality dispositions has changed, this will express itself in differences in the central tendencies of aggregate choices made among available alternatives; some groups will flourish at the expense of others, through the operation of electoral voting, expansion or contraction of membership, or other choice mechanisms (buying and selling, raising money through donation, energy commitments by members). If the psychosocial compromise of a group that emerges as popular involves norms that differ from those that had been previously institutionalized, personality-induced normative change is under way. Of course organizational competition and selection can be induced by a decline in the institutional viability of dominant organizations without change in personality frequencies, but even when the process is set in motion by institutional factors, the aggregate choice mechanism will reflect the influence of genotypic personality dispositions and bring about an adaptive compromise that includes their needs for expression.

This process is in effect a socially institutionalized form of the variation-selection model; it includes the presumption that there is individual variation in ideological preference, that such preferences will be expressed in the decision to join or participate in an organization, and that decisions in the aggregate will select the ideological solutions to be culturally propagated. From this perspective, the process has two particularly interesting features. When there is widespread discontent with existing institutions, representing institutionally or personality-induced inadequacy in the fit between norms and motives, religious or political organizations offering diverse solutions often proliferate; the multiplication of variants is itself an adaptive response to the breakdown in previous compromise formations (see Wallace, 1956). The proliferation represents the opportunism of those who sense the problem and the population-wide need for a solution not dictated by existing norms; they seize the permissive occasion to create a distinctive compromise they and their fellows find personally satisfying, which they offer to the public for wider support. The opening, the occasion itself, stimulates persons to attempt innovation. The multiplicity of solutions offered to the public, as organizational ideologies designed to attract membership or endorsement, permits a wide array of possibilities to be considered in the competition and enter into the selective process.

Another interesting feature is that when the selective process has resulted in the establishment of a new psychosocial adaptation as dominant for a population, some of the unsuccessful variants will remain in existence. Normative pluralism allows organizations to create distinctive ecological niches for their self-selected membership even when they do not represent the majority choice, and an organization unsuccessful in one competition may survive as a representative of a solution that may later prove adaptive, in cultural "revival." In other words, diverse psychosocial solutions of potential adaptive value are often stored not merely as cultural memories but as ongoing organizations, often small and sectarian in nature, that are ready to expand when conditions are more propitious to their message. Zaretsky (1971) has argued that American spiritualist churches have had this kind of history over the last 130 years: expanding in times of crisis, contracting afterwards, but surviving as a resource to meet future needs.

3. *Successful innovation within the existing opportunity structure.* This is involved in both cultural drift and organizational compromise-selection, but it is here referred to in its most discontinuous form: a sudden "breakthrough" so widely recognized as advantageous that it is quickly imitated on a large scale or otherwise legitimized without effective resistance. Some of the great advances in science, technology, economic production, and political and military organization were of this type. They entailed the creative exploitation of generally recognized existing possibilities, exploitation that had not been previously imagined but were not outside existing normative standards. Since they did not directly oppose existing norms but rather maximized established values in novel ways, they could gain immediate acceptance, but their widespread emulation made previous adaptations obsolete and eroded the norms that went with them. Henry Ford's innovation of mass production could be seen as an example of this process; so could the Beatles' innovation in musical entertainment and men's hair style. In both cases innovation brought massive monetary reward from enthusiastic consumers, which had a legitimizing effect in itself but also stimulated large-scale imitation that eventually altered normative standards in a major way.

This also occurs outside economic production and consumption. In politics, for example, when a charismatic figure is elected head of state, the success embodied by his office inspires emulation of the innovative adaptation represented by his charismatic public posture. In contemporary American culture, with its high value given to novelty and its mass communication media, any novelty regarded as worthy of media attention is likely to be widely imitated and may alter prevalent psychosocial adaptations. In such a culture, there is an established pattern of a vanguard (person or group) that takes the first step in developing a new style that attracts attention, and the masses who respond to the successful innovation with endorsement and imitation.

All three of these processes are usually involved in personality-induced change. Cultural drift, for example, often prepares the ground for change, shifting norms toward receptivity of innovative breakthroughs and the selection of certain group ideologies over others. Successful exploitation of opportunities permitted by the normative environment attracts imitation in the processes of cultural drift and organizational competition as well as in innovative breakthroughs. Groups differing in sociocultural development are likely to lean more or less heavily on these several processes. For example, a fairly high degree of institutional differentiation is required for the normative pluralism that allows organizational competition and selection. Where institutions are relatively undifferentiated, personality-induced change is more likely to occur through cultural drift. Where communications are rapid and widespread, the successful innovation is more likely to be publicized as a breakthrough and a model for imitation.

Recognizing their differences and complex interdependencies, these three processes taken as a group suggest that changes in normatively acceptable psychosocial adaptations can and do occur without deviance and opposition. There can be no doubt that deviant behavior is a source of change (see Parsons, 1949) and that social conflict often accompanies change. But it is a fallacy of the institutionalist viewpoint to dichotomize behavior as conformist or deviant and to see change as a disruption of ongoing adaptation rather than as a part of it (see Levinson, 1959; Buckley, 1967). In the model presented here, cultural drift, organizational competition, and successful innovation-imitation are continuously active processes by which motives selectively influence the direction of evolutionary change, always seeking better fit with the sociocultural environment.

11

A Cost-Benefit View of
Psychosocial Adaptation

In this chapter we return to the basic purposes of a comparative psychology of human populations, formulate some of the fundamental questions of culture and personality in terms of the evolutionary framework advanced in the foregoing chapters, and ask: What must we know to answer those questions, and what would we do with the answers if we had them? A theoretical formulation is only valuable if it guides empirical research in significant directions; here I attempt to foresee the directions and assess the significance of the research implied by population psychology as an evolutionary theory of culture and personality.

Questions for a Population Psychology

In Chapter 1 I asserted that one of the three basic questions of culture and personality is: How are psychological differences between populations related to the sociocultural environments of those populations? This can now be reformulated in terms of the evolutionary model developed so far, with particular reference to the types of psychosocial adaptive compromise described in Chapter 9. The reformulation generates the series of questions that follow.

What factors account for variations in patterns of psychosocial adaptation among human populations? The evolutionary model leads us to reject simplistic causal answers to this question. Our model begins with the phenotypic social behavior seen by ethnographic observation, which represents a "compromise" between the genotypic dispositions that constitute the personality system of individuals and the normative pressures in their sociocultural environment. The terms of this compromise, having been worked out in earlier generations as operative norms of phenotypic behavior through selective feedback from both dispositional and normative pressures, are selectively reworked at the level of individual development in the deliberate socialization of childhood and adolescence, in adult role taking and role performance, and in the operation of social sanctions and incentives. The resultant phenotypic forms of conformity, far from merely reflecting institutional demands, are actively created by individuals in response to the motives and norms they experience. As psychosocial adaptations they are selective accommodations to the sociocultural environment, reflecting opportunistic exploitation of its available possibilities for personal satisfaction. These accommodations may stabilize, but they are also full of potentialities for change induced by institutional or personality factors. Every point at which adaptive fit between norm and motive is selectively reached is a point at which change can take place. As soon as one side of the compromise is altered, introducing negative feedback, a better fit is sought through the processes outlined in Chapter 10. In many, if not most populations, change is continual; better fits are always being sought; and stability refers to a relatively slowly changing adaptation. Stability is always dependent on the adaptive behavior of individuals and on the selective conditions set by their genotypic personality dispositions, which cannot be eradicated by normative pressures.

Given the multiplicity of selective processes by which each adaptive compromise is attained, the diversity of such compromises among human populations cannot be attributed to a single set of factors acting through a straightforward causal mechanism. Each instance of phenotypic fit between norm and motive must be seen as an evolved product incorporating information about past and present environments in a concise formula for action that indirectly represents the pressures through which it was historically created. Accounting for cross-cultural variation in psychosocial adaptation, therefore, can mean reconstructing historically the processes of variation, feedback, and selection by which each variant evolved to its present form. It can also mean elucidating the processes by which it is currently maintained and propagated. A full understanding necessarily requires both historical reconstruction and the analysis of current function, but the latter is a more realistic aim for comparative analysis. Accounting for synchronic variations in pattern of psychosocial adaptation means research into the contemporary social and psychological functions of those patterns, with the understanding that their contents can only be partly explained without reference to the historical conditions under which they developed.

The concept of an adaptive psychosocial pattern as an evolved compromise implies that such patterns are overdetermined, in the sense in which Freud (1900) said dreams are overdetermined—that their observable form represents the final common pathway for multiple pressures seeking expression. Having survived selective accommodation to environmental and genotypic features at so many points in social process, psychosocial patterns have been shaped by numerous constraints, some of which continue to be involved in their maintenance. It is thus possible to trace a pattern back to influencing factors in several directions, each of which might be taken as "causal" without an understanding of the selective processes involved. Concretely, the individual in his pattern of social conformity has at least two "reasons" for his behavior: It allows him satisfaction of private motives and it accords with what is socially prescribed. In addition, it may well be consistent with the personal standards he internalized through deliberate socialization by his parents, and it is likely to have an ideological justification in a religious or ethical doctrine. These diverse sources converge in providing support for his pattern of behavior. Though each factor might seem to constitute an adequate explanation in itself, and in the case of a particular individual not all factors are necessarily involved, all contributed to the history of the pattern and all are involved in its maintenance as a population characteristic rather than an idiosyncrasy. Its overdetermined nature, by diversifying the grounds for its social acceptability and popular appeal and by a reinforcing consistency in influencing the individual, contributes greatly to its stability as a pattern of psychosocial adaptation.

What factors account for change in psychosocial adaptation within a human population? This question requires the diachronic perspective of the previous chapter, which necessarily involves reconstruction of the process by which one pattern of psychosocial adaptation was given up and a new one evolved. The factors operating as selective agents must be elucidated, with particular attention to which changed first and what effects its change had on the sequence of events. Overdetermination can be seen as a conservative force because individuals tend to be oversocialized; they are wedded to an established adaptive pattern through multiple motives and pressures acting at different points in their development toward a convergent effect. The result is what might be called "overconformity," in which the individual's conformity is in response to contemporaneous social norms *and* his own inner standards *and* his own material interests *and* his emotional needs *and* an institutionalized ideological system—all converging in the same phenotypic behavior.

It might appear that this convergence guarantees the high level of stability that some functionalists have assumed to be necessary for the operation of the social system. In the present view, however, there is no such assumption. On the contrary, it is assumed that both individuals and sociocultural institutions can tolerate a wide range of behavior patterns and adaptive styles without disruption or breakdown; they are therefore capable of entering into many types of unfavorable compromises until opportunities arise for better compromises. An unfavorable compromise should produce discernible symptoms, possibly of a compensatory nature, indicating that a societal goal or widespread individual motive has been sacrificed, but such symptoms can be chronic without occasioning serious disruption or breakdown. As the institutional environment and frequencies of genotypic dispositions change and individuals seek to maximize their advantages within the constraints of their internal and external environments, adaptive compromises more favorable to one of the compromised factors will replace older psychosocial adaptations. This kind of change is expectable in any human population. Individual personalities and sociocultural institutions are a good deal more flexible than functionalist formulations with equilibrium concepts usually imply. Comparative research on psychosocial adaptation must divest itself of the a priori assumption that any particular adaptive pattern is essential to the maintenance of an equilibrium without which an imagined chaos or psychosis would prevail. Stability is never absolute; change is not equivalent to disruption; and stressful conditions are regularly endured when better alternatives are unavailable.

How are the stabilized patterns of psychosocial adaptation characteristic of a population related to the consciously experienced satisfactions and frustrations of its members and to the incidence among them of behavior disorders indicating chronic psychic stress or tension? Do some patterns of psychosocial adaptation afford their members more satisfaction or generate differing frequencies of behavior disorders than others? These questions move toward the cost-benefit orientation of this chapter, with the emphasis on psychic, as opposed to social, cost and benefit (see Etzioni, 1968, pp. 622–632). On the assumption that patterns of psychosocial compromise, however adaptive in environmental terms, vary widely in their impact on psychic functioning, we can ask whether some patterns more than others take a toll on the individual that finds expression in his subjective emotional state and in the probability of his manifesting a behavior disorder. If comparative research were to reveal covariations of this type, the discovery would have important policy implications. Similar questions can be asked from the social side: *How are the stabilized patterns of psychosocial adaptation characteristic of a population related to its relative success or failure in attaining institutional goals, and to its relative frequency of social conflict patterns?*

This brings us to the final and perhaps most important question: *How are institutional success and failure related to the psychological condition of population members and what part does psychosocial compromise play in mediating such relationships?* In other words, are sociocultural institutions and the psychological characteristics of their individual participants in a complementary relation such that institutions succeed in achieving their goals only through adaptations involving individual constraints that result in suffering and behavior disorder? Conversely, if individuals are permitted greater personal choice and expression in their environment, does this necessarily involve a sacrifice of societal or institutional goals? Or is it that the suffering and behavior disorders of individuals are more frequent where institutional regulation is slack? Finally, is it possible to identify *optimal* psychosocial adaptations that maximize institutional success and personal satisfaction while minimizing social conflict and behavior disorders? Are such optimal adaptations empirically discoverable or only hypothetically conceivable? The significance of such questions for the mental health and social welfare of human beings is obvious; if investigators in the field of culture and personality could provide answers they would help solve fundamental problems underlying public discussion of societal goals. The kind of research that would be needed to attack these problems is taken up in the following section.

Data Requirements for Comparative Research

Our discussion so far has been in the abstract. We now turn to a consideration of the kinds of information we would need about each human population and its sociocultural environment to answer the foregoing questions. In outlining these requirements I am making the assumption that culture and personality research will not reach mature form until we are able to compare institutional and psychological functioning across the full cultural range of human populations and to find, in such comparisons as well as in historical studies, empirical regularities in the covariations of personality distributions with sociocultural environments.

The categories of data required are shown in Table 11.1. Each category needs to be explained in terms of what kind of description it refers to and what relations it might have with the other categories.

1. *Institutional goals.* This refers to the official publicly accepted goals of social action in a given institutional domain—economic, political, religious, etc. Some of those goals can be panculturally defined (*e.g.,* collective subsistence, security from danger, reproduction, cultural transmission), whereas others are culture-specific in their institutional definition (preservation or expansion of structures, maximization of cultural values), although linked to larger human purposes universal to the species. Comparative analysis would seek to identify those common, pancultural goals against which the institutions of culturally diverse populations could be comparatively assessed in terms of their relative success in goal attainment (category F6). But the first order of data required would be an ethnography of the institutions in each cultural context so that it would be possible for the analyst to understand the relations of the official goals of the institutions in local context to the panculturally defined goals in terms of which his indicators of success and failure would be constructed.

2. *Institutional rules and sanctions for role performance.* A closely related order of data supplied by institutional ethnography concerns the

TABLE 11.1. *Categories of data required for comparative psychosocial research.*

Sociocultural environment:

A. Institutional goals
B. Institutional rules and sanctions for role performance
C. Situational norms for reacting to institutional and motivational pressures

Personality distributions:

D. Phenotypic patterns of response in social situations
E. Genotypic dispositions (normally distributed)

Hypothesized outcomes of personality-environment interaction:

F. Level of success in attaining institutional goals
G. Consciously experienced satisfactions and frustrations of population members
H. Behavior disorders (rare in frequency but stable over time)

rules for behavior in the roles that make up the public definition of the individual's institutional environment and the positive and negative sanctions designed to maintain conformity to the rules. These rules and sanctions constitute the official instrumentality by which institutional goals are attained through the actions of individual men. They are, in effect, the public ideals of role performance and the legal or quasi-legal mechanisms through which those ideals are enforced. For the individual, who often does not understand the institutional goals, the rules and sanctions concerning his role performance are the widest aspects of his institutional environment that he can perceive; they comprise the normative pressures he experiences.

3. *Situational norms for reacting to institutional and motivational pressures.* This category of data concerns the actual rather than ideal norms governing individual behavior in the face-to-face situations of his immediate life space, for example, in situations of work, dispute, love-making, teaching. These norms represent compromises between the institutional rules for role performance and the individual's personal motives, worked out in the culture of the small group that selectively redefines institutional constraints and gives them a workable form. This type of ethnographic data has rarely been used in comparative analysis, but it is essential for psychosocial comparison to represent the proximal normative environment of the individual. Collecting it requires breaking the environment of the role down into component face-to-face situations with their own normative structures. As compromises to which individual motives have manifestly contributed, these normative structures reflect the psychosocial adaptive patterns characteristic of the population.

4. *Phenotypic patterns of response in social situations.* This is the psychosocial adaptation looked at from the side of the individual, as opposed to that of the normative environment, and involves data on how aggregates of individuals in fact behave (*e.g.*, their average rates of normal and deviant activity) in the face-to-face situations making up their lives. Insofar as the personality phenotype is closely fitted to situational norms, quantitative data of this type will assume the form of a J-curve, with most individuals conforming to those norms most of the time.

5. *Genotypic dispositions.* These comprise the internal environment of the individual, analogous to the external (sociocultural) environment in that phenotypic behavior must be adapted to it. Unlike the external environment, however, genotypic dispositions necessarily vary from one individual to another, and it is probably safest to imagine them as being normally distributed in a population. Their central tendencies reflect the socially standardized environmental components in their individual development, but there is a considerable range of variation around these central tendencies, reflecting the effects of genetic and experiential variants. Unlike phenotypic behavior patterns, which are pushed toward J-curves by normative pressures, genotypic dispositions vary more extremely and exert pressures of their own on social behavior. Such dispositions cannot be directly observed; they must, paradoxically, be inferred from phenotypic behavior patterns to which they contribute but in which they appear transformed by the terms of the adaptive compromise with situational norms.

6. *Levels of success in attaining institutional goals.* This requires the construction of indicators for comparative institutional analysis based on data concerning the "performance" of the institution in achieving its goals. In economics, indicators such as Gross National Product and per capita income have been used; in political studies, various measures of political stability and integration. Whatever the value of these particular measures, they are attempts to assess the goal-attainment of institutions, and such attempts are necessary to answer questions concerning the relation of costs and benefits in societal and individual functioning. Ways must be found to assess comparatively the social value or beneficial outcomes produced by similar institutions in different populations. From the present theoretical perspective, such outcomes represent the aggregate performance of individuals and therefore reflect their behavior patterns as well as the institutional arrangements within which they function. Differing psychosocial adaptations in the same institutional domains may produce varying degrees of success in achieving institutional goals.

7. *Consciously experienced satisfactions and frustrations of population members.* This kind of data would enable us to assess comparatively the relative frequency of positive and negative subjective emotional states that have become stabilized in a population. Like the previous category, it represents an outcome of the patterns of psychosocial adaptation, but

an outcome in the subjective judgments of individuals, whose responses would be aggregated for comparison of populations.

8. *Behavior disorders.* This category includes all of the forms of deviant behavior such as crime, suicide, psychoses, neuroses, and psychosomatic disorders that are characteristic of only a small number in a population but are nonetheless regarded as distinctive of that population by virtue of the stability of their frequencies over time, particularly in comparison with other populations. Despite their rarity in the population, these behavior patterns might represent outcomes of psychosocial adaptations that generate conflict and stress in the individual for which there is no readily available legitimate avenue of discharge. It could be that what is experienced as conscious dissatisfaction for the majority results in behavior disorder for a minority and that the proportions of these outcomes of psychologically "bad" compromises are related positively over time and among populations.

A comparative approach would involve collecting data in each of these categories for culturally diverse human populations and examining the relations of the categories to each other cross-culturally and over time. In a cost-benefit analysis, social costs and benefits would be defined in terms of relative success in attaining institutional goals, psychological costs and benefits would be defined in terms of relative position on a satisfaction-frustration continuum and the frequencies of behavior disorders of various types. One objective of comparative analysis would be to make generalizations about the relations of psychological and social costs and benefits to each other and to the institutional and personality variables that contribute to and represent the patterns of psychosocial adaptation. Another would be to discover to what extent optimal conditions are possible—whether costs can be minimized and benefits maximized on both sides simultaneously.

Conclusions

It would be pretentious to do more than outline a future cost-benefit analysis of psychosocial adaptation at this point in the history of culture and personality research. The potential value of such an analysis should be evident from the foregoing discussion, but we do not currently have the data necessary to conduct it. Of the eight categories of data, however, seven seem clearly obtainable with methods at our disposal. The one kind that is not obtainable is evidence concerning genotypic personality distributions, due to methodological difficulties that have plagued the culture and personality field for decades. The problem of obtaining this evidence is in my opinion the greatest obstacle to the development of a comparative psychology of human populations. In the next section of this book I examine this problem and propose a means of solving it.

Part IV

The Study of Individual Dispositions in Social Settings

12

Strategies in Personality Study

In 1936 Ralph Linton, contemplating the problem of studying personality cross-culturally, complained, "It is unfortunate that we have no exact, objective techniques for identifying psychological types" (p. 484). Thirty-five years later, we have a multitude of personality tests for which exactness and objectivity are claimed, but the major obstacle to a comparative psychology of human populations remains the lack of dependable instruments for diagnosing the individual case. The contemporary anthropologist seeking a method of personality assessment for comparative study finds that: reputable personality psychologists do not agree on which method is best for measuring any particular disposition; different methods of measuring the "same" disposition correlate poorly or not at all, yielding differing distributions of results for the same group of individuals; and there is doubt and disagreement about the extent to which the methods tap enduring dispositions of the person or his reactions to the immediate conditions under which behavior is sampled. In fact, social and personality psychologists are currently engaged in intense and fundamental self-criticism regarding the validity of their methods (see Rosenthal, 1966; Berg, 1967; Mischel, 1968; Yarrow, Campbell, and Burton, 1968; Rosenthal and Rosnow, 1969).

The methodological plight of personality psychology is well portrayed in *Personality Tests and Reviews* (Buros, 1970), a massive compendium based on the *Mental Measurements Yearbooks*. Of the 513 personality tests developed over the past 40 years (96 projective and 417 nonprojective tests), more than three-quarters are still in print and "are still being sold." This durability might lead one to believe that they have proven their worth. But the compiler tells us:

The size of the monograph [*Personality Tests and Reviews*] . . . reflects the tremendous interest and activity of psychologists in assessing personality. In no other area of testing has there been such an overwhelming flood of articles, books, dissertations, research monographs, and tests. Personality tests are generally long-lived and obsolesce very slowly. Paradoxically, the area of testing which has outstripped all others in the quantity of research over the past thirty years is also the area in which our testing procedures have the least generally accepted validity. . . .

The vast literature on personality testing has failed to produce a body of knowledge generally acceptable to psychologists. In fact, all personality instruments may be described as controversial, each with its own following of devotees (pp. 20, 25–26).

Buros is critical of the Minnesota Multiphasic Personality Inventory (MMPI), most widely used of nonprojective personality tests, saying that it "is probably just as controversial, if not more so, than it was ten or twenty years ago" (p. 26). Turning to other instruments, he states:

The Rorschach, kingpin of all personality tests judging by the vast amount of material written on it, is another example. This monograph reports 3,747 references (over 530 are doctoral dissertations) for the Rorschach, with a current output of about 120 references per year. This vast amount of writing and research has produced astonishingly little, if any agreement among psychologists regarding the specific validities of the Rorschach. It is amazing to think that this voluminous research and experiential writing over a period of nearly half a century has not produced a body of knowledge generally accepted by competent psychologists. Even among the Rorschach disciples, there are various schools of thought, each with its own following. (A recent book describes five "American Rorschach systems.") It is easy to understand that we must expect always to have believers among us—persons who have the will to believe in a particular instrument or theory—but it is difficult to understand why the research has been so unproductive.

The sterility of the research and experiential writing on the Rorschach and the MMPI is also applicable to other personality tests which have generated fewer publications. In no case, however, has the accumulated research produced an enduring body of generally accepted knowledge concerning the validities of the test under study. We are still at the stage where every test, regardless of its merits and deficiencies, is considered useful by some and useless by others (p. 26).

The demoralization among personality researchers occasioned by this situation is reflected in the concluding section of the comprehensive review of the personality testing literature by Sechrest:

It is the contention of the writer that what is needed in the field of personality assessment is more imagination and inventiveness, which is not a way of saying that what is needed is more of the same thing we already have. . . .

There are . . . many other available measures that represent only changes on the themes provided by other tests. . . . While some such measures may be mildly interesting, it seems unlikely that any will provide a badly needed breakthrough in personality assessment methodology. In the estimation of the writer, the individual with an assessment problem will do well to think about it from many different angles before he adopts one of the currently available, standard measures. A fair appraisal of the research literature would justify the conclusion that any reasonably well thought out new method would not be likely to be measurably worse. It would not have to be remarkable to be better (1968, pp. 607–608).

The student of culture and personality is thus in a very different position from that of biomedical investigators seeking to make cross-population comparisons of individual characteristics. The epidemiologist investigating the distributon of malaria or anemia, for example, can depend on the laboratory analysis of blood samples for valid diagnostic results at the individual level; reliable procedures have already been developed and accepted by the scientific community before he begins his comparative study. In comparative personality study, however, we cannot assume that the diagnostic problems have been solved in the psychological laboratory or clinic; there are no procedures that have gained full acceptance in the relevant scientific community, and those of widest currency are used *faute de mieux* for reasons other than their demonstrated validity in assessing personality dispositions. The anthropologist who takes a personality test to the field on blind faith and then has the results subjected to blind analysis by an experienced psychologist is acting out a diagnostic charade based on an analogy with medical research that does not yet accord with the facts in our field. Thus we have no choice but to become our own personality psychologists, delving deeply into the methodology of personality assessment to rethink the central problem of distinguishing operationally between the behavioral properties of individuals and their environments.

Recent methodological work in psychology reveals that the behavior measured in psychological experiments and testing studies is strongly, sometimes overwhelmingly influenced by the interactive settings in which observation and measurement takes place. Thus subjects present themselves in a socially valued light to the investigator, meet what they sense to be his expectations, become acquiescent or secretive about themselves or interested in topics he has questioned them about—all in response to aspects of the social situation in which investigator and subject communicate. Of course it was recognized long ago in motivational arousal experiments that something as apparently inconsequential as the phrasing of instructions for a Thematic Apperception Test could influence thematic content in the responses, but in recent years psychologists have become increasingly and more systematically aware of the many *unintended* influences of this nature (response sets, experimenter effects, test artifacts) that are affecting their results, Insofar as they are interested in generalizing from the assessment situation to other situations in the individual's life, this is a matter of great concern to them.

The recognition by psychologists that the assessment situation is a complex social interaction can only be viewed as a healthy development, but what are its implications for interpreting the results of previous personality studies? As a matter of fact, it helps make discouraging sense of their results, for correlations between dispositions sometimes reach fairly high levels when a single type of instrument (*e.g.*, paper-and-pencil questionnaire, projective test, interview, teachers' ratings) is used but hardly ever when different kinds of instruments are used for each disposition. This, together with the low or zero correlations between differing measures of the "same" disposition, suggests that each type of instrument represents a distinctive social situation that elicits distinctive and consistent patterns of behavior (Mischel, 1968; Yarrow, Campbell, and Burton, 1968). In other words, the behaviors that personality psychologists regard as symptoms of person-specific dispositions have not shown the expected transsituational generality. This evidence calls into question the fundamental assumptions and research strategies of personality psychology.

There are several ways of reacting to this pattern of evidence. One is to disbelieve it or reject the generality of its implications, as some personality psychologists probably would do. But the conclusion stated above has been reached independently by several highly responsible investigators reviewing hundreds of studies, including those done with great care and awareness of the methodological problems involved by psychologists sympathetic to the dispositional view. The sheer volume and variety of research carried out by personality psychologists who believe in a dispositional theory is so great that it is reasonable to expect that if both theory and research strategy were correct, they would have turned up solid evidence of transsituational dispositions; such evidence is conspicuously lacking. The canons of inference and validation that personality psychologists have imposed on themselves do not allow this general finding to be dismissed.

Another way of reacting to this fact is to conclude that the dispositional view of individual behavior is wrong and to seek consistency primarily in situations. This position is congenial to behaviorists of the Skinnerian and social-learning orientations and to sociologists who try to explain social behavior wholly in terms of normative pressures operating in interpersonal settings. Mischel (1968) has presented the case from a social-learning perspective. He argues that the assumption of dispositions underlying observable behavior seems plausible because we tend to make global judgments about ourselves and others, thus organizing perceptually the disparate behaviors of an individual, but that the assumption has been contradicted by the evidence from systematic research. It is more in accord with what we already know to assume that the behavior of an individual is *not* consistent from one type of situation to another and that it tends toward consistency only when the environmental factors eliciting it and maintaining it are relatively stable, in extremely similar situations of assessment or real life. The search for underlying dispositions of a general nature should be abandoned, according to Mischel, in favor of detailed analysis of overt behavior in specific situations and of the contingencies in those situations that are currently eliciting and rewarding the behavior. The goal of such analyses is more effective decision making and technique in the assessment and treatment of behavior disorders, on the basis of what is already knowable. Thus Mischel offers a strategy for maximizing the utility of presently available data and techniques; he, and others of his persuasion, reject investigative strategies that seek to go beyond the limits of present knowledge and procedures to discover more fundamental regularities, insofar as such strategies involve positing the existence of dispositional entities for which there is as yet no empirical support.

Mischel's approach is pragmatic, and he effectively challenges the relevance of clinical psychology as currently practiced to effective diagnosis and therapeutic improvement. But clinical goals and those of scientific explanation are separable, and his program is for an immediate technology of behavior change, like animal husbandry and plant breeding before the advent of Mendelian genetics, rather than a deepening understanding of behavioral processes in the individual. From a scientific point of view, he is premature in rejecting the dispositional view, even if it has not yielded as accurate predictions as a purely inductive approach to individual behavior. It is valuable to know that the weight of a mental patient's folder is a better predictor of his return to the hospital than a battery of psychological tests, but we may be interested in knowing more about him than the probability of rehospitalization; for example, we may want to *explain* not only his rehospitalization but his history of mental disorder.

Some explanatory goals may be unattainable at present, but we can devise new procedures for moving toward them, and in doing so we are not without guidelines for the more advanced disciplines that deal with relations between organisms and their environments. Regarding the problem of individual disposition versus environmental situation, for example, we might consider protective coloration in fish and amphibia. Flatfish, squids, and octopuses can change color quickly according to the conditions of illumination in their background. One could study them carefully and discover the situations in which they were pale and those in which they were dark so that prediction was perfect, and one could manipulate illumination so as to control their skin color at will. But having achieved perfect situation-specific prediction and control, one would not yet understand how the animal manages to change color.

Research at the cellular level reveals that in the flatfish the change is produced by the movement of minute granules of pigment within the cells of the epidermis: when the pigment is concentrated at the center of the cell the animal looks pale, and when it is spread throughout the cell the animal looks dark. In squids and octopuses pigment is contained in small elastic bags, that, when round, cover a small area and leave the animal pale, but when flattened into a disc shape by a series of radially arranged muscles (each supplied by a nerve fiber), they cover a large part of the surface and make the animal dark. The apparently discrete situation-specific responses are thus properly explained by a single mechanism in the organism that provides for both, and no amount of situational analysis could produce this understanding. It is not unreasonable to expect that such mediating processes may be discovered in the adaptive response patterns of man, and this is one argument against prematurely foreclosing the search for dispositions underlying diverse situational responses. Dispositional theories of personality have made little headway toward confirmation in research to date, but they have by no means been conclusively falsified.

This argument suggests a third reaction to the negative evidence from personality studies, questioning their methodology rather than their theoretical basis. In the pages that follow I shall reexamine the assumptions underlying the research tradition, initiated by Hermann Rorschach in 1921 and developed by Henry Murray and his co-workers (1938) at the Harvard Psychological Clinic, in which psychoanalytic theory and psychological testing methods were brought together for personality diagnosis. At the heart of this critique is the recognition that in observable human behavior there are almost always reflections both of the pressures the individual experiences in his immediate environment *and* the tendencies generated by his prior experience and genetic constitution. Personality testing seemed to offer a means of disentangling the two by controlling the immediate environment so that more durable tendencies would express themselves, "uncontaminated," in behavior. It has now become clear that there is not as much control of environmental pressure in psychological tests and experiments as was promised. "Contaminating" influences are present, and they vary not only from one psychological measurement situation to another, but also from psychological measurement situations to other situations in the person's life. This jeopardizes valid inference from the observed behavior to tendencies of a more general nature, leaving the findings of personality research interpretable in terms of the situational approaches of sociological reductionism and Skinnerian behaviorism. We need a different strategy for disentangling personal disposition and situational influence in the study of personality.

This problem is not peculiar to the study of human behavior; the confounding of enduring individual disposition with response to the proximate situation occurs wherever, through the adaptive processes of evolution, "fit" has been achieved between organism and environment. This confounding is the epistemological consequence of adaptation; it is the way in which the behavioral products of evolution are presented to the senses of the scientific observer. The central difficulty in the effort to disentangle the respective contributions of organism and environment to adaptive behavior is that adaptation can be achieved in a variety of ways. Adaptation always involves incorporation of environmental information into the response repertoire of the organism, but the information may be incorporated through phylogenetic or ontogenetic processes. If the information is incorporated wholly in phylogenesis, natural selection acting over many generations produces an innately fixed response system that is adaptive. But phylogenetic processes may have evolved developmental flexibility for the organism so that it can respond differently to variations in environmental stimulation and supplies. In animals, flexibility can involve the activities of the sense organs, which read the current environment for variations and initiate variable (even if only reflexive) responses. In the higher animals, developmental flexibility involves individual information storage and retrieval (memory and learning processes) as well as sensation, so that the individual organism can respond more variably and accurately to larger segments of environmental information. In all organisms, however, a great deal of environmental information has been incorporated phylogenetically; even a developmentally flexible response pattern is an innate capacity evolved out of interaction with a variable environment.

Thus there are different mechanisms of adaptation, but it is not always easy to tell which one accounts for an observed response pattern, and this leads to serious errors of inference. Suppose we were investigating coloration in a population of flatfish on the assumption that an animal's color is an innately fixed response to the illumination in its normal environment. Having made this assumption we take one snapshot of each fish in its setting and discover a strong correlation between the paleness or darkness of the fish and the amount of illumination in its setting. We conclude that we were right: There are pale fish and dark fish, their differences in coloring having developed through natural selection in settings of different illumination. Our method of data collection failed to take account of the possibility of flexible response in coloration, so it lead us to a false conclusion based on facts. A different method would have yielded the additional fact that each flatfish varies in color over time and can shift rapidly from light to dark. Our mistake was in presuming that the environmental information contained in the adaptation between skin color and illumination had been encoded and fixed in the past, with appropriately protective coloration being transmitted through the genes. What the genes do transmit, however, are the capacities for the individual animal to obtain contemporary information regarding illumination and to respond differentially. Thus our snapshot data reflected the past phylogenetic experience of flatfish as well as their responses to the conditions of their surroundings at the moment the snapshot was taken, but in a form in which the two influences could not be distinguished. Similar examples of premature and one-sided judgments in the heredity-environment controversy abound in the human sciences.

Research should be based on the recognition that observed adaptation can be attained through several mechanisms, each of which needs to be investigated before a final conclusion is reached. The problem is one of devising data collection strategies for determining to what extent the environmental information that leads to action is located in dispositional structures of the individual organism (and therefore based on individual or phylogenetic experience of past environments) or in the current environment as the organism experiences it through his vital processes (*e.g.*, sensation, nutrition).

Biological research has long been concerned with making such determinations and has a number of established strategies for doing so. Although it is beyond the scope of this discussion and the competence of its author to review these in detail, three broad kinds of approaches will be presented schematically in terms of their relevance to the study of personality and sociocultural environment.

The "physiological" strategy. In this approach the starting point is the individual organism, whose responses are assessed over a range of conditions, some of which are environmentally induced, in order to arrive at a "normal" or baseline rate of responding. Marked deviations from the baseline following upon experimental interventions or other environmental events can be attributed to environmental influence with greater reliability than if a response baseline had not been carefully established. Simple measurements like body weight, heart beat, blood pressure are not constant, even over a single day; they vary with the action of the digestive system, the cycle of sleep and wakefulness, activated and non-activated states of the nervous system, the effects of alcohol, barbiturates and other drugs, and so forth. To obtain a stable baseline measure from which deviations can be reliably attributed to environmental influence, it is necessary to sample the normal range within which the assessed values fluctuate—over the diurnal cycles of activity and digestion, over lengthier time periods believed to involve regular or irregular fluctuation, and in a variety of activated conditions that the investigator or subject can manipulate. When a normal range of fluctuation has been established through research not only for a particular individual but for a population or a species; when this range has been demonstrated to have specified limits that are rarely transgressed by individuals, individual assessment can be drastically reduced to a single unrepeated response measure, such as body weight. But when the normal range of fluctuation has not been established and when the limits of its individual and temporal variability are unknown, unrepeated measurement on a group of individuals may well confound their inter-individual variation with their intra-individual variability, yielding highly unstable response measures. It is not merely repeated assessment that is necessary for stable measures, but assessment over a range of conditions known to vary endogenously and environmentally for the normally functioning individual. The baseline obtained in this way can serve as a stable background against which the effects of conspicuous environmental interventions can be studied, although the baseline itself is not necessarily explained thereby (as discussed below).

The "ecological" strategy. In this approach, an environment serves as the starting point, and a variety of species of organisms is studied in relation to it. Detailed knowledge of a particular environment and its resources for survival make it possible to identify species-specific adaptive responses as characteristic of the organisms rather than the environment (in the broader sense) and then to work back to the structures in the organism that make it respond to the environment differently from coresident species. Cognitively (and simplistically), the environment is the ground against which the varieties of species-specific behavior reveal themselves. It must be emphasized, however, that knowledge of an environment can only be a starting point for disentangling dispositional and situational factors in adaptation. This is partly because species that differ grossly (*e.g.*, herbivores and carnivores) do not inhabit the "same" environment, and when their more proximate ecological niches are investigated, the confounding of disposition and situation recurs. It is also partly because different populations of the same species inhabiting different environments may vary, indicating that the adaptive patterns that distinguish them from other species in the original environment are developmentally flexible rather than genically fixed. Thus the ecological strategy leads toward study of microenvironmental adaptation (involving the other two research strategies discussed here) as well as toward comparative studies of varying environments occupied by a given species.

The "embryological" strategy. The focus here is on the growth patterns of the individual organism, and investigation begins with careful observation of those patterns and the environmental matrix within which they occur. The advantage of this method is that at least some adaptive responses can be observed from their initial occurrence in the life of the organism, and evidence can be obtained concerning the extent to which they develop "spontaneously" or "endogenously"—that is, independently of environmental conditions surrounding the organism—or are contingent on certain environmental events. If a response pattern regularly occurs before the organism is exposed to the environmental conditions with which the response is associated in the mature individual, the investigator is alerted to the possibility that the information leading to action is encoded in the genes or acquired in prenatal or early postnatal experience. Observations of development often show that a response varies concomitantly with certain external events or that its growth and organization varies among individuals or populations with the presence or absence of certain types of stimulation, thus identifying environmental determinants. It usually becomes necessary to perform experiments in which environmental as well as anatomical and biochemical conditions are systematically altered, in order to make more decisive judgments about the complex determination of growth and development patterns. But a great deal can be learned by tracing an adaptive response from its observable inception through its normal course of growth and its transactions with environmental events.

These research strategies are not used in isolation from each other, although biologists usually specialize in only one of them; each line of approach raises questions about adaptive processes and structures that can only be answered by recourse to the others. They provide complementary methods of making inferences concerning the relative contributions of disposition and proximate environment to observed adaptive behavior; none of the methods is dispensable.

Psychologists have been strongly influenced by these biological research strategies and have applied them to the more elusive phenomena of human and animal behavior. The use of the "physiological" approach by behavioristic psychologists of the Skinnerian school (although without an interest in mediating processes) and the employment of the "embryological" approach by ethologists are familiar contemporary examples. In psychology, however, the adherents of different approaches are intellectually isolated from each other, and complementarity is rarely realized. Furthermore, the "ecological" strategy, which in biology is most closely connected with the integrating perspective of evolutionary theory, is least developed in psychology because experimental and clinical traditions have dominated psychological research. Personality study might have been expected to develop an ecological approach in which differences among individuals are revealed against the environmental settings common to their life situations, but it has in fact largely restricted its data gathering to the environmental settings of the psychological clinic, laboratory, and classroom.

To explain the particular course that personality research has taken since the pioneering work of Murray *et al.* (1938) would require a lengthy digression into the intellectual history and sociology of the field. Suffice it to say that as personality psychology has expanded over the past three decades, it has been subjected simultaneously to the pressures of producing diagnostic results for clinical psychiatry and meeting the methodological standards of experimental psychology and psychometrics. Both sets of pressures have operated to reduce the amount, diversity, and naturalness of the evidence collected from each individual assessed, putting severe constraints on the development of any research strategy aimed at disentangling disposition and situational reaction. Personality testing has tried to be for psychiatry (and business) what intelligence testing has been for education: a predictive device, useful in mass selection, that doubles as a research method. This effort has not been notably successful, and it seems unlikely that personality assessment as it is presently carried on will teach us as much about the dynamics and development of personality as decades of intelligence testing did about cognitive processes—which was not very much. There has been little serious consideration of whether the inexpensive and convenient procedures favored by testers represent an appropriate scientific approach to personality as theoretically conceived, and if not, what alternatives would be more appropriate. It is now necessary to reevaluate the testing strategy from an investigative viewpoint, putting aside considerations of expense, diagnostic convenience, and psychometric tradition, in the search for the best means of identifying personality dispositions in observable behavior.

In reevaluating the testing approach to personality study, nothing is more critical than the initial step from clinical psychoanalysis, the source of our major personality theory, to the projective techniques that were intended to represent psychoanalysis in academic and clinical psychology. As Murray *et al.* (1938) put it, "Our work is the natural child of the deep, significant, metaphorical, provocative and questionable speculations of psychoanalysis and the precise, systematic, statistical, trivial and artificial methods of academic personology" (pp. 33–34).

Years, later, despite the influential advocacy of projective techniques in psychoanalytic circles by Rapaport, Schafer, Holt, and others (*e.g.*, Rapaport, Gill, and Schafer, 1945; Schafer, 1948, 1954, 1967), it was possible for a leading personality psychologist deeply involved in both projective testing and psychoanalysis to review the literature and conclude:

> Although several interesting and encouraging attempts have been made to demonstrate the utility of some portion of psychoanalytic theory in understanding or interpreting some segment of projective-technique response, a rational and carefully specified bridge from psychoanalytic theory remains a hope for the future—it is definitely not an accomplishment of the past (Lindzey, 1961, p. 128).

Thus, although projective techniques were originally designed to operationalize psychoanalytic concepts, they represent such a different methodology that it is necessary to talk of building bridges between the two approaches. It is my contention that the initial step from psychoanalysis to the test-interview-experiment battery of Murray *et al.* (1938) involved a sacrifice of the advantages accruing to the "physiological," "ecological" and "embryological" strategies that are built into the clinical method of psychoanalysis.

In the next chapter I try to take a fresh look at the process of clinical inference in psychoanalysis, to see if it is not possible to base on psychoanalysis a method of investigating personality that is more effective than the testing approach.

13

Psychoanalytic Clinical Method

The extensive efforts of academic psychologists to test psychoanalytic hypotheses, originating in the 1920's and crystallized into their present form by Sears' (1943) *Survey of Objective Studies of Psychoanalytic Concepts,* have proceeded on the assumption that psychoanalysis as developed by Freud was a valuable theory attached to a scientifically worthless method. In this chapter I argue that psychoanalysis represents a valuable method for studying personality that must be properly understood before attempting to assess the validity of its theoretical propositions, and that there are methodological advantages in psychoanalytic clinical procedures that point the way to a more adequate personality psychology than we have at present.

In making this departure from established thinking on the subject, I am bolstered by a number of considerations, not the least of which is that academic research on psychoanalysis has so frequently been disappointing and even on its face has seemed to do so little justice to the topic under investigation. This is partly due to ignorance, as Holzman suggests:

> Another factor in the controversy over the validity of psychoanalysis is that many sophisticated investigators have a poor knowledge of psychoanalysis. . . . There seems to be an expectation that these psychologists, their shallow acquaintance with primary source materials notwithstanding, will be able to make compelling translations of psychoanalytic theories or assertions into research proposals (1970, pp. 6–7).

The primary source materials, as interpreted by Gedo and Pollock (1967), show that throughout its development by Freud, theoretical

185

advances in psychoanalysis were responses to problems encountered in the application of existing clinical technique. Freud emphasized this methodological primacy, as in the following quotation from an encyclopedia article published in 1923.

> Psychoanalysis is the name (1) of a procedure for the investigation of mental processes which are almost inaccessible in any other way, (2) of a method, (based upon that investigation) for the treatment of neurotic disorders and (3) of a collection of psychological information obtained along those lines, which is gradually being accumulated into a new scientific discipline (1923b, p. 235).

These considerations alone would lead one to suspect that psychologists had prematurely dispensed with its clinical method when they began conducting research on psychoanalysis. My own experience in training at a psychoanalytic institute suggests not only that its procedures are the strongest part of psychoanalysis but also that they are not adequately portrayed in the published literature. Psychoanalytic case histories are usually so condensed and addressed so narrowly to an ingroup audience of fellow clinicians, who need not have the procedures explained to them, that they present a false image of doctrinaire judgments based on fragmentary evidence. This image prevails among behavioral science investigators, and psychoanalysts have done little to provide corrective information. It is thus necessary to examine in some detail the way psychoanalysts work in order to find out what scientific contributions their method might make to the comparative study of personality.

In undertaking an examination of psychoanalytic method, one is immediately confronted with the old controversy between the research goals of discovering general laws and of understanding the individual case, the nomothetic and idiographic approaches respectively. Psychoanalytic clinical investigation has usually been seen as idiographic, whereas psychological research is explicitly nomothetic, and the two orientations have been regarded as supplementary at best and often incompatible. In the following section I argue that a proper understanding of idiographic work in psychoanalysis is essential to the construction of a sound scientific methodology for the study of personality. It will become clear, however, that psychoanalysis departs importantly from the standard model of individual case study in abnormal or clinical psychology and that its departures represent the most promising lines of methodological development for personality research.

Basic Inference Procedures in Psychoanalysis

Psychoanalysis as investigation has been most frequently regarded from the outside as a kind of behavioral science case study, parallel to the ethnography, the community or organization study, the clinical case study in psychology. In this type of research, each pattern of action is shown to be connected to other actions in a structure of exchange or communication, functional interdependencies of behavior, an ideational system of shared or idiosyncratic meanings. The result is an understanding of a particular person, group, or institution as a distinctive and coherent organization of interconnected parts. That this applies to the psychoanalytic approach to personality cannot be doubted, but it is not the whole of it. A central feature of psychoanalytic work is the temporal dimension, which brings it closer to historical case study and to the "event analysis" or "process" studies of social anthropologists such as Turner (1967, 1968) and Swartz (1968). The psychoanalytic use of temporal sequence in individual behavior, however, is quite distinct and is the proper starting place for an examination of inference procedures in psychoanalysis.

First, it must be noted that psychoanalysis[1] consists of 45- or 50-minute sessions conducted four or five times a week for eleven months of the year and carried on for at least three years. That means approximately 200 sessions a year and a total of at least 600 sessions. Personality assessment or diagnosis goes on throughout that period. Contrary to a widespread impression, the focus of psychoanalytic observation is not on reconstruction of early life experiences but on what is happening during each of the 600 sessions and on the processes of change over the period of their occurrence. Thus psychoanalytic observation is a study of ongoing process ranging from the microscopic events of the session to the macroscopic trends of the entire period. (Freud's theory of this process includes the idea that the patient inevitably regresses in analysis to certain infantile patterns of behavior that activate significant memories from his early life; the analyst, therefore, deals with such childhood material only as the patient introduces it into their current relationship, as it becomes part of the ongoing process.)

The psychoanalytic method is based on the technique of free association. The "fundamental rule" for the patient in analysis is that he should say whatever comes into his mind regardless of how offensive, trivial, or silly; the analyst does not actively question the patient, though when he becomes silent the analyst may urge him to report what he is thinking. The basic unit of psychoanalytic observation is the associative sequence, a sequential chain of the patient's spoken thoughts. The content of the thoughts or ideas produced under these conditions varies enormously: current preoccupations; something that happened last night; a dream or dream fragment; bodily sensations while lying on the couch;

1. In the context of this book, *psychoanalysis* refers to the "mainstream" Freudian psychoanalysis represented organizationally by the American Psychoanalytic Association and the International Psychoanalytic Association.

reactions to the analyst's appearance, clothes, office furniture, or wall decorations; emotional feelings; childhood memories; an incident in the waiting room; the difficulties of free associating; the concerns that led to treatment; and so forth. The analyst's interest is in what connects one reported idea with those next to it in sequence. Why does idea A lead to idea B? Why does a train of thought move in the particular direction that it does? The psychoanalytic theory of associative thinking was set forth by Freud in Chapter 7 of *The Interpretation of Dreams* (1900); it cannot be fully recapitulated here, and even an adequate description of how it is used in the analytic situation would require an excessively long account for our present purposes. I therefore present in sparse outline some of the basic working assumptions that guide psychoanalytic inferences concerning free association.

1. There are determinate psychological connections between adjacent ideas in an associative sequence, even when these ideas have no apparent (conscious) relevance to one another from the point of view of the patient or an outside observer.

2. The connections are determined not only by simple contiguity in the patient's prior experience but by their remembered relevance to deep-seated motives.

3. When ideas closely connected to deep-seated motives have been excluded from consciousness (repressed owing to their unacceptability to the self), they are replaced in associative sequence by ideas more remote from those motives, producing an "illogical" association that can only be understood in terms of the unconscious connection.

4. When a train of association leads toward an idea closely connected to an unconscious motive, the sequence will be interrupted by the patient, through a lapse into silence or a sudden upsurge of apparently groundless anxiety or emotional feelings or an abrupt change of posture or conversational approach ("resistance").

5. When the analyst offers an interpretation of the interruption in terms of its motivational relevance, and when that interpretation gives recognizable expression to the excluded idea, the patient will be able to associate to it and bring to consciousness ideas that are closer to the unconscious motive.

6. Close observation of the free associations of a patient without interpretation by the analyst provides indications of the unconscious motives connecting ideas. The analyst postpones interpretation until the indications have become strong enough (through repetition of types of sequential behavior, *e.g.*, the ideas that repeatedly precede interruptions) for him to reach a tentative conclusion on which the interpretation can be based.

These procedures constitute the core of psychoanalytic work, and skill in using them in the analytic situation is the aim of psychoanalytic training. Several points about this procedural core must be stressed. First, its basis is an associational theory of thinking and its basic data are ideas produced sequentially in association with one another. Hence temporal sequence is central to the inference process. Second, in the course of analytic work over at least 600 sessions, the analyst has the opportunity to observe the patient repeat similar associative sequences many times in the same situation before arriving at a final judgment concerning their motivational meaning. As Gedo and Pollock state, "The analyst must have sufficient time to validate his observations and interpretations in the course of the numerous repetitions of the analysand's characteristic responses" (1967, p. 562). Finally, in observing the patient's response to his own interpretation, the analyst obtains feedback concerning the validity of his inference. As Greenson says, "We need the patient's responses to determine the validity of our interpretation" (1967, p. 39). If the feedback is negative, the analyst will alter his inference and make a different interpretation the next time an interruption of association (resistance) occurs. Thus psychoanalytic observation is interventive and has a self-correcting process built into it.

What has been described so far is the basic unit of psychoanalytic inference, and it is present at every stage in the analytic process. It is not simply repeated endlessly, however, but is a building block in larger temporal units—the session, the week, the analytic phase, and intermediate units of idiosyncratic length. In each of these, the inference procedure based on the Freudian model of the associative sequence is applied. The analytic observer asks, why does behavior pattern A lead to behavior pattern B? Why does the patient's behavior in analysis move in the particular direction it does? And he seeks the answer in indicators of unconscious process connecting and influencing that movement. A discussion of each type of unit, with hypothetical examples, follows.

The session. Although the 45- or 50-minute session ("hour") sometimes contains one uninterrupted flow of associations, more frequently resistance provides junctures within the session. Taking the entire session as a unit, the analyst examines the relation of its component associative sequences. It may be, for example, that a new patient is consciously apprehensive about revealing certain thoughts currently on his mind. He arrives late for the session, appears nervous, and finds on lying down on the couch that his mind goes blank. He can think of nothing to say. The analyst simply comments on his apprehension (an interpretation), which seems to relax the patient, and he begins to associate but then stops short of revealing some thoughts about which he seems to be ashamed. Sensing this, the analyst asks if he is afraid of how the analyst will react to his revelation. This interpretation serves to remind the patient that he will not be punished for whatever he says in analysis and makes him aware of his fear; he then talks about and associates to the (consciously suppressed) thought. Another example: A patient comes to his session preoccupied with thoughts about himself and his psychological difficulties. He talks freely, and his associations move rapidly toward memories of a terrifying incident in his life. Suddenly he stops and says how uncomfortable he is on the couch; he writhes about, complaining of pain in his back. The analyst interprets this as resistance (the content of the interpretation would depend on previous events), after which the patient remembers a dream he had last night that seems to be responsible for his preoccupation today. He recounts the dream and associates to it.

In both these hypothetical examples the patient's different responses to the fundamental rule of free association early and later in the session can only be understood in relation to events preceding and following a particular series of associations; the associative sequences of each session together form a sequence for analysis. Inference concerning the session as a unit is assisted by observation of the characteristic (repeated) behavior of the patient in many sessions. Some patients, for example, characteristically ruminate about superficial concerns during the entire session and then mention emotionally charged events or issues when they are on their way from the couch to the door. Some are completely silent at the beginning of every hour and build up to a crescendo, while others become inhibited toward the end, preparing for a dreaded separation. These patterns of the whole session are noted and interpreted in the same manner as the smaller steps within the associative sequence.

The week. Analytic sessions on successive days may be associatively linked; the most familiar example is the analyst's interpretation of Day 1, which becomes the day residue (the instigation) for a dream that night, which is recounted and associated to on Day 2. Major emotional events in an analytic session are likely to have reverberations in subsequent days, which makes the week a convenient unit of analysis. Like the session, the week has definite structural properties, notably a beginning and an end, to which patients respond. Just as some patients are chronically early or late for their sessions or chronically inhibited or uninhibited at their end, so the gap of two or three days between weeks produces characteristic behavior patterns. Some patients become upset at the impending separation toward the end of the week, whereas others have a hard time getting back into free association at the beginning of each week and are only able to overcome resistance by its end. Reviewing a week, the analyst detects associative connections between sessions and a sequential movement throughout the week, as the patient moves toward or away from dealing with a highly charged emotional issue.

The analytic phase. A temporal unit of an entirely different sort is contributed by the psychoanalytic theory of clinical technique, which conceptualizes the entire process of psychoanalysis in terms of an invariant sequence of phases of varying length. The exact definitions and boundaries of these phases are by no means agreed upon by all analysts, but the following five represent a reasonable common denominator:

1. *Establishment of the therapeutic alliance.* In this phase interpretation is focused on fostering self-observation in the patient and on establishing a sense of companionship in the analytic work between the patient-as-self-observer (his "observing ego" as opposed to his "experiencing ego") and the analyst.

2. *Analysis of resistance and defenses.* As the patient begins to be emotionally involved and regressed in analysis, his defenses become mobilized to prevent deeper involvement and more regression, and these defenses manifest themselves as resistances to free association, which the analyst interprets.

3. *Development of the transference neurosis.* With the retreat of the initial defenses, the patient regresses to infantile modes of thinking and feeling about the analyst, based on his unconscious experience in childhood. He begins to reproduce in his sessions microcosmic versions of behaviors influenced by the intense conflicting motives and emotions experienced in childhood toward parents and siblings (and the resultant internalizations), but now intruded into his relationship with the analyst. This is the transference neurosis, which the analyst's interpretations gradually bring into the forefront of conscious attention.

4. *Analysis of the transference neurosis.* When it becomes full-blown, the transference neurosis must be analyzed; each aspect of the central infantile conflict must be reexperienced with great intensity in relation to the analyst and mastered by gradual discharge of the emotional energies that had been trapped in the confines of a child's unconscious fantasies, as adult consciousness is extended to that experience. This is known as "working-through." The analyst's interpretations in this phase link neurotic behavior toward the analyst with motivational conflicts of childhood origin.

5. *Termination.* In the final phase, the patient faces the loss of the analyst as an object of attachment and this often requires another round of working-through, with special attention to the unconscious meanings of separation from a parental object.

Psychoanalysts have some general expectations about how much chronological time each of these phases takes, although it is also expected to vary from one case to another, so the analytic observer makes an assessment of what phase his patient is in at the moment, whether it is taking more or less time than normal and why, and how much progress is being made toward the next phase. Since a phase can last more than a year, its connection with what went before is of a different order from the connections in the associative sequence, the session and the week, but there are profound similarities. The defenses manifested early in the analytic process are related to the deep-seated motives brought to consciousness later in the same way as the "illogical" association of ideas is related to the unconscious connection between them. The latter can be seen as a microcosmic form of the former, or the analytic process as a whole can be seen as the analysis of a single associative sequence extended over a long period of time. The dynamic model of associative thinking constructed by Freud and applied by him to defensive processes in dreams, jokes, and slips of the tongue (as well as in literature and religion) is used by the working analyst to understand long-term trends in the behavior of his patient as the latter makes his way through the sequential phases of the psychoanalytic process.

In making inferences about these longer units of behavior, the analytic observer is guided by the elaborated premises of Freudian theory. He assumes a set of determinate relations between the personality structure of the patient and his behavior in analysis. Thus he assumes that the defenses built into the patient's character structure and used by him in other situations will enter into analysis as resistances. Or to put it an-other way, he assumes that the resistances manifested in analysis are representative of the patient's enduring defensive structure. He further assumes that the transference neurosis represents in current microcosm the residues in personality structure of the conflicting motives experienced in the childhood situation. As debatable as some of these theoretical assumptions may be to a skeptic, the analytic observer has many opportunities to check on their validity in each case.

Intermediate units. There are other temporal units in psychoanalysis to which the associative model of inference is applied, but they are peculiar to the individual case. They tend to be longer than the week but shorter than the analytic phase. For some patients, for example, a vacation period is particularly salient because they experience the month-long separation as a severe deprivation, or a release from imprisonment, or in some other idiosyncratic way that is anticipated in analytic sessions beforehand and has consequences for many sessions afterwards. In such cases, the way in which the patient reacts to the vacation period in successive years can be a sensitive indicator of analytic progress and personality change. Other temporal markers include unique events in the patient's environmental situation—a death in the family, a divorce or love affair, an occupational success or failure—which by arousing or gratifying certain motives bring certain ideational material to the fore and help mobilize or eliminate certain resistances. Events of this nature may be partly responsible for promoting or preventing movement in the sequence of analytic phases. This is also true of events in or surrounding the analytic process: a particular dream or memory, or the appearance or disappearance of a symptom, or the discovery of a fact about the analyst's personal life, or a particular encounter in his waiting room, may trigger a sudden shift in functioning in the analysis. It is not that such internal or external events cause change in any enduring sense but that they may be closely enough associated with discernible movement in the analysis to be convenient boundary markers in the inference process.

The analyst may find it makes sense to divide the analysis into idiosyncratic phases marked by certain dreams, love affairs of the patient, emotional outbursts in analysis, and so forth. Some experienced analysts consider the first dream a significant event usually dividing one phase from another; others look upon the patient's first dream of the analyst as himself as an event of this sort. There is obviously room for subjective preference in the definition of these intermediate units, but the important question is not where the boundary goes but what kind of case can be made for a before-after change due to the elimination or mobilization of defenses. Evidence of this comes from the close examination of analytic sessions and weeks before and after the alleged marker. If a change clearly did follow upon the particular event, and the ideational content of free association and resistance before and after connected it with that event, this would support the hypothesis relating that marker to an unconscious connection between the two time periods in analysis. Here again the dynamic theory of associative thinking provides the model of inference concerning the processes of change over substantial periods of time.

From this presentation it should be clear that psychoanalytic observation provides a type of detailed data from which inferences concerning time series of varying scope are possible. The sequence from free association to resistance to interpretation to free association, for which Freud provided a theoretical model of analysis, is discernible in the brief components of the analytic sessions. By analogical extension based on the same dynamic model of mental functioning (*i.e.*, the model of motivational conflict and defense), it can also be identified in longer intervals ranging from a single session to more than a year. Temporal units of varying length are not only understood in terms of the same basic principle but can be assembled for diagnostic inference, short units fitting within the longer and contributing fine-grained evidential detail concerning long-term trends. It is possible, for example, to compare one analytic phase (or other time period) in the analysis with another by focusing on associative material from sessions and weeks drawn from each of them, seeking indications of the relative strength and quality of resistances, the bringing to consciousness of certain motives and the fantasies associated with them, the deepening of regression and use of more primitive defenses in resistance, the development of transference, and so forth.

The analyst has associative material to make day-by-day, week-by-week assessments that provide building blocks in inferences concerning long-term trends. And while the primary focus of the analyst is on what goes on in the analytic sessions themselves, which he observes directly, he can (and does) also divide the material according to the level of consciousness and behavioral functioning it represents and its place in the life situation of the patient, creating a number of separable data streams for longitudinal inference. Dreams, for example, can be studied over time by themselves (along with the associations to them) to see if they confirm the inferences based on behavior in the analytic situation as a whole. The same is true for the patient's reports of his symptoms (phobias; anxieties; hypochondria; depression; bodily conversions; psychosomatic manifestations such as asthma, ulcers, rheumatoid arthritis), the appearance, disappearance, and relative severity of which can be charter over a substantial period of time, examined microscopically in relation to events in analysis (including particular ideational material recorded in associative sequence) and in the patient's life situation as he reports it. Still another separable data stream is the patient's reported behavior in his life situation, for example, in the marital or occupational spheres, which can also be examined longitudinally for indications of change in the relative strength of particular motives.

A point that is often missed in behavioral science discussions of psychoanalysis is that while the procedures of analytic inference are guided by the Freudian theoretical system, they are also severely disciplined by the mandatory examination of these separable streams of longitudinal data, which are checked against one another in the process of making a diagnostic judgment. The analytic observer is prevented from converting a doctrinaire hunch into a definitive assessment by the necessity of examining whether it is upheld by trends in the patient's dreams, symptoms, and social behavior outside the analytic situation. This procedure is particularly important in answering a question raised above: How does the analyst confirm the theoretical assumptions that resistances in free association represent the patient's characteristic defenses and that the transference neurosis represents the central conflicting motivational forces of the patient's unconscious mental functioning? The answer is that the analyst has a variety of data available to him to check on the validity of those assumptions in each individual case He has evidence concerning the consistency of conflicts experienced and defenses used across the several behavioral domains mentioned, plus the patient's memories of behavior and experience in past life situations extending back to childhood. Psychoanalytic training develops the skill of examining these lines of evidence in fine-grained detail and checking them against one another; this is an important supplement to the longitudinal analysis of the directly observed associative material in the analytic situation.

In this section I have attempted to show the role of longitudinal inference procedures, based on the dynamic model of associative thinking, in psychoanalysis. I have deliberately emphasized the temporal aspect of psychoanalytic assessment because it is so often overlooked or taken for granted in comparing psychoanalytic observation with other methods of personality assessment and because I believe it produces evidence concerning behavioral dispositions that is unmatched by the research procedures of academic psychology. Even without applying the Freudian inference procedures to the data from a psychoanalysis, an observer examining the data would certainly be able to make many reliable judgments concerning the behavioral characteristics of the patient, seeing his repeated reactions, cyclical changes and progressive alterations played out over hundreds of hours. The sheer quantity of data collected in a single observational frame and its extension over such long periods of time yield inferences about personality (not necessarily Freudian, but based on psychoanalytic data) with a *face validity* that is usually lacking in the data produced by standard research instruments such as tests or interview schedules.

But the use of psychoanalytic inference procedures does contribute several additional dimensions of validity. The linkages between ideas shown in the microscopic examination of the patient's associations contributes a phenomenological validity to assessment because it shows how a particular event or self-perception is connected with other ideational material in the patient's subjective system of thought or cognitive structure. Observation of the effects of the analyst's interpretations on resistance and subsequent associations, as well as the effects of events in and out of analysis on longer-term trends in behavior, contributes quasi-experimental data concerning the validity of motivational assessments. Comparison of defensive patterns across temporal units of varying scope from a few minutes to more than a year contributes convergent validity concerning the consistency and strength of these patterns, And comparison of different lines of evidence—from dreams, symptoms, outside social behavior in analytic sessions—adds convergent validity regarding consistency of changing behavior patterns across levels of consciousness and behavioral functioning and across environmental domains. In all of this the longitudinal quality is central, but it is not the only strength of psychoanalytic inference, as the following section demonstrates.

Research Strategies Embedded in the Clinical Method

To what extent are the inference procedures of psychoanalysis generalizable to investigations conducted in other types of settings? I attempt to answer this question by considering first how the biological research strategies discussed in the preceding chapter are embedded in the psychoanalytic clinical method. My argument is that the method developed by Freud employs all three of those strategies and represents a solution to the problem of disentangling enduring individual disposition from reaction to proximate environmental pressure in the observation of the adaptive behavior of humans. When the clinical procedures have been examined as investigative strategies embodying certain principles for the collection of data, it will be easier to imagine how these principles, as opposed to their concrete embodiments in psychoanalysis, can be applied to other situations in which data can be collected.

The "physiological" strategy. By observing a single individual repeatedly over a long period of time, the analytic observer is able to establish a "normal" baseline of the patient's behavioral response, from which marked deviations can be noted in relation to their possible causes and consequences as the analytic process goes on. By the end of the first 200 hours (if not earlier) the analyst has observed the patient under varying conditions originating in the analytic situation and in his life outside analysis. He has seen how the patient habitually responds to the week-long intensity and weekend break of analysis, to the frustrations occasioned by the analyst's failure to gratify motives that are expressed in the sessions, to the demands and opportunities of his job and marital situation, and to the ups and downs of social stimulation and satisfaction in his total life situation. The patient's typical cycles and other rhythms and recurrences of emotional mood, adaptive performance, and internal struggle have had a chance to manifest themselves under the microscope of free association.

An assessment of personality based on the first 200 hours provides a baseline of typical response sequence within the idiosyncratic temporal units displayed by the individual patient as well as in terms of the more standard temporal structure of psychoanalysis. In the context of such an assessment, a particular behavior at one point in time can be seen as occupying a position in an observed temporal order rather than as indicating a static attribute. Thus an expression of anger or sadness would not be taken to indicate a personality trait of hostility or depression but rather understood in terms of the conditions and behaviors recurrently preceding and following it. The latter type of inference might lead the observer to realize that the anger or sadness was not a stable characteristic of the person but only characteristic of his behavior at one point in a recurrent sequence of reaction to certain kinds of events. In other words, the baseline assessment derived from extended observation in psychoanalysis protects the observer from incorrectly assuming that a manifest behavior seen at one point in time is representative of a stable trait, a pitfall common in personality tests.

The psychoanalytic assessment of behavior against a baseline established for each individual over a variety of conditions, each of which involves temporal complexity, is in principle similar to the method of operant conditioning devised and widely applied by B. F. Skinner and his students. If one regards the effects of the analyst's interpretations (and other less controlled events) and their sequelae as analogous to experimental intervention, it becomes clear that psychoanalysis operates with an experimental, or at least quasi-experimental, approach to the collection of data on personality. In psychoanalysis, however, the observed behavior (the associative material) is analyzed into numerous dimensions of content instead of just a single one, and, in contrast to operant conditioning, the behavioral data are used to diagnose dispositional entities rather than being of interest in and of themselves.

Emphasis must again be given to the point that the "physiological" strategy is not being used when assessment is merely repeated, as in the test-retest tradition of personality measurement. Retesting as such does not involve systematic sampling of environmental and endogenous conditions known to vary normally for the individual; such sampling is required to form an accurate baseline, from which changes can validly be attributed to events that repeatedly vary with the behavior. In monitoring a person's preoccupations on a day-to-day basis, psychoanalytic observation covers the entire range of conditions in which he functions, approaching the conditions phenomenologically, through the patient's associations rather than through independent study of environments. The regularities that emerge soon give the analyst detailed evidence concerning the patient's subjective experience in these environmental settings as well as in the analytic sessions so that when irregularities occur their origin is usually clear. Thus, when an analyst has had a patient in treatment for some time, he has no difficulty distinguishing between short-term emotional fluctuations within that patient's normal range of reactions to normal environmental events, and behavioral alterations outside that normal range, associated with unusual events or with signs of fundamental personality change.

The form that the "physiological" strategy takes in psychoanalysis needs further explanation. The psychoanalytic situation is a very special one for the patient because in it he is guaranteed that he will not be chastised for whatever he says and that no one else will hear it. These guarantees plus the trust involved in the therapeutic alliance, the patient's desire to get well, and some of the regressive features of the situation (the doctor-patient relationship, the prone position on the couch) combine to foster in the patient a willingness to reveal in his associations thoughts, feelings, and wishes that he would conceal in other settings. In this respect, psychoanalytic observation must be thought of as taking place under a "relaxed" condition of the organism, in which normal constraints are temporarily lifted, as in physiological observation under special conditions designed to reveal the underlying structure and functioning of the organs and processes being investigated.

To summarize, psychoanalytic observation is not experimental in the strict sense, but observation is conducted under a special "relaxed" condition of the organism, in which normal environmental constraints are suspended; observation is longitudinal, producing a time series of assessment points, and it also samples the effects of stimulation from the normal range of environmental settings in which the individual functions; the observer intervenes and makes assessments before and after; early observations on behavioral recurrences of idiosyncratic length and environmental range permit a baseline assessment distinguishing stable from fluctuating features of behavioral response. Most of these characteristics of the "physiological" strategy in psychoanalytic observation, which contribute heavily to the face validity of clinical assessment of personality, are not present in academic personality research.

THE "ECOLOGICAL" STRATEGY

Psychoanalytic clinical ecology begins with the formal structure of the psychoanalytic situation: the fee-paying doctor-patient relationship as defined in our society; the special demands of the psychoanalytic relationship, including the patient lying prone on the couch while the analyst sits out of sight behind his head; the frequent sessions at the same hours, the need to be on time, the monthly bills; the relative anonymity of the analyst; and of course the fundamental rule of free association. These are virtually constant for all analytic patients regardless of who the analyst is. For each particular analyst there are other structural features that are constant for his patients but not for others: the physical arrangement and surroundings of his office, including the arrangement of furniture and decorations in his office and waiting room; whether he shares an office with other physicians; the proximity of his office to other analysts and the probability of meeting other analytic patients; the proximity to toilets; the difficulty of parking or getting transportation to the area; location in a specific part of town with particular characteristics. And of course there are the analyst's unique personal attributes: his appearance, age, sex, height, facial features, body build, clothing; his voice and accent; his style of dealing with patients; and so forth. The psychoanalytic observer becomes a specialist in the details of these constant features, for they form the background against which individual differences in the personalities of his patients are revealed.

At the beginning of the analytic process, the patient's handling of these formal features can be very revealing, for it is then that several arrangements must be made concerning the patient's case and his need for analysis, the time of appointments, the fee, becoming acquainted with the basic procedures of lying on the couch and free associating, and so forth. The experienced clinician who has seen many patients react to and handle these aspects of the situation begins noting idiosyncratic behavior patterns immediately. The patient's initial presentation of himself to the analyst, his handling of the authority relationship between them, his first attempts at free association, his reactions to the unfamiliar surroundings and procedures—all become diagnostic data. The unfamiliarity and ambiguity of the situation are sources of diagnostic strength, for they insure that the patient's initial behavior will reflect his own dispositions rather than reactions to environmental pressures. There are such pressures in the situation, but the analyst who has seen numerous patients cope with them can readily distinguish idiosyncratic reaction patterns from the common denominator. Some patients, for example, evidence a great deal of concern about the inconvenience of appointment times; some are habitually late; some take an open interest in the analyst's appearance or private life, while others avoid any mention of the analyst in their associations. The analyst's clinical skill in "listening to the patient" begins with his attention to every detail in the patient's initial structuring of the ambiguities inherent in the situation.

Ambiguity and constancy of stimuli are central features of projective personality tests, but they are used somewhat differently. In psychoanalysis, the entire interpersonal situation is in observational focus, whereas in testing there is a distinction between responses to the test stimuli themselves and "off-stage" reactions to the testing situation, which are regarded as data only if the material is being used for "clinical" assessment as opposed to psychometric investigation. In projective testing the aim is to make explicit every aspect of the investigation except the visual or verbal test stimuli themselves and the purpose of collecting responses to them, lest ambiguity lead to variable testing conditions and destroy the constancy of the situation from person to person. The aim is to elicit a sample of the individual's fantasy life. In psychoanalysis, however, there is a bare minimum of explicit procedural rules, and the rest of the situation is deliberately ambiguous so that the internally motivated preferences of the patient can express themselves over many aspects of the situation. The aim is not merely to elicit fantasy in an unstructured visual or verbal field but also to make of the psychoanalytic situation an unstructured interpersonal field that the patient structures from the resources of his own personality.

To study the patient's structuring of the ambiguities of the psychoanalytic situation, the analyst not only acquaints himself with the situation itself, with particular reference to the boundaries between objective reality and ambiguity, but also keeps his own behavior as constant and ambiguous as possible. The analyst is himself part of the "projective test," and if he acts differently to different patients or intrudes himself too much on the interaction between himself and a patient, he destroys a valuable source of information about the unique dispositional characteristics of each individual. There is some disagreement among psychoanalysts (see Greenson, 1967) as to how far one becomes a "blank screen" without jeopardizing the therapeutic alliance with the patient. All agree, however, that in the early stages of analysis the analyst keeps interpretation and intrusion to a minimum, to allow behavioral tendencies in the patient to express themselves openly.

The analyst and the analytic situation may form a blank screen (or perhaps more accurately, a textured screen) on which the patient's personality is projected, but the screen is usually not static. Early in the analysis, while the patient is becoming acquainted with the situation, his associations may be focused on formal and procedural features such as the timing of appointments, the waiting-room arrangement, the doctor-patient role relationship, and the strangeness of talking while lying on a couch. Even at this stage the analyst is examining associations to these features in terms of where they lead, what they reveal not only about how the patient deals with this situation but what motives concerning the analyst he brings into the situation consciously or unconsciously. But as time goes on the procedural and formal features become familiar and recede from the associative material, as the relationship with the analyst becomes increasingly the conscious and intense focus of attention and emotional involvement. The analytic situation as social and physical structure becomes the background against which deeper aspects of personality structure are revealed.

The goal of the analyst as observer and therapist is to create conditions under which the patient will impose on the ambiguous relationship between them behavior patterns reflecting his strongest unconscious motives concerning self and others. The patient's intrapsychic structure of motives is to become overtly expressed in his behavior toward the analyst in the transference. It should be noted that this goal of bringing latent dispositions into observable behavior is common to all scientific studies of individual organisms and is essential to make valid inferences about dispositional and environmental contributions to adaptive behavior. The psychoanalytic version of this strategy operates on the assumption that latent personality dispositions were formed in childhood and are unconsciously influencing adult behavior and can be brought to observable expression in the analytic situation. This process depends not only on the ambiguity of the situation but on two other factors: the regression-inducing features of psychoanalysis and interpretations by the analyst. Regression to childhood ways of thought, feeling, and action is induced first by the prone position of the patient (which interferes with normal adult postural controls) and by the normal tendency to treat a doctor as a parental figure, then by the analyst's refusal to act like a gratifying parent, which raises the intensity of the patient's irrational infantile motives relative to his adult rationality and control. The analyst's interpretations serve to bring the aroused unconscious motives gradually to the patient's conscious attention as the regression proceeds so that the usual ways of avoiding recognition of these motives (by defending against them) are hindered by analysis of resistance.

When this procedure is successful, the patient, rather than responding in his usual ways to social environments, constructs a phenomenal environment from the powerful motivational and cognitive forces of his unconscious mental apparatus, and it is this subjectively constructed environment that is at the center of psychoanalytic interest, both therapeutic and investigative. Psychoanalysts consider it most important that the conditions of analysis foster a purely subjective transference and transference neurosis with minimal interference from external reality so that the patient's own infantile motives can be observed in action and treated. The essential skills of the analyst are seen as eliciting and analyzing these subjective tendencies in "pure culture," so to speak, and the clinical analyst usually seeks to deepen his experience and knowledge along these lines rather than broadening his area of expertise. Hence the introduction of any changes in the traditionally minimized environment of the analytic situation for therapeutic or investigative purposes is met with strong opposition and becomes a matter of debate. Hence the sometimes exaggerated but understandable rejection by psychoanalysts of investigative intrusions like tape recording into the analytic session, and their view of personality testing as so diluted as to be virtually unrelated to their own work. Psychoanalysts observe individual behavior in a specialized environmental setting that elicits latent dispositions that, following Freud, they believe to be "almost inaccessible in any other way."

The "embryological" strategy. Discussion of the other two strategies embedded in psychoanalysis has touched on the "embryological" as well. For the analytic observer, psychoanalysis is a developmental process, similar to the transitions of normal personal development, involving the phases outlined in the previous section, studied longitudinally over a period of three or more years. If it is successful in its therapeutic goals, structural change in personality is achieved. The analyst's focus is on the development of the transference neurosis from its inception at the onset of analysis through its growth and peak period and its resolution in the analytic working-through and termination. Even apart from its important theoretical assumptions about the relation of the transference neurosis to childhood conflicts and their developmental resolution, psychoanalytic observation embodies an embryological strategy of data collection, for it follows an individual over a period of time and in an observational context in which a directed process of change is going on. Events associated with advancing and retarding that process become manifest in the longitudinal attention to both the individual's behavior patterns and the environmental factors to which he is exposed (as phenomenologically mediated through his associations).

The advantages of this embryological strategy are that one can disentangle environmental from endogenous contributions to developmental

process by observing the temporal sequence of environmental and behavioral events and patterns. This is no less true of psychoanalysis than
of other detailed longitudinal approaches to development. The strength
of psychoanalysis is that this embryological strategy is combined with
"physiological" and "ecological" strategies for the valid detection of dispositional contributions to the normal adaptive behavior of human
adults. The question we must now ask is how the psychoanalytic clinical
method of assessing personality can be generalized to settings outside
the doctor's office without sacrificing the research strategies that give
psychoanalytic inferences their validity.

14

The Couch and the Field

What can we learn from psychoanalysis that can be used in the comparative study of personality and sociocultural environment? In the previous chapter I suggested that psychoanalysis is first and foremost "a procedure for the investigation of mental processes," and that this procedure in its standard clinical form contains a solution to the central problem in personality assessment, that of distinguishing between the enduring behavioral dispositions of individuals and their reactions to transient environmental conditions. If psychoanalytic clinical method does indeed solve that problem, it deserves careful examination, for—as I argued in Chapter 12—the confounding of enduring disposition with situational reaction in observable behavior is inherent in adaptation and has given rise, in the field of culture and personality, to the dispute over sociogenic and psychogenic interpretations of cultural behavior.

Examining psychoanalytic method with some care in the preceding chapter indicated that its greatest strength as an assessment procedure— longitudinal observation of ongoing process, opportunities for quasi-experimental inference over varying temporal units, the elicitation of highly motivated interpersonal behavior in a known environmental context—are usually absent in psychological testing. In attempting to transform psychoanalysis into psychometric assessment procedures, personality researchers have eliminated the major means by which analysts establish the validity of their clinical judgments. If psychoanalysis is to be of use in personality research it is as a method employing certain strategies of personality assessment that should be carefully preserved. This method itself, as developed and primarily used in a specialized therapeutic context that maximizes its distinctive procedural advantages, may not appear to lend itself to widespread use outside that context, let alone in other cultures. But by moving beyond the concrete details of the classic psychoanalytic situation to the principles of diagnostic inference embodied in it, we can view psychoanalysis as a generalizable methodological solution to the problems of personality assessment.

How can the principles of psychoanalytic methodology be used to investigate personality in the wide variety of situations and cultural contexts in which human life is lived? This difficult question must be faced at the outset, for only if these principles are widely usable can the psychoanalytic approach, which has proved so illuminating clinically and has produced our most promising theory of human personality, offer us help in the comparative study of personality and sociocultural environment. The present discussion of this question is focused on the study of personality in cultural contexts different from our own, although it has implications for nontherapeutic studies in our own culture, and it therefore begins with consideration of psychoanalytic anthropology.

Most psychoanalytic writing on other cultures, beginning with Freud's *Totem and Taboo* (1913), have involved no serious attempt to apply the clinical method of psychoanalysis. They are what the psychoanalyst David Rapaport called "as if" analyses, in which the standards of evidence used in clinical interpretation are suspended in order to speculate about the meaning and function of exotic material that has a source outside the psychoanalytic situation. Rapaport commented, "Peculiarly enough, the psychoanalysts who were interested in these more 'practical' sciences [anthropology and sociology] very quickly forgot the 'as if' character of their analyses" (Rapaport 1944, p. 181). These numerous works, often using already published data, are sometimes plausible and often provocative, but have little to tell us about the cross-cultural applicability of psychoanalytic method.

Other psychoanalytic writings, perhaps those most influential in anthropology, have been based on interaction between an analyst and one or more persons of another culture, in an attempt at some approximation, however remote and truncated, of psychoanalytic data collection. The first such attempt was that by Géza Roheim, an anthropologist and practicing psychoanalyst who worked among Central Australian aborigines, Normanby Islanders in Melanesia and (more briefly) Somalis in Aden, and the Yuma Indians, during the years 1929 to 1931. In Roheim's first report (1932) on his field research he described and illustrated the kinds of data he collected: series of dreams, with associations, from informants whom he interviewed repeatedly and whose reactions to himself he noted; observations of children playing with and without the dolls he introduced; observations of child rearing and other kinds of interpersonal behavior. Rather than adopting the unintrusive stance of the psychoanalyst or trying to create a controlled and constant situation in which to meet all persons, which would have been very difficult, Roheim

was both active anthropological interviewer and psychoanalytic impro-
viser, exploring the use of different techniques in a variety of settings.

Since 1932, some 15 to 20 psychoanalysts and anthropologists with
psychoanalytic experience and interests have done field work among non-
Western peoples with the explicit intent of conducting psychoanalytic
investigations. Their methods have been diverse.[1] Some have continued
or elaborated upon one of the techniques first used by Roheim; others
have attempted psychotherapy, usually in a clinic or hospital setting;
still others have used a clinical interview, often focused on life history
and sometimes supplemented by projective tests. There is much variation, not only in the amount of understanding shown of the culture in
which their work with individuals was embedded, but even in the way
of approaching those individuals. For example, Ortigues and Ortigues
(1966), who saw patients coming to a hospital for psychiatric treatment
in Dakar (Senegal), criticize Parin, Morgenthaler, and Parin-Matthey
(1963) for seeking out persons among the Dogon (in Mali) and paying
them for participation in group interviews conducted along psychoanalytic lines. No consensus on how to collect psychoanalytic data in a
non-Western culture has emerged from these studies, and no one has
produced results impressive enough to command the emulation of others
in this field.

Apart from their internal disagreements, studies in psychoanalytic anthropology have from the beginning satisfied neither psychoanalysts nor
anthropologists because they seemed not to meet the standards of investigation in either field. Despite increased sophistication on the part of
some and efforts to remedy the flaws of earlier work, this problem remains: Psychoanalytic anthropology for the most part strikes anthropologists as inadequate anthropology and psychoanalysts as inauthentic psychoanalysis. Professional prejudices are involved here, but there are also
cogent criticisms that cannot be dismissed.

From the viewpoint of anthropology, much psychoanalytic anthropology is based on superficial or misguided field work, or both. Although
there are notable exceptions,[2] many investigators have spent too little

1. Representative of the resulting literature are works by Erikson (1939, 1943),
Jules and Zunia Henry (1944), DuBois (1944), Dorothy Eggan (1949, 1952, 1961,
1966), Devereux (1951, 1967, the latter including a bibliography of his other publications), Parin, Morgenthaler and Parin-Matthey (1963), Morgenthaler and Parin
(1964a, 1964b), Boyer (1962, 1964), Prince Peter (1965), and Ortigues and Ortigues
(1966), LaBarre (1970). The work of Anne Parsons (1969), on Italians and Italian-
Americans rather than non-Western peoples, has an important place in this literature.
I omit reference to the works of psychological anthropologists such as Mead, Bateson,
Whiting, Spiro, and Caudill, which are referred to elsewhere in this book.

2. Anne Parsons' work (1969) is the best example so far of how ethnographic
understanding and competence in the vernacular language can help psychoanalytic
field work. Boyer (1962, 1964) is a psychoanalyst who, with his anthropologist
wife, has spent an exceptional two years (over a 13-year period) with the Mescalero
Apache Indians.

time in the field and have made no effort to learn the native language, usually working through interpreters or the local colonial or trade language. They have frequently worked only with a few very acculturated persons who could speak a European language or with indigenous deviants and healers, without becoming sufficiently acquainted with others to understand how the persons they worked with differ. They have sometimes confused individual with institution in their published analyses, failing to distinguish between the persons studied and the groups and institutional patterns in which those persons function, and they have often characterized cultural norms in terms derived from psychopathology. Yet from the viewpoint of psychoanalysis, much psychoanalytic field work is only "as if" analysis, eliminating many of the features of psychoanalytic method, particularly the length of the analytic relationship and the verification of inferences concerning subjective meaning through associative material. The solution of course lies in the statement by Hartmann, Kris, and Loewenstein (1951) that "data collected by anthropological field work and psychoanalytic observation will have to be combined," but the data of both types must be adequate at the outset.

The most obvious remedy to these deficiencies is to meet the standards of both anthropological field work and clinical psychoanalysis with literal completeness, to carry out a complete ethnographic study and then psychoanalyze individuals from the society studied in the same way individuals are analyzed in our own society. This proposal deserves serious consideration before any alternatives are examined, for if we move on to alternatives hastily, sooner or later the question will arise: Why not do the full job?

Psychoanalysis and Ethnography Compared

In attempting to examine this proposal, I have found it useful to make parallel considerations of ethnographic field work and clinical psychoanalysis in terms of three components: the investigator, the situation, and the subjects. Throughout this parallel treatment the primary question is how and to what extent the psychoanalytic clinical method can be imported into ethnographic field work as practiced by anthropologists or as it might be redesigned for psychoanalytic investigation.

Let us first consider the investigator. The psychoanalyst is a person whose primary interest is in inner experience, who has undergone personal analysis and submitted himself to carefully supervised training emphasizing skill in applying a standard method to different persons, and who in training and after is encouraged to make his own subjective reactions (positive and negative) to his patient a major focus of his analysis. The anthropologist is usually a person whose primary interest is in the outer world of shared social and cultural reality in an exotic

context, who undergoes an intellectual training predicated on the assumption that contexts differ so much among cultures that only general
guidelines to field method can be provided, who is encouraged to develop his own interests and works unsupervised in the field from the
beginning, and who takes professional pride in befriending the people
he works with and attaining a sympathetic understanding of their viewpoint, through participation as well as interviewing. The potential in-
compatibilities are many, resulting from the recruitment, training, and
professional self-images of persons in psychoanalysis and anthropology.
The psychoanalyst is likely to approach a novel cultural context impa-
tiently, seeing it as an obstacle to getting into intrapsychic material
rather than as an opportunity for investigation. The anthropologist may
be unwilling or unable to engage in the self-analysis required by psychoanalytic work, because it involves confronting his own hostile and ex-
ploitative feelings toward the people he is working with, or because it
threatens the unexamined defenses in his own personality that helped
determine the intellectual interests represented by his field work. These
difficulties do not hold for all investigators, but they indicate illustratively
that if data are to be collected that will meet the present standards of
both disciplines, there is a problem—not necessarily insuperable—about
who is to do it. Either some very exceptional anthropologists must be
trained as psychoanalysts or some unusual psychoanalysts must collabo-
rate with ethnographers and be prepared to spend long periods of time
in the field.

The situations in which psychoanalysts and ethnographers collect their
data also differ drastically. In contrast to the analyst, the ethnographer,
on his own initiative, lives with or near his subjects all day long and has
varied contacts with them as interviewer, visitor, friend, sometime em-
ployer, dispenser of medicine, driver, fictive kinsman. Although the
ethnographer is asked for help, he does not ordinarily use this as an
occasion for investigation but rather goes to his subjects when they are
not in a state of dire need, to request their assistance in his research
venture. How different this is from the therapist-investigator, whose help
is sought by a needy patient and who then insists on substituting understanding for gratification! If classical analysis is to be conducted, it
must be done outside the ethnographic situation, either by a psychoanalyst who is not the ethnographer or by an ethnographer-psychoanalyst
who does ethnography in one community and then shifts to another for
psychoanalytic work with patients.

Finally, there are the subjects of investigation. The heart of the issue
here is whether the people studied by anthropologists are analyzable.
In assessing analyzability, the psychoanalyst is considering aspects of
ego functioning: motivation and capacity for self-observation, ability to
postpone gratification; tolerance for analytic regression and the upsurge

of strong affects; reality-testing, quality of object relations, potential for developing a transference neurosis, and so forth. The anthropological evidence, as I read it and have experienced it, indicates that these ego functions are extremely variable cross-culturally and are in fact the most interesting and important aspects of personality variation among human populations. If I am right, there are few grounds for assuming *a priori* that a non-Western population contains individuals who are analyzable in the usual sense. Recent attempts at clinical work by psychoanalysts in non-Western cultures—Boyer (1964) among the Mescalero Apache, Morgenthaler and Parin (1964a, 1964b) among the Dogon of Mali, the Ortigues (1966) in Senegal—provide no support for a more optimistic view. My own general description of personality patterns in Africa (Le-Vine 1970b) illustrates the basis for this skepticism. Two characteristics by themselves—concreteness of thought and a strong reliance on projection as a defense—would make analysis of an ordinary (unschooled and rural) African difficult if not impossible, for both would stand in the way of his developing the verbal self-awareness required for analysis. In fact, I know of no evidence indicating that classical psychoanalysis is possible in non-Western populations except with urbanized and highly literate individuals whose capacities for abstract thought and self-description along Western lines have already been developed to an extraordinary degree. It may be that this is true of European and American populations as well.

Our brief examination of the proposal to combine ethnography and psychoanalysis in their fullness, meeting the current evidential standards of both, has suggested a number of difficulties. Investigators in the two disciplines differ extremely in training and personality, and the situations in which they collect their data are not compatible. By interdisciplinary collaboration, retraining of researchers and proper sequencing and placement of the two activities, these differences might be resolved. It would be possible, though not easy. In considering the human subjects of such investigations, however, the specter of sheer impossibility looms large. It is unlikely that many of the people in whom we are interested are analyzable by strict criteria, and they are unanalyzable for reasons that make them particularly interesting to psychoanalytic theory. Some psychoanalysts might be tempted to dismiss these unanalyzable tribal and peasant peoples as being psychologically not significantly different from the ego-defectives and psychotics in our society who are already being studied from a psychoanalytic point of view, but this does not accord with the facts. We are speaking here of individuals who are well adapted to the sociocultural environments in which they function and who represent a large proportion of the world's population. Some of their adaptations and life-styles resemble those that predominated in human history until a few hundred years ago. If psychoanalysis aspires to be a general psychology of the human species, ways must be found to collect acceptable psychoanalytic data from individuals who are not suitable patients for classical analysis.

It is worth noting at this point that even if classical analysis were universally applicable, the central problem of method in psychoanalytic anthropology would not be solved, for the numbers of individuals that could be analyzed, and their representativeness, would not be adequate to make generalizations about a population for cross-cultural comparison, and the number of populations that could be studied so intensively would be too few for comparative generalization. Thus sociological considerations combine with strictly psychoanalytic ones to make the task of devising satisfactory new field methods imperative.

Guidelines for Comparative Psychoanalytic Research

Can a cross-culturally applicable method of data collection be devised that preserves the crucial features of psychoanalytic personality assessment in the context of an intensive ethnographic field study? This is partly an empirical question, requiring a great deal of exploratory research for its answer. On the basis of presently available knowledge and the examination of psychoanalysis presented so far, however, a methodological framework for such research can be formulated and is presented here and in the next three chapters. First, a statement of some basic principles to serve as guidelines for the development of new methods:

1. Individuals, and only individuals, can be psychoanalyzed. Customs, institutions and organizations cannot be, and any attempt to do so involves dispensing with those elements in the clinical method that give psychoanalytic assessments their validity. There is a fundamental issue at stake here. *Personality* refers to the organization of behavior of the individual human organism. If it makes sense to think of personality as an organized system of interdependently functioning parts—and I believe this is at least as plausible as it is for social and cultural systems—it requires as intensive an investigation (in a culture and personality study) as the sociocultural environment that surrounds it. Investigators in the culture and personality field, including those in psychoanalytic anthropology, have usually been so interested in interpreting culture that they have neglected to devote as much time and effort to studying the complexities of individual personality as they have to examining culture patterns of possible psychological relevance—despite the availability of psychoanalysis as a model of intensive clinical investigation. In the view taken here, intensive personality study is essential rather than optional in culture and personality field work, since psychosocial interpretations without it remain speculative, and psychometric approaches to personality have insufficient validity.

2. There is no consensus in clinical psychoanalysis about how it might be applied outside the standard clinical situation or which of its elements

are most important to preserve in any such application. Psychoanalysts agree on the value of their method in its original form, but they do not agree on what constitutes its central defining characteristics. Some say that the analysis of a transference neurosis is central to psychoanalysis, and any procedure that precludes the development of such a neurosis should not be called "psychoanalytic." Others say that a full transference neurosis is not always achieved, even in psychoanalytic treatment, that the analysis of transferences onto the analyst is central to psychoanalysis, and that any method that elicits transferences in clearly observable form should be considered psychoanalytic data collection. Still others put their greatest emphasis on the analysis of resistances to free association, which they regard as the *sine qua non* of psychoanalytic investigation. Perhaps it would be most accurate to say that analysts disagree about which elements could be dropped from psychoanalysis in its nonclinical application without eliminating the possibility of obtaining psychoanalytic data. Some analysts working on infants (*e.g.*, Spitz, 1965, Wolff, 1963), from whom verbal associations are not obtainable, have used what they regard as psychoanalytic principles in the observation of infants and mother-infant interaction, though no single accepted method has emerged. Thus the development of a method for cross-cultural psychoanalytic research will have to proceed without an unequivocal mandate from the clinical practitioners of psychoanalysis.

3. The operative goal of psychoanalytic method is to detect the respective contributions to the observable behavior of an individual of two thought processes, those termed primary and secondary by Freud (1900), and to understand the relations between the two processes in the individual's responses to the environmental situations that make up his life. Secondary process thought, sometimes referred to as logical or directed thinking, is the processing of accurate environmental information, according to logical rules and for manifestly adaptive ends. It is found in its purest form in the survival-oriented activities of normal mature adults when they are awake and alert. Primary process thought is attuned to needs affectively experienced rather than to accurate sense perceptions, and it represents them metaphorically rather than according to logical rules, directed less toward adaptive goals (which involve environmental change) than toward immediate subjective satisfaction from the mental representation itself. It is dominant in the mental functioning of small children, in the dreaming of adults, in expressive activities of many kinds, and in hallucinations. Primary process thought is in the service of the irrational motives, pleasure-seeking and moralistic, which become partly excluded from consciousness in the course of individual development but continue to influence the operations of the personality system. Secondary process thought is in the service of adaptation to environmental reality, including the demands and opportunities of the

social and cultural systems, and it exerts a rationalizing influence on individual behavior.

One of the best explications of this distinction can be found in Jean Piaget's early work, *The Language and Thought of the Child* (1926):

> Psychoanalysts have been led to distinguish two fundamentally different modes of thinking: *directed* or *intelligent thought,* and *undirected* or, as Bleuler proposes to call it, *autistic thought.* Directed thought is conscious, *i.e.,* it pursues an aim which is present to the mind of the thinker; it is intelligent, which means that it is adapted to reality and tries to influence it; it admits of being true or false (empirically or logically true), and it can be communicated by language. Autistic thought is subconscious, which means that the aims it pursues and the problems it tries to solve are not present in consciousness; it is not adapted to reality but creates for itself a dream world of imagination; it tends, not to establish truths, but so to satisfy desires, and it remains strictly individual and incommunicable as such by means of language. On the contrary, it works chiefly by images, and in order to express itself, has recourse to indirect methods, evoking by means of symbols and myths the feeling by which it is led.
>
> Here, then are two fundamental modes of thought, which, though separated neither at their origin nor in the course of their functioning are subject, nevertheless, to two diverging sets of logical laws. (*Footnote:* There is interaction between these two modes of thought. Autism undoubtedly calls into being and enriches many inventions which are subsequently clarified and demonstrated by intelligence.) Directed thought, as it develops, is controlled more and more by the law of experience and of logic in the stricter sense. Autistic thought, on the other hand, obeys a whole system of special laws (laws of symbolism and immediate satisfaction) which we need not elaborate here. Let us consider, for instance, the completely different lines of thought pursued from the point of view of intelligence and from that of autism when we think of such an object as, say, water.
>
> To intelligence, water is a natural substance whose origin we know, or whose formation we can at least empirically observe; its behavior and motions are subject to certain laws which can be studied, and it has from the dawn of history been the object of technical experiment (for purposes of irrigation, etc.). To the autistic attitude, on the other hand, water is interesting only in connection with organic wants. It can be drunk. But as such, as well as simply in virtue of its external appearance, it has come to represent in folk and child fantasies, and in those of adult subconsciousness, themes of a purely organic character. It has in fact been identified with the liquid substances which issue from the human body, and has come, in this way, to symbolize birth itself, as is proved by so many myths (birth of Aphrodite, *etc.*), rites (baptism, the symbol of a new birth), dreams and stories told by children (pp. 63–64).

The free associations of the psychoanalytic patient reveal secondary process thought so long as they present a chain of associations that appears to the analyst and the conscious self of the patient to be logical and "objective" (*i.e.*, environmentally accurate, based on mechanical contiguities); but when an idea appears that is not related to the one before it by logical implication or an obvious perceptual connection, or when the chain is interrupted or terminated by the patient himself, the influence of primary process ideation has been detected. The psychoanalyst, by analyzing these resistances to free association, seeks to bring to consciousness primary process material concerning unconsciously conflicting motives. In ordinary adult life, however, primary process material often becomes manifest: in nighttime dreaming; in daydreaming; and when an individual is experiencing fatigue, the effects of drugs or intoxicants, or emotional stress. On such occasions, realistic appraisal of the environment is suspended in favor of intensely experienced subjective imagery and associations related overtly or metaphorically to deep-seated motives.

The relative proportions of primary and secondary process thought vary greatly in these situations, as they do in the several phases of the analytic process. The patient entering analysis manifests much less primary process material than he does when in the throes of the transference neurosis, although even in the former situation the experienced clinician can detect signs of unconscious influence through small distortions of reality and in resistance to free association. Similarly, in ordinary life situations there is, for example, a much greater proportion of primary process material in a nighttime dream than in a daydream or in mental functioning while slightly intoxicated; but these are matters of degree, and both processes are always represented and always at work. Thus the nighttime dream is revised and given logical organization through the operation of secondary process before its final recall the following day, and even the economic behavior of normal adults will reveal a primary process component to someone in a position to assess its subjective significance to the individual. Psychoanalytic method is designed to identify the components of primary process thought, representing unconscious motives, and secondary process thought, representing environmental rationality, in the behavioral functioning of individuals; and this task should be considered central in the application of the method to life situations beyond the therapeutic and in other cultures.

4. A psychoanalytic research method that is to assess personality through distinguishing operationally between primary and secondary process components of behavioral functioning must include at least three elements, representing the "ecological," "physiological," and "embryological" strategies discussed in the preceding two chapters:

The first requirement is a situational context that can serve as the psychosocial equivalent of the classic psychoanalytic situation and become a frame in which to observe an individual over time. Apart from being a recurrent feature of his life during the period of observation, the situational context must involve interpersonal behavior directed toward a sufficiently limited and stable field of social objects so that these objects can be independently appraised by the observer as features in the environment to which the individual is responding. If the observer is to distinguish between primary and secondary process components of behavioral response, he must know in detail the reality of the environmental situation to which the individual is responding so that he can determine where rational adaptation ends and unconscious motivation begins. Unless the situational context is to be contrived by the observer in the manner of a psychological experiment, a therapeutic intervention or a personality test, knowing the situational context entails intensive ethnographic research concerning the social expectancies, norms, and cultural concepts relevant to behavior in that context.

Observation in a suitable situational context must first provide a baseline assessment of the individual's response patterns over time and over conditions in which the balance of primary and secondary process material varies recurrently within a certain range. This adds another context or background against which to view the individual's behavior, the context established by his own patterns of repetition and behavioral continuity. Since it may be expected that conditions such as fatigue, stress, and frustration will bring about temporary alterations in the relative proportions of primary and secondary process material manifesting themselves, observing the individual over a variety of such conditions should yield information about the nature of unconscious motives as well as a more stable ground against which future departures will stand out.

From the baseline assessment onward, longitudinal observation of the individual should have a developmental context; it should be focused on a process of directed change. Change occasions some degree of stress, frustration, or personal disruption, bringing out for examination primary process material that would otherwise remain hidden in a well-established adaptation to routine conditions. The process of directed change should be externally defined by a temporal marker of obvious psychosocial significance, which might be a termination point like a developmental goal in infancy or childhood, or a starting point like a stressful event and its sequelae, or a transitional phase. The more objective the temporal structure of the observation period, the more easily it will reveal individual differences along a developmental continuum. Furthermore, observation in the developmental context should include both environmental events (possible determinants) and behavioral events (including deviations from baseline response patterns), noting their sequential relations over time, in order to test hypotheses about the relative contributions and interactions of environmental factors and unconscious motives in the process of change.

The recommendations for research embodied in this set of guidelines should be viewed as necessary but not sufficient conditions for a widely applicable psychoanalytic method. Although such a method will have to be developed empirically, we can envision a range of possibly sufficient conditions by considering what situational contexts are available for its application. This question is explored in the following chapters.

15

Universal Categories and the
Translation Problem

The search for natural situations in which psychoanalytic observation might be possible brings us to a problem with which anthropologists have long been preoccupied, that of identifying those universal features of human life that act to limit and channel behavioral variation among individuals and populations and therefore recommend themselves as "natural units" for cross-cultural comparison. In this quest for what Kluckhohn (1953) called "universal categories of culture," the goal of making comparative generalizations has sometimes appeared to be incompatible with the evidence of cultural variation. There is no lack of obvious universals of human nature, culture, and situation, but ethnographic investigations of specific cultures reveal such a variety of distinctive and intricate systems of social interaction and belief that the constraints of universals do not seem to account for much of what the investigator sees. In response to this problem, some anthropologists adopted a relativistic position, rejecting in effect the relevance of universals to the ethnographic task of obtaining a full account of the subjective organization of interaction and belief peculiar to a cultural group. Others took a comparative viewpoint, using a single set of categories for all cultures despite the arbitrariness involved. Relativism in its extreme form foreclosed the possibility of cross-cultural generalization, whereas comparativism courted the danger of ethnocentrism in viewing other cultures.

Kluckhohn (1953) gave this problem prominence in anthropological discussion, reviewed past attempts to solve it, and suggested that linguistics had developed an effective solution that could be generalized to other aspects of culture. The linguistic solution was to have identified the operative constraints on variation in human speech, reflecting biological and cognitive limits for the species, and to have used these sets of limited options as units for descriptive investigation. Kluckhohn (1953, pp. 521–522) recommended that cultural anthropologists turn their attention to the "invariant points of reference supplied by the biological, psychological and sociosituational 'givens' of human life," including those suggested by psychoanalysis, and use them as units or categories for organizing ethnographic data. Anthropologists concerned with individual development such as Margaret Mead (1939, Mead and McGregor 1951) and John W. M. Whiting (1941; Whiting and Child 1953), had already been doing this (in very different ways), but their categories tended to be either specific to a particular phase of developmental immaturity or insufficiently grounded in objective universals to find the widespread acceptance accorded linguistic units like the phoneme. Kluckhohn's proposal did not succeed in forcing the desired breakthrough or even in redirecting most ethnographic research, but it did help stimulate numerous attempts to develop a "new ethnography" that could achieve the formal elegance and intersubjective agreement of structural linguistics and reconcile the need for comparison with the empirical diversity of cultures.

Hardly any of these attempts involve a classification of major components of the human situation in the style of Florence Kluckhohn's value orientations concerning the relations of man to man, nature and time (1954; Kluckhohn and Strodtbeck 1962). Instead, their emphasis is on well-established or clearly demonstrable anchor points in human anatomy, physiology, speech or other communicative structures, for specifiable (even microscopic) dimensions of cultural variation. In formal semantic analysis (Hammel, 1965) lexical units of speech are used to approach folk nomenclatures and taxonomies in domains such as kinship, plants, animals, colors, and diseases, where the referents of speech can be objectively identified independently of the speaker; the aim is to reveal the principles underlying each indigenous classification through a replicable procedure in which the objective referents serve as a background for observed variation. Goodenough (1970), in discussing kinship terminology, argues that universal categories with their sets of limited options can be inductively arrived at by repetition of these culture-specific analyses in diverse cultural contexts. Berlin and Kay (1969) arrived at a semantic universal through the inductive study of 24 languages, showing that although humans can make a large number of perceptual discriminations of color, basic color terms in speech are few and highly structured cross-culturally. Their findings indicate that functional or psychological factors put severe constraints on cultural variability in this domain. Once the pancultural range of variability in a given domain has been inductively specified, the sets of possible alternatives provide units for a full and comparable ethnographic description in any cultural context. Such units take on a larger cultural meaning, as Goodenough (1970) suggests, when they are related to functional (adaptive) criteria operating in that domain. When the functional association is missing, formal semantic analysis can be a sterile academic exercise rather than a significant attempt at comparable description of cultural variation.

Other novel approaches to ethnography have used (or proposed using) the human body, its external activities or internal processes, as anchor points, usually with some relevance to communication. Birdwhistell's *kinesics* (1952) represents an early attempt to extend linguistic analysis to the gestures that accompany or substitute for speech. Harris (1964) showed that a system for the comparative analysis of behavior (primarily nonverbal) could be built upon basic units consisting of observable bodily motions and their environmental effects, aggregating them into larger units of greater temporal scope and applicability to a cultural group. Unlike the semanticists, Harris believes that intersubjective comparability can be achieved directly, without concern for the subjective cultural categories of indigenous taxonomies, and his system of *actonics* is designed to demonstrate this point. The restriction of actonics to nonverbal behavior, however, makes the confrontation with semantic analysis less direct than intended. Ekman, Sorensen, and Friesen (1969), psychologists investigating nonverbal behavior, claim a semantic universal in facial displays of emotion, supported by inductive evidence from six cultures and based on the "association between facial muscular movements and discrete primary emotions, although cultures may still differ in what evokes an emotion, in rules for controlling the display of emotion, and in behavioral consequences" (p. 86). They provide a categorical scheme for the comparative analysis of nonverbal behavior (Ekman and Friesen, 1969). Watson and Nelson (1967) have proposed that the bodily orifices, as the points of exchange between the human organism and its environment, could serve as plausible anchor points for comparable ethnographic description of culturally and psychologically meaningful behavior. Chapple (1970) suggests the basic physiological rhythms of the human body as anchor points that are idiosyncratically and culturally structured and significant in human communication.

These attempts at finding universal units for cultural comparison have to deal with two problems that are of direct relevance to a possible psychoanalytic ethnography: the problem of objective structure and the problem of translation. Objective structure refers to a species-wide constraint on behavior that is unequivocally identifiable regardless of cultural context and is therefore suitable as a background or frame for observations that will be comparable across cultures. The problem of translation refers to the difficulty of adequately interpreting behavior observed in a given frame without additional contextual material. These problems require clarification before specific proposals for psychoanalytic ethnography can be sensibly made.

The problem of objective structure is an aspect of the general perceptual phenomenon of figure and ground as discussed by Gestalt psychologists. The figure-ground phenomenon refers to the human tendency in visual perception to identify a bounded form against a background more easily the sharper the boundary and the greater the contrasts in light and hue between the form and its background. Scientists, like all human perceivers, are in the position of having to identify bounded entities of some kind in relation to larger, more amorphous environments, but they do this as a self-conscious process of intellectual construction rather than through the unreflective act of sensory perception. The distinction between organism and environment is of this order, and is usually considered one of the less problematic examples in science. In behavioral science (as discussed in Chapter 12) the distinction between individual behavioral disposition and its sociocultural environment is very problematic and has engendered a good deal of disagreement. Part of the psychoanalytic solution to this problem (presented in Chapter 13) is to facilitate the observation of idiosyncratic behavior by knowing in detail the situation in which individuals are observed and by holding that situation as constant as possible for the individuals in it. In this "ecological" approach, the individual's behavior stands out against the background of the situation, in contrast with the previously observed behavior of other individuals in approximately the same situation. This resembles in principle the "contrast within a frame" approach of linguistics. In phonemic analysis, for example, the human speech apparatus provides the species-wide background, constraining variation within certain biological limits, and a language is observed (through systematic interviewing of informants) to contrast with other languages in the sounds it selects as meaningful entities.

For objective structures to serve as backgrounds or frames in the observation of variation, they must be intermediate in the constraints they put on behavior. If they overstructure behavior, there is no observable variation, whereas if they impose loose or ambiguous constraints, variation may be so great as to blur the distinction between culture-specific "figure" and species-wide "ground." In the ideal intermediate case, the universal frame provides a set of limited options, permitting variation of specific kinds within a specific range. Structural linguistics has been particularly successful in identifying such sets and developing upon them a method for making comparable observations of behavioral variations that can be clearly related to the operating principles of languages as normative systems. Even in linguistics, however, the sets of limited options were not arrived at by deduction from a knowledge of the anatomy of speech but had to be empirically discovered through comparative study of behavior, involving scientific trial-and-error, as Goodenough (1970) has indicated. This is partly because variation is constrained not only by the speech apparatus but also by less observable structures of human information processing, which result in a less extensive range of phonemic variation than would be theoretically possible on the basis of anatomy alone (see Greenberg, 1966). Without neurophysiological knowledge of these structures, it was necessary to study their behavioral effects. The same point is made by Berlin and Kay's (1969) study, which shows that the basic color vocabulary of human languages is much more restricted than the human capacity for discriminating colors perceptually. The lesson to be drawn from this research experience is that we should not expect to generate universal categories for the observation of psychologically significant behavior purely on the basis of an *a priori* theoretical analysis which takes account only of biosocial "givens;" they must be generated inductively through research.

Whatever categories of behavior may be empirically discovered for the cross-cultural description and analysis of personality systems, it cannot be assumed that they will entail constraints on individual dispositions as clearly evident as those of linguistic units on the cultural norms governing sound and grammar in speech. As conceptualized in psychoanalysis and related theories, personality dispositions seem too complex, too general and trans-situational, too idiosyncratic, and too dependent on connotative meanings to be easily reduced to sets of limited options. While humans can be put into experimental situations that limit their options drastically, it has proved difficult to generalize from their observed behavior to the other situations in which their lives are normally lived. We cannot assume that the meaning of an observed act is adequately given or specified by the objective structure of the situation in which it takes place, and this raises the probelm of translation.

If the meaning of an act is not "exhausted" by the situation in which it is observed, the question arises of how its meaning on one occasion can be compared with its meaning on another occasion. Facial expressions are interpretable across cultures, according to Ekman and Friesen (1969), in terms of primary emotions to which they are linked in universal subcortical programs, but each culture has its own "display rules" that act to constrain affective expression in the face, and individuals have idiosyncratic patterns of using the display rules in their own affective behavior. A single instance of a facial expression may be correctly interpreted in its primary affect (joy, surprise, fear, anger, disgust-contempt, sadness, *etc.*) without knowing the culture or the person. To understand that expression as it would be understood by another person from the same culture, however, it is necessary to know the cultural display rules according to which, for example, a derisive laugh might be interpretable as contempt or sadness rather than joy. To understand that expression as it would be interpreted by someone who is well acquainted with the person making it, one would have to know his personal style of emotional expression, in which, for example, expressiveness is so muted that a smile is a significant departure from habitual stolidity. If the objective structure of the situation does not exhaust the meaning of an act, information on the cultural and personal contexts in which that act occurred must be applied in order to translate the act, in its cultural and personal significance, into a scientific description comparable with descriptions of similar acts in different contexts. Omitting such contextual information guarantees misinterpretation of the act and mistranslation into the common data language.

In the search for features of the human situation in which to anchor psychoanalytic observation, the problems of objective structure and translation must be kept in mind. While we are seeking universal categories that not only provide a common background but also entail limitations on the range of options, we must recognize that the cross-cultural interpretation of individual behavior in psychological terms is likely to require extensive contextual data on the cultures and persons involved, to achieve the translatability that is essential for comparable descriptions.

A Bicultural Research Method

The most important practical conclusion to be drawn from the preceding discussion is that a proposal to solve the problem of objective structure by offering a new set of universal anchor points for comparable psychoanalytic ethnography is of relatively little value without a solution to the more difficult problem of translation. The difficulty is that if the translation problem is taken seriously, solving it can become an end in itself, as indeed it is for those anthropologists who aim only to understand the rules and beliefs that constitute another culture and translate them into a language of scientific observation. In studying the personality system, however, we have to go beyond deciphering the cultural code, an essential first step, to understand the subjective meanings encoded in the individual's organization of behavior. The job demands so much of an outside investigator that it may never be carried out in more than a few cultures. The solution I propose is for collaboration between two behavioral scientists, one from the culture being studied and one from outside, in translating the psychological data collected by the indigenous behavioral scientist into a comparable data language, by explicating the contexts that give the individual's behavior its cultural meanings.

This proposal is based on the facts that psychoanalysis, psychological anthropology, and developmental psychology are becoming international, with small but increasing numbers of non-Western investigators, and that these behavioral scientists are uniquely equipped to make cultural translations of psychological material from individuals of their own cultural backgrounds. The non-Western behavioral scientist, like other highly educated persons of the same origin, began learning a European language and European conceptual categories while he was still a child and continued this learning through many years of schooling and higher education, often completing it with several years of residence in a Western country. His knowledge of English (or French, Spanish, Portuguese) and its style of thought is much better, if less self-conscious and formal, than the knowledge of his language that a Western ethnographer could acquire in two years of field work. The outside ethnographer not only works systematically at understanding the structure, style, and usage of the indigenous language but also becomes socialized into using it the way native speakers do in his intensive contacts with them. In all but a few cases, however, this socialization does not last long enough, or begin early enough, to go beyond a level of fluency at which many vernacular connotations of psychological significance are constantly being missed. The indigenous behavioral scientist, particularly if he has lived abroad, is more completely "biculturated" and—in his early experience with his own culture—is biculturated in a way that is more relevant to psychological work in that culture.

In terms derived from psychoanalytic ego psychology, the ego of a person raised in a non-Western culture who has acquired a high level of Western education may be thought of as split into two parts, one containing the knowledge and skills necessary for participation in the indigenous culture, the other containing knowledge and skills required for participation in a Western culture, particularly in its intellectual life. He can switch from one to the other of these adaptive modes according to environmental demands. But the two parts are qualitatively different because of the ages at which they were acquired and their means of acquisition. The indigenous ego has its roots in the total experience of infancy and early childhood, much of it nonverbal; it developed through participation, including language learning, in the contexts of home and community and contains residues of emotionally significant and formative experiences up to the time at which higher education or career occasioned separation from the indigenous environment. The Western ego, by contrast, originated in the restricted context of learning a foreign language in school and was broadened through increasing intellectual knowledge of Western ideas and institutions and the increasing need to use Western patterns of thought in school and other institutional settings. Its interpersonal content depends on the amount of experience with Westerners and their life-styles at home and abroad.

His indigenous ego permits the behavioral scientist of non-Western origin to understand—automatically, effortlessly, and unreflectively—verbal

and nonverbal communications expressed according to the cultural rules
he internalized early in his life. The indigenous contexts from which
these behaviors derive their communicative significance are part of his
personality and available for his use in understanding persons of the
same background. This gives him a tremendous advantage over the
foreign investigator. It does not necessarily mean, however, that the non-
Westerner is ready to translate the significance of the understood behaviors into the Western language or into the behavioral science categories he has encoded in his Western ego. Unless he has had occasion
for intensive and systematic introspection of a cross-cultural kind, he is
likely to find much of what he understands in communicating with those
of similar origins very difficult to express adequately in Western linguistic
and intellectual categories. Part of this difficulty stems from the inadequacy of those categories, which require revision to describe non-Western concepts of behavior and personality in a direct and comprehensive
way. But it is due in larger part to the relatively unreflective quality of
his indigenous communication, as with the ordinary native speaker of a
language who speaks according to the rules but cannot tell a foreigner
what those rules are. Another way of putting this is that the indigenous
and Western egos of the behavioral scientist are cognitively different.
Meanings in the indigenous ego are encoded in experiential, context-
embedded terms (*enactive* and *ikonic* representations, in the terminology
of Bruner *et al.* 1966), whereas meanings in his Western ego are encoded in abstract, verbal terms (*symbolic* representation), corresponding to their functional origins in his life history. Translation can only
occur through a process akin to that preliminary aspect of psychoanalysis
in which the ego of the patient is "split" into its experiencing and observing functional components, so that the latter part can report on the
former (Sterba 1934, 1940; Greenson 1967).

Translating from his indigenous culture's system of meanings to the
Western language in which his scientific communication is carried on
thus poses an intrapsychic problem for the non-Western behavioral scientist, but its solution can be facilitated by interpersonal collaboration. In
the therapeutic or working alliance of psychoanalysis, the analyst allies
himself with the patient's observing ego, encouraging it to grow through
focusing attention on what the patient is experiencing at the moment
and making efforts to express it in words. Insofar as this is successful, the
patient develops a strengthened capacity for self-observation and self-
description that is his collaborative link with the analyst in their common work; the analogous relationship between student analyst and his
supervisor has been called the "learning alliance" (Fleming and Benedek,
1966, p. 53). The non-Western behavioral scientist could use a similar
kind of "working alliance" with a foreign investigator, to help him translate the implicit rules by which behavior is assigned meaning in the con-

textual structures of his indigenous ego into the explicit description terminology of his Western ego. Of course not all behavioral scientists of
non-Western origin would need this help, just as many patients come
into analysis with well-developed observing egos. But the collaborative
translation of systems of meaning can provide a comparability for psychological investigation that is unlikely to be achieved without it.

In working with a foreign collaborator on the problem of translating
the cultural rules for interpreting communication in his own culture, the
non-Western behavioral scientist is forced to put into words implicit
understandings that he may never have verbalized previously (and which
less sophisticated persons of his cultural background cannot express
verbally) and to make translations of these words into the European language that communicate the original meanings adequately. This is a trial-
and-error process during which the non-Westerner may make many false
attempts to translate and the Westerner many attempts to rephrase the
translation in ways that seem incorrect or imprecise to his collaborator.
From this process comes an increasing specification of the indigenous
rules so that the denotation and connotation of vernacular terms in
various contexts become more and more explicit. By adopting the position of the learner who needs to be socialized into the culture through
a knowledge of explicit rules and where they do and do not apply, the
foreign investigator acts as the guinea pig for the original translation,
testing it out by using it as his only guide to hypothetical (or real) sequences of communicative behavior that can be evaluated as culturally
appropriate or inappropriate by the non-Western investigator. This
process is of course very similar to the questioning of linguistic informants by foreign linguists, who make implicit grammatical rules explicit
by constructing sentences that can be evaluated by informants as correct
or incorrect usage.

The close parallel of this process with linguistic interviewing and its
resemblance to conventional ethnographic interviewing raises the question of why it could not be carried on with relatively uneducated informants of the indigenous culture. The answer is that it could, if the
only purpose were to construct a "grammar" of interpersonal communication, but in the present context such a grammar is only a first step, permitting more accurate assessment of the behavior of individuals in a
particular cultural group. The purpose of the grammar is to make explicit the culturally defined options in the individual's life situations, and
the normative and other cultural values associated with each of the options, so that in observing the behavior of an individual of the same cultural background, the behavioral scientist becomes consciously aware of
the terms by which he (his indigenous ego) gives it an automatic cultural interpretation. The grammar is a medium of translation between
the context-embedded experiencing of his indigenous ego and the verbal

concepts of his Western ego, a European key to the terms of his indigenous communicative experience. As such, it functions as a heightened
observing capacity, similar to the observing ego in psychoanalysis, designed in this case to translate the meaning of an act from one cultural
context to another for description in comparable terms.

The grammar should be thought of, not as a fixed and definitive set of
rules that could be adequately applied by anyone to behavior in the
culture, but as a device to enable the non-Western behavioral scientist
to extend his conscious verbal awareness of the conventions by which he
automatically communicates in indigenous settings. This process of extension can only be considered completed when he is able to translate
adequately into the Western language of scientific discourse the behavioral data on which a personality assessment is based. The task of developing the grammar must begin before the study of individual personalities but will continue, perhaps indefinitely, as new behavioral
material brings to attention previously untranslated understandings encoded in the indigenous ego. For this reason, the working alliance should
also continue into work with individual persons. For the indigenous behavioral scientist, building the grammar is recapturing the cultural context in his childhood experience and transforming it into an intellectual
communication. Insofar as this experience was not entirely conscious and
is shared with others of his group, it forms the basis of an empathy with
them that is invaluable in clinical work and can become a research instrument through the collaboration with a foreign investigator.

Summary and Conclusions

This chapter has been concerned with two problems in the collection of
psychoanalytic data from culturally diverse human populations, which
I call the problems of objective structure and of translation. The problem
of objective structure refers to the identification of pancultural categories for the observation of psychologically significant behavior. Anthropological attempts to identify universal categories for comparison of
cultural (as opposed to psychological) characteristics have frequently
followed structural linguistics in anchoring units for comparison in features of human biology or communication that are universally observable as stable background frames against which behavioral variation of
a limited range stands out. The human range of variation in such frames
is established not merely by an *a priori* assessment of constraints inherent
in the biological or communicative apparatus but through empirical research in diverse cultures.

Consideration of how to adopt this approach for psychoanalytic ethnography leads to the problem of translation, since it is unlikely that any
conceivable set of universal categories could provide data on personality

that would not require cultural and personal contextual information to become interpretable in psychoanalytic terms. Even data collected within the framework of a suitably identified universal category will have to be translated to convey its cultural and individual meanings in a language of scientific description. The amount of knowledge of cultural and linguistic context a person must have to be able to understand social behavior as an average native of that culture understands it is so great that a foreigner might never get past that stage, to understanding how a native understands his own behavior (consciously and unconsciously) in more than one culture in a lifetime.

In these terms, the problem of translation seems an almost insuperable obstacle to carrying out such investigations in more than a handful of cultures. But an alternative to the traditional foreign ethnographer approach is proposed that involves collaboration between an indigenous non-Western behavioral scientist, who aims to collect comparable psychoanalytic data from individuals of his own cultural background, and a foreign behavioral scientist (probably Western, at this point in time), to develop a "grammar" of indigenous meanings through which the data on individuals can be translated into a comparable descriptive language. Such a method would have an obvious ethnocentric slant at first, though perhaps less so than conventional methods, and it would be amenable to development toward a more universal language of discourse for personality psychology. In any event, the problem of translation must be solved in a moderately satisfactory way before new proposals of solutions for the problem of objective structure can be taken seriously. Having dealt with translation here, however imperfectly, I turn to objective structures in the next chapter.

16

Psychoanalytic Ethnography:
Structures for Comparative Observation

In this chapter I suggest four different types of universal (or quasi-universal) structures as observational frames: the bodily symptoms of affective reactions; the circadian (daily) rhythms of activity and inactivity; developmental phases in the course of individual life from birth to death; and bureaucratic institutional structures of Western origin. Throughout the presentation of these suggestions I assume the bicultural approach to the problem of translation as the preliminary method of explicating the cultural contexts in which individual behavior is assigned communicative significance. It is proposed as a means of increasing the cross-cultural comparability of psychological material without reducing such material arbitrarily and prematurely to a set of formal operations.

Bodily Manifestations of Affective Reactions

Nothing is more characteristic of psychoanalysis than its concern with emotions or affects (which are conceived of in psychoanalytic theory as mental representations of drives) and their relations to the organization and functioning of personality. In understanding a person from a psychoanalytic point of view it is essential to know the affective terms in which he experiences himself and others, for these are keys to his unconscious conflicts and in particular to the influence of unconscious, primary-process dispositions on his ability to use rational, secondary-process thought in social functioning. The experiencing of fear, rage, sadness, surprise, joy, disgust, shame, or sexual arousal in situations where they are culturally inappropriate (inappropriate according to the standards of environmental reality in his ecological niche) is an indication that a personal motive of some strength and depth is affecting the individual's adaptation to his sociocultural environment. In the psychoanalytic situation this is seen when associations to ideas of little conscious importance to the patient lead to an upsurge of one of these emotions, or when a trivial act by the analyst or someone in his waiting room triggers an intense affective response. Primary process thought is organized by *affective* connections rather than logical or perceptual ones.

From an ethnographic viewpoint affects appear to be extremely variable across cultures. Some groups have publicly sad funerals, others gay ones; Americans weep at films that bring forth roars of laughter from Africans. Anthropological experience indicates that populations differ widely in the conditions that evoke affective reactions from them, in the intensity and style of their emotional expression, and in the reactions of others to emotional displays (Ekman and Friesen, 1969). Furthermore, these observable variations seem to be controlled by complex, subtle systems of symbols that are culture-specific and difficult to compare systematically. Tomkins (1962–1963) and Ekman and Friesen (1969) claim, however, that there are discrete primary emotions common to all humans by virtue of their neuromuscular structure; certain facial muscles are activated by grossly similar affective experiences in all cultures. No matter how variable the cultural patterning of affects, their modes of expression have a common biological substratum.

This biological substratum also manifests itself in the observable bodily symptoms of more intense affective reactions, for example in weeping, blushing, anxiety or stress reaction, and (with qualifications) sexual arousal, and nauseation, which I propose as suitable anchor points from which to initiate a comparative study of affects. The intensity of reactions that involve such symptoms makes them impossible to ignore in a general consideration of human affects and suggests that they represent extreme and less disguised manifestations of the emotions that activate facial expressions. They may not constitute a "royal road to the unconscious" but they are at least discernible paths from the social surface of individual behavior that promise to lead in that direction.

There are several advantages to this set of anchor points, the first of which is the obvious translatability of words for bodily symptoms (tears, change in facial color and warmth, rapid heart beat, cold sweat, penile erection, vomiting, and nausea) into any language with unequivocal denotative reference. (Despite the "obviousness" to an outside investigator, any difficulty in translating these into a particular language or some equivocality in the nearest translation, would in itself be a starting point for a cultural investigation of psychological significance.) Second, there is the (presumed) universality not only of the symptoms themselves but of their connections with some affective states, not necessarily the same ones in all cultures. This might seem most questionable in the case of blushing, which is sometimes thought of as peculiar to light-skinned peoples, but my experience with very dark-skinned Africans indicates they not only perceive facial darkening in others and increased warmth in their own faces but interpret these as symptoms of what might be roughly translated as "embarassment." Pending further evidence it seems safe to assume that blushing is a possible affective symptom for all human populations (see Darwin 1965, pp. 315–320). Nausea and vomiting seem to me more questionable as universal affective symptoms, but only comparative research of the type proposed here will answer this question. In the meantime the assumption of universality for these bodily symptoms of affective reactions is not unreasonable.

Individual occurrences of these symptoms are observable and memorable, making them suitable topics for interviewing. A person tends to know when he is experiencing the symptoms and often understands their relation to the ideational component of the affect and to the conditions that aroused it. This is true of weeping, less so of blushing (in that a person can blush without being aware of it), and least true of the stress reaction, which may only reach self-awareness when it is quite intense (although less intense levels can be detected by an investigator through measurement of the galvanic skin response or heart beat). Everyone has consciously experienced the symptoms at some time in his life but no one is aware of all of them whenever they occur. Similar variability holds for observation of the symptoms by another person; if one weeps, blushes, or vomits in public, it is likely to be noticed by others (though blushing might be overlooked in some situations); whereas if one becomes sexually aroused, nauseated, or anxious, it will probably not be noticed at moderate intensity. The point is that all of the symptoms are potentially observable by self and others, and their connections to affects are part of the common culture in which persons communicate, so they are subject to the self-monitoring and self-controlling processes of personality functioning.

When the symptoms have reached the threshold of awareness, an individual is likely to remember the event for some time (unlike facial expressions) because of the rarity of experiences at that level of intensity. The rarity is also variable among types of reactions, individuals, and populations, but everyone can remember vividly some time when he experienced intense bodily concomitants of affective reactions and other incidents in which he observed those symptoms in others.

Though they may be memorable, public displays of affective reactions with bodily symptoms are usually inconsistent with cultural norms concerning the maintenance of composure in adults (except for tearfulness at funerals and ritual vomiting in some cultures). Insofar as an adult is striving to maintain his composure, such a display occurs "in spite of himself," breaking through his conscious control like a slip of the tongue but with more obvious significance. With the exception of sexual arousal in culturally appropriate situations, it usually constitutes a mild disruption in psychosocial functioning, a small but significant disequilibrium, following which he attempts to regain his composure and restore his equilibrium. From the viewpoint of the investigator of personality, affect display is all the more significant because it is a mild violation of adult cultural norms, for it is more likely to represent an intense emotion and less likely to be feigned. Paradoxically, the affect that breaks through into behavior when a person weeps, blushes, or trembles in violation of composure norms, often indicates the operation of internalized social controls, such as remorse, embarassment, fear of authority or public exposure. In such cases it is the thought of transgressing or failing to meet the standards by which one evaluates himself that triggers an affective reaction beyond the bounds of self-control. The study of bodily symptoms in affective reactions, then, leads ultimately to the moral constraints operative in the personality system. (Sexual arousal and nauseation are likely to lead into other areas of personality functioning.)

There is also a developmental aspect to these reactions. Affective displays of an "excessive" character are more frequent and more tolerated among children than among adults because children have not yet acquired the capacity to experience emotions without expressing them at full intensity; as they grow older, the maintenance of composure in public, even when emotions are aroused, becomes possible and expected. Thus reactions like weeping, blushing, or trembling in an adult who usually meets the standards of composure operative in his cultural environment can be seen as temporary regressions on a line of development along which he had moved in the course of growing up, and they can reveal residues of childhood dispositions persisting in the organization of his personality. (See A. Freud, 1965, on the concept of developmental lines.)

SUMMARY

The commonly observable bodily symptoms (such as weeping, blushing, trembling) of intense affective reactions can provide a series of anchor points from which to begin the comparative study of affective experience. The symptoms are appropriate for this because they are sensory events that can be identified in any language, probably occur in connection with affect in all humans, and are infrequent and visible enough to be remembered with relative ease. They are thus suitable topics for cross-cultural conversation. Discovering the diverse cultural and psychological contexts in which these symptoms occur (or are narrowly avoided) should yield comparable information relevant to the understanding of personality structure and development. This comparable information, collected according to procedures discussed in Appendix A, could become the framework with which to approach the varieties and complexities of affective experience in human cultures. This is one approach; there are other situational contexts with distinctive normative backgrounds and points of entry into the social surface of personality, to which we turn in the following sections.

Daily Cycles of Activity and Inactivity

The advantages of the psychoanalytic situation for the ecological observation of personality are due in large measure to its bounded location in time and space. The repeated sessions of identical length in an identical room constitute (with the other situational constants of the analyst-patient relationship) a uniform background against which to observe different persons in their cycles and transformations during years of analysis. A natural analogue to the psychoanalytic or any other investigator-controlled situation is not easily found; the attractiveness of artificially structured settings for observing individual behavior has always consisted in their reduction of the overwhelming complexity and variation encountered in natural social settings. Human activity, however, is not a featureless continuity, as anthropologists long ago recognized in dealing with annual cycles of agricultural work and migratory food quest and their associated rhythms of culturally organized behavior. Natural punctuations in the temporal stream of individual behavior occur at many levels, but none is more basic than that of the 24-hour activity cycle, rooted in man's biological nature, which in its brevity and repetition resembles the psychoanalytic hour and forms a convenient unit for ethnographic description and comparison.

The universality of the 24-hour day as a cyclical framework in which human behavior may be comparably studied has not gone unnoticed by anthropologists and other behavioral scientists. In the ethnographies of *Six Cultures: Studies of Child Rearing* (Whiting, 1963), for example, four of the six accounts contain chapters entitled "Daily Routine" in which the typical day of a family in the community is described. The psychological ecology of Barker and Wright, as exemplified in their book, *One Boy's Day* (1951), uses the day as the temporal unit for describing (in massive detail) the environmental settings of individual behavior. In the viewpoint taken here, however, the 24-hour day is considered not simply as a unit in which behavior patterns and their environmental settings happen to repeat themselves but as reflecting biological rhythms that have concomitants in mental activity.

Man shares with the higher vertebrates a number of physiological cycles that involve mental activity and have behavioral effects. There is, for example, a basic rest-activity cycle (BRAC) involving visceral, somatic, and neurological variations that have been documented during sleep and are correlated with dreaming. Kleitman (1969) states:

> [The] BRAC increases in duration, in proportion to body size, in the course of phylogenetic and ontogenetic development. In the rat, the "biological hour" equals 10 to 13 minutes; in the cat, about 30; in the monkey, 45; in man, about 90; and in the elephant, about 120 minutes. The BRAC lengthens from birth to maturity in all species exhibiting the cycle—in man, from 50 to 60 minutes in the infant from 85 to 95 minutes in the adult (p. 34).

Although the evidence for the operation of the BRAC in wakefulness is not so good as that cited above for sleeping, Kleitman and other investigators in this field believe it operates throughout the 24-hour day, modifying psychophysiological functioning during the waking as well as sleeping hours. In waking, the nonactivated phase of the cycle (which can be altered by external stimulation) manifests itself in fatigue and drowsiness.

At the level of the 24-hour day, it is obvious that the alternation between sleep and waking involves a cyclical variation in gross motor and mental activity, and research has shown its association with cycles in the electrical activity of the brain and in numerous other physiological and biochemical indicators (*e.g.*, body temperature, blood sugar, endocrine secretions). (See Kleitman, 1963; Kales, 1969; for less technical presentations, see Luce and Segal, 1966; Chapple, 1970.) All of these cycles are roughly synchronized with each other and with 24-hour earth rotations in what are called *circadian* rhythms, to emphasize their approximate nature. The factors accounting for synchronization (*e.g.*, light variations, social interaction, awareness of time) are the subjects of continuing research, but two facts are clear: cycle duration varies from one human individual to another and tends to be highly consistent for a given adult individual; social communication and living routines are importantly involved in synchronizing the circadian cycles of different individuals with each other and with 24 hours under experimental conditions of continuous darkness (Aschoff *et al.*, 1971).

The mental concomitants of human circadian rhythms have been studied to some extent. In sleep, they involve the dream states associated with the REM (rapid-eyeball-movement) phases of the BRAC. During wakefulness, they are discernible as variations in the performance of simple tasks requiring motor and intellectual alertness (*e.g.*, dealing cards, multiplying numbers). Summarizing an extensive and varied literature, Kleitman (1963) states:

> Most of the curves of performance can be brought into line with the known 24-hour body-temperature curves, allowing for individual skewing of

the curves toward an earlier or later, rather than a midafternoon, peak. For each individual there probably exists a drowsiness temperature level, above which it is easy to remain awake and below which it is progressively harder to do so (p. 161).

The speed and accuracy of task performance is low early in the morning, rises to an idiosyncratic midday peak, and declines thereafter as the time for sleep approaches—all in correspondence with the rise and fall of body temperature. Hartmann, a laboratory investigator of sleep and dreams, makes the following comments about the thought processes that might be involved in the BRAC and circadian cycles:

> In psychoanalytic terms, it is tempting to consider the 90-minute cycle to be related to the id—it appears early, does not alter in response to external factors, and is clearly associated with the primitive, primary process activity of dreaming; however, the 24-hour sleep-wake cycle can be related more closely to the ego—it develops later, apparently as an *adaptation* to the terrestrial day, and it is superimposed on the earlier 90-minute cycle.
>
> Knowledge of the 90-minute cycle may also have practical psychological implications. It is quite possible that such a cycle could be demonstrated in daily functioning on psychological and psychomotor tests, if tests of sufficient sensitivity were available. For instance, one might expect a tendency toward an increase of daydreaming or loosening of associations every 90 minutes, or an increase in primary process thinking (1968, p. 285).

The panhuman universality of the rhythms discovered in studying Western subjects has often been taken for granted, partly because they are grossly similar to those of other mammals and partly because—at least in the case of the circadian rhythms—they are obviously adaptive for all human populations inhabiting environments where there are daily variations in sunlight and darkness. Most of the variability studied has been experimentally induced rather than customary, but the possibility of cross-population differences has come in for some consideration. Kleitman (1963, pp. 191–192) checked on travelers' impressions that inhabitants of the northern coast of Norway hardly sleep in the summer when there is daylight most of the time; he found that a sample of persons from one community average about one hour less sleep in the summer than in the winter. In a review of the literature on 24-hour sleep cycling, Webb (1969) notes a difference in average sleep time between two samples of Americans aged 6 to 18 years of age, one studied in the period 1910 to 1912 and the other in 1963 to 1964; he suggests a historical shift but does not report its direction or probable course. He makes the following theoretical speculation:

> I suspect that there are at least four complex interactive factors that may lead to sustained individual differences in sleep length: (1) genetic-constitu-

tional factors; (2) early experiences, such as parental attitudes and behavior controls; (3) variables of the chronic subclinical physiological state, such as differences in the nutritional, endocrine, and blood systems; and (4) intrapsychic and chronic environmental stressors, such as anxiety or work demands (p. 56).

Unfortunately, empirical evidence is lacking. Concerning cultural differences, the lack of evidence moves Webb to humor:

> The general pattern from age 5 years in the Western world is biphasic sleepwaking: a long waking period with one roughly seven- to eight-hour sleep period. (No one yet has exploited a foundation to study the "siesta" pattern of the tropical and subtropical cultures, although at various odd moments, I am most tempted) (p. 58).

We know there are some cross-cultural variations in sleeping customs, the post-prandial "siesta" being the most striking deviation from our own adult habits, but it is not yet known whether this affects the circadian rhythms of psychophysiological functioning in any substantial way. The range of variation in sleep-awake cycles may turn out to be significant, but it is certainly restricted. In the West African groups I know, for example, people still do most of their sleeping at night despite a daytime nap, and this seems to be generally true of "siesta cultures" (see Taub, 1971). Yet there appear to be more extreme differences in the way sleep is managed for infants and children, and present information does not tell us whether this permanently affects some of the circadian rhythms. Nutritional and genetic factors are other possible sources of variance. There is much cross-cultural physiology to be done here, without unwarranted exploitation of funding agencies.

Despite the gaps in present knowledge on this subject, I will venture the following statements. In all human populations there is an activity cycle organized on a daily (24-hour) basis, which includes shorter-term cycles of rest and activity. The daily cycle is universally divided into a sleeping phase, most of which is at night, and a predominantly waking phase, which is longer than the sleeping phase and may or may not be punctuated by a nap. If it is not punctuated by a nap, it is punctuated by rest phases of a fairly stable number and duration, often associated with eating, drinking, and social interaction. However these sleep-wake and rest-activity alternations are organized in the 24-hour day, the differences in psychophysiological functioning between sleep and waking and between rest and activity can be presumed universal for the human species until proven variable. (This presumption is based on the fundamental nature of the metabolism-linked cycles of brain waves and neuromuscular activity revealed by biological research.) For all humans, then, sleep is a state of the organism sharply differentiated from waking; within both sleep and wakefulness there are cycles of activated and nonactivated phases. In sleep, activation involves dreaming; during wakefulness, activation involves an alert orientation to the environment, nonactivation, fatigue and relaxation. These cycles represent organic programs and have "demand" qualities such that prolongation of the activated or nonactivated phase at the expense of the other leads to compensatory functioning.

The ideational content of mental activity varies with these cycles. In sleep, the activated phase is marked by the dominance of primary process ideation in vivid visual hallucinations (dreams); in wakefulness, generally distinguished by a strong sensorimotor orientation to the environment, it is in the nonactivated phase (often augmented by fatigue resulting from exertion in the previous phase) that the controls of secondary process thinking are loosened, and primary process ideation manifests itself. Thus observable shifts in thought processes accompany the physiological cycles of activity and inactivity common to all humans in their daily lives. The modes of physiological, ideational, and behavioral functioning specific to activated and nonactivated phases in sleep and wakefulness, and their biologically determined cyclicity in the 24-hour day and shorter periods, provide a universal structure against which cultural and individual differences can be meaningfully observed. The daily activity cycle and its component short-term cycles constitute a proximal biopsychological context in which lives are led and ethnographic observation can be carried out.

To develop the potential of the 24-hour day as a pancultural situational context for psychoanalytic observation, it is necessary to create an "ethnography of the daily cycle," a description of the cultural norms and beliefs relevant to the individual's management of his own activity and inactivity at different phases in the cycles that comprise his day. Such a description would include the social expectations concerning the temporal organization and ideational concomitants of sleep, work, eating and drinking, recreation, social interaction, and sexual discharge in the daily life of each major social category of person. It would also include the cultural categories with which a person conceptualizes his own daily rhythm and the cultural standards by which he evaluates his own performance and needs as he experiences them daily. Once the semantics of daily activity were understood, it would be necessary to find out, through participant observation, how much individual variation there is in conforming to the cultural rules and standards, and how persons react to deviation by themselves and others. In brief, an ethnography of the daily cycle would first be comprised of descriptions of the ideal day for each category of person, what was observed as the actual day in central tendency and deviation, and the ways in which persons responded to the discrepancy between ideal and actual. One focus would be on the duration and intensity of activities, effort expended and depth of relaxation, the demands of task performance, the release experienced in recreational pursuits, and the stimulation experienced from food and drink. An important feature would be the extent to which there was cultural recognition of psychophysiological features such as the rest-activity cycle, reduced performance early and late in the wakefulness phase, compensation effects when cycles are disrupted, and so forth. Another focus would be on cultural beliefs concerning nighttime dreams, daydreaming, and other ideational phenomena associated with specific phases in the daily cycle.

In examining the ideational aspects of the daily cycle, a major goal would be to assess the relative dominance of primary and secondary process thought enjoined by cultural norms at different phases in the cycle. It is of particular interest to discover to what extent cultural institutions, or cultural forms that are positively valued if not completely institutionalized, legitimize regressions during the waking hours from secondary process thinking to primary process ideation, and when they do, what is the permissible content of the primary process material. Does the normative organization of the daily cycle permit the emergence into social interaction, during nonactivated phases of functioning, of unconscious motives in fantasy and other forms, and if so, what motives are permitted expression? In cultures without a siesta, the period between the end of work and the evening meal is often a conspicuous time for such license, particularly if drinking is prevalent; where the siesta is culturally programmed, such a period might come later in the day. But it would be wrong to prejudge culturally approved regressions except to consider them expectable features of the daily cycle. In this ethnographic part of the investigation, the focus would be on the legitimization of regression and on the permissibility of expressing certain kinds of thoughts; the process of regression and the psychological significance of ideational content, however, can only be understood through the study of the individual.

This ethnography of the daily cycle, which incidentally might provide much more psychologically relevant material for cultural comparison than current ethnographic description does, could be pursued in a particular culture until it was well enough known to the team of investigators (indigenous and foreign) to be used as a reliable contextual background for identifying idiosyncrasies of daily activity, that is, until the matching of any one individual's daily activity cycle against the cultural norms as generally practiced threw light on his distinctive features with a high degree of face validity. This is analogous to the experienced analyst's use of his familiarity with the realities of the clinical situation and with the variations in patients' responses to identify with confidence the distinctiveness and adaptiveness of a particular patient's reactions. The daily cycle in a culture is a great deal more complex than the psychoanalytic situation, but it is much more intrinsically interesting as an object of general scientific inquiry, and the indigenous behavioral scientist is already familiar with it as a participant, so he is not starting from ignorance. His familiarity, however, would have to be made explicit, extended to social categories he had not experienced and extended as well to developmental aspects such as the ways in which children were socialized to culturally appropriate cyclical behavior. When a satisfactory ethnographic description of the cultural organization of the daily cycle was achieved, it could be used as a situational frame for the observation of individuals. The panhuman cycles of psychophysiological functioning and the cultural beliefs and rules about daily functioning can be seen as constraints within which the individual fashions his daily cycle; insofar as the investigator is acquainted with these constraints, he can detect the individual's own contribution to the periodicity of his observable daily behavior.

In studying the individual within the biopsychological frame of the daily cycle as semantically and normatively organized in his cultural group, the aims of research would be to detect in his personally organized daily cycle personal preferences indicative of enduring behavioral dispositions beyond the simple desire to conform, and to obtain samples of behavior revealing primary and secondary process functioning as they naturally occur in his daily cycle. These samples must be large and representative enough to permit assessment of the personal dispositions that account for the repetitive patterns of daily behavior during the period in his life. The latter aim must be seen as an ideal goal, the attainment of which must involve research strategies to be worked out in the field. Insofar as this goal can be attained, the study of the individual in his daily cycle would provide a cross-sectional view of his personality that could be repeatedly obtained at a number of points in a longer-term segment of his life, for the assessment of change and development on which a more valid diagnosis of personality depends.

While it is not possible to solve, in advance of field research, the problems of data collection posed by these research aims, the aims can be spelled out in more specific detail. There is an ambitious program of psychological data collection involved here, but it is not the relatively unfocused amassing of observational material that Barker and Wright (1951) illustrated. On the contrary, observation is to be sharply focused along certain lines that are of special importance in the psychoanalytic theory of personality—though without a necessary commitment to that theory. First and foremost, the focus is always on the contents of consciousness as manifested in social behavior during a particular phase of activity or inactivity. The field investigator's primary problem is to develop a relationship with the person he is studying through which he can gain access to the conscious thoughts that accompany his actions. This can be provisionally imagined as some locally meaningful variant or amalgam of the ethnographer-informant and therapist-patient relationships. In the context of that companionship, during certain phases the investigator will be aware of the person's thoughts, because he will be communicating them as he experiences them, in conversation. In other phases, the thoughts will not be spontaneously communicated, and the investigator can ask the person what he is or was thinking at the time of the action. As in all observation of behavior, it is not realistic to expect a completely forthright reply so that greater weight may be given to spontaneous than elicited responses. The operating assumption, however, is that the thoughts accompanying action will become manifest, if not at the time or in response to an inquiry then in a more relaxed or regressed phase of the daily cycle, when some of its hidden associations may manifest themselves as well. The investigator will record the actions and communicated thoughts (including dream reports) of a person, treating their sequence in a day as a flow of associations—constrained rather than free, but constrained by external realities known to the investigator—until their repetitive cycles become predictable to him. This observational record will constitute the basic material for analytic assessment.

The first type of analysis of this material will be in terms of primary and secondary process thought at different phases in the cycles. All behavioral material, including dream reports, is a composite of these two ideational processes, but the focus is on how much one or the other contributes to a particular stream of behavior. This assessment is based on judgments as to how an idea is represented in a communicative act, how ideas are connected with one another in a sequence, and how ideas are related to reality.

How is an idea represented? This question refers to the way an idea is represented in a communicative act, in terms of cognitive dimensions that differentiate primary from secondary process thinking and students of cognition have dealt with in various distinctions: concrete vs. abstract; preoperational vs. operational thought (Piaget); enactive, ikonic, and symbolic representation (Bruner, Olver, and Greenfield, 1966); sensory vs. ideological poles in symbolic systems (Turner, 1969). Primary process operates through imagery rather than through the use of words in clearly designated areas of (denotative) reference, and this imagery is predominantly visual and charged with affect, although the quality of the affect may be disguised. It has been termed hallucinatory and autistic ideation, and also poetic, lyrical, metaphorical, or mystical ideation. The visual imagery often entails immediately perceived aspects or parts of things (which stand for other things) and personifies intense affects by referring to animals or parts of the human body, without an explanation of the context in which the representation should be understood. The use of proverbs in conversational speech, common in many African cultures, is an example of an institutionalized form of primary process representation.

Because this type of representation is conventional in many groups, its use by an individual cannot be directly attributed to drives, as in Freud's (1900) theory of dreams, but it is nevertheless important to estimate how much of a person's experience is being represented this way. Such an estimate can be made more reliably by an indigenous behavioral scientist than an outside investigator, because people try harder to explain themselves to foreigners, giving up the more difficult metaphors of vernacular speech.

How are ideas connected with one another? The question here is whether the connection between ideas adjacent in associative sequence is logical or environmental, as judged by the indigenous behavioral scientist who has acquainted himself with the local reality context, or affective —the latter being characteristic of primary process. This kind of assessment, central in the psychoanalysis of free associations, may not be so easy to make in all phases of naturalistic observation, but there will be phases in which association is sufficiently spontaneous and unconstrained to permit such judgments.

How are ideas related to reality? Reality-testing is a characteristic of secondary process thought, but it is suspended when primary process takes over. This is Freud's way of conceptualizing the hallucinatory quality of dreams and, to a lesser degree, other imaginative forms of mental production. To the extent that the imaginary is presented as true or that what is wished or feared is presented as an immediate reality or that the present is not distinguished from the past or future, primary process is operating. The suspension of reality-testing involves a regression of the ego from secondary to primary process ideation. In the ethnography of the daily cycle, the question is under what conditions is such a regression (however limited) permissible and with what content; in the study of the individual, the inquiry is into the conditions, repetitiveness, depth, and content of actual regressions in the individual and their consequences for his daily adaptation.

These three questions are starting points for distinguishing between primary and secondary cognitive process in the behavioral material recorded by the investigator in the context of the daily cycle. Operational criteria of a more definitive kind will emerge from empirical research.

The second line of analysis is focused on larger units of activity, perhaps whole phases of a cycle and even the entire day. It asks the question: What does the person's recorded activity reveal about the quantity and quality of his hedonic (pleasure-seeking) goals, moral inhibitions, and adaptive competence—and their interrelations? Psychoanalysts would formulate this in terms of the personality structures, id, superego, and ego, but at this level of analysis, operating outside Western culture, it is best to make the question of structuralization an empirical one, with the answers emerging from the data rather than imposed upon it.

In seeking to answer this question, evidence is aggregated from the detailed material of the first line of analysis. Primary process ideation reveals the operation of hedonistic and moralistic motives and their conflicts; secondary process thinking reveals competence; and the ebb and flow of these thought processes within a phase and over the daily cycle indicates the relations between motivational conflicts and the conflict-free sphere of adaptive functioning. This last point requires explanation. One of the foci of analysis is the extent to which primary process ideation interrupts secondary process thinking, indicating an interference with adaptation by motives made powerfully disruptive through conflict. The questions to be raised are: To what extent is adaptation to external reality free of interference from motivational conflict? To what extent do adaptive considerations control daily functioning, postponing the expression of hedonic and moralistic motives to phases in which they do not interfere with adaptation and moderating their intensities? To what degree are conflicting and contradictory motives and adaptive dispositions synthesized in behavior and made consistent in cognition, and what kinds of competence (psychoanalytic terms: ego synthesis, quality of defenses) are revealed in these processes? This list of questions could be extended to ask everything necessary for a psychoanalytic assessment at one point in time. From the examination of material in this line of analysis, it should be possible to arrive at preliminary judgments concerning the kinds of motivational and adaptive dispositions involved, the ways in which these dispositions are represented cognitively—for example, in relation to representations of self and significant others—and the necessity and adequacy of positing mental agencies or structures to account for the ideational content of daily functioning. Based on data concerning the ideational concomitants of the daily cycle, these judgments should permit comparison across cultures.

The two lines of analysis described so far are at different levels of generality and are, therefore, important to distinguish for purposes of this analytic exposition, but they would clearly overlap in operation. A third overlapping line of analysis would be focused on representations of self and others, as they appear in primary and secondary process ideation and as they occur in relation to specific hedonic, moralistic, and adaptive dispositions. This analysis would result in judgments concerning conceptions of self, conscious and unconscious, and relations with objects, including those in the contemporaneous interpersonal environment and those in the subjective representational world. Since self and object relations are a primary feature of the next two observational frames to be presented, they will not be discussed further here.

This discussion has carried us far beyond psychoanalytic ethnography into psychoanalytic observation of the individual to illustrate how the daily activity cycle could be used as an observational frame, analogous to the analytic session, for the repeatable collection of sequential data on the ideational processes of the person in relation to an ecological context. Many vital questions, including those concerning how the daily cycle could be sampled, have been left unanswered and must remain matters for empirical inquiry, but the following sections will suggest the wider context in which this microscopic approach could be used.

Development in the Life Cycle

Psychoanalysis is a developmental process with an initial problem (the patient's dissatisfaction with his own functioning), a goal (the re-solution of infantile motivational conflicts interfering with his functioning), and a sequence of phases through which these intrapsychic conflicts are imposed on an interpersonal situation and brought to consciousness for re-solution. These features—the problem, the goal, the interpersonal situation, and the sequence of phases—constitute the common structural background for the observation of developmental process in diverse patients. They provide the points of reference for the longitudinal assessment of personality stabilities and changes. Psychoanalytic observation in natural settings must also be longitudinal and have analogous points of reference constituting a structural background or frame in which individuals can be compared.

Anthropologists long ago recognized that development in the life cycle was a possible basis for cross-cultural comparison. In ethnography, this has most often resulted in compressed descriptions of ceremonies and other customary institutions associated with each culturally recognized phase in ontogeny, from pregnancy to death; only rarely, however, have such data been compared across cultures or analyzed theoretically. In the field of culture and personality, development—particularly during immaturity—has been a major research interest for more than 40 years, and numerous comparative studies have been carried out. Although the majority of these studies were heavily influenced by psychoanalytic theory and they have produced a great deal of evidence on variations in child rearing patterns and their possible correlates in parental roles and adult personality, few have treated development as a process requiring intensive longitudinal observation synchronized to the real time of the process itself. The intensive study of ongoing process has recently been developed in anthropology, not by anthropologists concerned with ontogeny and influenced by the longitudinal perspectives of clinical psychoanalysis and ethology but by those concerned with religion and politics (Turner, 1967, 1968, 1969; Swartz, Tuden, and Turner, 1968). (Some of Turner's studies deal with ontogenetic problems, but from social and cultural points of view rather than that of the individual.) Cross-cultural studies of socialization have tended to be too ambitious in their aims and too modest in their methods to undertake the intensive longitudinal study of developmental process in real time.

In the work of Erikson (1959), psychoanalysis has produced the most comprehensive and detailed conceptualization of the life cycle, as a whole and in the relations among its differing phases. Erikson's formulation is full of hypotheses worthy of testing, although some doubts might be raised about the pancultural applicability of the concepts involved in his stages. Other psychoanalytic ego psychologists have also made notable contributions to theory and conceptualization of development in the life cycle, many of them appearing in the annual *Psychoanalytic Study of the Child;* the most useful of them, in my opinion, is Anna Freud's (1963, 1965) concept of *developmental lines.* These theoretical and conceptual innovations, however, do not replace the methodological approach of clinical psychoanalysis to the collection of data and the making of inferences about development.

A comparative method applying principles of psychoanalytic observation and assessment to naturally occurring developmental processes of relatively short duration would require the four following steps:

1. *Identification of the process.* The division of the individual human life into units of developmental process is necessarily somewhat arbitrary, however naturalistic the intent, and reflects the aims and assumptions of the investigator. The present aim is to find short-term natural analogues to psychoanalytic process that are identifiable in ontogeny in all human populations. This suggests first of all demonstrable panhuman biological constraints on behavioral performance and directional change, constraints that in their universality can provide a constant structural frame for observation like that provided by the controlled ecological context of the psychoanalytic situation. At the most superficial level, such constraints are obvious in the growth processes of infancy and early childhood, in the processes of parenthood (including mating, reproduction, pregnancy, parturition, infant care), and in the functional decline of senescence. They are much less clear in later childhood, adolescence, and middle age, although a better knowledge than I have of developmental trends in metabolic processes and biochemical activity might clarify them. In the absence of better information, I will venture the guess that it would be difficult to identify biological constraints on behavior powerful enough to serve as observational frames for comparative personality study between about the age of five and the onset of mating, and (for mature adults outside of parenthood) until menopause for women and the decline of old age for men. A major exception may be the process of mourning for the death of a person to whom one was emotionally attached, which, according to the evidence assembled by Pollock (1961), has phylogenetic roots indicated by the parallel mourning reactions of the higher vertebrates. Other exceptions could no doubt be produced,

were the biological evidence assembled to support them. For the moment I will consider only those biological constraints on behavior obvious to a nonbiologist like myself.

For purposes of focused observation, the constraints should limit the goals and directions of developmental change for all humans, and in line with the psychoanalytic analogy, the goals must have some observable interpersonal content. The development of attachment to mother in infancy, the development of maternal and paternal behavior in young adulthood, the process of adapting to loss or separation from a loved one once attachment has occurred—these are developmental processes with adaptive goals that have interpersonal content and are constrained by human biology and ecology to a limited set of options. The interpersonal behavior observed reflects intrapsychic dispositions operating within biologically restricted directions.

The manifestation of intrapsychic dispositions in interpersonal behavior is the result of another essential ingredient, the psychosocial instability occasioned by the biological process, so that a fixed adaptation to the environment cannot be maintained from the beginning to the end of the developmental period. The psychoanalytic patient, by virtue of his malfunctioning and dissatisfaction, is often in a somewhat unsettled state even before he seeks treatment. Once he begins, he finds that his normal defenses are maladaptive in the psychoanalytic situation, because the analyst will not gratify his emotional needs, and this induces a regression to more primitive defenses in his repertoire; the regression is also fostered by the ambiguity and novelty of the situation and his prone posture on the couch. The maladaptation, psychic disequilibrium, and regression bring forth the primary process material associated with the primitive defenses and the unconscious motives with which they are in conflict, and they enable the analyst to observe signs of the unconscious conflicts to be brought into conscious awareness. Without the disruption in the person's normal functioning, the unconscious conflicts would remain hidden. This is essential for psychoanalytic observation, and its absence in much personality research is a major basis for psychoanalytic skepticism about studying personality outside the therapeutic situation. But developmental events and processes also induce psychic disequilibria, maladaptive responses and regression, through the operation of endogenous or exogenous factors posing novel adaptive problems and arousing intense affective reactions that disrupt the ordinary defenses of everyday life. This psychosocial instability, induced by biological events or social demands, is thus a defining characteristic of the developmental process suitable for psychoanalytic observation.

Two other criteria for identifying an appropriate developmental process must be emphasized, although they have been implied in the foregoing. First, the process should be defined by unequivocal temporal markers at its beginning or end so that a period of synchronized observation can be unequivocally established. Second, the duration of the process should be such that the investigator can make repeated observations at its beginning, middle, and end. This ordinarily will mean it should last no more than a few years, which is true of most clearly marked biological transitions anyway.

Summary: Development in the life cycle does not present itself to the investigator in segments as demarcated and controlled as the psychoanalytic treatment process. It is nevertheless possible to identify universal units of developmental process with biologically limited options for the direction of behavioral change, in which psychosocial instability makes latent dispositions manifest themselves in observable interpersonal behavior and which have unequivocal temporal markers and limited enough duration to make longitudinal observation of ongoing process feasible. The development of infant attachment to mother, the development of maternal and paternal behavior in young adulthood, and the adaptation to separation or loss, were mentioned as examples; they will be dealt with in more detail below.

2. *Ethnography of the developmental process.* Once the unit of process has been identified, the first step is to investigate the cultural concepts, rules, institutions, and expectations that surround it in as many cultures as possible, to discover the range of options that actually occur within the previously known biological constraints. This requires a much more detailed ethnography of development than we have seen to date, for it must be focused on the adaptive problem and developmental direction and goal as specifically as the conceptualization of the developmental process dictates. As in the ethnography of the daily cycle, the aim of this field work is to find the cultural constraints in a particular setting that limit the options available to an individual in responding to the panhuman situation defined by biology. In this case, however, change is not cyclical but directional, toward a goal, and the ethnography must cover the entire period of development and its component phases. The major tasks will be to understand and explicate the semantics of that developmental process and the norms of proper response throughout its course.

3. *Observation of the individual.* When the cultural and social contexts in which the individual responds to the biological process are adequately understood, it is possible to undertake investigation of individuals undergoing that process. With the biological and cultural constraints on individual response already known to the investigator, he is able to identify with confidence those options selected by the person studied that reflect dispositional contributions from his personality to overt behavior. The instability of psychosocial functioning experienced by the person during the period of observation makes his actions in selecting among the limited range of options particularly revealing of

his intrapsychic dispositions, for the anxiety associated with the instability is likely to foster a developmental regression to earlier modes of
functioning accompanied by primary process ideation. The primary
process material should expose unconscious motives and their conflicts
that would not be revealed when adaptation was stable and psychic
equilibrium well maintained by smoothly functioning defenses.

The method of collecting data on an individual undergoing a developmental process is dependent on the nature of that process—on the age
at which it occurs, the accessibility to observation of its behavioral manifestations, the duration of the process as a whole and its distinguishable
phases, the kind of relationship possible between the investigator and
the person while he is undergoing the process, and so forth. As a general approach, however, I propose the use of the daily activity cycle
outlined in the previous section, to be established before the onset of
the process as a baseline measure and then examined frequently enough
during the process to provide comparable material on each of its phases.
Whatever is going on with a person biologically, intrapsychically, and in
his psychosocial adaptation during a developmental transition must manifest itself in alterations of his daily cycles of sleep and wakefulness, rest
and activity, and in the ideational concomitants of those alterations, appearing as shifts in the content of dreams, daytime fantasies, conversational concerns. The observational focus on the daily cycle is a way of
charting these alterations over time as deviations from the baseline condition sampled prior to the onset of the process. In the developmental
context the ideational content of particular interest is that which represents other persons; the issues of attachment, separation, and loss in
relation to those persons; and the anxiety and other affects and signs of
disturbance experienced in connection with those issues. The developmental context gives the study of the daily cycle its *raison d'être* as a
means of monitoring the psychological course of a developmental
process and taking soundings in each of its phases. The observational
frame of the daily cycle, used repetitively and with a number of persons within the larger framework of the developmental process, com-
bines elements of the "physiological," "embryological," and "ecological"
strategies (discussed in Chapters 12 and 13) in a manner resembling
that of psychoanalysis, and it provides the basis in data for inferences
of comparable validity.

The discussion of observational method so far has been primarily applicable to adults and older children, because infant development can
be and has been effectively studied longitudinally with a straightforward
observational approach, there being relatively little gap between latent
dispositions, insofar as they are stable, and overt behavior. The more
difficult question is how an assessment of personality made in adulthood (*e.g.*, in the transition to parenthood or on the death of a spouse)

relates to psychoanalytic hypotheses concerning the effects of childhood experience on adult behavior. Reconstructive evidence can only be indirect and partial without the direct observation of infants and children themselves, but it is equally important. During the developmental process the investigator will have observed behavioral stability and change, and he will have a basis for drawing some conclusions about which aspects of the person's manifest behavior are more resistant to change in the face of stress and environmental influence; these are more likely to reflect dispositions formed in childhood. Second, the regressions occasioned by developmental instability and anxiety will have given the investigator an opportunity to sample the person's primary process ideation reflective of unconscious motives and their conflicts, which are hypothesized in psychoanalytic theory to represent residues of early experience. Third, through affective associations, the developmental events may have reactivated memories of significant events in early life that became topics of conversation. Thus this type of developmental assessment does allow some inferences concerning the dispositional residues in personality of earlier stages in development, but these inferences must also be tested in direct research on the earlier stage as well.

Direct research on infancy and early childhood conducted over a limited timespan involves individuals other than those being studied as adults; any connections inferred between one person's early experience and another's adult personality require assumptions concerning environmental and developmental similarities between those persons that must be supported by empirical evidence. The lack of this kind of evidence in culture and personality research has been a major source of skepticism regarding its developmental hypotheses. It is very difficult to obtain convincing evidence, but the problem is not hopeless. In my view, the answer will be found in carrying longitudinal investigation of child development forward from infancy to the period of childhood, perhaps four to six years old, in which verbal representations of motives and social objects become accessible to investigation, while at the same time pushing inquiries into adult memories back to that same period. The convergent evidence thus obtained on the phenomenology of that period should bring to light the ways in whch early experience has been affectively and cognitively registered at a point before the development of operational thought. The construction of a research instrument based on the early work of Piaget and applied to a sample of Hausa children in Nigeria is described in a paper by LeVine and Price-Williams (1970).

4. *Comparison across cultures.* The material collected according to the method outlined above would result in a personality description sufficiently rooted in universal features to be comparable across cultures. The arguments concerning universal features as observational frames have already been presented; recapitulating them here would add noth-

ing to their weight, since only empirical study can provide the crucial test. My own confidence that observation of short-term developmental process can produce cross-culturally comparable psychoanalytic evidence has been strengthened by the work of Pollock (1961, 1962, 1972) on the process of mourning and that of Ainsworth (1967, 1969) on the development of attachment in infants. Each has identified panhuman elements in those processes and used observational evidence (from clinical psychoanalysis in the case of Pollock and naturalistic observation on the ethological model in the case of Ainsworth) to generate a sequence of observable phases that hold not only for our own culture but at least one other (Orthodox Jews for Pollock, the Ganda of East Africa for Ainsworth). A great deal of psychoanalytic publication, most recently represented by a book on parenthood edited by Anthony and Benedek (1970), and especially its biological chapter by Kaufman (1970), convinces me that similar potentialities exist in the developmental processes of parenthood.

Bureaucratic Institutional Structures

The final observational frame to be proposed in this chapter departs from the biological roots of the others and points the way toward a different kind of structural background that will be treated less extensively here than its importance merits. This proposal recognizes that biological features are not the only structural constancies common to much or all of humanity. In psychoanalysis, the institutional structure of the fee-paying, doctor-patient, consulting-room relationship is a central part of the normative environment in which observation is conducted. This has always seemed to be one of the most culture-bound aspects of psychoanalytic observation, for the investigator can hardly export a Western set of norms to a people who have very different but equally institutionalized therapist-patient relationships. Yet a formal social structure provides a strong background, more detailed than any biological feature, against which diagnostic idiosyncrasies are revealed. Unlike the biological reactions and processes discussed above, institutional structures ideally constrain overt behavior through explicit normative prescriptions and proscriptions to a narrow set of options, while necessarily allowing variation in the manner or style of conformity. The explicitness of formal norms and their relevance to the most observable aspects of psychological functioning in overt behavior make them valuable frames for the comparable observation of individuals. The difficulty is that they vary so widely across cultures.

Certain institutional structures have become so widespread in the world that they are absent only in the most remote hinterlands of a few countries: the bureaucracies of Western origin operating in schools, hospitals, post offices, and other government offices everywhere. While their Western origin would seem to make them alien in many places, in fact it merely represents the common historical background from which they have diverged in mixing with local traditions. (The background is not quite uniform, since European and American colonial powers had differing bureaucratic traditions, but these differences can be documented and the original form introduced into a non-Western area can be reconstructed in detail.) In most non-Western countries the divergence from Western norms, beginning with the replacement of colonial supervisors by local ones, has taken place recently enough that the original norms are still recognized regardless of whether they are still followed. There is thus a rough comparability of structural background: Schools and hospitals everywhere have the same organizational goals, similar physical settings (classrooms, clinics, wards), similar formal role relationships (teacher-pupil, doctor-nurse-patient), with official definitions that are nearly identical.

The original goals, settings, and formal role prescriptions act as a common framework of constraints within which variation has been considerable and against which variation is conspicuous. Furthermore, these bureaucracies have come to play a vital role in the lives of individuals in many or most parts of the world. Western schooling replaces indigenous education as essential preparation for adult life; hospitals and dispensaries are turned to for medical needs; post offices become essential communication links in the maintenance of kin and other social relationships over distance; increasing numbers of persons spend large segments of their waking hours occupying bureaucratic positions or seeking employment in them. They are thus appropriate situations in which to make comparable observations of individual behavior.

A method for diagnosing personality dispositions through the observation of bureaucratic behavior would follow the same steps outlined earlier. Most important would be a careful ethnography of the institution, revealing the local norms and formal and informal expectations that govern its operation and form the proximal environment of the person, limiting his options for action in some areas and providing opportunities in others. When this is done, it would be necessary to identify not only the rhythms of activity and relaxation but also the critical points in the operation of the institution at which individuals acted in such a way as to reveal in their observable behavior the motives that lay behind their relationships toward others in that setting and their concepts of self and others. It is easiest to imagine critical points of this kind in a hospital where bureaucrats must continually respond to emergencies and crises, to the intense needs of patients in distress, and to the grief and anger of mourners. In the hospital, too, there are unique opportunities for longitudinal observation of patients under stress, as the studies of surgery patients by Janis (1958) have so effectively shown (see also Janis and Leventhal, 1968).

Opportunities for comparable psychological observation within a naturally structured observational frame exist not only in hospitals and other bureaucratic settings but in any institutional structure of a single historical origin that has diffused to diverse cultural groups. This is an extension for comparative personality study of the principles contained in the method of controlled comparison as formulated by Eggan (1954). A widespread religion can be used as a common framework for comparing diverse groups, as Geertz (1968) did in comparing the divergent Islams of Morocco and Indonesia. Where the common historical origin is unequivocal, the investigator can have some assurance that his categories of comparison are naturalistic rather than invented.

In this chapter I have tried to show that the major objections to a psychoanalytic anthropology—that psychoanalytic data can be collected only in the classic therapeutic situation and that the data might not be comparable across cultures—can be met in principle. The search for natural situations, common to all human populations, in which data might be collected according to procedures embodying the basic inference strategies of psychoanalysis, has not proved hopeless. Biological research and comparative social science uncover constants of the human situation that can serve as suitable backgrounds for the study of individual personality; these have been illustrated in the methods proposed. In all cases, ethnography must provide the intermediate observational framework, the shared symbolic and interactional contexts through which the individual experiences human universals and their limitations. The procedures outlined raise many questions that cannot be effectively answered before empirical exploration, but in the next chapter I deal with a specific problem, religious symbolism, of interest to anthropology and psychoanalysis alike, and indicate how these procedures might be used to solve it.

17

Religious Symbols and
Religious Experience

Freud's *Totem and Taboo* (1913) established the relevance of psychoanalysis to the study of religion. Though skeptical of Freudian interpretations of particular religious patterns, anthropologists have turned and
returned to psychoanalytic concepts and theory for help in making sense
of the religious symbolism with which their field work confronts them.
Recently, despite the generally inhospitable climate in anthropology and
sociology for psychoanalytic explanations of culture, a number of accomplished students of comparative religion—Beidelman (1964, 1966b), Bellah (1965), Richards (1956), Spiro (1965, 1966, 1967), Turner (1967,
1968, 1969), and Wilson (1971)—have applied, or discussed the application of, psychoanalytic concepts to ethnographic data on religion. I do
not review this literature here but instead deal with what appears to be
the primary problem they have encountered: understanding the psychological meaning of a religious symbol, the unexpressed and possibly
inexpressible meaning that connects the symbol as part of a cultural system with the emotions it arouses in individuals. If the methods outlined
in the previous chapter are to be of value in the comparative study of
personality, they should be able to contribute to the understanding of
religion and also enrich thereby their assessment of individual personality. To put it another way, if a method of personality assessment is
effective, it should simultaneously shed light on an individual's religious
experience and reveal the psychological factors involved in maintaining
and changing a religious system.

The methodological heart of the problem is that the native informants
on whom ethnographers depend to explain the conventional meanings in
their belief system cannot offer effective interpretations of many important ritual symbols; they cannot decode the symbol into words that con-

nect its observable attributes with the affective contexts in the individual in which it evokes a response. In this respect, as Turner (1967) and Geertz (1968) have recognized, the ethnographer is in the position of the psychoanalyst confronted by a dream that the dreamer does not understand—except that the analyst has an established method for dealing with it. As Geertz (1968, pp. 107–114) discusses it, there are two related aspects to this problem: First, there is the inherent incompatibility of the religious experience itself with reporting that experience to an investigator; during the experience one cannot report, and after the experience, the memory of it undergoes secondary revision, being assimilated to rational or commonsensical (secondary process) modes of thought. Second, a religious belief can have two cultural forms, the one in which it is experienced in ritual (and which is so difficult to decode), and the other in which it is part of routine, commonsense cognition; and the relation between these two forms (for example, the amount of influence of the first on the second) varies among individuals and populations.

Anthropologists have devised a number of solutions to this problem. Beidelman (1964, 1966b) operates by detailed examination of the ritual and ideological contexts in which symbols recur, using some Freudian assumptions about body imagery as his guiding hypotheses. He has demonstrated that if the ethnographic description is thorough enough, it is possible even for someone other than the ethnographer to decode selected symbols in psychoanalytic terms. Turner (1967, 1968, 1969) uses the observation of ritual process, assembling detailed information on the semantic and interactive contexts in which a particular sequence of ritual events take place, to uncover meanings of the symbols involved (*i.e.*, their positions in the semantic and interactive contexts accessible to the ethnographer) that go beyond the consciously expressed interpretations of informants. He believes that further decoding of these symbols is desirable but outside the competence of anthropologists. Spiro (1965, 1967) argues that the understanding of religious symbols requires the anthropologist to undertake psychological studies of religious participants (*e.g.*, a person undergoing exorcism of a spirit, novitiates undergoing training in a monastery), and he uses ethnographic-clinical observation and projective testing as methods of study.

None of these solutions has yet proven to be entirely satisfactory. Turner (1967, pp. 32–40) is quite explicit about the limitations of his method for penetrating the psychological meaning of symbols. Beidelman (1970, p. 524) suggests the need for future "intensive and detailed analyses" of individuals, using psychological method. Spiro (1965), has been using such methods in a long-term psychosocial investigation of Burmese religion; his publications so far represent data only from the preliminary phase of the first serious field study of religious symbolism in its psychological dimensions. Geertz (1968) poses the problem in such a way (summarized above) as to question whether it can be solved, but neither he nor the others suggest that it can be ignored.

If the anthropologist's problem resembles that of the psychoanalyst confronted by a dream his patient cannot explain, how does the analyst solve it? He gets the patient to associate to the dream. But what does he do with the information? How does he decode its symbolic content? In their clinical work as opposed to their "as if" analyses of exotic culture patterns, all psychoanalysts would agree with Erikson (1958) that "a symbol is a symbol only when it can be demonstrated to be at work." Rapaport (1944, in Gill, 1967, p. 188) states:

> It appears that meaning is one of the concepts of psychoanalysis that we use and misuse more than others. What do we mean by meaning? We ask about a dream, "What is the meaning of it?" What do we mean? I submit that we mean, "How does that dream fit into the psychic continuity of the individual who dreamed it?" We don't imply anything else in our query about "meaning," so far as I can see. . . . The concept of the meaning of a symptom or an idea or a symbol or a dream brings it into a certain place in the psychological continuity.

Parallel to the "psychic continuity" of the individual in analysis is what Erikson (1958) calls the "evidential continuity" maintained by the analytic observer through the methods outlined in Chapter 13. Understanding a symbol from a psychoanalytic point of view involves understanding its functions in maintaining, restoring or altering states of equilibrium in the personality system of the individual. The psychoanalytic method is in this sense analogous to the method of Turner, which uses the observation of ritual behavior in process to establish the functions of symbols in the social and cultural systems of groups. It requires the intensive longitudinal attention to the individual in his psychological and social functioning that Turner gives to groups in their collective functioning.

On the basis of this psychoanalytic view of symbolic meaning, it is possible to construct an approach to religious symbolism. The first tenet of this approach is that (in accordance with the guidelines of Chapter 14) it is applicable only to individuals; it will establish the subjective meanings of a cultural symbol for the particular individual studied, not for other members of the group, who may or may not share those meanings. Its operative focus, as emphasized in the foregoing chapters, must be on the respective contributions of primary and secondary process thought to be the observed flow of ideational and behavioral material; this is the concrete observational context in which the symbol must eventually be placed in order to decode its personal meanings. The procedures to be followed have been suggested in the previous chapter and include the working alliance of bicultural and foreign investigators, the ethnographic study of affects, and a series of observational frames based on daily activity cycles, developmental processes and formal institutional structures. I shall consider briefly how each of the research strategies of psychoanalysis—"physiological," "embryological," and "ecological"—as embodied in the proposed procedures, can contribute to understanding the psychological meaning of a religious symbol.

A Psychoanalytic Approach to the
Study of Religious Experience

The "physiological" perspective. From this point of view, the person's religious behavior and experience would be placed in the context of his cycles of functioning and deviations from those cycles. The functioning of the individual would be longitudinally assessed through the repetition of data collection within the observational frame of his daily activity cycle. The data from each observational period would be analyzed in the cognitive terms presented in the previous chapter (diagnostic of primary versus secondary process ideation), in terms of the trichotomy of pleasure-seeking, moral constraint, and adaptive competence, and in their representations of self and others. Observation would be repeated, at some interval to be determined, until the cycles manifested themselves clearly; these would form the material for the baseline assessment. Observation would be resumed at various intervals consistent with maintenance of the relationship between observer and person studied, to detect deviations from the baseline patterns and their concomitants in conditions internal or external to the individual. A major focus of analysis would be the occurrence of regression from secondary to primary process thought and along other developmental lines; and the conditions precipitating such a regression, its functions in resolving or avoiding motivational conflict and in restoring states of equilibrium in cyclical functioning. At every point in this collection and analysis of data, the occurrence of religious activity and religious thought content (in dreams as well as waking life) would be noted and eventually understood in its sequential contexts within the temporal structure of individual functioning.

The "embryological" perspective. This point of view would be provided by framing the observational program just described within the larger temporal structure of a developmental process such as parenthood (from courtship through infancy of the first child) or mourning for the loss of a loved one, in which there are objective events and fairly clear adaptive goals around which to organize observation. Soundings would be taken at different phases in the developmental process, which has several advantages as a contextual background against which to understand religious experience: It is disruptive of normal functioning, occasioning psychological instability and possibly stress against which everyday defenses may be inadequate; and it often involves recourse to ritual activity (see Turner, 1968), which can serve as another structural frame for the observation of individual behavior. Spiro (1965), following Hallo-well (1938), has proposed that religion offers individuals culturally con-stituted defenses to help resolve their intrapsychic conflicts, and Pollock (1972) shows the utility of this concept in understanding rituals intended to deal with the process of mourning. In the developmental perspective it would be possible to discover if individuals did use religious symbols for such defensive functions and in relation to what events, what motives and conflicts activated by events, and with what consequences not only for the restoration of equilibrium but for possible adaptive or maladaptive change away from a previous psychosocial equilibrium.

The *"ecological"* perspective. This is the integrating perspective in which the individual is compared with others in the same environment for differences in stable functioning, response to unusual events, and developmental change—differences that would indicate the contribution of person-specific (as opposed to situation-specific) dispositions to observable behavior. The *sine qua non* from this point of view is a thorough knowledge of the environment, in this case the semantics and normative expectations of the sociocultural environment in which the daily and developmental functioning of the person is embedded so that the individual's motives are not confused with the pressures of his situation. This requires an ethnography (described in the previous chapter) methodologically identical to the standard kind but with a different substantive focus, one given by the biopsychological structures of the daily activity cycles and the developmental processes of the life cycle and by the formal institutional structures of bureaucracies (and perhaps other social forms). The ethnography would entail the expected place of various religious symbols, activities, and experiences in daily life and the various segments of the life cycle, and the ecological analysis would require comparing individuals in the ways in which they met and deviated from these expectations. Individuals would also be compared in their observable affective reactions to religious symbols, in the daily and developmental ideational contexts of such reactions, in the ways in which they integrated religious elements into their daily functioning, and in the antecedents and sequelae of religious activity during the instability of a developmental process. The question would be: How do different individuals use religion in their own personality functioning, and if they use it differently, what in their social positions or personality dispositions accounts for the difference?

This bare outline, which is all that an *a priori* discussion can and should produce, indicates the several personal contexts in which religious symbols could be placed in an attempt to understand their psychological meaning, their connections with the affective experience of individuals. What this approach has to recommend it is its realistic conception of the combination of rational-adaptive and metaphorical-affective modes of experience in individual personality functioning, and of the psychoanalytic method as a means of uncovering the distinct operations of the two modes and their relations in the sequential analysis of individual ideation. This conception, promulgated by Freud (1900) in his distinction of primary and secondary process, has been frequently forgotten by his followers in their analyses of religious phenomena.

What this approach has against it, however, is the specter of its sheer impossibility as a set of field procedures which, though they utilize skills most professional anthropologists have or could acquire, might involve individual data collection on a scale that could not be tolerated in field relationships. The monitoring of individual functioning without therapeutic intent, however valuable scientifically, may prove both unworkable and unethical in some or all cultural contexts. In developing his method, Freud, like so many other scientists, tried it first on himself, and then constructed it in such a way that it was closely tied to the voluntary collaboration of the patient, not only in seeking treatment but in doing the analytic work at every step of the process. Psychoanalysis is less something that an analyst does to a patient than something a patient does to himself under the guidance of an analyst. The latter is less a surgeon than an obstetrician. In his proposal for an expansion of psychoanalytic observation, the role of the non-Western behavioral scientist is crucial, exploring the use of this method through his own self-monitoring and then devising locally meaningful methods of guided self-monitoring that would help solve the complex scientific and ethical problems involved. The self-aware persons of various cultures who are also participants in their traditional religious systems can, with proper guidance, contribute uniquely to the translation of the experience with religious symbols into universally comprehensible descriptions.

Although this approach has not yet been tried in research, I shall attempt to illustrate its potential contribution to the understanding of witchcraft, using published materials and my own field experience. Witchcraft may seem peripheral to the subject of religious symbolism, but most anthropologists regard witch beliefs as part of the magic-religious belief system of a people (e.g., Mair, 1969; Wilson, 1971). As cultural images of malevolence that are mobilized in the public behavior of witchcraft accusations and confessions, those vivid and widespread beliefs—found with varying symbolic content among pre-industrial peoples everywhere—have received attention from anthropologists and historians working in virtually every part of the world.

Witchcraft Accusations and Psychological Structure

This heading is a deliberate paraphrase of "Witch Beliefs and Social Structure," an article in which Monica Wilson (1951) traced the differences in the evil acts attributed to witches by two African groups to the differing normative demands made by their kinship and community structures. In the ensuing decades, the growing ethnographic literature on Africa and elsewhere has been focused on the social context of witchcraft. A basic axiom of this literature is that, as Middleton and Winter (1963, p. 1) put it, "these beliefs are social, not psychological, phenomena and must be so analyzed." Without rejecting the demonstrations by Evans-Pritchard (1937) and Gluckman (1944) that witch beliefs provide cognitively consistent explanations of misfortune and may also prevent social disruption of greater magnitude than the witchcraft accusations themselves, social anthropologists have shown that in populations believing in witchcraft, accusations tend to be associated with features of the social structure, for example, competitive relationships unregulated by normative prescription or recurrent schisms in communities or descent groups (see Douglas, 1970, for a review and some additional social-structural suggestions). Most of the explanations offered strongly imply the operation of psychological processes,[1] but these are rarely explored, because the study of such processes is not regarded as appropriate for social anthropology (see Devons and Gluckman, 1967, pp. 240–253). It is of course an appropriate task for culture and personality research, and that is why I take it up here. More important than the scientific division of labor, however, is that social-structural explanations of witchcraft, with individual experience and psychological process left out, are incomplete and therefore inadequate, as I hope to show in the following illustrations.

My first illustration comes from 16th and 17th-century England, for which the recent writings of Macfarlane (1970a, 1970b) and Thomas (1970, 1971) give us an exceptionally clear picture of witchcraft beliefs and accusations.[2] Thomas states, "My approach will be primarily sociological, and I shall have to omit any consideration of intellectual or psychological aspects of the subject. Any fully satisfying explanation of English witchcraft, would, of course, have to take account of them as well" (1970, p. 47). In fact, however, the hypothesis that he and Macfarlane present and support with evidence is a *psychosocial* hypothesis

1. It has been a standard exercise in teaching culture and personality to demonstrate that some of the British social anthropologists who most emphatically reject psychological explanations of culture—and particularly of ritual—do in fact posit intrapsychic phenomena that closely resemble Freudian concepts such as ambivalence, guilt, displaced hostility, projection—but that they prefer to discuss them as if they could occur independently of the individual's psychological organization. I omit this demonstration from the present discussion because I assume that the formerly doctrinaire "psychology taboo" has been replaced by a healthy skepticism about the demonstrable relevance of specific psychological factors, combined with a recognition that the problem of symbolism will ultimately require psychological understanding for its solution.

2. Thomas' extensive study of English magic (1971), with a section on witchcraft (pp. 435–583), became available to me after this chapter was written. It elaborates and adds to his earlier discussion rather than revising it.

in which psychological factors play a central role. The Thomas-Macfarlane formulation is summarized briefly in the following paragraphs.

From medieval times to the early 18th century, there was a legitimate place for witchcraft beliefs and accusations in the official framework of English religious and legal institutions. Throughout this period, however, there were also legitimate and widely used alternatives to witchcraft in explaining misfortune and seeking recourse for injury; accusing someone of witchcraft was only one of several options available to a victim of misfortune. Though the institutional environment was more favorable to witchcraft accusations at some times than at others, their rise and fall in English history—and particularly their apparently sharp increase in the 16th century and rapid decline after the middle of the 17th—cannot be attributed simply to the imposition of official policies from above by the central authorities of church or state. The phenomenon can be understood only by examining the factors in community life that led individuals to make witchcraft accusations, rather than choosing other courses of action, more frequently in one era than another.

Before the Reformation, the Catholic Church in England provided numerous ritual precautions, including the use of holy water and the sign of the cross, to ward off evil spirits and malevolent magic, and priests helped their parishioners in this regard. People generally regarded themselves as protected against witchcraft, but anyone who thought he was bewitched could find recourse in church ritual without undertaking legal prosecution. These practices were officially denounced and effectively eliminated after the Reformation; Protestant preachers reaffirmed the power of evil but left a bewitched person with a choice between resorting to counter-magic, which was prohibited and had to be clandestine, and legal prosecution, which was approved and eventually supported by civil legislation (in 1542, 1563, and 1604). Under these conditions, witchcraft accusations and prosecutions naturally increased, but their subsequent ups and downs are not correlated with major shifts in legal or ecclesiastical mandates concerning witchcraft. Between 1542 and 1736 there were only 16 years (1547 to 1563) when a witchcraft statute was not in force, but most of the known prosecutions occurred between 1560 and 1680, including some that were brought in the years when there was no relevant statute (Macfarlane 1970a, p. 14). As Macfarlane states: "The institutionalization of the punishment of witches can be seen as a 'necessary' cause of witchcraft prosecutions, but it is not a 'sufficient' one" (1970a, p. 20). With the exception of one organized anti-witch crusade (1645 to 1647), the trials of witches during those 120 years "originated at a local level" and "reflected local animosities" (Thomas 1970, p. 58). They also reflected the effects of social change, particularly the breakdown in village communalism and the concomitant shift of charitable functions from the local community to extra-community institutions (primarily the workhouse). When old and new normative expectations about local charity coexisted and competed, they generated the animosities that give rise to witchcraft accusations; once the shift of functions was completed and the new expectations were established as the community consensus, animosities were less frequently generated and accusations waned. At the same time, rising skepticism about witchcraft among the educated classes, who were represented in trials as judge and jury, made prosecution more difficult and execution less likely, thus virtually eliminating witchcraft trials in many areas some 50 years before the statute was repealed in 1736. In villages that experienced the tension of conflicting expectations about charity after that date, violence against alleged witches (now treated as a criminal act) erupted occasionally until late in the 19th century.

This is the broad historical picture. From 1560 to 1680, the period of frequent accusations, we find from Macfarlane's study of three Essex villages and less systematic data on other parts of England, that those prosecuted (and in many cases executed) for witchcraft were predominantly women over 50 years of age (or their husbands) who were poorer unrelated neighbors of their alleged victims but not from the poorest segment of society. Typically, the accused witch had previously been refused a favor by her neighbor who, when a sudden misfortune befell him later, blamed it on the grudge she bore him for his refusal and initiated a prosecution against her for witchcraft. Macfarlane (1970a, pp. 168–176) provides detailed data on this from Essex, and Thomas (1970, pp. 62–63), indicates it was true in other parts of England as well; the latter states the psychosocial hypothesis succinctly:

> Witch beliefs . . . arose at a time when the old tradition of mutual charity was being sapped by the introduction of a national Poor Law. This made the model householder's role essentially ambiguous. The clergy still insisted on the duty of local charity, whereas local authorities were beginning to forbid householders to give indiscriminate alms at the door. It is this unhappy conjunction of private and public charity that accounts for the uncertain light in which contemporaries viewed the poor. On the one hand, they hated them as a burden to the community and a threat to public order. On the other, they still recognized it was their Christian duty to give them help. The conflict between resentment and a sense of obligation produced the ambivalence which made it possible for men to turn begging women brusquely from the door and yet to suffer torments of conscience after having done so. This ensuing guilt was fertile ground for witchcraft accusations, since subsequent misfortune could be seen as retaliation on the part of the witch. The tensions that produced witchcraft allegations were those generated by a society which no longer held a clear view as to how its dependent members should be treated; they reflected the ethical conflict between the twin and opposing doctrines that those who did not work should not eat, and that it was blessed for the rich to support the poor (p. 67).

Thomas describes the case of an accused witch named Christian Shirston in Somerset, who in 1530 was denied ale and milk by three neighbors, each of whom in turn became the victim of a mysterious disaster: in one case, for example, a cow gave blood and water instead of milk. He states:

> When shutting the door in Christian Shirston's face, her neighbors were only too well aware of having departed from the accepted ethical code. They knew they had put their selfish interests before their social duty. When some minor accident overtook them or their children it was their guilty conscience that told them where to look to find the source of their misfortunes (1970, p. 63).

Macfarlane confirms this in his Essex study.

> It was usually the person who had done the first wrong under the old ideals of charity who felt himself bewitched. . . . [An] accusation of witchcraft was a clever way of reversing the guilt, of transferring it from the person who had failed in his social obligation under the old standard to the person who made him fail. Through the mechanism of the law, and the informal methods of gossip and village opinion, society was permitted to support the accuser (1970a, pp. 196–197)
>
> Thus it could be argued that the emotion that lay behind witchcraft accusations arose largely from discord within individuals, within people who felt the demands of the old communal values and the power of the old sanctions, while also realizing the practical necessity of cutting down or re-directing their relationships (1970b, p. 94).

Macfarlane quotes a seventeenth-century poet, Sir Francis Hubert, who recognized the dynamics involved:

> Besides, when any Errour is committed
> Whereby wee may incurre or losse or shame,
> That wee our selves thereof may be acquitted
> Wee are too ready to transfer the blame
> Upon some Witch: That made us doe the same.
> It is the vulgar Plea that weake ones use
> I was bewitch'd: I could nor will: nor chuse.
> But my affection was not caus'd by Art;
> The witch that wrought on mee was in my brest.
> (Macfarlane, 1970a, p. v)

Thomas and Macfarlane thus locate the immediate cause of the witchcraft accusation in the intrapsychic experience and functioning of the individual accuser: He experiences conflict between selfish interest and moral duty and, having allowed the former to be expressed in action at the expense of the latter, feels guilty. The subsequent occurrence of misfortune arouses the guilt—or the experience of uneasiness, anxiety, or discomfort associated with it—to a level at which the individual cannot tolerate it for long. The witchcraft accusation is a reinterpretation of the moral situation that reduces his guilt feelings and permits him to solicit social validation of his status as a victim rather than an agent of malevolence. If Thomas and Macfarlane are right, witchcraft accusations in this period cannot be adequately accounted for without taking account of psychological structures in the personalities of individuals.

Let us begin with the individual's refusal to give food, drink, or other requested help to his poorer neighbor. This refusal was a departure from previously established custom, but the person refused usually had a reputation as a malevolent and unneighborly person, and the man who turned her away was subject to no punishment from the authorities or the community. Any uneasiness he experienced after his refusal, therefore, could not be based on a realistic fear of punishment. Sometimes the old woman was heard to pronounce a curse as she was leaving, but in other cases

> It was not necessary for the suspected witch to have given evidence of her malevolence. The victim's guilty conscience was sufficient to provoke an accusation, since, when a misfortune occurred, his first reaction . . . was to ask what he had done to deserve it. When, in 1589, a Southampton tanner's pigs expired, after having "danced and leaped in a most strange sort, as if they had been bewitched," he recalled how on the previous day the Widow Wells had come to his door on two occasions, "there sitting (and) asking nothing; at length, having not given anything to her [we may underline his assumption that something should have been], she departed." On the basis of the next day's occurrences, he warned her that "if he took any hurt by her afterwards he would have her burned for a witch." Yet there is no evidence of any expressed malevolence on her part at all (Thomas, 1970, pp. 63–64).

It may be argued that in a community in which belief in the power of curses is strong, it would be reasonable, even realistic, for a man to believe that a deprived old woman would curse him even if he did not hear the curse; but if so, why refuse to give her what she wants? In an earlier period, according to Macfarlane (1970b, p. 93), people were indeed too afraid of curses to deny gifts to the poor, and the curse was a sanction enforcing communal sharing in the village. One might think it would be a choice between giving to the witch if one feared her curse, and refusing her if one did not. That men who refused her nevertheless worried about being cursed suggests the operation of an unconscious factor, like the guilt that Thomas mentions, which did not enter awareness at the time of refusing but influenced subsequent patterns of reaction. Such men apparently consciously thought themselves free to refuse, only to discover that they were troubled after having done so—despite the absence of threat from the alleged witch or anyone else.

Concerning the subsequent misfortune or injury, Macfarlane (1970a) states, "In many cases it is impossible to tell whether the injury or the specific realization that one was likely to be bewitched came first" (p. 111). In the typical cases that he and Thomas discuss, however, it appears that while the refusing neighbor may have been consciously or unconsciously anticipating retribution for his unneighborly act, it was not until the injury or misfortune occurred that he formed the conscious judgment of being bewitched. The misfortune, which could be as serious as a death in the family or as minor as cream failing to turn to butter or the death of a chicken, precipitated the accusation of witchcraft.

From a psychoanalytic point of view, the processes involved may be seen as follows. The initial instance of the woman coming to the door aroused a conflict between two motives, one associated with a new ideology of individualism but which was experienced as selfish greed by the villager, and the other associated with traditional values and experienced as the internal demand to act morally. By refusing her, the villager conformed to the new code of conduct, pushing his moral qualms out of consciousness, at least temporarily. He nevertheless unconsciously experienced his act as one of selfish greed for which punishment was deserved. The villager's perception of the act as a violation of his own moral ideals established its place and strength in his memory. Cognitively, it became embedded in a network of associations relevant to ideas of retribution and malevolence. Affectively, it gave rise to feelings of unease or anxiety that made the memory more difficult to keep out of consciousness and more likely to be revived by relevant associations.

Then the misfortune occurred. Macfarlane (1970a, pp. 203–204; 1970b, p. 88) emphasizes that witchcraft was not the only explanation of misfortune available to 16th- and 17th-century English villagers; but he and Thomas argue that it was the explanation most likely to be selected by someone experiencing unconscious guilt over an unneighborly act. In psychoanalytic terms, there are several factors to be considered here. The guilty person's memory of his act put him into an uncomfortable state of heightened sensitivity to ideas of retribution, from which relief would be welcomed. When the misfortune occurred, its unpleasant nature revived the memory of the greedy act through a series of connecting associations such as the following: unpleasant event inflicted on me—punishment—wrongdoing—my own recent wrongdoing. Sometimes the nature of the unpleasant event itself strengthened the associative chain by an additional "clue," as when a man who refused a woman a quart of milk found that his cow gave blood instead of milk or that the cream would not turn to butter; the "punishment" directly suggested the "crime" by the associative link involving "milk." In other cases, however, the temporal contiguity of the events was enough, given his emotional state, to trigger a similar chain of associations.

To draw the conclusion that a misfortune following a misbehavior must be causally related to it, as punishment to crime, is to function cognitively at a level that Piaget (1932) calls "immanent justice," which is characteristic of the moral judgment of young children. Since the English villagers presumably functioned generally at higher levels, I suggest that the stress of the unpleasant event occasioned a regression to childlike thought processes in which normal criteria for assessing evidence were suspended. This temporary and restricted regression was facilitated by the rumors of neighbors who reported that they had been afflicted for refusing the woman and by the "cunning man" (diviner) who, when consulted, tended to strengthen and legitimize any suspicion the person might have.

Thus, with some help from others, the person reached the firm conclusion that he was being punished for his moral violation. Since he unconsciously felt he deserved the punishment and had been troubled about his selfish act, it might be thought that the idea of his being punished would reduce his emotional discomfort and restore his equilibrium. In fact, it had just the opposite effect, because the misfortune was taken as a signal of his culpability, which could no longer be excluded from consciousness, and of a punishment process that had been set in motion but might not (according to local belief) end with a single act of vengeance. In his heightened state of moral anxiety, the villager still had some options other than a witchcraft accusation. He might, for example, have made a kind of public confession as an attempt to purge himself of guilt feelings. If he had gone to the clergy to confess they might have given him moral support, but they claimed no power to stop the effects of witchcraft. His fellow villagers, however, might not even have been willing to give him moral support for a confession of sin, since they were committing similar "sins" in accordance with the new morality—something which he implicitly acknowledged when he turned the old woman away. Though confession might have afforded him relief, the social conditions were not sufficiently favorable for him to select that avenue of discharge. The accusation of witchcraft, however, offered him the kinds of advantages characteristic of a true "culturally constituted defense" (Spiro, 1965). It provided an explanation in which the accuser's selfish greed is far outweighed by the malevolence and destructiveness of the witch, his minor sins of omission contrasted with a vengeful act of much greater magnitude, involving murder, mayhem, or the destruction of property. Belief in such an explanation permits the individual to feel that he has been wronged so much more than he has done wrong that he deserves to see himself as victim rather than sinner. When he is able to believe this explanation wholeheartedly, through the avenues described below, then he experiences relief from the emotional reaction (anxiety and unease associated with guilt feelings) activated by his original trans-

gression and reactivated at a heightened level by the subsequent incident of misfortune.

The attractiveness of the witchcraft explanation as a defense mechanism that reduces guilt feelings does not mean it was adopted automatically by the afflicted individual. On the contrary, there is the evidence
that such persons usually discussed the explanation with their neighbors,
recounting the sequence of events and getting in return not only the
neighbor's judgment on the facts but also other stories about the vengeful acts of the alleged witch. The "cunning man" also functioned to validate private suspicion as public fact. In these encounters with neighbors
and the cunning man, the would-be accuser might be seen as regressing
in another way, resembling that described by Freud (1921) in *Group
Psychology and the Analysis of the Ego:* In submitting his ideas for validation, he was taking the role of a small child whose parents define for
him what is true and false, real and unreal. Although in normal life the
villager generally fulfilled this reality-testing function for himself, his
urgent need for a socially acceptable defense that would relieve his
anxiety induced him to solicit the aid of others in this case—to replace
his judgment with theirs. When they confirmed his suspicions, he was
ready to make a public accusation.

The encounters with neighbors and the cunning man, and subsequently with juries and judges, have another side to them. Each time the
accuser told his story he was, in effect, confessing his transgression of
traditional morality and receiving implicit absolution from others in the
community and those of higher authority. They not only confirmed that
he was more sinned against than sinning, thereby validating his defensive
belief, but also gave public (if tacit) sanction to his original refusal of
alms. The accuser repeated the guilt-reducing defensive behavior in
public at least until his part in the trial was over, and perhaps afterward
as well among friends and neighbors. (It should also be mentioned that
each public hearing and trial involving a case of this kind must have had
an effect on all those who witnessed it—helping them with their own guilt
about ceasing to give alms.) We have no way of knowing from the historical evidence how permanent and effective these performances were in
reducing the experience of guilt.

This analysis has merely spelled out in detail the psychological implications of the Thomas-Macfarlane formulation, showing the processes that
must have been operating if the hypothesis put forward by these careful
historians is correct. There are several conclusions to be drawn:

1. The witchcraft accusation serves a psychological function for the
accuser, in this case (rural England 1560 to 1680) reducing the anxiety
associated with moral guilt to a tolerable level. In making the accusation,
the accuser is constructing, from the opportunities available in his socio-

cultural environment, a personally satisfying defense against guilt feelings—a function performed by neurotic symptoms and character traits in the classical Freudian theory of neurosis. The psychological meaning of the accusation for the person making it *is* the functions it serves in his personality system, not only for the management of motivational conflict and emotional tension but also in terms of the maintenance or alteration of stable dispositional structures ("institutions of the mind") that have a long developmental history.

2. The psychological functions of the witchcraft accusation can only be understood by attributing an enduring dispositional structure to the individual, a moral ideal that acts as a motive in relation to his other motives (such as greed), and operates selectively to help determine how he responds to an environmental stimulus, how he evaluates his response, what emotions he experiences after having evaluated it, how he encodes the evaluated response and the evoked emotions in his memory, and how he responds cognitively and affectively to subsequent events that might revive the memory. The historians in this case found it necessary to posit a disposition that is complex in its psychological functions, involving the processes of motivation, perceptual judgment, emotional reaction, memory, and thinking. This kind of stabilized and complex disposition is conceptualized in psychoanalysis as psychic structure. The particular kind of structure we have been discussing—involving moral judgment, self-policing, guilt reaction—is referred to by psychoanalysts as *superego*. While discussions of the superego often seem unduly abstract, it is hard to see how one can account for the historical materials reviewed without positing a complex dispositional structure like superego that operates as an agency within the personality in relation to its other structures.

If we had observational data of the type proposed earlier on accusers and nonaccusers in an Elizabethan village, it would be possible to know how each individual responded in thought and action to other situations in his life that posed moral dilemmas and might evoke self-accusatory anxiety, as well as to situations that put him under different kinds of emotional stress. If these observations were analyzed against the background of each individual's pattern of adaptation when not under stress, assessments could be made of the psychological differences between accusers and nonaccusers that might have contributed to their different use of the opportunities for witchcraft accusation offered all of them by the religious and legal institutions in their common environment. We could then determine whether these psychological differences required or justified the inference of dispositions, either at the relatively superficial level of motives and their conflicts (the "dynamic" point of view in psychoanalysis), or tensions and their reduction (the "economic" point of view), or at the deeper level of stabilized agencies (the "structural" point of view). If the same type of observational data, similarly analyzed, were available for communities in 16th-century continental Europe, where witchcraft accusations differed in both belief content and social organization from those of England (Trevor-Roper, 1967), and for colonial Massachusetts, where both similarities and differences are evident (Demos, 1970), it would become possible to inquire whether the cross-cultural differences in the patterns of witchcraft accusation were in any way attributable to personality differences between the populations involved.

3. The personality disposition (or structure of dispositions) required to account for the psychological function of witchcraft accusations in the individual must also be seen as a factor contributing to their frequency during and after their peak period in English history. Personality dispositions in the accuser made an active contribution to the causal chain leading from refusal of alms to execution of the witch, and therefore should be held responsible, along with other factors, for rates and patterns of witchcraft accusations as social and historical phenomena in this period. Key facts in this regard are that even at the period of greatest ambiguity about alms and greatest frequency of accusations, there were objective (socially and culturally valid) options for refusing alms without being punished and for interpreting misfortune as due to causes other than witchcraft. Both requests for alms and personal misfortunes were very frequent at that time, and the evidence suggests many individual differences in patterns of responding to both situations. Some persons were better able to cope with their neighbors' requests, either by yielding or by experiencing less guilt after rejecting them, and some persons were less prone to use witchcraft as a defense mechanism for managing the motivational conflict and emotional reaction aroused by misfortune. Thus the frequency of witchcraft prosecutions was partly dependent on the frequency in the population of those personality dispositions that made some people more susceptible to moral conflicts, guilt reactions, and the witchcraft defense.

Thomas (1970, 1971) implies that the decline in witchcraft accusations is largely attributable to the institutionalization of the workhouse and other formal governmental arrangements for taking care of the poor and elderly; so villagers found themselves less and less frequently facing difficult choices between duty and desire and consequently freer to pursue their individual economic advancement. This hypothesis entails a change in the frequency only of the situations that elicit guilt reactions and the witchcraft defense, not in the frequency of susceptible persons. I will argue, however, that the latter also occurred—that as time and social change went on, there were fewer villagers with such susceptibilities and more persons whose moral standards permitted or demanded "selfish" individualistic behavior to such a degree that even if they had been put in the same situation that earlier evoked moral conflict, they would not have experienced conflict or its psychological sequelae. This argument finds support in Macfarlane's contention (1970a, pp. 201–204) that the decline in witchcraft prosecutions accompanied a decline in the "acceptance of the mystical link between individuals in which one person's well-being was dependent on the attitude of others" (1970a, p. 204). The villager's representation of himself as mystically interdependent with his neighbors was at the basis of both his responsiveness to their requests for alms and his tendency to believe that their malevolence alone could magically cause him physical injury.

In psychoanalytic terms this involves a symbiotic representation of the boundary and relationship between self and others and constitutes a dispositional characteristic (of the ego) of a more fundamental type, in which the superego structure mentioned above is embedded. A person with a symbiotic representation of self-other relations will have developed a superego in which the evaluation of actions and the activation of guilt feelings are primarily dependent on the maintenance of emotional and material transactions between himself and others; an interruption in the flow of transactions (*e.g.*, by his refusal of alms) that provokes ill feelings in a neighbor leads (through regression) to the judgment that her vengeful attitude alone—which is experienced as part of the self—is wreaking punishment upon him. The witchcraft accusation, however defensive in its origin and regressive in its content, is also a first step toward increased individuation, in which the accuser and other persons are socially supported for refusing alms; this is also indicated by the recurrent belief that witches not only make requests but are also excessive in their offers of material and emotional help to their neighbors. In later generations, I argue, fewer individuals experienced their neighbors in this symbiotic mode; more villagers distinguished sharply between their own individual welfare and attitudes and those of others in their community and were therefore less susceptible to moral conflicts about individualism and to magical beliefs about the malevolence of their neighbors.

Such a major change, though associated with socioeconomic trends such as the development of contract law (Max Gluckman, personal communication), cannot be seen as merely altering the social situations in which people functioned, for it must have involved a transformation in the unconscious representation of self that is a fundamental aspect of the personality genotype. This suggests that other changes (*e.g.*, in family structure) were also taking place in that period to alter the pattern of infantile and childhood experience so as to produce a larger proportion of less symbiotic, more individuated persons. This hypothesis, then, assigns a significant role in the 17th century decline in witchcraft accusations to change in the frequency of personality dispositions. It deserves intensive historical research not only in its direct relevance to religion and magic, but also because if true it would further an understanding of the psychological "preparation" for subsequent urbanization and industrialization that occurred in rural England but probably has not occurred in the villages of Africa and other non-Western areas.

So far we have been discussing psychological structures that manifest themselves as social behavior in emotional reactions and in the defensive resolution (the witchcraft accusation) of the motivational conflict that evokes those reactions. There is another side to witchcraft, however, involving more purely intellectual or cognitive structures that are no less "psychological" but are more accessible to conscious awareness in the person who has them. Macfarlane (1970b) reports:

> On the surface, the villagers of Hatfield Peverel were practical, "rational," farmers and craftsmen. . . . Yet . . . we are enabled to see, through the series of confessions recorded for the Assizes of 1566 and 1579, some of their secret fears and thoughts. . . . It immediately becomes clear that overlapping with the ordinary physical world was a sphere inhabited by strange, evil creatures, half-animal, half-demon. A world full of "power," both good and evil. This cannot be dismissed as a delusion or fantasy of a minority; it appears to have been fully credible to all the villagers and to the presiding magistrates, who included the Queen's Attorney, Sir John Fortescue (later Chancellor of the Exchequer) and Thomas Cole, Archdeacon of Essex (1970b, p. 96).

A century later, however, the counterparts of those eminent magistrates did not find witch beliefs and accusations credible and frequently dismissed the charges. Trevelyan (1942, pp. 256–259) describes the rise of "the questioning spirit of science" among the English upper classes in the years 1660 to 1700 and states that "in the later years of the century, the reaction of educated minds to charges of witchcraft was very different from what it had been a short time before" (p. 258). He adds, "It was lucky for the witches that England was still aristocratically governed" (pp. 258–259), and quotes Sir John Reresby's account of a witch trial in 1687 at which, though the evidence against the woman seemed strong to the believers (apparently ordinary people), it was disbelieved by the men of education, Sir John and the judge who reprieved her. In the historical portrait painted by Trevelyan, the oppressive ecclesiastical preoccupations of Cromwellian England fostered a reactive secularism and skepticism in the subsequent Restoration period that was strongly reinforced by the development of experimental (physical) science and official scientific societies. A critical, skeptical, empirical approach to natural phenomena, even within the framework of religious orthodoxy, became the hallmark of an educated man, and education was restricted to the upper classes.

Thus antagonism to belief in witchcraft and other forms of "superstition" began with the aristocrats and gentry and worked its way down gradually, particularly in the rural areas. In the middle and late 17th century, when witchcraft accusations were declining in places like Essex, there were significant differences in witch beliefs between persons of different class status. Since those of higher status served as judges and jurors, they were in a position to dismiss witchcraft prosecutions. Of equal or greater importance, however, is that the local gentry could withhold social validation of a villager's private suspicions in the period preceding formal court proceedings. The accuser might obtain support for his suspicions from other villagers but not from those of highest social position, whose opinion would have legitimized them for the court and in his own eyes. It must be assumed that the decline in witchcraft accusations came about not only because high-born skeptics ran the courts, but also because they played a major role in defining social reality for the villagers. Their skepticism carried with it the prestige of their social position and was therefore likely to convince at least some villagers that their suspicions were groundless—as well as unacceptable to a court of law.

Skepticism about witch beliefs, however related to cultural trends in religion and science, reflects deep-seated personal standards of credibility that deserve closer attention from a psychological point of view. The skeptic may share the motivational conflicts of the believer but cannot accept the same defensive resolution of them. The motivational conflict that Thomas and Macfarlane attribute to accusers is, in fact, not unique to them, for guilt over refusing to help the needy is common enough even in contemporary Western society. Nowadays this conflict would be most commonly experienced in relation to a less affluent kinsman rather than a neighbor, but it does occur, and people often choose to put individual interest over the recognized (if ambiguous) obligation to provide assistance, and subsequently feel guilty about it. The difference is that contemporary Westerners cannot accept the belief that their needy relatives are bewitching them, even when personal misfortune follows their refusal of help and even though the belief offers a desirable reduction of guilt feelings. They prefer to justify or rationalize not helping their kinsman by claiming that he is undeserving or that those who have a greater obligation to help him are not doing so; or they may exaggerate the aid they have given him or argue that their obligations to closer kin prevent them from giving; or they may avoid meeting him socially or even thinking about him. They may even imagine that the refused kinsman is more angry at his refusers than he really is, and then use his presumed anger as a pretext for breaking off relations with him—which resembles the English witchcraft cases of four hundred years ago.[3]

But contemporary Westerners will not allow themselves to believe in the magical malevolence of the guilt-arousing person, because they have autonomous and internal standards of credibility based on physical evidence, according to which witchcraft explanations are outrageous nonsense that could only be believed by children, madmen, and superstitious foreigners. The Restoration gentry rejected witch beliefs at a time when they would not have been considered insane if they had believed them; so we must assume that they found them repugnant despite their availability as personally advantageous and socially acceptable defense mechanisms, and despite the likelihood that the gentry were experiencing the same motivational conflicts that led to accusations among the villagers. To account for their behavior, we need to posit a personality disposition of a cognitive type that includes rules of evidence (in psychoanalytic terminology, the reality-testing function of the ego) and that operates with sufficient independence of the dispositions accounting for motivational conflict to be able to select certain defense mechanisms and reject others according to their conformity with its rules. Thus skepticism and belief should be seen as reflecting different cognitive dispositions in the individual personality.

When Trevelyan refers to the "questioning spirit of science," it is easy to draw the conclusion that individuals acted skeptically in the 17th century simply because they had been educated in the methods and findings of physical science. But in our own day there are people in America, Europe, Africa, and elsewhere who have had this exposure and nevertheless believe in a variety of supernatural phenomena. Furthermore, it has long been accepted in social anthropology that scientific beliefs and witch beliefs can exist in one person; the former explain "how" and the latter "why." A person may understand bacterial infection but still believe he was selected for infection by a witch who bore him a grudge. In the case of the 17th-century skeptics, however, we are confronted with individuals who rejected this form of coexistence; they applied their scientific standards of credibility to the domain of witchcraft accusations and rejected the latter as superstition. In so doing, they revealed not

3. Some of the same conflicts occur nowadays at the level of the wider community, the national society, in which members of the more affluent social segments experience guilt over the plight of the poor and defend themselves against it by adopting the belief that the poor are undeserving, by isolating themselves from exposure to information about poverty, or by exaggerating the significance of private charity in alleviating the situation. Insofar as such persons exaggerate the menacing and violent attributes of the poor and advocate counter-violence against them, they are manifesting in a different cognitive context the defensive resolution involved in the witchcraft accusations of Elizabethan England.

simply knowledge but a way of using it in relation to the phenomena of experience and imagination that differentiates them from their ancestors and the contemporaneous villagers. It is this way of using the empirical approach in everyday life that should be seen as a personality disposition, a psychological structure in which even comforting suspicions must pass tests of empirical evidence.

If psychological study were to show that even under personal stress these individuals did not adopt witchcraft explanations, we would be able to assess the extent to which the reality-testing capacities of the ego dominated adaptive reactions in the face of motives pressing for immediate satisfaction. If the domination were as far-reaching as we have reason to suspect, it would strengthen the inference that scientific education alone does not explain their skepticism. This level of cognitive control over motives and emotions is such a fundamental aspect of personality that it must have antecedents in individual development reaching back before the age at which scientific concepts (*e.g.,* of causality) could be acquired. To put it another way, the psychological disposition we are discussing involves, as a central part of the self-representation, a sharp distinction between objective reality (as experienced through the senses) and subjective imagination, so that even under contrary pressures the distinction cannot be suspended without embarassment or self-deprecation. Here again, as with the emotional aspect of witchcraft, we come back to the representation of the self as a controlling principle in personality organization and to the sharpness of the boundaries between inner and outer sources of experience as a feature that differentiates those for whom witch beliefs are possible from those for whom they are not. I suggest again that issues of individuation are involved, that the relevant psychological dispositions have their origins in early experience patterns that prepare the individual for the acquisition of a scientific or other intellectual attitude toward natural phenomena as a central feature of his self-representation. If this hypothesis is right, changes in the environmental conditions in which infants and children were raised must have preceded the development of skeptical individuals. This leads me to expect that the early environments of children changed first in the upper classes and later among yeomen and peasants—an expectation that could be tested in historical research.

In this lengthy excursion into history I have argued that two types of psychological structures were involved in English witchcraft accusations, one that manifested itself in emotional reactions and defenses against motivational conflict, the other entailing standards of credibility and reality-testing, and that they were differently organized in the self-representations of believers and nonbelievers. Although I may have strained the historical evidence to its limits, the analysis illustrates how data about individuals as actors in religious environments can be used to clarify the

ways in which they selectively use and alter those environments. Much
of my argument simply spells out psychological processes implicit in the
work of anthropologists. For example, Monica Wilson (1951) refers to
witch beliefs as the "standardized nightmares of a group," and the contents of those beliefs in two African groups are shown to stem from
motives (sexual and oral-possessive) that are suppressed by social norms
in the respective groups. Thus her study would be more correctly entitled, "Witch Beliefs and Social Structure *As Experienced by the Pondo
and Nyakyusa*." The italicized addition would emphasize that a description of the social structure with all its normative pressures would not
suffice to predict which of those pressures is subjectively experienced in
such a way that the motives it suppresses would be attributed to witches
in institutionalized belief. The selective operations of personality and
psychosocial process have been relegated to a "black box" between social
structure and belief. It is the aim of this chapter to show what kind of
light a psychoanalytic approach can throw into this black box. We now
turn to African witchcraft, on which—in contrast to that of England—
ethnographic work is still possible.

"Paranoia" and Witchcraft in an African Community

Our exploration of English witchcraft during two centuries of social
change showed how much there is to be learned about the psychological
basis of cultural symbolism from an approach that examines witchcraft
accusations as events in the lives of individuals. It also illustrated how
accounts of witchcraft accusations could be used to throw light on the
personality structures of individual accusers and those with whom they
conversed. We may never have enough data on individuals who lived
more than 300 years ago to answer all the questions raised by that exploration, but there are many peoples elsewhere for whom witchcraft
accusations are contemporary and can be studied more fully. In drawing this second example from my own field work among the Gusii people
of Kenya, I am able to frame the questions for psychoanalytic research
in a context that illustrates more concretely the tasks set for the investigator. At the same time I hope to show that neglect of those tasks involved in the intensive study of individuals, leaves psychological interpretations of witchcraft open to serious question.

Witchcraft and measures taken to counteract it were major preoccupations in Nyansongo, a Gusii community of about 200 persons, and in
surrounding communities, when I worked there in 1955 to 1957. Gusii
beliefs and practices concerning witchcraft resemble those of many other
African peoples, though they have distinctive features as well (see
LeVine, 1958, 1962, 1963; LeVine and LeVine, 1966, pp. 92–104). In
Nyansongo, as elsewhere in Africa, witchcraft accusations strike the

anthropological observer as an important institutional medium for the expression of social tensions, particularly antagonisms within the local community, despite the fact that witchcraft is no longer a legally punishable offense (and that accusing someone of witchcraft can be). In studying this small community over an 18-month period, I became convinced that its members' behavior with respect to witchcraft beliefs and accusations should be seen not merely as characteristic of the sociocultural environment in which they functioned but as reflecting a disposition in their personalities. The most obvious aspect of this disposition, partly because the Nyansongans recognized it themselves, lay in its motivational dynamics, that is, in the defense mechanism of projection, in which the individual's own hostility was attributed to others in the form of witchcraft accusations. Previous ethnographic observers had noted this phenomenon elsewhere in Africa. Evans-Pritchard (1951), for example, stated that "Azande are well aware of what psychologists call projection, that when a man says that another hates him and is bewitching him, it is often the first who is the hater and the witch" (p. 100).

For a number of reasons it seemed appropriate in the Gusii case to go beyond noting the presence of projection and apply the term "paranoid" (LeVine and LeVine, 1966, p. 190). In psychoanalytic theory, projection is the central defense mechanism in the clinical syndrome of paranoia, and long before my field work, behavioral scientists had been using the adjective "paranoid" loosely to describe persons, groups, and situations dominated by the suspicions and accusations to which projected hostility gives rise. Furthermore, Whiting and Child (1953, pp. 269–276) had shown that from the Freudian conception of paranoia could be derived developmental hypotheses that found support in correlational evidence linking cross-cultural variations in witch beliefs with child rearing practices. Most important, however, there were striking descriptive similarities between paranoid patients in the West and Nyansongans: Both blamed others for their misfortunes, believed in the secret malevolence of those around them (with lurid fantasies about their activities), maintained a suspicious and unrevealing attitude toward potential enemies, and were concerned about their own vulnerability to being poisoned or magically attacked by secret enemies. Hence Nyansongans were "paranoid." Despite the superficial plausibility of this diagnosis, I now believe it needs to be reexamined in terms of the approach to religious experience and symbolism proposed in this chapter, with attention to its general implications for the use of psychoanalytic concepts like "paranoia" in the comparative study of religion.

In this reexamination, there is value in reviewing in this context some of the methodological principles presented earlier. First, there is the principle that only individuals can be psychoanalyzed, not institutions. For the ethnographic observer, this means that the beliefs and norms concerning witchcraft that were handed down to the current generation are to be viewed as part of the institutional environment and context in which they function. These beliefs and norms were selectively developed and selectively institutionalized by earlier generations, partly on the basis of their own personality dispositions, but through a complex series of events that cannot (for most African societies) be reconstructed on the basis of available evidence. We could speculate about the personality dispositions that contributed to these events, but there is no possibility of obtaining the historical data necessary to test these speculations. Rather than waste his analytical skills on ingenious but speculative interpretation of witch beliefs and practices, the investigator should focus on how observable individuals exploit that aspect of their institutional environment for their own private purposes.

Given a certain set of institutions, individuals will use them in different ways at a single point in time. Gusii brides, knowing that in traditional Gusii belief women who are witches try to recruit their daughters-in-law into the company of witches and that this practice constitutes acceptable grounds for divorce, frequently use this claim as a means of dissolving their marriages. There is reason to suspect that in some cases the girl simply dislikes her husband or her mother-in-law, knows her father would ordinarily refuse to consider her personal preferences as opposed to the bridewealth he will have to return on dissolution of the marriage, and makes the witchcraft accusation to force his compliance. Is such a girl "paranoid" or simply clever? The point is that (as discussed in Chapter 9) when a set of beliefs or practices become institutionalized, it becomes available for manipulation by those who find in it not (or not only) the primary (psychic) gain involved in its symbolic content but secondary gains derived from its status as part of the institutional structure of society. For the bride referred to, the witchcraft symbolism itself may be irrelevant to her purpose, which is to get out of the marriage any way she can. It cannot be assumed, therefore, that conformity to institutional norms of belief and practice reflects personality dispositions related to the institutionalized symbolism; this must be demonstrated through the study of individuals.

A second principle concerns the psychological functions of religious behavior as opposed to its appearance or social consequences. In likening an ethnographically observed pattern of individual behavior to a clinical syndrome identified in psychoanalysis, one must demonstrate not only behavioral similarity but also that the observed behavior has similar functions in the personality systems of those individuals manifesting it. Paranoia and paranoid schizophrenia, for example, are not conceptualized in psychoanalysis as patterns of behavior but as complex personality disorders with interrelated dynamic, psycho-economic, structural, and developmental properties, each of which requires investigation. The use of projection as a mechanism of defense refers to the dynamic aspect of personality functioning, having to do with how motivational conflict is managed. In psychoanalytic discussions of paranoid psychopathology, projection is discussed in its relations with other aspects. Thus, for example, projection in that context includes the conversion of sexual (particularly sadistic homosexual) impulses toward others into their perceived hostility toward the self; the homosexual wishes are related to the resolution of the oedipus complex in childhood. Projection may conceivably be used as a defense mechanism by nonpsychotic persons in our own and other cultures and it may or may not be involved in the deeper interdependencies of the classical paranoid syndrome, but these are empirical and important questions. If projection is embedded in a different structure of interdependencies, serves different functions in that structure, and has a different developmental history, it is necessary to investigate these and discover what they are. Once that is done, it is possible to consider whether calling the observed behavior "paranoid" is accurate or misleading.

Another way of putting this is to say that projection as a defense mechanism is widely used by normal persons and is easily observable in highly competitive and other stressful social situations, whereas clinical paranoia or paranoid schizophrenia is found in rare individuals whose projective tendencies are very general, are not due to situational pressures, and are related to a series of sexual and other behavioral dispositions originating in early childhood. In both cases, environmental conditions have occasioned a regression to the use of projective thinking, but the normal person is capable of recovering when the stress is removed or of compartmentalizing the projection in his life in a way the paranoid person is not. The question of whether the normal person under stress regresses to a projective fantasy that includes the same sexual and other content found in the paranoid delusion is an empirical one, and I assume there is great individual variation in this regard.

Finally, there is the principle of making inferences regarding personality dispositions and their organization through careful attention to the relative contributions of primary and secondary process thought to observable behavior (in this case, to witchcraft accusations). The term *paranoid* in psychopathology implies a delusional system and a sharp break with reality that may or may not be present in the Africans we are observing. This is where our attention must first be focused: If witchcraft accusations are possible without a sharp break in reality, under what external and internal conditions do they occur and what kind of thought processes do they involve? We now turn to examine this question in the case of Nyansongo.

There is a remarkably consistent set of beliefs about witches that is shared not only by the residents of Nyansongo but, so far as I can tell,

by most other Gusii communities as well. Although these beliefs are part
of a nonliterate tradition, they appear as structured and constant from
one individual to another as if they were published scripture. Each individual interviewed used different anecdotes from personal experience to
illustrate the shared beliefs, but there was minimal disagreement about
how witches operate: They are women who run naked at night with
firepots, knocking on houses, exhuming and eating corpses, magically
killing their enemies, *etc.* (see LeVine, 1963, for a fuller description).
These shared beliefs, together with the norms concerning appropriate
behavior toward witches and in response to bewitchment, constitute a
cultural system—part of the sociocultural environment handed down to
the Gusii of today by their ancestors. I found little evident skepticism
about these beliefs, despite the influence of Christian missions. One
young man with public health training told me he believed that witches
could only kill by poisoning one's food, not by magic, but he seemed to
be alone in that belief at that time. Yet witch beliefs were certainly not
equally salient for everyone in Nyansongo, and there were those who,
while not challenging the existence and power of witches in general,
tended to reject or minimize specific accusations of witchcraft. And there
were others who, like the bride mentioned above, seemed to be consciously using witchcraft accusations to manipulate others' fears without revealing their own state of belief. We can nevertheless assume that
traditional witch beliefs form part of the institutional environment in
which all Nyansongans function; our question is how do they use that
environment for their own purposes.

In reviewing the variety of witchcraft accusations in Nyansongo as
individual phenomena, I find it makes sense to distinguish between public accusations, which are rare, and private gossip, rumor and suspicion, which are relatively frequent. On the public side, I begin with what
the Gusii call *ebarimo enene* (literally "big madness"), which though
recognized in fact, never occurred in Nyansongo while I was there (although it did occur in the surrounding area). It is important because it
resembles a paranoid reaction more closely than any other behavior I
observed. The term in Gusii is applied to an affliction in which an adult
man attacks those around him verbally and physically, usually trying to
kill them with a machete before he is restrained; it differs from simply
running amok in that it is recognized as a chronic condition, involving
recurrent outbursts and strange behavior inbetween. People are afraid
of persons so afflicted and are relieved when they are taken away by the
authorities. The hallmark of the affliction in Gusii eyes is its indiscrimi-
nateness: the person attacks not only his enemies but anyone nearby, he
does it when sober and not only when drunk, and he violates not only
norms prohibiting assault but also and more significantly those against
sexually abusive speech. He is aggressively suspicious and may openly

accuse people of bewitching him—between as well as during outbursts—
but these accusations are not taken seriously, despite the fact that Gusii
believe his condition to be usually caused by witchcraft. Once people
stigmatize a man with the diagnosis of *ebarimo enene*, they discount his
allegations as the ravings of a madman. Thus even in the context of this
"paranoid" community, the rare and flagrant case of what would probably be diagnosed as paranoid schizophrenia in our own society stands
out as being delusional by their own standards. Gusii have standards of
credibility and procedures for applying them to witchcraft accusations,
and the psychotic cannot meet them.

Another kind of public accusation is a formal hearing conducted by the
elders of the community for the purpose of settling a dispute involving
witchcraft allegations. This is the contemporary version of the witch
trial, which in the past would have included subjecting the defendant to
ordeals and executing her (or him) if found guilty. Nowadays such hearings have no legal authority to punish and are authorized by the local
chief to effect a voluntary settlement of the dispute underlying the accusations; the elders involved take it as their duty to make the disputing
parties see what they have done wrong, to advocate a just solution to the
real dispute over land or property or whatever, and to warn everyone
against engaging in witchcraft or sorcery. This was the line taken in the
one hearing that occurred in Nyansongo during 1955 to 1957. It did
become public during that hearing that a certain woman was widely
believed to be a witch, but the elders minimized her contribution to the
case at hand. What was never made public, however, was that the elders
had conducted an earlier private investigation and had arrived at the conclusion that witchcraft was not responsible for the death of the respected
elder whose widow was making the accusation. The complicated details
of that case are beside the point, but the criteria used by the elders in
such an investigation are highly pertinent. They included an autopsy in
which swollen visceral organs were taken as signs of witchcraft, an investigation of whether the dead man had quarrelled with someone generally considered to be a witch, and a question as to whether he had
committed a sexual or property offense that might have brought magical
retribution not involving witches. Thus the elders applied established
standards of evidence and credibility before arriving at a judgment; if
an accuser's case did not meet these standards, as was true in the case
I observed, the accusation was publicly discredited.

The elders of the community and descent group seemed generally dis-
posed during 1955 to 1957 to discredit witchcraft accusations, not so
much on grounds of credibility as on the pragmatic ground of maintaining peace among local groups through the settlement of their disputes. They regarded these accusations, which in the absence of legal
punishment could only lead to retribution by sorcery and more mutual

suspicion, as disruption of the social order they were responsible for maintaining. They therefore refused to endow accusations with the validation of their authority and prestige. In that respect they looked beyond the immediate and real issues of the case at hand to the larger reality of social tension produced by socioeconomic change and acted (on the basis of rational considerations about which they were not entirely frank) to discourage accusers. It is noteworthy that accusers, though they might run from one adjudicative authority to another, were eventually persuaded to interpret their misfortunes in terms other than witchcraft and to settle their disputes, if only temporarily; in most cases, accusations were stopped long before they reached a stage at which the public hearing would even be considered. Nyansongo accusers, like the English villagers discussed in the previous section, solicit social validation of their private suspicions, particularly from those they respect; and they regressively put their leaders and other neighbors in the position of doing their reality-testing for them, to the benefit of the community as a whole. In this situation the interaction between primary- and secondary-process thinking becomes social process, and the synthetic function attributed to the ego in psychoanalysis is exercised by those in authority.

To put this somewhat differently, Nyansongans in positions of authority and responsibility—homestead heads, lineage and community elders, chiefs and members of the tribunal courts—saw their duty as resolving disputes among those they governed, and this meant asserting their moral influence against the credibility of specific witchcraft accusations. This left the governed relatively free to express their suspicions, knowing they would sooner or later be disciplined by those whose judgment they trusted more than their own. Having expressed themselves in what was publicly considered a disruptive way, however, they thereby called their suffering to the attention of authorities who might give help even if they dismissed the witchcraft allegation. Insofar as they gained a favorable judgment in a property dispute, for example, the discredited accusation could be deemed successful as a tactical maneuver in litigation. Although litigation was extremely frequent in Nyansongo, I do not mean to reduce witchcraft accusations entirely to such secondary gains, but to suggest that a full understanding of their recurrence in the face of authoritative discouragement must include consideration of these gains. Nyansongo accusers were usually persons under severe stress (for instance, with multiple deaths in the family) who might well have regressed to a projective defense—culturally constituted if not officially encouraged at the time—that helped alleviate their suffering, but their choice of targets for projection and their attempts to involve authority might have been dictated by motives with both self-aggrandizing and projective components.

Another, more frequent, form of public accusation illustrates the division in the community between "irresponsible" accusers and their more skeptical superiors. At funerals, the widow, daughter, mother, or sister of the deceased almost invariably made accusations of witchcraft—usually with veiled references to specific neighbors—in the lament she chanted as visitors came to pay their respects. Although these might reveal suspicions actually entertained by the whole family, they were never taken seriously because women are permitted to react emotionally to bereavement without suffering the consequences. The men remain silent at a funeral; if one of them voiced a suspicion of witchcraft it would be regarded as a terrible breach between neighbors that could lead to ligitation for slander and other counter-measures. Women are, in fact, expected to react more violently and emotionally than men to any kind of stress, but their behavior—if kept within prescribed limits— is often socially discounted by the men responsible for managing the affairs of patrilineage and community.

The limits in regard to funeral behavior are frequently transgressed after a particular type of death—that of a married woman in a polygynous family who had only one or no children so that her father must return a large part of the bridewealth originally received at her marriage. The addition of this economic burden to the emotional impact of her death usually makes her blood kinsmen extremely angry, and the anger becomes formulated as outrage because her co-wives killed her by witchcraft. At the funeral, her male kinsmen restrain their anger, but the women grab the deceased's movable property (*e.g.*, grain from her granary) and destroy whatever immovable property she had, so that her alleged murderers cannot profit by her death. This is resisted by the widower's family, and violence erupts that eventually involves the authorities and litigation in court. At most funerals, however, the women keep their emotional expression within the bounds of chanted witchcraft accusations, which are "excused" for them under the ritual circumstances.

The public witchcraft accusations discussed so far—those of "madmen," those presented at public hearings conducted by the elders, and those at funerals—show how little public validation such allegations receive from the influential men of the community. Most accusations that come out into the open can be and are dismissed as the ravings of a madman, the outburst of an irresponsible woman under emotional stress, or the defensive maneuvering of a party to a property dispute—which allows the elders or influential men to shift the grounds of public decision-making from the accuracy of the accusation itself to the alleviation of the friction or sense of grievance that made it a threat to the social order: Restrain or expel the madman; ignore the woman and give her time to calm down; settle the property dispute through judicial process. This policy operates to manage and contain social tensions, while allowing people to retain their private defensive fantasies. Through the social dynamics described, secondary-process thinking remains in ultimate control of the community's social adaptation, though it is recurrently threatened by witchcraft accusations.

The private forms of witchcraft accusation in Nyansongo are much more frequent and less easily defined than those that manifest themselves publicly. One way of looking at these private forms is as steps along a path that leads to the public arena. As in Elizabethan England, in Nyansongo the accuser has a suspicion that is reactivated by misfortune; he discusses the suspicion with close friends or kinsmen who may or may not validate it; he consults diviners and other magical specialists who probably do validate it; he consults someone of higher local prestige to acquire the final confirmation needed for a public hearing. The witchcraft claim is sometimes quickly quashed by neighbors and kinsmen. For example, a senior man dies leaving a substantial debt to someone outside the community. The rumor that he has been killed by anti-theft magic goes rapidly around and hardly anyone shows up to bury him, fearing they will be killed by the magic. When his survivors begin claiming he was bewitched by a man with whom he had a boundary dispute, they are already aware that most of their potential supporters think otherwise. If they stubbornly press ahead with the witchcraft charge, some responsible elder will finally persuade them to forget about witchcraft and pay the debt to prevent their own deaths, but in most cases the dramatic negation at the burial is sufficient in itself.

Gossip about witchcraft, produced by land disputes, mysterious and multiple deaths and other misfortunes, is constantly circulating and being supported (if only briefly) or invalidated by informal influence processes that reflect local standards of credibility applied to the projective fantasies of aggrieved or deprived individuals. In applying these standards, community residents recognize that participants in a dispute and bereaved persons make accusations that are not acceptable to those less involved. They assert less biased judgments against those whose judgment is obviously affected by emotion. For example, there were three women in Nyansongo whose constantly belligerent and unneighborly behavior fitted the traditional Gusii image of witches and who were widely suspected. Accusations directed at anyone else were regarded with skepticism, particularly if made by someone engaged in a property dispute with the target of his accusation. Accusations directed at one of the three suspected witches were questioned in terms of the proof produced, the presence of impartial witnesses, alternative explanations, and so forth. The homestead head is frequently called upon to deal with witchcraft suspicions among his wives, and he usually responds as other Gusii leaders do, by attempting to correct inequities among them while rejecting or minimizing the witchcraft charges. Thus much of the less public activity concerning witchcraft is basically similar to the more public forms in being centered on the dynamics of social validation and resulting in an informal consensus to discredit or ignore the accusations before they become grounds for action.

In the most private sphere of belief, that of the individual's conscious thoughts, witchcraft suspicions of a detailed and vivid nature seem to lead a more active existence unchecked by the harsh light of public skepticism. Here is where the important questions for psychological research are located. It sometimes seemed that a witchcraft accusation was largely a hostile defensive response to misfortune, and it could be taken as reflecting a personality disposition simply on the grounds of its repetition in reaction to various misfortunes when other reactions were clearly possible. But informants claimed to have harbored suspicions of particular neighbors and kinsmen for many years, interpreting numerous events in terms of them, and sharing their suspicions with others only when particular misfortunes reactivated the fear associated with these suspicions, at which time they would also resort to protective magic. In some cases these suspicions, among half-brothers, could be traced back to witchcraft accusations between their mothers, who had been co-wives competing for the favor of the same husband (see LeVine, 1962). Thus the sons had grown up with these suspicions as part of their cognitive apparatus, ready to be invoked when trouble struck. This raises the question of whether these men had compartmentalized "delusional systems" or at least defensive fantasies as an integral part of their personalities, and if so, how did they operate in the context of a nonpsychotic adjustment, that is, what were the conditions that evoked and suppressed the use of these fantasies in social behavior and kept it within adaptive bounds?

A related question concerns the relation of emotional reactions and their ideational representatives to this set of private suspicions. Nyansongan discussions of witchcraft accusations touch on many powerful emotions: jealousy, hostility, grief, and fear on the part of the accuser; oral greed, vengefulness, sexuality on the part of the witch. How are these emotional components psychologically organized in relation to the cognitive defense of the suspicions? For example, Gusii describe themselves as afraid of the dark (in contrast with the neighboring Kipsigis, who used to take military advantage of this by attacking the Gusii at night), "because" they are afraid of the witches running about, and Nyansongans do indeed stay indoors most nights. To what extent does this fear, which is inculcated in children at an early age, provide an emotional basis for witch beliefs that cannot be eradicated later in life? Nyansongans of both sexes agree that women are much more afraid than men of the dark, and even of the dusk when they imagine they see fearful shapes while collecting firewood. Does this mean that fear plays a larger role in the formation of witchcraft suspicions among women than men?

These questions suggest areas that would have to be explored psychologically to understand the meaning and function of witchcraft accusations for Nyansongans. The ethnographic data indicate that in Nyansongo and neighboring communities there are at least five different behavioral styles with respect to witchcraft accusations, each of them implying a different functional organization of dispositions relevant to witch belief: There is the recognized "madman," for whom accusations are part of his indiscriminate pattern of retaliation against delusional enemies; there is the responsible elder, who adopts a skeptical public attitude about specific accusations and does not engage in divisive quarrels; there is the younger or less responsibly-minded man who, while using the skeptical attitude to keep peace at home, becomes involved in property disputes, angry litigation, and—when misfortune strikes—witchcraft accusations; there are the normal married women, who are freer than men with the display of their emotions, including hostility, and quicker to make witchcraft accusations under the pressure of domestic quarrels and bereavement; finally, there are the particularly quarrelsome women who know they are reputed to be witches and may think of themselves as such. For each of these types, the subjective meaning of witchcraft accusations and their psychological functions in defense, in the discharge of tension, in maintaining a self-representation, is likely to be different; and there should be concomitant differences in their developmental histories to account for these differences. If this is so (and these types can only sample rather than exhaust the range of individual variation), the various symbols in Gusii witch beliefs must vary among individuals in their salience, evocative power, and personal significance. It is the task of the psychoanalytic method I have proposed to describe this psychological variation in response to a shared set of cultural symbols.

It is obvious that to describe Nyansongans as "paranoid" begs the questions left unanswered by the conventional ethnographic research I conducted among them. The present exploration showed that there are rational controls on projective fantasy, operating through social processes in the community, but that witch beliefs and accusations nevertheless continue to serve a variety of personal functions (most of them inadequately understood) for its varied residents. The next step in psychosocial understanding can only be achieved by investigating directly the place of these beliefs and accusations in the lives and developmental histories of the individual residents themselves. When this has been done, not only for witch beliefs but other aspects of religious experience and symbols, and not only in one culture but in several, it will be possible to assess the value of this approach.

In studying witchcraft accusations psychoanalytically, our aim would be not only to understand the psychological functions of the symbols involved in witchcraft beliefs and rituals but also to understand the individual's uses of those symbols, beliefs, and rituals as symptoms of personality dispositions and structures that might distinguish his population from others. If, for example, it were to turn out that the witchcraft accusations of Elizabethan villagers were frequently based on guilt reactions whereas those of Nyansongans were more frequently based on anger, or that those who rejected witchcraft explanations in the two communities did so for very different reasons, these differences might be indicative of major differences in personality between the two peoples, differences that should manifest themselves in other domains of social behavior. In this sense the symbol-using religious behavior of the individual is taken, like his dreams or neurotic symptoms, as a road into unconscious parts of his personality, but parts that, for all their idiosyncratic patterning, are similar for those who participate in the same cultural institutions.

This long road into the unconscious begins with what psychoanalysts call the "adaptive point of view" and what has been referred to here as "ethnographic investigation," that is, the explication of the environmental reality, with all its constraints and options, in which the individual functions. Only then can one proceed to the functional analysis of the "dynamic" and "psycho-economic" points of view, in which sequential information about the individual is examined for evidence of unconscious motives, conflicts, and defenses and their relationship to tension and its reduction in emotional reactions. Once these cognitive and emotional patterns are understood in environmental context, it is possible to investigate their organization in higher-order dispositional stabilities of "psychic structure"—the "structural" point of view in psychoanalysis. When enough evidence has been collected on the individual's functioning in diverse situational contexts to confirm a structural diagnosis, the developmental origins of the structure can be considered, that is, to what extent does it reveal residues of early experience in developmental context? Here, independent observational studies of child development may be required to supply data on the typical lines which psychological growth follows in that population. Thus the road which begins with individual participation in a religious institution may end with an understanding of how the psychological development of the individual made that pattern of participation both possible and probable.

Part V

Conclusions

18

New Directions in Culture and
Personality Research

This book has undertaken a reexamination of the intellectual foundations
of research on culture and personality, a diagnosis of its major problems,
and an attempt at constructing a coherent framework for their solution.
The field of culture and personality is peculiar in that it attracted a
great deal of interest in its early days (before 1950) as an area of importance to anthropology, psychology, education, and psychiatry; generated
sound theoretical statements and highly controversial research studies;
and then lost the interest of all but those who specialize in one of its
topical foci, such as the socialization of the child or comparative psychopathology. In the past 20 years each of these specialized areas has produced an extensive research literature, exploring and redefining the complexities of child development, mental disorder, and expressive behavior
in cross-cultural terms. Each specialty is on the way to becoming a subdiscipline of its own, as divergent from other branches of culture and
personality as psychology is from anthropology. However diverse these
research efforts, they draw their inspiration from a common set of problems identified by the original theorists of culture and personality, and
they are afflicted by overlapping and interrelated methodological difficulties. In this book, therefore, I have attempted to clarify the premises
from which research on culture and personality springs and to explore
in detail the bases for an integrating theory and methodology that will
provide coherent guidance for diverse investigations. Rather than describe empirical studies and review research findings, I have focused on
the goals of culture and personality as a behavioral science and on
strategies for attaining those goals.

In the first section of the book I began by giving preliminary (and
conventional) definitions of "culture" and "personality" and then sug-

gested that the field designated by their juxtaposition as "culture and personality" was defined by its attention to three problems: the psychological differences between populations, the origins of such differences in individual development, and the relations of such differences to sociocultural environments. These are problems that require empirical data from diverse human populations for their solution, but investigators in the culture and personality field tend to *assume* that there are psychological differences between populations, largely on intuitive and experiential grounds (explored in Chapter 2). The movement from assuming on experiential grounds that populations differ in personality dispositions to demonstrating it systematically has been a major aspect of scientific development in culture and personality research, and the types of evidence used in systematic comparison are also reviewed in Chapter 2.

The critical overview of existing theory and method in the second part of the book showed how the various theoretical tendencies in the field are not seriously in contradiction with each other or with the perspective of evolutionary theory, from which many of them are descended. A plausible theoretical integration seems possible, given some reassessment of the contrast between institutionalized and deviant behavior (Chapter 6), but disagreements about method, shared with personality psychology, pose greater obstacles to cumulative and decisive empirical research. In the third part I proposed that culture and personality study should eventually become a "population psychology," analogous to population biology, in which individual psychological characteristics are statistically aggregated and compared across populations in relation to the characteristics of sociocultural environments. The applicability of this analogy, and particularly of the Darwinian variation-selection model, was considered in detail, after which I outlined the units and processes involved in a plausible evolutionary model of culture-personality relations. Then I attempted to foresee the calculation of psychological and social costs and benefits that research based on this model would produce and how it might contribute to a comparative assessment of psychosocial adaptation (Chapter 11). Such grandiose goals cannot be approached, however, until the problem of assessing individual personality dispositions is solved, and that problem was considered in the final section of the book.

The difficulties of personality assessment, which must be overcome before unambiguous cross-population comparisons can be made and before the causes and consequences of population differences can be properly investigated, lie in the inevitable confounding of enduring disposition and response to environmental pressure in observable social behavior. If internal motive and environmental demand lead to the same response, as they do in the case of adaptive fit, observed responses can be attributed either to psychological disposition or immediate environmental pressure according to the theoretical inclination of the investigator. The challenge to the investigator is to design a program of observation through which he can locate the information that leads to response. How much of it comes from the immediate situation (as an outside observer might perceive it) and how much of it is already in the organism before encountering the situation? The biological research strategies for answering this kind of question were outlined (Chapter 12) and their embodiment in the clinical method of psychoanalysis were discussed in some detail (Chapter 13). The conclusion reached is that Freud's clinical method involved more effective and valid procedures for making inferences about the presence and operation of personality dispositions than the personality tests that have been used to operationalize his constructs. I recommended designing research methods based on Freudian clinical principles but applied to universal human situations that supply structural frames for naturalistic observation; Chapters 14 to 16 and Appendix A contain proposals for conducting this kind of observation in anthropological field investigation. Finally, I tried to show how these methods might deal with the understanding of religious symbols, a problem of particular interest in contemporary social anthropology.

The evolutionary model of culture and personality and the method proposed for the study of psychosocial adaptations have some definite implications for the future directions of research in this field. A population psychology must eventually operate along the lines of epidemiology, in which distributions of individual characteristics in populations are studied in both contemporaneous and historical relationships, to discover their correlates (potential causes and consequences) and means of transmission. At present, this type of research must be seen as a future goal toward which culture and personality studies should be progressing rather than one that is currently attainable. To be sure, a great deal more could be done with the psychological interpretation of available statistical data on crime, suicide, alcoholism, mental illness, psychosomatic disorders, and responses to public opinion polls—in comparing national populations as well as their ethnic components. Such an effort, however, would serve primarily to raise important questions rather than answer them, for in the absence of reliable personality indicators, these data are often interpretable in purely sociological as well as psychosocial terms. It is only when we have reliable indicators of personality dispositions, analogous to laboratory tests for the diagnosis of disease, that we shall be able to operate as the epidemiologists do, charting variations in incidence across nations and historical periods and identifying environmental determinants in their co-variations. In the meantime we must concentrate a large proportion of our effort on developing the diagnostic instruments that will make comparison possible.

In developing these diagnostic instruments, the most useful model in biological research is to be found not in medicine but in ethology, where investigators sensitive to the properties of both organisms and their environments have worked out research strategies involving naturalistic observation for disentangling the contributions of each to the adaptation of the individual animal. Naturalistic observation of individual humans responding to their environments over time at different stages in the lifespan can produce the kind of data we need to draw conclusions about the species-wide range of human response and to make valid personality assessment possible.

The direct study of individuals, following the proposals of Chapters 14 to 17, involves an enormous amount of data collection. It might well be wondered whether in this direction could lie such an extended detour into clinical investigation for culture and personality research that it might never return to the main road of comparative population studies. I believe this detour is necessary regardless of the risks involved, since the premature pursuit of statistical comparison leads toward greater ambiguity about psychological factors in social behavior rather than greater certainty. There are, however, grounds for some optimism about the possibilities of generating objective and widely applicable methods and quantifiable data from intensive clinical observation. The work of Luborsky (1970), for example, has produced the symptom-context method for making objective assessments of the meaning of neurotic symptoms in associative material drawn from psychoanalytic sessions; this seems directly applicable to psychoanalytic data collected in other situations as well, and could form the basis of a comparative method. And the work of Ainsworth (1967), referred to earlier, shows how longitudinal observation of infants and their environments generates regularities that could ultimately be used in a comparative assessment procedure. It is only from this intensive study of individuals, to discover how they use and react to cultural features in their psychological functioning and development, that reliable personality indicators will come.

A final word must be added about history. There are limitations to comparative studies, and epidemiologists as well as other students of human populations have made some of their greatest advances by using time series data on a single population over successive periods of history. While it is impossible to obtain new samples of behavior from past generations, psychologically informed historical research has several unique advantages as a complement to contemporaneous studies. It gives us an empirical basis for assessing the stability and malleability of behavior patterns that may reflect personality influence, and it enables us to examine co-variations among successive generations of the same population, where many more factors may be held constant than among different populations. Many theoretically sophisticated questions that cannot be answered by synchronic research can at least be explored in diachronic inquiry, and explored with increasing insight and relevance, as anthropological studies of culture and personality—using the clinical microscope—supply more precisely framed questions.

Appendix A. A Comparative Method for the Study of Affective Reactions

The initial procedure of discovery would be an interview, translatable into any language, in which an individual would be asked to report and explain incidents in which he manifested the bodily symptoms of affective reactions (see pp. 372–378) and saw other people manifesting them, and to give his understanding of the cultural rules and expectations concerning such reactions. In reporting specific incidents, he would give details of the situation that elicited the reaction, his thoughts and feelings at the time (if it were his own reaction; if someone else's, the words and gestures that accompanied it), and what happened afterward (e.g., internal or external conditions that reduced or terminated the reaction, acts of restitution based on its ideational concomitant). In reporting the cultural rules, he would indicate the conditions under which such reactions were expected to occur, their socially acceptable and unacceptable aspects, and how people would react to them overtly and covertly under a variety of conditions. Although these rules might be not ordinarily talked about and therefore not readily accessible to verbal formulation, the discussion of specific incidents should make at least some of them manifest. Furthermore, the bicultural research method outlined in Chapter 15 would mean that the first use of the interview in a given culture would be with the indigenous behavioral scientist as informant, using his working alliance with a foreign investigator to probe the rules built into his own ego in detail sufficient to make a foreigner understand them.

The problem of the implicitness of these rules is nonetheless great enough to warrant several approaches to a solution, all of which could be incorporated into the intervew. One approach would be to ask about locally familiar fantasy media that might elicit the reactions: oral narratives, films and other public entertainments, and religious performances. This would be done as part of an effort to assess the general frequency of the reaction in the normal life of the individual (which is likely to vary by sex, age, and social status as well as culture), but it would also indicate if the elicitation of these reactions had become institutionalized in the cultural life of the group, which might make them somewhat more available to verbal discussion. Another approach would be to ask about each of a series of locally comprehensible situations which elicit the reactions in some cultures and ask the person if he could imagine himself so reacting if he were in that situation. This list of situations would include obviously culture-bound reactions from a variety of cultures; it could be based on exploratory work with the interview in a few cultures and then added to as more groups were studied. In accordance with the linguistically based method described by Goodenough (1970, pp. 107–111), culture-specific responses would be accumulated until the range of cultural variation was exhausted, at which point it would be possible to make some generalizations about similarities and differences in affective reactions. Similarities between culturally diverse groups might represent pancultural universals or psychological resemblances between a restricted set of groups. Knowledge of the total range of eliciting conditions would be formulated as constraints on the alternatives from which human groups can select evokers of intense affective reactions. It would then be possible to describe each culture's unique cluster of selections in a way that would directly expose its similarities and differences with other cultures.

This interview procedure would be but a starting point for understanding the complex grammar of emotions in a culture and cross-cultural variations in such grammars. It would not aim at reducing the complexity and variation to its physiological roots but rather at using the latter as frames for comparative study. It is easy to talk about eliciting or evoking conditions, but understanding and translating what makes the people of a given culture weep involves delving deeply into the system of symbols to which they are affectively attached. In this type of ethnographic investigation the developmental perspective provides another frame in which the data on affective reactions can be comparably described, and one of special significance from a psychoanalytic viewpoint. The interview would concern not only adult males and females but children at various stages of life, and adults in transitional phases, life crises or stress conditions that are within the range of cultural expectation, and it would have to be administered to persons in those stages and phases. Thus anchored in the life cycle, the data on norms concerning the evocation of bodily symptoms would yield specific information about the experience of disruption in developmental situations as well as about the acquisition of the adult norms and their ideational concomitants (*e.g.*, moral constraints). The result would be more refined bases for comparison.

Field observations of affective reactions in natural social settings by the indigenous and foreign behavioral scientists would supplement and check on the interview material. Experimental studies could also be profitably pursued, at least for the anxiety or stress response, in which physiological measures (galvanic skin response, heart beat) are obtainable independently of self-report, and can be evoked by fantasy materials projected on a screen (Lazarus, 1966). Films or pictures involving significant cultural themes could be constructed and ranked as evokers of physiological response in the original group for which they were designed and in other groups. Ultimately, conclusions would be drawn about cultural similarities and differences in the conditions evoking the responses, the magnitude of the response, and the acknowledgment of the associated affect in the person's report on himself.

This discussion is sufficient to indicate the promise of this approach to a comparative ethnography of the life situations in which persons function. One of the givens of individual functioning is the capacity for affective response, and one range of situations is defined by the cultural norms regarding affective expression in public. A systematic description of the cultural contexts in which bodily symptoms of affects are evoked, displayed and interpreted can not only be made comparable across cultures but can establish a normative background against which the idiosyncratic patterns of affective response, at the surface of the personality, stand out and can be diagnosed.

References

Ainsworth, Mary
  1967. *Infancy in Uganda*. Baltimore: Johns Hopkins University Press.
  1969. Object relations, dependency and attachment: a theoretical review of the infant-mother relationship. *Child Development* 40:969–1025.
Alland, Alexander
  1967. *Evolution and human behavior*. Garden City, N.Y.: Natural History Press.
Allport, Gordon W.
  1954. *The nature of prejudice*. Cambridge, Mass.: Addison-Wesley.
  1968. The historical background of modern social psychology. In G. Lindzey and E. Aronson, Eds. *Handbook of social psychology*, vol. 1. Cambridge, Mass.: Addison-Wesley.
Allport, G. W., and Postman, L.
  1947. *The psychology of rumor*. New York: Holt.
Anthony, E. James, and Benedek, Therese, Eds.
  1970. *Parenthood: psychology and psychopathology*. Boston: Little, Brown.
Aschoff, J., Fatranska, M., and Giedke, H.
  1971. Human circadian rhythms in continuous darkness: entrainment by social cues. *Science* 171:213–215.
Ashby, W. R.
  1952. *Design for a brain*. New York: Wiley.
Bandura, Albert
  1969. Social-learning theory of identificatory processes. In D. Goslin, Ed., *Handbook of socialization theory and research*. Chicago: Rand McNally.
Barber, James D.
  1968. Classifying and predicting presidential styles: two weak presidents. *Journal of Social Issues* 24: 51-80.
Bargery, G. P.
  1934. *A Hausa-English dictionary and English-Hausa vocabulary*. London: Oxford University Press.
Barker, Roger and Wright, Herbert
  1951. *One boy's day*. New York: Harper & Row.
  1955. *Midwest and its children*. Evanston, Ill.: Row, Peterson.

Barkow, Jerome
    1970.   Hausa and Maguzawa: processes of group differentiation in a rural area of North-Central State, Nigeria. Unpublished Ph.D. dissertation in Human Development, University of Chicago.

Barry, H. H., Child, I. L., and Bacon, M. K.
    1959.   Relation of child rearing to subsistence economy. *American Anthropologist* 61:51–63.

Bartlett, F. C.
    1932.   *Remembering: a study in experimental and social psychology.* Cambridge: Cambridge University Press.

Bateson, Mary Catherine
    1968.   Insight in a bicultural context. *Philippines Studies* 16:605–621.

Becker, Howard S.
    1970.   *Sociological work: method and substance.* Chicago: Aldine.

Beardslee, D. C. and Fogelson, R. D.
    1958.   Sex differences in sexual imagery aroused by musical stimulation. In J. W. Atkinson, Ed., *Motives in fantasy, action and society.* Princeton: Van Nostrand.

Beidelman, T. O.
    1964.   Pig (*Guluwe*): an essay on Ngulu sexual symbolism and ceremony. *Southwestern Journal of Anthropology* 20:359–392.
    1966a. Swazi royal ritual. *Africa* 36:373–405.
    1966b. The ox and Nuer sacrifice: some Freudian hypotheses about Nuer symbolism. *Man* 1:453–467.
    1970.   Some sociological implications of culture. In J. McKinney and E. Tiryakian, Eds. *Theoretical sociology,* New York: Appleton-Century-Crofts.

Bell, Norman, and Vogel, Ezra, Eds.
    1968.   *A modern introduction to the family.* New York: The Free Press.

Bellah, Robert
    1965.   Father and son in Christianity and Confucianism. *The Psychoanalytic Review* 52:236–258.

Benedict, Ruth
    1934a. Anthropology and the abnormal. *Journal of General Psychology* 10: 59–80.
    1934b. *Patterns of Culture.* Boston: Houghton Mifflin Co.
    1938.   Continuities and discontinuities in cultural conditioning. *Psychiatry* 1:161–167.
    1946.   *The chrysanthemum and the sword.* Boston: Houghton Mifflin Co.
    1949.   Child rearing in certain European countries. *American Journal of Orthopsychiatry* 19:342–50.

Berg, Irwin A.
    1967.   *Response set in personality assessment.* Chicago: Aldine.

Berlin, Brent, and Kay, Paul
    1969.   *Basic color terms: their universality and evolution.* Berkeley and Los Angeles: University of California Press.

Birdwhistell, Ray
    1952.   *Introduction to kinesics.* Louisville: University of Louisville.

Boyer, L. Bryce
    1962.   Remarks on the personality of shamans with special reference to the Apaches of the Mescalero Indian reservation. In W. Muensterberger

and S. Axelrod, Eds. *Psychoanalytic study of society,* vol. 2. New York: International Universities Press.

1964. Psychological problems of a group of Apaches: alcoholic hallucinosis and latent homosexuality among typical men. In W. Muensterberger and S. Axelrod, Eds. Psychoanalytic vol. 3. New York: International Universities Press.

Briggs, Jean
1970. *Never in anger: portrait of an Eskimo family.* Cambridge, Mass.: Harvard University Press.

Brim, Orville G.
1959. *Education for child rearing.* New York: Russell Sage.
1966. Socialization through the life cycle. In O. G. Brim and Stanton Wheeler, Eds. *Socialization after childhood.* New York: Wiley.

Bruner, Edward
1956a. Cultural transmission and cultural change. *Southwestern Journal of Anthropology* 12:191–199.
1956b. Primary group experience and the process of acculturation. *American Anthropologist* 58:605–623.

Bruner, J. S., Olver, R., and Greenfield, P. M.
1966. *Studies in cognitive growth.* New York: Wiley.

Brunswik, Egon
1956. *Perception and the representative design of psychological experiments.* Berkeley: University of California Press.

Buckley, Walter
1967. *Sociology and modern systems theory.* Englewood Cliffs, N.J.: Prentice-Hall.

Buros, Oscar
1970. *Personality: tests and reviews.* Highland Park, N. J.: Gryphon Press.

Burton, Roger, and Whiting, John W. M.
1961. The absent father and cross-sex identity. *Merrill-Palmer Quarterly* 7: 85–97.

Campbell, Angus, Converse, Philip and Miller, Warren
1960. *The American voter.* New York: Wiley.

Campbell, Donald T.
1961. The mutual methodological relevance of anthropology and psychology. In F. L. K. Hsu, Ed., *Psychological anthropology.* Homewood, Ill.: Dorsey Press.
1966. Variation and selective-retention in sociocultural evolution. In H. Barringer, G. Blanksten, and R. Mack, Eds. *Social change in developing areas: a reinterpretation of evolutionary theory.* Cambridge, Mass.: Schenkman.
1969. Definitional versus multiple operationalism. *et al.* 2:14–17.

Chapple, Elliott D.
1970. *Culture and biological man.* New York: Holt, Rinehart and Winston.

Child, Irvin L.
1968. Personality in culture. In E. F. Borgatta and W. W. Lambert, Eds. *Handbook of personality theory and research,* Chicago: Rand McNally.

Clausen, John
1966. Family structure, socialization, and personality. In L. W. Hoffman and M. L. Hoffman, Eds., *Review of child development research,* vol. 2. New York: Russell Sage Foundation.

Clausen, John, Ed.
  1968.   *Socialization and society.* Boston: Little, Brown.
Cottrell, Leonard
  1969.   Interpersonal interaction and the development of the self. In D.
          Goslin, Ed., *Handbook of socialization theory and research.* Chicago:
          Rand McNally.
Cronin, Constance
  1970.   *The sting of change: Sicilians in Sicily and Australia.* Chicago: Uni-
          versity of Chicago Press.
Darwin, Charles
  1965.   *The expression of emotions in man and animals.* Chicago: University
          of Chicago Press. (First published London: John Murray, 1872.)
Dawson, Richard, and Prewitt, Kenneth
  1969.   *Political socialization.* Boston: Little, Brown.
Demos, John
  1970.   Underlying themes in the witchcraft of seventeenth-century New
          England. *American Historical Review* 75:1311–1326.
Devereux, George
  1951.   *Reality and dream: psychotherapy of a Plains Indian.* New York:
          International Universities Press.
  1967.   *From anxiety to method in the behavioral sciences.* The Hague:
          Mouton.
Devons, Ely, and Gluckman, Max
  1967.   Conclusion: modes and consequences of limiting a field of study. In
          M. Gluckman, Ed., *Closed systems and open minds: the limits of
          naivety in social anthropology.* Chicago: Aldine.
DeVos, George
  1961.   Symbolic analysis in the cross-cultural study of personality. In
          B. Kaplan, Ed., *Studying personality cross-culturally.* Evanston, Ill.:
          Row, Peterson.
DeVos, George, and Hippler, A.
  1969.   Cultural psychology: comparative studies of human behavior. In
          G. Lindzey and E. Aronson, Eds., *Handbook of social psychology,*
          vol. 4. Cambridge, Mass.: Addison-Wesley.
Douglas, Mary, Ed.
  1970.   *Witchcraft confessions and accusations.* London: Tavistock.
DuBois, Cora
  1944.   *People of Alor.* Minneapolis: University of Minnesota Press.
Duijker, H., and Frijda, N.
  1960.   *National character and national stereotypes.* The Hague: Mouton.
Durkheim, Emile
  1951 (1895).   *Suicide.* Glencoe, Ill.: The Free Press.
Edgerton, Robert B.
  1970.   Method in psychological anthropology. In R. Naroll and R. Cohen,
          Eds., *A handbook of method in cultural anthropology.* Garden City,
          N. Y.: Natural History Press.
Eggan, Dorothy
  1949.   The significance of dreams for anthropological research. *American
          Anthropologist* 51:177–198.
  1952.   The manifest content of dreams: a challenge to social science.
          American Anthropologist 54:469–485.
  1961.   Dream analysis. In B. Kaplan, Ed. *Studying personality cross-cul-
          turally.* New York: Harper & Row.

1966.   Hopi dreams in cultural perspective. In G. von Grunebaum and R. Caillois, Eds. *The dream in human societies.* Berkeley and Los Angeles: University of California Press.

Eggan, Fred
1954.   Social anthropology and the method of controlled comparison. *American Anthropologist* 56:743–763.

Ekman, Paul, and Friesen, Wallace
1969.   The repertoire of nonverbal behavior: categories, origins, usage and coding. *Semiotica* 1:49–98.

Ekman, Paul, Sorensen, Richard, and Friesen, Wallace
1969.   Pan-cultural elements in facial displays of emotion. *Science* 164:86–88.

Erikson, Erik
1939.   Observations on Sioux education. *Journal of Psychology* 7:101–156.
1943.   *Observations on the Yurok: childhood and world image.* University of California Publications in American Archaeology and Ethnology.
1958.   The nature of clinical evidence. *Daedalus* 87(4):65–87.
1959.   *Ego identity and the life cycle.* New York: International Universities Press.

Etzioni, Amitai
1968.   *The active society: a theory of societal and political processes.* New York: The Free Press.

Evans-Pritchard, E. E.
1937.   *Witchcraft, oracles and magic among the Azande.* London: Oxford University Press.
1951.   *Social anthropology and other essays.* New York: Free Press.

Fadipe, N. A.
1970.   *The sociology of the Yoruba.* Ibadan: Ibadan University Press.

Fiske, Donald W.
1971.   *Measuring the concepts of personality.* Chicago: Aldine • Atherton.

Fleming, Joan, and Benedek, Therese
1966.   *Psychoanalytic supervision.* New York: Grune and Stratton.

Freud, Anna
1963.   The concept of developmental lines. *Psychoanalytic Study of the Child* 18:245–265.
1965.   *Normality and pathology in childhood.* New York: International Universities.

Freud, Sigmund
1900.   *The interpretation of dreams.* (Standard Edition, vols. 4 and 5.) London: Hogarth.
1913.   *Totem and taboo.* (Standard Edition, vol. 13.) London: Hogarth.
1916–17.   *Introductory lectures on psychoanalysis,* Part III. (Standard Edition, vol. 16.) London: Hogarth.
1921.   *Group psychology and the analysis of the ego.* (Standard Edition, vol. 18.) London: Hogarth.
1923a.   *The ego and the id.* (Standard Edition, vol. 19.) London: Hogarth.
1923b.   *Psychoanalysis* (an encyclopedia article). (Standard Edition, vol. 18.) London: Hogarth.
1930.   *Civilization and its discontents.* (Standard Edition, vol. 21.) London: Hogarth.

Fromm, Erich
1941.   *Escape from freedom.* New York: Farrar & Rinehart.

Fromm, Erich, and Maccoby, Michael
   1970.   *Social character in a Mexican village.* Englewood Cliffs, N. J.:
           Prentice-Hall.
Gedo, John, and Pollock, George
   1967.   The question of research in psychoanalytic technique. In B. Wolman,
           Ed., *Psychoanalytic techniques.* New York: Basic Books.
Geertz, Clifford
   1968.   *Islam observed.* New Haven: Yale University Press.
Gill, Merton M.
   1967.   *The collected papers of David Rapaport.* New York: Basic Books.
Gluckman, Max
   1944.   The logic of African science and witchcraft. *Human Problems in
           British Central Africa* 1:61–71.
   1963.   *Order and rebellion in tribal Africa.* London: Cohen & West.
Goffman, Erving
   1959.   *The presentation of self in everyday life.* New York: Doubleday
           Anchor.
   1961a. *Asylums.* New York: Doubleday Anchor.
   1961b. *Encounters.* Indianapolis: Bobbs-Merrill.
   1963.   *Behavior in public places.* New York: Free Press.
   1967.   *Interaction ritual.* New York: Anchor Doubleday.
Goodenough, Ward
   1970.   *Description and comparison in cultural anthropology.* Chicago:
           Aldine.
Goody, Jack, Ed.
   1958.   *The developmental cycle in domestic groups.* Cambridge: Cambridge
           University Press.
Gorer, Geoffrey
   1943.   Themes in Japanese culture. *Transactions of the New York Academy
           of Sciences,* Ser. II, 5:106–124.
   1948.   *The American people.* New York: W. W. Norton.
Gorer, Geoffrey, and Rickman, John
   1949.   *The people of Great Russia.* London: Groset.
Goslin, David, Ed.
   1969.   *Handbook of socialization theory and research.* Chicago: Rand
           McNally.
Gray, R. and Gulliver, P., Eds.
   1964.   *The family estate in Africa.* London: Routledge and Kegan Paul.
Greenberg, Edward S., Ed.
   1970.   *Political socialization.* New York: Atherton.
Greenberg, Joseph
   1966.   *Language universals.* The Hague: Mouton.
Greenfield, Patricia M., and Bruner, J. S.
   1969.   Culture and cognitive growth. In D. Goslin, Ed., *Handbook of sociali-
           zation theory and research.* Chicago: Rand McNally.
Greenson, Ralph
   1967.   *Technique and practice of psychoanalysis,* vol. 1. New York: Inter-
           national Universities Press.
Hallowell, A. Irving
   1938.   Fear and anxiety as cultural and individual variables in a primitive
           society. *Journal of Social Psychology* 9:25–47.

1954. Psychology and anthropology. In J. P. Gillin, Ed., *Toward a science of social man*. New York: Macmillan.

1955. *Culture and experience*. Philadelphia: Univ. of Pennsylvania Press.

Hammel, Eugene, Ed.
1965. Formal semantic analysis. Special publication, *American Anthropologist* 67 (5): Part 2.

Hanks, L. M.
1949. The locus of individual differences in certain primitive cultures. In S. Sargent and M. Smith, Eds. *Culture and personality*. New York: Wenner-Gren.

Harris, Marvin
1964. *The nature of cultural things*. New York: Random House.

Hart, C. W. M.
1954. The sons of Turimpi. *American Anthropologist* 56:242–261.

Hartmann, E.
1968. The 90-minute sleep-dream cycle. *Archive of General Psychiatry* 18: 280–286.

Hartmann, Heinz
1958. *Ego psychology and the problem of adaptation*. New York: International Universities Press.

Hartmann, Heinz; Kris, Ernst; and Lowenstein, Rudolph
1951. Some psychoanalytic comments on "culture and personality." In G. Wilbur and W. Muensterberger, Eds., *Psychoanalysis and culture*, New York: International Universities Press.

Henry, Jules and Zunia
1944. Doll play of Pilaga Indian children. *Research Monograph 4*, American Orthopsychiatric Association.

Holzman, Philip
1970. *Psychoanalysis and psychopathology*. New York: McGraw-Hill.

Inkeles, Alex
1955. Social change and social character: the role of parental mediation. *Journal of Social Issues* 11:12–23.

1959. Personality and social structure. In R. K. Merton, L. Broom, and L. Cottrell, Eds., *Sociology today*. New York: Basic Books.

1961. National character and modern political systems. In F. L. K. Hsu, Ed., *Psychological anthropology*. Homewood, Ill.: Dorsey.

1963. Sociology and psychology. In S. Koch, Ed., *Psychology: study of a science*, vol. VI. New York: McGraw-Hill.

1966a. Social structure and the socialization of competence. *Harvard Educational Review* 36:265–283.

1966b. The modernization of man. In M. Weiner, Ed., *Modernization: the dynamics of growth*. New York: Basic Books.

Inkeles, Alex and Levinson, D. J.
1954. National character: the study of modal personality and sociocultural systems. In G. Lindzey, Ed., *Handbook of social psychology*, vol. II. Cambridge, Mass.: Addison-Wesley, pp. 977–1020.

1968. National character: the study of modal personality and sociocultural systems. In G. Lindzey and E. Aronson, Eds., *Handbook of social psychology*, second edition, vol. 4. Cambridge Mass.: Addison-Wesley, pp. 418–506.

Janis, Irving L.
 1958. *Psychological stress.* New York: Wiley.
Janis, Irving L. and Leventhal, Howard
 1968. Human reactions to stress. In E. F. Borgatta and W. W. Lambert, Eds., *Handbook of personality theory and research.* Chicago: Rand McNally.
Kales, Anthony, Ed.
 1969. *Sleep: physiology and pathology.* Philadelphia: Lippincott.
Kaplan, Bert
 1961. Editor's epilogue: a final word. In B. Kaplan, Ed., *Studying personality cross-culturally.* Evanston, Ill.: Row, Peterson.
Kardiner, Abram
 1939. *The individual and his society.* New York: Columbia University Press.
 1945. *Psychological frontiers of society.* New York: Columbia University Press.
Katz, Jay
 1963. On primary and secondary gain. *The Psychoanalytic Study of the Child* 18:9–50.
Kaufman, I. C.
 1970. Biologic aspects of parenthood. In E. J. Anthony and T. Benedek, Eds., *Parenthood: psychology and psychopathology.* Boston: Little, Brown.
Kleitman, Nathaniel
 1963. *Sleep and wakefulness,* revised edition. Chicago: University of Chicago Press.
 1969. Basic rest-activity cycle in relation to sleep and wakefulness. In A. Kales, Ed., *Sleep: physiology and pathology.* Philadelphia: Lippincott.
Kluckhohn, Clyde
 1953. Universal categories of culture. In A. L. Kroebeor, *Anthropology today.* Chicago: University of Chicago Press.
Kluckhohn, Clyde, and Murray, Henry A., Eds.
 1948. *Personality in nature, society and culture.* New York: Knopf.
Kluckhohn, Florence
 1954. Dominant and variant value orientations. In C. Kluckhohn and H. Murray, Eds., *Personality in nature, culture and society.* New York: Knopf.
Kluckhohn, Florence, and Strodtbeck, Fred L.
 1962. *Variations in value orientations.* New York: Harper & Row.
Koestler, A.
 1961. *Lotus and the robot.* New York: Macmillan.
Kohlberg, Lawrence
 1969. The cognitive-developmental approach to socialization. In D. Goslin, Ed., *Handbook of socialization theory and research.* Chicago: Rand McNally.
Kohn, Melvin L.
 1967. *Class and conformity: a study of values.* Homewood, Ill.: Dorsey.
LaBarre, Weston
 1970. *Ghost dance: the origins of religion.* New York: Doubleday.
Langton, Kenneth P.
 1969. *Political socialization.* London: Oxford University Press.

Lasswell, Harold
  1930. *Psychopathology and politics.* Chicago: University of Chicago Press.
  1948. *Power and personality.* New York: W. W. Norton.
  1968. A note on "types" of political personality: nuclear, corelational, developmental. *Journal of Social Issues* 24:81–91.
Lazarus, Richard S.
  1966. *Psychological stress and the coping process.* New York: McGraw-Hill.
Lee, S. G.
  1968. Spirit possession among the Zulu. In J. Beattie and J. Middleton, Eds., *Spirit mediumship and society in Africa.* London: Routledge and Kegan Paul.
Leighton, Alexander, Lambo, T. A., et al.
  1963. *Psychiatric disorder among the Yoruba.* Ithaca: Cornell University Press.
LeVine, Robert A.
  1958. Omoriori: smeller of witches. *Natural History* 67:142–147.
  1959. Gusii sex offenses: a study in social control. *American Anthropologist* 61:965–990.
  1962. Witchcraft and co-wife proximity in southwestern Kenya. *Ethnology* 1:39–45.
  1963a. Witchcraft and sorcery in a Gusii community. In J. Middleton and E. Winter, Eds., *Witchcraft and sorcery in East Africa.* London: Routledge and Kegan Paul.
  1963b. Behaviorism in psychological anthropology. In J. Wepman and R. Heine, Eds., *Concepts of personality.* Chicago: Aldine.
  1966a. *Dreams and deeds: achievement motivation in Nigeria.* Chicago: University of Chicago Press.
  1966b. Outsiders' judgments: an ethnographic approach to group differences in personality. *Southwestern Journal of Anthropology* 22:101–116.
  1970a. Cross-cultural study in child psychology. In P. Mussen, Ed., *Carmichael's manual of child psychology,* third edition, vol. II, pp. 559–612.
  1970b. Personality and change. In J. Paden and E. Soja, Eds., *The African Experience.* Evanston, Ill.: Northwestern University Press.
LeVine, Robert A., Klein, Nancy, and Owen, Constance
  1967. Father-child relationships and changing life-styles in Ibadan, Nigeria. In H. Miner, Ed., *The city in modern Africa,* New York: Praeger.
LeVine, Robert A., and LeVine, Barbara B.
  1966. *Nyansongo: a Gusii community in Kenya.* New York: Wiley.
LeVine, Robert A., and Price-Williams, D. R.
  1970. Children's kinship concepts: preliminary report on a Nigerian study. Paper presented at the American Anthropological Association Meeting.
Levinson, Daniel J.
  1959. Role, personality and social structure in the organizational setting. *Journal of Abnormal and Social Psychology* 58:170–180.
Lewin, Kurt
  1935. *A dynamic theory of personality.* New York: McGraw-Hill.
Lewis, I. M.
  1971. *Ecstatic religion.* Hammondsworth, England: Penguin Books.

Lindzey, Gardner
    1961.   *Projective techniques and cross-cultural research*. New York: Appleton-Century-Crofts.

Linton, Ralph
    1936.   *The study of man*. New York: Appleton-Century-Crofts.
    1945.   *The cultural background of personality*. New York: Appleton-Century-Crofts.

Luborsky, Lester
    1970.   New directions in research on neurotic and psychosomatic symptoms. *American Scientist* 58:661–668.

Luce, Gay Gaer, and Segal, Julius
    1966.   *Sleep*. New York: Howard-McCann.

MacAndrew, Craig, and Edgerton, R. B.
    1969.   *Drunken comportment: a social explanation*. Chicago: Aldine.

McClelland, David C.
    1958.   The use of measures of human motivation in the study of society. In J. W. Atkinson, Ed., *Motives in fantasy, action and society*. Princeton: Van Nostrand.
    1961.   *The achieving society*. Princeton: Van Nostrand.

McClelland, David C., Atkinson, J. W., Clark, R. A., and Lowell, E. L.
    1953.   *The achievement motive*. New York: Appleton-Century-Crofts.

McClelland, David C. and Winter, David G.
    1969.   *Motivating economic achievement*. New York: Free Press.

Macfarlane, Alan
    1970a. *Witchcraft in Tudor and Stuart England*. London: Routledge & Kegan Paul.
    1970b. Witchcraft in Tudor and Stuart Essex. In M. Douglas, Ed., *Witchcraft confessions and accusations*. London: Tavistock.

Maddi, S.
    1968.   *Personality theories: a comparative analysis*. Homewood, Ill.: Dorsey Press.

Mair, Lucy
    1969.   *Witchcraft*. New York: McGraw-Hill.

Mayer, Philip, Ed.
    1969.   *Socialization: the approach from social anthropology*. London: Tavistock.

Mead, Margaret
    1928.   *Coming of age in Samoa*. New York: William Morrow.
    1930.   *Growing up in New Guinea*. New York: William Morrow.
    1932.   An investigation of the thoughts of primitive children with special reference to animism. *Journal of the Royal Anthropological Institute* 62:173–190.
    1935.   *Sex and temperament in three primitive societies*. New York: William Morrow.
    1939.   *From the South Seas*. New York: William Morrow.
    1953.   National character. In A. L. Kroeber, Ed., *Anthropology Today*. Chicago: University of Chicago Press.
    1954.   The swaddling hypothesis: its reception. *American Anthropologist* 56:395–409.
    1964.   *Continuities in cultural evolution*. New Haven: Yale University Press.

Mead, Margaret, and McGregor, F. C.

1951.   *Growth and culture.* New York: Putnam.

Mead, Margaret, and Metraux, Rhoda
1953.   *The study of culture at a distance.* Chicago: University of Chicago Press.

Mead, Margaret, and Wolfenstein, Martha
1955.   *Childhood in contemporary cultures.* Chicago: University of Chicago Press.

Middleton, John, and Winter, Edward, Eds.
1963.   *Witchcraft and Sorcery in East Africa.* London: Routledge and Kegan Paul.

Miller, Daniel R., and Swanson, G. E.
1958.   *The changing American parent.* New York: Wiley.

Miller, Neal E., and Dollard, John
1941.   *Social learning and imitation.* New Haven: Yale University Press.

Minturn, Leigh, and Lambert, W. W.
1964.   *Mothers of sex cultures.* New York: Wiley.

Mischel, Walter
1968.   *Personality and assessment.* New York: Wiley.

Morgenthaler, F. and Parin, P.
1964a. Ego and orality in the analysis of West Africans. In W. Muensterberger and S. Axelrod, Eds., *Psychoanalytic study of society,* vol. 3. New York: International Universities Press.

1964b. Typical forms of transference among West Africans. *International Journal of Psychoanalysis* 45:446–449.

Murray, Henry, *et al.*
1938.   *Explorations in personality.* New York: Oxford University Press.

Mussen, P. H., Ed.
1970.   *Carmichael's manual of child psychology,* 3rd ed. New York: Wiley.

Naroll, Raoul
1970.   What have we learned from cross-cultural surveys? *American Anthropologist* 72:1227–1288.

Nimkoff, M. F., and Middleton, R.
1960.   Types of family and types of economy. *American Journal of Sociology* 66:215–225.

Ortigues, M. and Ortigues, E.
1966.   *Oedipe Africain.* Paris: Plon.

Parin, Paul, Morgenthaler, F., and Parin-Matthey.
1963.   *Die weisen denken zuviel.* Zurich: Atlantis.

Parker, Seymour
1960.   The Wiitiko psychosis in the context of Ojibwa personality. *American Anthropologist* 62:603–623.

Parsons, Anne
1969.   *Belief, magic and anomie: essays in psychosocial anthropology.* New York: Free Press.

Parsons, Talcott
1949.   *The social system.* New York: Free Press.
1964.   *Social structure and personality.* New York: Free Press.

Parsons, Talcott, and Shils, Edward, Eds.
1951.   *Toward a general theory of action.* Cambridge, Mass.: Harvard University Press.

Piaget, Jean
  1926.   *The language and thought of the child.* London: Routledge and Kegan Paul.
  1932.   *The moral judgment of the child.* London: Routledge and Kegan Paul.
Pollock, George
  1961.   Mourning and adaptation. *International Journal of Psychoanalysis* 42: 341–361.
  1962.   Childhood parent and sibling loss in adult patients: a comparative study. *Archive of General Psychiatry* 7:295–305.
  1972.   On mourning and anniversaries: the relationship of culturally constituted defensive systems to intrapsychic adaptive processes. *Israel Annals of Psychiatry,* 10:9–40.
Prince Peter of Greece and Denmark
  1965.   The psychological testing of Todas and Tibetans. In M. Schur, Ed., *Drives, affects and behavior,* vol. 2. New York: International Universities Press.
Pringle, J. W. S.
  1951.   On the parallel between learning and evolution. *Behavior* 3:175–250.
Rapaport, David
  1944.   The scientific methodology of psychoanalysis. In M. Gill, Ed., *The collected papers of David Rapaport.* New York: Basic Books.
Rapaport, David, Gill, M., and Schafer, Roy
  1945.   *Diagnostic psychological testing.* Chicago: Year Book Publishers.
Read, Margaret
  1959.   *Children of their fathers: growing up among the Ngoui of Nyasaland.* New Haven: Yale University Press.
Richards, Audrey I.
  1956.   *Chisungu.* London: Faber and Faber.
Riesman, David
  1950.   *The lonely crowd.* New Haven: Yale University Press.
Roheim, Géza
  1932.   The psychoanalysis of primitive cultural types. *International Journal of Psychoanalysis* 13:1–224.
  1943.   *The origin and function of culture.* New York: Nervous and Mental Disease Monographs.
  1950.   *Psychoanalysis and anthropology.* New York: International Universities Press.
  1969.   The psychoanalytic interpretation of culture. In W. Muensterberger, Ed., *Man and his culture: psychoanalytic anthropology after Totem and Taboo.* London: Rapp and Whiting.
Rosenthal, Robert
  1966.   *Experimenter effects in behavioral research.* New York: Appleton-Century-Crofts.
Rosenthal, Robert, and Rosnow, Ralph, Eds.
  1969.   *Artifact in behavioral research.* New York: Academic Press.
Sapir, Edward
  1938.   Why cultural anthropology needs the psychiatrist. *Psychiatry* 1:7–12.
Schafer, Roy
  1948.   *The clinical application of psychological tests.* New York: International Universities Press.
  1954.   *Psychoanalytic interpretation in Rorschach testing.* New York: Grune & Stratton.

1967. *Projective testing and psychoanalysis.* New York: International Universities Press.

Schneider, David M., and Sharp, Lauriston
1970. The dream life of a primitive people: the dreams of the Yir Yoront of Australia. *Anthropological Studies* 1, American Anthropological Association.

Schooler, Carmi, and Caudill, William
1964. Symptomatology in Japanese and American schizophrenics. *Ethnology* 3:172–178.

Sears, Robert R.
1943. *Survey of objective studies of psychoanalytic concepts.* New York: Social Science Research Council.

Sechrest, Lee
1968. Testing, measuring and assessing people. In E. F. Borgatta and W. W. Lambert, Eds., *Handbook of personality theory and research.* Chicago: Rand McNally.

Segall, M. H., Campbell, D. T., and Herskovits, M. J.
1966. *The influence of culture on visual perception.* Indianapolis: Bobbs-Merrill.

Shibutani, T.
1961. *Society and personality: an interactionist approach to social psychology.* Englewood Cliffs, N.J.: Prentice-Hall.

Singer, Milton
1961. A survey of culture and personality theory and research. In B. Kaplan, Ed., *Studying personality cross-culturally.* Evanston, Ill.: Row, Peterson.

Smith, David, and Inkeles, Alex
1966. The OM scale: a comparative socio-psychological measure of individual modernity. *Sociometry* 29:353–377.

Spindler, George
1955. *Sociocultural and psychological processes in Menomini acculturation.* Berkeley: University of California Publications in Culture and Society, vol. 5.
1968. Psychocultural adaptation. In E. Norbeck, D. Price-William, W. McCord, Eds., *The study of personality.* New York: Holt, Rinehart and Winston.

Spindler, George, and Spindler, Louise
1961. A modal personality technique in the study of Menomini acculturation. In B. Kaplan, Ed., *Studying personality cross-culturally.* Evanston, Ill.: Row, Peterson.

Spiro, Melford E.
1957. *Kibbutz: venture in utopia.* Cambridge, Mass.: Harvard Univ. Press.
1958. *Children of the kibbutz.* Cambridge, Mass.: Harvard University Press.
1961a. Social systems, personality and functional analysis. In B. Kaplan, Ed., *Studying personality cross-culturally.* Evanston, Ill.: Row, Peterson.
1961b. An overview and a suggested reorientation. In F. L. K. Hsu, Ed., *Psychological anthropology.* Homewood, Ill.: Dorsey.
1965. Religious systems as culturally constituted defense mechanisms. In M. Spiro, Ed., *Context and meaning in cultural anthropology.* New York: Free Press.
1966. Religion: problems of definition and explanation. In *Anthropological approaches to the study of religion.* ASA monograph 3. London: Tavistock.

1967. *Burmese supernaturalism: a study in the explanation and reduction of suffering*. Englewood Cliffs, N.J.: Prentice-Hall.

Spitz, Rene
1965. *The first year of life*. New York: International Universities Press.

Sterba, Richard
1934. The fate of the ego in analytic therapy. *International Journal of Psychoanalysis* 15:117–126.
1940. The dynamics of the dissolution of the transference resistence. *Psychoanalytic Quarterly* 9:363–379.

Strangman, Eugene
1967. Achievement in fantasy: a study of achievement imagery in the TAT stories and dream reports of American adolescents. Unpublished Ph.D. dissertation in Human Development, University of Chicago.

Straus, Jacqueline H., and Straus, Murray A.
1953. Suicide, homicide and social structure in Ceylon. *American Journal of Sociology* 58:461–469.

Sundkler, Bengt
1948. *Bantu prophets in South Africa*. London: Oxford University Press.

Swartz, Marc J.
1968. *Local-level politics: social and cultural perspectives*. Chicago: Aldine.

Swartz, Marc J., Tuden, Arthur, and Turner, Victor W.
1968. *Political anthropology*. Chicago: Aldine.

Tapp, June L., Ed.
1971. Socialization, the law and society. *Journal of Social Issues* 27(2):1–229.

Taub, John M.
1971. The sleep-wakefulness cycle in Mexican adults. *Journal of Cross-Cultural Psychology*, 2:353–364.

Thomas, Keith
1970. The relevance of social anthropology to the historical study of English witchcraft. In M. Douglas, Ed., *Witchcraft confessions and accusations*. London: Tavistock.
1971. *Religion and the decline of magic: studies in popular beliefs in sixteenth and seventeenth century England*. London: Weidenfield and Nicolson.

Thomas, W. I., and Znaniecki, F.
1927. *The Polish Peasant in Europe and America*, vols. I and II. Chicago: University of Chicago Press.

Tomkins, Silvan
1962–1963. *Affect-imagery-consciousness*, vols. 1 and 2. Springfield, Ill.: Charles C Thomas.

Tooth, G.
1950. *Studies in mental illness in the Gold Coast*. London: His Majesty's Stationery Office, Colonial Research Publication No. 6.

Trevelyan, G. M.
1942. *English social history*. London: Longmans Green.

Trevor-Roper, H. R.
1967. *European witch-craze of the sixteenth and seventeenth centuries*. New York: Harper & Row.

Turner, Ralph H.
1956. Role-taking, role-standpoint and reference-group behavior. *American Journal of Sociology* 61:316–328.

Turner, Victor W.
  1967.   *The forest of symbols*. Ithaca: Cornell University Press.
  1968.   *Drums of affliction*. London: Oxford University Press.
  1969.   *The ritual process*. Chicago: Aldine.
Wallace, A. F. C.
  1952.   The modal personality of the Tuscarora Indians as revealed by the Rorschach test. *Bureau of American Ethnology Bulletin*, (150).
  1956.   Revitalization movements. *American Anthropologist* 58:264–281.
  1959.   The institutionalization of cathartic and control strategies in Iroquois religious psychotherapy. In M. K. Opler, Ed., *Culture and mental health*. New York: Macmillan.
  1961a. Mental illness, biology and culture. In F. L. K. Hsu, Ed., *Psychological anthropology*. Homewood, Ill.: Dorsey.
  1961b. *Culture and personality*, first edition. New York: Random House.
  1970.   *Culture and personality*, second edition. New York: Random House.
Watson, James B., and Nelson, Harold E.
  1967.   Body-environment transactions: a standard model for cross-cultural analyses. *Southwestern Journal of Anthropology* 23:292–309.
Webb, Eugene, Campbell, D. T., Schwartz, R. D., and Sechrest, L.
  1966.   *Unobtrusive measures*. Chicago: Rand McNally.
Webb, W. B.
  1969.   Twenty-four sleep cycling. In A. Kales, Ed., *Sleep: physiology and pathology*. Philadelphia: Lippincott.
Weber, Max.
  1947.   *The theory of social and economic organization*. Glencoe, Ill.: Free Press.
White, Leslie
  1949.   *The science of culture*. New York: Farrar, Strauss.
Whiting, Beatrice B., Ed.
  1963.   *Six cultures: studies of child rearing*. New York: Wiley.
Whiting, John W. M.
  1941.   *Becoming a Kwoma*. New Haven: Yale University Press.
  1961.   Socialization process and personality. In F. L. K. Hsu, Ed., *Psychological anthropology*. Homewood, Ill.: Dorsey.
  1965.   Effects of climate on certain cultural practices. In W. Goodenough, Ed., *Explorations in cultural anthropology*. New York: McGraw-Hill.
  1969.   Methods and problems in cross-cultural research. In G. Lindzey and E. Aronson, Eds., *Handbook of social psychology*, vol. 2. Cambridge, Mass.: Addison-Wesley.
Whiting, John W. M., Chasdi, E. H., Antonovsky, H. F., and Ayres, B. C.
  1966.   The learning of values. In, *People of the Rimrock: a study of values in five cultures*. E. Vogt and E. Albert, Eds., Cambridge, Mass.: Harvard University Press.
Whiting, John W. M. and Child, I. L.
  1953.   Child training and personality: a cross-cultural study. New Haven: Yale University Press.
Whiting, John W. M., Child, I. L. et al.
  1966.   *Field guide for the study of socialization*. New York: Wiley.
Whiting, John W. M., Kluckhohn, R., and Anthony, A.
  1958.   The function of male initiation ceremonies at puberty. In E. Maccoby, T. Newcomb and E. Hartley, Eds., *Readings in social psychology*. New York: Holt.

Whiting, John W. M., and Whiting, Beatrice B.
   1959.   Contributions of anthropology to methods of studying child rearing. In P. Mussen, Ed., *Handbook of research methods in child development*. New York: Wiley.
Wilbur, G. and Muensterberger, W., Eds.
   1951.   *Psychoanalysis and culture*. New York: International Universities Press.
Wilson, Monica
   1951.   Witch beliefs and social structure. *American Journal of Sociology* 56:307–313.
   1971.   *Religion and the transformation of society*. Cambridge: Cambridge University Press.
Witkin, H. A., Dyk, R. B., Faterson, H. F., Goodenough, D. R., and Karp, S. A.
   1962.   *Psychological differentiation*. New York: Wiley.
Wolf, Arthur
   1966.   Childhood association, sexual attraction and the incest taboo: a Chinese case. *American Anthropologist* 68:883–898.
   1968.   Adopt a daughter-in-law, marry a sister-in-law: a Chinese solution to the problem of the incest taboo. *American Anthropologist* 70:864–874.
   1970.   Childhood association and sexual attraction: a further test of the Westermarck hypothesis. *American Anthropologist* 72:503-515.
Wolff, Peter
   1963.   Observations on the early development of smiling. In B. M. Foss, Ed., *Determinants of infant behavior*, vol. 2. New York: Wiley.
Wrong, D. H.
   1961.   The oversocialized conception of man in modern sociology. *American Sociological Review* 26:183–193.
Yap, P. M.
   1969.   The culture-bound reactive syndromes. In W. Caudill and T. Y. Lin, Eds. *Culture and mental health research in Asia and the Pacific*. Honolulu: East-West Center Press.
Yarrow, Marian R., Campbell, John, and Burton, Roger
   1968.   *Child rearing: an inquiry into research and methods*. San Francisco: Jossey-Bass.
Young, Frank
   1965.   *Initiation ceremonies*. Indianapolis: Bobbs-Merrill.
Zaretsky, Irving
   1971.   To see and yet believe: spiritualist therapy. Paper presented at NIMH Conference on Anthropology and Mental Health.
Zborowski, Mark
   1949.   The place of book-learning in traditional Jewish culture. *Harvard Educational Review* 19:87–109.

Name Index

Subject Index